The Royal Commission on Legal Services

Chairman: Sir Henry Benson, GBE

FINAL REPORT

Volume Two

Surveys and Studies

Parts A and B, Sections 1–13

Presented to Parliament by Command of Her Majesty

October 1979

LONDON
HER MAJESTY'S STATIONERY OFFICE
£11 net

(2 parts not sold separately)

Cmnd 7648–1

ISBN 0 10 176481 2*

THE ROYAL COMMISSION ON LEGAL SERVICES

REPORT

Volume Two

Cmnd 7648—I

ISBN 0 10 176481 2*

CORRECTIONS

Page 304:
For "ANNEX 9.3" read "ANNEX 9.2"

Page 628 (Section 20, table of contents)
paragraph numbers:

Delete	*Insert*
20.83	20.81
20.85	20.83
20.86	20.84
20.87	20.85
20.88	20.86
20.92	20.90
20.93	20.91
20.95	20.93
20.97	20.95

October 1979

LONDON: HER MAJESTY'S STATIONERY OFFICE

Contents

PART A

Lists of Those who Assisted the Commission

Lists of Those who Assisted the Commission

For the reasons described in Volume I, paragraphs 1.18–1.20, the Commission drew a distinction between evidence of a general character and the accounts people gave of their personal experiences.

List 1 below gives the names of those individuals and organisations who submitted evidence, whether written or oral, of a general character. The majority of such witnesses agreed that their evidence should be made public and it has been deposited in the Public Records Office and in the Public Record Office of Northern Ireland, as well as in the libraries of the institutions listed in Volume I, paragraph 1.22.

Most witnesses gave written evidence only. Some gave oral evidence as well and others gave oral evidence only. The following system of symbols in list 1 denotes the public availability of evidence:

no symbol	written evidence only, publicly available
*	written evidence only, not publicly available
**	written and oral evidence, both publicly available
***	oral evidence only, publicly available
****	written evidence publicly available, oral evidence not publicly available

List 1, giving the names of those who submitted evidence of a general character, is arranged in alphabetical order, except for the names of individuals who gave oral evidence on behalf of an organisation; they appear below the name of the organisation concerned.

List 2 contains the names of all those who assisted the work of the Commission by giving information, receiving visits and in many other ways. It includes the names of those who gave the Commission information about personal experiences which the Commission regarded as submitted in confidence and which have not been published.

List 3 gives the names of those who assisted the Commission as consultants.

The Commission takes this opportunity to record its gratitude to all those individuals and organisations whose names appear in the three lists below.

LIST 1

Individuals and Organisations who gave Written and/or Oral Evidence to the Commission

D M Adams
Adamsdown Community Trust
Advisory Committee on Legal
  Education
Agricultural Mortgage Corporation
  Limited
Alban Deaf Association (Watford
  branch)
D M L Alexander
E M Alexander
Mrs E F Allan
G E Allan
**Master A E Anderson—Taxing
  Master of Northern Ireland
H F Andrews
G Applebey
*J Armstrong
Miss J M Arran
Articled Clerks Action Group
J Ashley, CH, MP
Associate Members Group
Association of British Factors
  Limited
Association of British Investigators
Association of Claims Assessors
Association of Consulting Engineers
Association of Corporate Trustees
Association of County Councils
Association of County Court and
  District Registrars
Association of Directors of Social
  Services
Association of District Councils
Association of District Secretaries
**Association of First Division Civil
  Servants—Legal Section
    C Furey
    J A Hornsby

Association of First Division Civil
  Servants—Legal Section (Customs
  and Excise Branch)
**Association of Law Costs
  Draftsmen
    D A Cole
    A E Gidney
    J B Harvey
    R Millward
Association of Law Teachers
Association of Liberal Lawyers
**Association of Local Advice
  Centres—Northern Ireland
    J Green
    Mrs M O'Shea
    W Patterson
Association of Magisterial Officers
Association of Metropolitan
  Authorities
Association of Scientific, Technical
  and Managerial Staffs
Association of Trade Protection and
  Debt Recovery Agents Limited
Automobile Association

C F Baden
E Bailey and Son
Sir George Baker, President of the
  Family Division
His Honour Judge Baker
H J Baldwin and Company Limited
Z Bankowski
A Banks and Company
**Bar Association for Commerce,
  Finance and Industry
    S Anderson
    J Keir
    M S Stewart, QC

5

Bar Association for Local
Government
Bar Council
Bar Students Working Party
J S Barnett
**Barristers' Clerks' Association
E Cooper
C B Harrison
Barrister on the North Eastern
Circuit
Barrow and Geraldine S Cadbury
Trust
P P Bartlett
A J Barton
***The Right Honourable Sir Garfield
Barwick, Chief Justice of
Australia
Bath Law Students Society
M Batley
Battersea Law Centre
The Bayswater Hostel Association
Limited
M Beach
N H Beach
Madame F E A Beets (France)
***Belfast Community Law Centre
A M McCullough
D Wall
A Bell
**The Benchers of the Honorable
Society of the Inn of Court of
Northern Ireland
Sir Frank Harrison
Lord Lowry, Lord Chief Justice
*A F Bennett, MP
*W A Bennett
F A R Bennion
A F Bessemer-Clark
*S P Best
G Bignell
G Bindman
Birmingham Housing Advice
Liaison Group
Birmingham Tribunal
Representation Unit

Bischoff and Company
R J Blair
J Blair-Gould
J C Blakeley
A E Blankensee (Australia)
*B H Bliss
*P Bocock
M R A Bolton
R Bond
M Boorer
Borough of Haringey
***Sir Wilfrid Bourne
The Bow Group
R Bowles
F J H Brackett
A V Bradbury
*Bradbury Controls Limited
Bremar Holdings Limited
Brent Community Law Centre
H M D Brett
L T Bridges
Bristol Polytechnic
Mr Justice Bristow
British Academy of Forensic
Sciences
British Actors Equity Association
British Association of Settlements
and Social Action Centres
British Association of Social
Workers
British Bankers' Association
*British Institute of International and
Comparative Law
British Insurance Association
British Insurance Brokers'
Association
British and Irish Association of
Law Librarians
**British Legal Association
S P Best
A Hilton
Mrs P Newman
Miss M H V Reckitt
G R Thomas
A Wexler

6

British Property Federation
British Waterways Board
Brixton Advice Centre
B J Brooke-Smith
T W Broomhead
I K R Brown
J Brown
*M C Brown
Lord Justice Browne
T E Browne
Brunel University
Lord Justice Buckley
L E Buckley
Building Societies' Association
His Honour Judge Bulger
*G B Bunker
***The Honourable Warren Burger,
    Chief Justice of the United States
    of America
E J C Burroughs
Bury and District Law Society
Mr Justice Bush

Cambridge Law Surgery
Camden Community Law Centre
Camden—Holborn and St Pancras
    South Labour Party
P Camp
M G Caplan
*J Carey
D Carson
*W B Caulfield
B I Cawthra
E A Cemernic
Certificated Bailiffs' Association of
    England and Wales
Chartered Institute of Patent Agents
C Chavasse
Check! Rights Centre
Chelmsford Auctions Limited
I D Cheyne
Child Poverty Action Group
****Chicago Title Insurance—Dominion
    Title Insurance Company Limited
    R Boyd-Pickens

R Flavin
Citizens Advice Bureau Legal
    Service—Kensington
Citizens Advice Bureau—Newcastle-
    upon-Tyne
***Citizens Advice Bureaux—
    Northern Ireland
    J Comerton
    Mrs C Gaw
    Mrs P Martin
    Mrs S Mawhinney
Citizens Advice Bureau—Pitsmoor,
    Sheffield
Citizens Advice and Information
    Office, City of Cardiff
City of Birmingham Polytechnic
City of London Solicitors Company
The Claims Bureau
M A Clancy
*Mrs P W Clegg
*F Cohen
A G Coles
College of Law
Miss M Colton
Commission for Racial Equality
Committee for Environmental
    Conservation
Committee of Heads of Polytechnic
    Law Schools
Committee of Vice-Chancellors and
    Principals of the Universities of
    the United Kingdom
Committee on Invisible Exports
Committee of London Clearing
    Banks
Conference of Chief Probation
    Officers
Conservation Society
Conservation Society (Bristol
    Branch)
Consultative Committee of
    Accountancy Bodies on behalf: of
    Association of Certified
    Accountants
    Chartered Institute of Public
    Finance and Accountancy

7

Institute of Chartered
Accountants in England
and Wales
Institute of Chartered
Accountants in Ireland
Institute of Chartered
Accountants of Scotland
Institute of Cost and
Management Accountants
Consultative Committee of
Accountancy Bodies—Ireland
on behalf of:
Association of Certified
Accountants
Institute of Chartered
Accountants
Institute of Cost and
Management Accountants
Consumers Association
Conveyancing and Legal Title
Limited
A Cook
L A Cook
***Sir Robin Cooke, New Zealand
F L Coombs
A J Cooper
*F A Couch
*T Coulon
***Council of Legal Education
(Northern Ireland)
Professor A E Astin
Professor C M Campbell
R D Carswell, QC
J H S Elliott
C C G McNally
Council of Her Majesty's County
Court Judges in Northern
Ireland
**Council of Her Majesty's Circuit
Judges
His Honour Judge McDonnell
His Honour Judge Sharp
His Honour Judge Trapnell
Council of The Stock Exchange
**Council on Tribunals
Professor K Bell

J M Hawksworth
D Hirst, QC
His Honour Judge Cox
C R Cradick
S M Cretney
Criminal Bar Association
J P Cunningham
*B Cutter

Darlington and Parkinson
Miss M R Davey
I Davidson, QC
J J S Davidson
D D Davies
D E J Davies
D R Davies
Major T G Davies
A E Davis
Clinton Davis and Company
F G Dearlove
**Lord Denning, Master of the Rolls
*W Dennis
Department of the Environment
Department of Prices and Consumer
Protection
F Deutsch
Devon and Exeter Incorporated
Law Society
*Viscount Dilhorne
Lord Diplock
G C Dixon
E H Dodson
D M A Doeh
The Doncaster and District Law
Society
Professor F E Dowrick
*A T Duckworth
Dudley and District Law Society
A Dutton
W E Dyke

Ealing Community Relations
Council
A Earnshaw
East Midlands Regional Group of
the Lawyers' Ecology Group

*East Sheen Advisory Council
*Mr and Mrs M G Edmonds
Lord Edmund-Davies
Miss J H Eedle
*Master J Elton
***Lord Elwyn-Jones, CH
Employment Appeal Tribunal
C P England
Equal Opportunities Commission
Mrs A Evans
J D Evans
Lord Justice Eveleigh
Executive Committee of the
    Northern Circuit Bar
*D C Eyre

Family Law Bar Association
Family Rights Group
Families Need Fathers
**Farrars' Building Chambers
    A. Huxley
S Farren
C E K Fear
Federation of Bangladesh
    Associations UK
J Fleet
J Flood
T N Flynn
Miss J Fookes, MP
Miss D Foreman
The Foy Society
The Honourable Samuel Freedman,
    Chief Justice of the Province of
    Manitoba
Free Representation Unit
Mrs A M De Freitas Sacchilary
J M Fryer
N Fricker, QC
B Fulwell

L Gabe
Lord Gardiner, CH
Miss J M Garrett
C D Geach
**General Council of the Bar in
    Northern Ireland

A Campbell
R D Carswell, QC
C M Lavery, QC
J M A Nicholson
J Pringle
General Foods Limited
General Medical Council
P W Genney
*K W Gilbert
J Gilchrist Smith
Gingerbread
A T Ginnings
*C Glasser
*Gloucestershire and Wiltshire
    Incorporated Law Society
P Goldenberg
I S Goldrein
J Goldring (Australia)
R C Goldsmith
K Goldstein-Jackson
*M J Goodall
A W B Goode
***Lord Goodman
M C Goodwin
Professor L C B Gower
H M Gowing and Sons
*P Graham
Grand Metropolitan Limited
R M K Gray
E Grayson
Greater London Citizens Advice
    Bureaux (Lawyers' Group)
Great Southern Group
J A Green
J V Greenlaw
*J Griffiths, QC
J L Griggs
*K W Grimes
H W Gristwood
P Grossman
M H Grundy
R H Gudgion
*Lord Guest
Guild of Surveyors
*K Gulleford

Hackney Council for Racial
Equality
Hackney Legal Action Group
Lord Hailsham, CH
R T Haines (USA)
Haldane Society of Socialist
Lawyers
*O Hallett
H B Hammer
Hampshire Legal Action Group
Miss K M Harding
Harlow Council
I T Harold
The Reverend Canon K Harper
Harrow Citizens Rights Group
Mrs A Harvey
Professor B W Harvey
*M Harvey
P Havemann
A Hawker
R Hazell
*His Honour Judge Head
Heads of Professional Bodies:
Chairman, Bar Association for
Commerce, Finance and
Industry
Chairman, Council of the
British Dental Association
Chairman, Council of the
British Medical Association
Chairman, Council of
Engineering Institutions
Chairman, Council of Science
and Technology Institutes
President, Chartered Institute
of Patent Agents
President, Institute of
Actuaries
President, Institute of Physics
President, Institution of
Mechanical Engineers
President, The Law Society
President, Royal College of
Surgeons of England
President, Royal Institute of
Chemistry

President, Royal Institution of
Chartered Surveyors
President, Pharmaceutical
Society of Great Britain
William Heath and Company
G Henderson
Oswald Henriques and Company
A group of barristers from the
Chambers of Piers Herbert
Herefordshire, Breconshire and
Radnorshire Incorporated Law
Society
G T Hesketh
R Hickmet
**The Judges of the High Court of
Justice
Lord Widgery, The Lord Chief
Justice of England
Mr Justice Ackner
Mr Justice Arnold
Mr Justice Oliver
The High Court Judges (Chancery
Division)
The High Court Judges (Family
Division)
J T Hills
*M Hinchliffe
*Ms E Hindmarsh
R C Hines
Hire Purchase Trade Association
Hodge, Jones and Allen
*Lord Hodson
Holborn Law Society
Home Office
Homes Conveyancing Centre
Homes Organisation
Lord Hooson
P J Horwitz
G B Hough
****House Owners Co-operative
Limited
S G Carter
K T Weetch, MP
House Owners Conveyancers
Limited

10

**Howard League for Penal Reform
    Dr D Acres, JP
    M Wright
*T Howard-Firth
 H S L House Owners Services
    Limited
*Miss G E Hunt
 P G Le M Hutchesson

Imperial Chemical Industries
    Limited
 C K M Imrie
**Incorporated Law Society of
    Northern Ireland
    J Comerton
    S M P Cross
    J G Doran
    S Lomas
    Miss T McKinney
    C C G McNally
Industrial Law Society
*F R Inglis
**The Inns of Court
    Lord Diplock
Institute of Conveyancers
**Institute of Legal Executives
    C A Broom
    L W Chapman
    G Huddy
    L Parr
Institute of Patent Agents
Institute of Practitioners in
    Advertising
***Institute of Professional Legal
    Studies—Northern Ireland
    Miss C Carr
    J H S Elliott
    A Gallagher
    J Maguire
    D Moloney
    J Russell
Institute of Public Loss Assessors
Institute of Shorthand Writers
Institute of Trading Standards
    Administration
H M Ireland

Irish Congress of Trade Unions

*Dr J E Jameson
 G S Jones
 M Joseph
**Justice
    M Bryceson
    P English
    G Godfrey, QC
    W Goodhart
    T Sargent
    P Sieghart
Justices' Clerks' Society

 A J Kambites and Others
*A Kammer
 R S Kelly
 M S Khan
 S A Khan
 Lord Kilbrandon
 M King
 C Kingsley
 W Knight

The Labour Party
*Miss J Lada-Walicki
*Mrs J E Laird
 Her Majesty's Land Registry
 Lane Neighbourhood Law Centre
 Reverend C A Larkman
 R Laugharne
*His Honour Judge Lavington
**Law Centres Working Group
    A Grana
    P Kandler
    P Lefevre
    N Walker
**The Law Society
    J L Barratt
    J L Bowron
    Sir Richard Denby
    C R Hewetson
    M D Holland
    P A Leach

11

Sir David Napley
Sir John Palmer
P G W Simes
Law Society Local Government
  Group
Law Society of New South Wales
K M Lawson-West
Lord Justice Lawton
Professor A D Lawton
A Layton
J L Lean
*D Leathard
**Legal Action Group
  G Bindman
  Lord Gifford
  O Hansen
**Legal Aid Advisory Committee of
  Northern Ireland
  Master A E Anderson
  Professor C M Campbell
  B G Finnegan
  His Honour Judge Higgins
  Miss S Murnaghan
  R E Scott
Legal Executives in the Isle of
  Wight
Leicester Legal Advice Centre
J Leigh Jennings
His Honour Judge Sir Ian Lewis
Library Association
P H Light
W A Limont
*C J Linsdell
J I Lishman
Liverpool Polytechnic
C Lloyd
London Advice Centre Group
London Association for Saving
  Homes
London Common Law Bar
  Association
London Criminal Courts Solicitors'
  Association
London Magistrates' Clerks'
  Association

**London Small Claims Court
  A Conway
  R Egerton
  Mrs A Hawkins
  M Loup
  E Woolf
London Solicitors' Litigation
  Association
London Trainee Solicitors' Group
J Loosemore and Company
**Lord Chancellor's Advisory
  Committee on Legal Aid
  Lord Hamilton of Dalzell
  A C Heywood
  H Hodge
  Lady Marre
  K Polack
  R E K Thesiger
  P W G Urquhart
  His Honour Judge White
Lord Chancellor's Department
Ms J Lucas, JP
M Lynch
C H Lyon

Professor J P W B McAuslan
*A B McCoubrey
C McCullough, QC
Lord MacDermott
J V Machin
I W Mackay
D McKibbin
C R Mackintosh
I A B McLaren
K J H Maclean
H G McLeave
J McMullen
*A McNeil
Magistrates' Association
*A Magnus
*J and C Malins
Manchester Law Society
Manchester Polytechnic
*March, Pearson and Skelton
Maria Colwell Memorial Fund
S B Marsh

12

L A D Martin
R M Martin
C D Mason
D C de Massey
**Masters of the Supreme Court
   Taxing Office
     Master G J Graham-Green
     Master Horne
     Master E J T Matthews, Chief
       Taxing Master
L D Matovu
J F M Maxwell
*Mrs G L May
P Medd, QC
*Medical Defence Union
***Mr Justice Megarry,
   Vice Chancellor
Lord Justice Megaw
L W Melville
N Menon
*Merrils, Ede and Gribble
Sir Robert Micklethwait, QC
Mid Surrey Law Society
S E Miller
Mirror Group Newspapers
His Honour Judge Miskin, QC
G Moffat
*M J G Moir
T Monk
D Montagu-Scott
R S Montgomerie
D T Morgan
*T S Morley (USA)
Mrs A P Morris
*Lord Morris
Mr Registrar D E Morris
*H R Morris
H A C Morrison
I A Morrison
Professor T H Moseley
*R T Moss
*G B Motion
S Muhammad
D Mulcock
G Mungham
Mrs S Murray

Sir David Napley
National Association for the Care
  and Resettlement of Offenders
**National Association of Citizens
  Advice Bureaux
    Mrs R Kohn
    A J Leighton
    Mrs R Martin
    Ms B Stow
    J Waldman
National Association of Citizens
  Advice Bureaux, Community
  Lawyers Group
National Association of
  Conveyancers
National Association of Probation
  Officers
National Association of Probation
  Officers (London Branch)
National Consumer Council
****National Conveyancing Guarantees
  Limited
    R Boyd-Pickens
    R Flavin
National Council for Civil Liberties
National Council of Social Service
National Council of Social Workers
  with the Deaf
National Federation of Consumer
  Groups
*National Federation of
  Neighbourhood Advice Centres
National Federation of Womens'
  Institutes
National House Building Council
****National House Owners Society
    S G Carter
    K T Weetch, MP
National Marriage Guidance
  Council
National Society for Legal and
  Financial Reform
National Union of Students
H W Neale
R H Neillands
*Mr and Mrs C Newbitt

13

J Newey, QC
C T Noel
E F Northcote
**Northern Ireland Consumer
    Council
        Ms B Hinds
        Mrs P Miskimmin
**Northern Ireland Legal Action
    Group
        J McGettrick
        J Meehan
*Northern Ireland Legal Quarterly
Northern Ireland Resident
    Magistrates Association
North Kensington Neighbourhood
    Law Centre
Nottinghamshire Law Managers'
    Association
Nottinghamshire Young Solicitors
    Group
Nuffield Foundation
E G Nugee, QC
Michael Nunn and Company
J Nutting and Others

Official Group on Legal Services
*M Ogden
Open University
D C Orgles
*N E Osborn
D J Ovenden
Oxford Law Course Advisory
    Committee
Oxfordshire Legal Action Group

Paddington Advice and Law Centre
I Partington
*Miss A E Pashley
A P H Peach
Dr D Pearl
J Pearce
Lord Pearson
*Ms R Pearson
D R Pedley
Master W Pengelly
P Pennant

*Mrs C E Perry
J E C Perry
Personal Rights Association
R G Peter
P Petrakis
*B W B Pettifer
*M A Pettit
*Ms K Philippson
Ms J Phillips
His Honour Judge Pickles
M D Piercy
Pimlico Neighbourhood Aid Centre
***Rear Admiral B C G Place
R Plane
Police Superintendents' Association
    of England and Wales
Polytechnic of North London—
    Department of Law
Polytechnic of the South Bank
*H F Porter
J G Porter
A A Preece
C Price, MP
Principal Registry of the Family
    Division
William F Prior and Company
Property Transfer Association
Prosecuting Solicitors' Society of
    England and Wales
G D Purnell

Queen Mary College, University of
    London—Faculty of Law
Queen's University, Belfast—
    Faculty of Law

*Viscount Radcliffe
Ramblers' Association
Real Estate Associates
*Miss J Rees
P Reeves
B C Reid
*E Rendall
C G Richmond
Rights of Women

Rio Tinto-Zinc Corporation
  Limited
D Robertson
W Robins
A G Robinson
Ms V L Robinson
W Rodgers, MP
A D Roper
*L F Rose
R I L Rose
M R Rose
A Rosen
Lord Justice Roskill
D A Rowlands
Royal Arsenal Co-operative
  Society Limited
Royal Institute of British Architects
Royal Institution of Chartered
  Surveyors
Royal Town Planning Institute

A Sachs
Sir Eric Sachs
Professor R Sackville
A F Sales
Lord Salmon
*P Sapsford
Save the Children Fund
N Scorah
Reverend M Scott
Scottish Young Lawyers'
  Association
*R P Seaman
E Seeley
R D Seligman
**The Senate of the Inns of Court and
  the Bar
    Mr Justice Browne-Wilkinson
    R D L Du Cann, QC
    J M Hillen
    D C Hirst, QC
    D B McNeill, QC
    M P Nolan, QC
    Sir Arthur Power
    Lord Scarman
    P E Webster, QC

Mrs W K Sewell
Shell UK Oil—Legal Division
H Shepherd
D Shirtcliffe
Shropshire Law Society
Shuttleworth, Dallas and
  Crombleholme
Simanowitz and Brown
Mrs M Simons
*R S Sinclair (USA)
C L Smith
*L Smith
Professor P Smith (USA)
W P Smith
*D Smout, QC
R H F Smyth
E A Snyder (USA)
P Soar
Society of Civil and Public Servants,
  Lord Chancellor's Department
  Section
Society for Computers and Law
  Limited
Society of Conservative Lawyers
Society of County Secretaries
Society of Labour Lawyers
**Society of Local Government
  Barristers
    R E C Jewell
    C H Ramsden
    N A L Rudd
Society of Pension Consultants
Society of Public Notaries of
  London
Society of Public Teachers of Law
Society of Stipendiary Magistrates
  of England and Wales
Somerset Law Society
R Southern
*Southern Office Machines Limited
Lord Justice Stamp
*T R Standen
Standing Conference of Asian
  Organisations in the United
  Kingdom
R Staunton

15

Stephenson and Farrow
Lord Justice Stephenson
B P Stone
*W G Strachan
A Strong
Students Representative
  Committee, Cambridge Law
  Faculty
Sunday Times
Supplementary Benefits Commission
M R Sutcliff
B T Sutcliffe

K M Talbot Alton
A C Taussig
Thamesdown and District
  Community Relations Council
*D W Thomas
P A Thomas
P Thompson
K Tomkinson
**Trades Union Congress
    G A Drain
    J F Eccles
    P Jacques
    T Mawer
    J Monks
    T Parry
Trainee Solicitors Group—Law
  Society
Triplan Interstructures Limited
*R W Tullie
V Tunkel
R Turner
R Tyson

United Kingdom Association for
  European Law
United Kingdom Federation of
  Business and Professional Women
United Lawyers' Association
*United States Department of
  Housing and Urban Development
University of Birmingham—Faculty
  of Law
University of Cambridge

University College of London—
  Faculty of Law
University College of Wales
University of Exeter
University of Leicester—Faculty of
  Law
University of Liverpool—Faculty
  of Law
University of London Union Law
  Group
University of Sheffield
University of Warwick

N D Vandyk
The Honourable Richard Vane
Dr M Vincent
C L Vincenzi

*J Wakeham, MP
A D Walker and Others
*W H Walker
Lord Justice Waller
Professor J N Walton
Wandsworth Rights Umbrella
  Group
*D Watts
*G P D'A Waud
J H Weatherill
K T Weetch, MP
Welfare Rights Group—Durham
**Wellington Street Chambers
    Lord Gifford
Welsh Consumer Council
J Wendon
*West and Son
West Country Young Solicitors
  Group
A Wexler
D Wheatley
C White
R C A White
Ms J Whiteman
B J Whitney
*A H Wicks
Lord Widgery, The Lord Chief
  Justice of England

*Lord Wilberforce
***Sir Richard Wild, late Chief
    Justice of New Zealand
*K Wilford
H W Wilkinson
Richard Williams
Rowland Williams
*J V Williamson
Ms H Wilson
C J B Wimberley
Mrs L Winetroube
W Wolfson
Women's National Commission
F O Wood

**Young Barristers Committee of the
    Bar Council
    J Barley
    J Nutting
    Sir Arthur Power
    N Purnell
    P Talbot
Young Lawyers Group for Cheshire
    and North Wales
Young Solicitors Group—Law
    Society

**Professor M Zander
R Zara

LIST 2

Individuals and Organisations who provided Information or who Assisted the Commission

Mr and Mrs L R Abbey
Abbey National Building Society
E K Abrahall
R R C Abrahams
Leo Abse, MP
Leo Abse and Cohen
Mrs B Ackroyd
R F Acraman
A A Adams
Mrs E M S Adams
F O B Adams
J Adams
T E Adams
J A Addison
F W Adkin
W J F Adkins
Alban Deaf Association (Luton Branch)
P C Alcock
M V Aldridge
A L Alexander
R Alexander
D A Alford
S T S Ali-Akbar
C S Allen
J E Allen
Mrs M Allen
P J Allen
Amalgamated Union of Engineering Workers
Mr and Mrs G C Amer
American Bar Association
American College of Trial Lawyers
Mrs H J Amesbury
R W Ammonds
A Anderson

D W Anderson
R Anderson
R B Anderson
Andrews & Co
G Andrews
J D Andrews
A K Angus
J Anscomb
B W Anslow
A J Anson
M Anwar
T F Archer
Mrs E Armstrong
C W Arnold
S A S Arnold
M Arnott
U Arrfelt (Sweden)
W G Ashton
J W Asquith
Association of Bristol Advice Centres
Association of Independent Businesses
Association of Local Authorities in Northern Ireland
E Aston
F Aston
Ms J Atkins
D N Atkinson
E A Austerberry
Miss P M Austin
R C Austin
Mrs Z Austin
C R Ayling
Mrs A Azriel

Mrs H Babington
J R Bacon
Miss L Bailey
Mrs A J Bailey
Mrs F E Bailey
V Bailie
A E Baillot
A Baird
G S Bajwa
J E S Baker (USA)
R Baker
R L Baker
Mrs A R Baldwin
B A Baldwin
Dr J Baldwin
Balham Law Centre
P D Ball
Balsall Heath Association
R S Banerjee
M J Banks
Mrs Y Banner
Barclay Trust
W Barcroft
A O Barker
Barlow, Lyde & Gilbert
A D Barlow
N F Barlow
Mrs P A Barnes
R M Barraball
D A Barratt
C D Barrett
G H Barrett
K Barron
F Bartholomew
C W Barton
Ms N R Bastin
Mrs M E Batchelor
Ms V Batchelor
Mrs G W Bates
J B Bates (USA)
Battersea Neighbourhood Aid
  Centre
Battersea and Wandsworth Trades
  Council
C V Batty
R G Baxter

J A Bazzani
Miss E Beardmore
L O Beasley
R E Beal
Miss E Beardmore
L O Beasley
Mrs D M Beaumont
Ms D Becker
D L Beckerman (USA)
Mrs P Beech
A F Beere
Belfast Solicitors Association
B W T Bell
C Bell
F Bell
J R A Bell
Bellenden Legal Advice Centre
Mrs R Belling
N Bellord
C A Bellows (USA)
Mrs M Benham
W G Benham
Dr R C Benians
J S Bennett
Mr & Mrs J Bennett
M E Bennett
Chambers of Patrick Bennett, QC
R A Bennett-Levy
J E Benns
Benwell Community Law Project
M Berkeley
N Berman
Mrs S Berridge
T Berry
His Honour Judge Best
W A Best
Mrs W M Best
N Beswick
D A Bettison
Mrs M Bews
H J Beynon
Mr and Mrs H J Bibby
E M Biggs
G H Biggs
J Biley
Mrs M Bindloss

19

L C Birch
Mrs M J Birch
W B Birch
D Bird
R J Bird
T D Birge (USA)
Mr Registrar M Birks
Mrs P Birmingham
Birmingham Law Society
Birmingham Law Society—Young
  Members Group
A H Bisset
Mrs R M C Black
Blackburn & Price Limited
Blackfriars Settlement
C B Blades
Mrs C Blain
Mrs D F Blencom
J A Blomley
R A Bluffield
Mrs D L Board
J G Boardman
Mrs J Bolding
Mrs I Bolt
Miss K T Bolton
K F Bone
Ms C M Boniface
Mrs A C Bonne
F Booth
P Bostic
Miss J H Bosworth
R N Botley
U G Bourke
E O Bourne
Mr and Mrs A J Bowen
Mrs J Bowen-Roberts
Bower, Cotton & Bower
R N Bower
P D Bowers
D Bows
Mrs A Boynton
Mr and Mrs I H Bradford
Bradford and Bingley Building
  Society
D M Bradley
J W Bradley

E Brady
Mrs R M Brandenburg
J G F Brandon
N R Brant
M S Branyall
Mrs A Bray
T J Brennan
Mrs L A Bridges
H Bridle
R J Brien
Mr and Mrs R I Briggs
Bristol Law Society
British Broadcasting Company
British Leyland Limited
British Standards Institution
Ms B M Broadbent
E H Bronstein (USA)
J Brogden
Ms R Brooke
J G Brooks (USA)
J S Brook-Smith
Mrs A Brown
A F H Brown
Mrs B J Brown
C D Brown
Mrs M Brown
M R Brown
Mrs O Brown
A J Brownhill
J G Bruce
T O Brugger
Mrs K M Bruton
R Bryan
D Bucknell
L H Buckham
Mrs G Buckley
C C Bulford
Bundesrechtsanwaltskammer
  (Germany)
H Bunting
J M Burchell (South Africa)
Mrs E M Burgess
Miss M K Burgess
Mrs P De Burgh Marsh
L R Burke & Co
J A Burnett

F G Burrage
A Burridge
Mrs B A Burrows
D M Burrows
J K Burrows
F Burton
L W Burton
Mrs E M Busi
H Butcher
J S Butcher
Mrs M Butler
Mrs P A Butler
Ms H Buttenweiser (USA)
C Button
H D Byers
Ms K Bygrave

J Cable
L Caddy
C R Cadman
B Cain
Caledonian Legal Advice Centre
Mrs D Calderon
G Callender
N Calvert
Cambridge House
    Legal Advice Centre
Camden Council of Social Service
Mrs A Cameron
H Campbell
J Campbell
J Campbell-Grant
Campus Legal Advice Centre
    (Birmingham)
Canning Town Legal Advice Centre
Canning Town Information Centre
W G Canning
J F Cannon (USA)
W K Cannon
J H Cant
W H Cantrill
D L Carey-Miller
Ms D Carlisle
L A Carlson (USA)
R Carne
Mr and Mrs L H Carpenter

J Carr
K A Carr
B Carroll
Mrs M D Carroll
Ms F Carson
D Carter
R Cartwright
R J Cary
R J Caselton
P Cashman
Mrs M A Cassford
C J Cavanagh (USA)
A Caville
P C Cena (USA)
Central Council for Education and
    Training in Social Work
Central Office of Information
Central Policy Review Staff
"Centre 70", Community
    Association Advice Centre
Centre for Interfirm Comparison
Centre for Socio-Legal Studies
R Cert
R J Chalk
Chambre des Notaires du Quebec
R Chandler
J F Chapman
Mrs D M Chapple
H Charles
T Charleton
A E Chave
Mrs E G Chenery
Mrs M Chesney
K S H Ching
S N Chisman
G S Christie
W B Christy (USA)
W Church
Citizens Advice Bureaux—Hull
Citizens Advice Bureau and Guild
    of Help, Southend
Clapham Law Centre
Clapham Legal Advice Centre
G I H Clare
R L Clare, Jnr (USA)
Mrs B M Clark

Mrs C Clark
E G H Clark
Mrs J D Clark
N J Clark
L Clarke
L R Clarke
P J G Clarke
R Clarke
R F Clarke
V A Clarke
W Clarke
Mrs J J Clarke-Govier
Miss M H Clegg
Miss P M C Clementi
Mrs G W Clifton
Mrs S Coamer
J Coates
Mrs L Cobb
M P Cocker
Mr and Mrs R J Cocking
A Cohen
B R Cole
D Coleman
Mrs M Coles
V F Collier
F W Collingbourne
C J Collins
Mrs G Collins
Mrs K Collins
W P Collins
F Collum
J S Colyer, QC
Commission of the European
  Communities
Committee on Civil Legal Aid and
  Advice (Eire)
Community House Law Centre
Mrs C A Compton
F A Conch
Coningham Road Advice Centre
Contact Legal Clinic—Cheltenham
Mrs J C Cook
C H E Cooper
Mrs D J Cooper
D N Cooper
F T Cooper

N Cooper
Co-operative Union
J Coppack
B L Corbett
A P Corke
W F Cornes
Mrs P M Cornish
V Costanzo
His Honour Judge Cotton
P F Coughlan
Council of Engineering Institutions
Council of Legal Education
Council of Local Education
  Authorities
J D Coventry
Coventry Legal and Income Rights
  Service
Coward Chance
Cowles and Company
B P Cox
S Cray
S Crayread
R M Creegan
R J Cridlan
K D Crisp
J F Cronin
Mrs A Crosley
Lord Cross
Mrs D I Cross
Mr and Mrs J E D Crossley
Lieutenant Colonel R J Crossley
A M Crossman
C R Crowe
Mrs K E Crump
H Cullimore
S Cumming and Son
W B Cumming
G P Cunliffe
Mrs N B Curling
J F Curran
D R Currer
Currie & Sons Limited
Mrs D V Curry
A E Curtis
E A L Cushion
P J Cutting

22

Sir William Dale
Dalkeith Knitwear Limited
D Dalton
P Dalton-Golding
His Honour Judge Daly Lewis
M J Dalziel-Jones
Dame Colet House
L H Daniels
Mrs C E Darbon
J R Darby
S E Davey
His Honour Judge David, QC
J E David
A G R Davies
C Davies
Mrs D Davies
F Davies
I C Davies
S Davies
T Davies
T R Davies
Ms V M Davies
D S Davis
S C Davis
I Davidson, QC
Mrs M E Davison
C A Dawson
T E Deacy (USA)
C Deakin
Miss E E Dean
J B Debley
Ms S Decker (USA)
Mrs P De Derbrech
Mrs E G Deeth
Mrs D Delaney
Ms S Dement (USA)
R de Normanville
F G Dent
L P Dent
Mrs E Denton
Department of Education and
    Science
Department of Education—
    Northern Ireland
Department of Finance—Northern
    Ireland

Department of Housing and Urban
    Development (Washington DC)
Department of Justice (Eire)
Department of Justice (New
    Zealand)
F Derbyshire
Mrs H M Derrick
Major R L Derverell
P Deverell-Stone
E A Devereux
Dewlands Park Residents
    Association
G P Dews
E Dicker
G N Dickinson
W D Dickinson
R E Dickson
W L Diedrich (USA)
P J Digby
Ms M Diment
Miss M Dinsdale
Mrs D A Diprose
M Dobbs & Company
F B Dodds
J Dodwell
J Doe
Mrs E Doloughan
Mrs T Dowd
Downham Legal Advice Centre
J Doyle
T H Drane
Miss W A Drew
Mrs D Drewett
G Drewry
J W Drinkwater
G Driver
D M Druce
Mr and Mrs Drummond
Mrs C Dubery
Mrs P Dubery
Dudley Road Legal Advice Centre,
    Birmingham
L W Duffen
H J Duffus
D R Duggleby
M Dun

23

P Duncan, Attorney General,
   South Australia
R G Duncan (USA)
Chambers of Victor A C Durand,
   QC
A J Dwek

East Greenwich Legal Advice
   Centre
H Eastham
J T Eccles
P H Edmonds
Mrs I Edson
Mrs A E Edwards
A J Edwards
Dr E A Edwards
Mrs H Edwards
H D Edwards
Mrs H M Edwards
Sir Martin Edwards
R L Edwards & Partners
T D Edwards
E Edwards Son & Noice
Mrs A Egerton
F Egerton
K W Eidman (USA)
E A Eist
J C Elamcusa
Electrical Electronic
   Telecommunication and
   Plumbing Union
John Elliot, Wallace and Company
Messrs Ellis and Company (Zambia)
His Honour Judge Ellison
D Ellwanger (USA)
Miss J Elson
W Elwell
B F F Ely
S G Ely
W V G Emery
J Epstein
Mrs N Epstone
A I Esslemont
Mrs E M Evans
G Evans
H T Evans

Mrs M Evans
Chambers of Thomas M Evans, QC
A Even
G Ewart

Fabian Society
The Faculty Office of the
   Archbishop of Canterbury
J M Fakes
Chambers of Peter Fallon, QC
Family Service Unit
C J Farr
K S Farr
K Farrar
W A Farrell (USA)
H D Farrer
Chambers of Colin Fawcett, QC
E Fear
Federal Ministry of Justice
   (West Germany)
Federation of Wholesale and
   Industrial Distributors
J E Fellows
Ms J Ferguson
Councillor H Ferguson-Jones
W Ferguson
P T Fernando
E Finan
J S Finch
Miss A Finlay
Mrs T M Firbank
A Fisher
D J Fisher
E Fisher
T Fisher
Mrs W Fisher
W Fisher
Fishers Limited
B R Flint
J E Flynn
Foreign and Commonwealth Office
G W Foreman
D T W Forsyth
D Foster
E Foster
Foster, Wells and Coggins

R J Foulger
J Fowler
Chambers of James E Fowler
R Fox
Mrs E D Foxall
Mrs F M France
Chambers of Hugh E Francis, QC
Miss U E Fraser
C A Freestone
Freshfields
Mrs E Frost
Friendship House Advice Bureau

E Gabbay
Mrs E Galea
R D Gall
Mrs P H Galloway
W A Galpin
J Gannon
J E Gardner
S Gardner
S Gardner
T J Gardner
Mrs J Gare
Garratt Lane Law Centre
Mrs E Garratt
F Gathe
Mrs V C De Gavino
W F Geake
G Geary
G Gee
Mrs M M Geenty
I Geffen
General Council of the Bar in Eire
General Dental Council
Ms H Genn
Mrs D Gent
Mrs A P Gentry
F J Gentry
E V George
V George
J J Gething
Mrs E Gibbard
A C Gibbins
C Gibbons
Chambers of Michael Gibbon, QC

Mr R Gibson
R E Gilbert
A Giles
E R F A Giles
K W Giles
Mrs L M Giles
Mrs J Gillen
J Gillings
Mrs R C G Gillunter
Mr and Mrs S J V Gilson
G W Gissing
M Gladstone
Miss I Gledhill
G L Goddard
J W Goddard
J Godson
E M Godwin
Lord Justice Goff
W M Goldsbrough
S A Goldsmith
R R Goldstone
S Goldstone
P Gonnella
His Honour Judge Goodall
D H Goodall
R Goodchild
J V Goodfellow
J Gordon
Mrs G C Gordon
L K Gordon (Australia)
R Gordon
Mrs J A Gorman
A Gornall
K Goryn
Miss C Gosling
D Gosling
B K Gossain
L J Gostling
G P Gough
F J Gould
Mrs A Gozzi
D Graham
L Graham
Mrs N Graham
S N Graham
Mrs F Grant

25

Mrs I D Grant
J Grant
R V Gray
W E Gray
Greater Manchester Legal Services
  Committee
A Greaves
D Greaves
C V Green
E Green
E L Green
F Green
Mrs M I Green
Professor R T Green
H J Grenitser
Chambers of William P Grieve,
  QC, MP
H Griffin
His Honour Judge Griffith-Jones
E C Griffiths
G T Griffiths
R F B Grimble
A C H Groom
Miss E J Grubb
W E Gumb
R A Gunn-Smith
S K Gupta
Mrs E Guthery
C Guy
K J Guy

D J Habgood
Hackney Advice Bureau and Law
  Centre
E Haftke
B C Haggett
R G D Hale
J E Hales
Halifax Building Society
Sir Basil Hall, Treasury Solicitor
E Hall
H S Hall
Mrs K Hall
R D Hall
Mrs Hall
Mr and Mrs Hall

C R Halpern (USA)
Mrs L P Hamblyn
N Ham
E H Hamilton
G Hamilton
Mrs M M Hamilton
Mrs S A Hamilton
M Hammerson
A V Hammond and Company
G Hamp
D Hancock
M T Hancock
Mrs T J Hancock
Professor J F Handler (USA)
Handsworth Law Centre
D J Hanlin
Mrs C M Hann
J B Hanson
A K Hanton
Mrs R L Hanwell
Harbottle and Lewis
S Hardaker
E E Hardcastle
P Harding
J R Hardon
Dr D C Hardwick
L V Harker
C A Harkin
Mrs N G Harper
P Harper
Mrs M Harrhy
B T Harris
D Harris
D L Harris
D W Harris and Company
Dr H R Harris
Ms L Harris
M D B Harris
A E Harrison
D M Harrison
E Harrison
J G Harrison
P Harrison
Mrs K T Harte
N Hartley
B W Harvey

26

M Harvey
Mrs P G Harvey
R W Harvey
Harvey and Marron
S Hashim
Ms E Haskew
G H Hathaway
S Hawkins
S R Hawkins
R Haworth
W Haydn-Trezise
Mrs V Hayes
R Hayden
Miss S Haynes
T J G Haynes
Mrs F I Hayter
Mrs B Healey
E F Healy
D Hearne (USA)
Mrs A V Heath
K G Heaven
Miss A M Heawood
J P Heawood
M J Hedges
Mrs V H Hedges
J Hedley
H Hely-Hutchinson
Ms A J Hemmi
C W Henderson
A Hepper
W Hepple
Miss S Herbert
Ms L Herbst
Hermer and Flacke
I Hermer
W J Herring
Mrs A Heselton
B Hewett
N Hewson
Miss P Hewson
J R Hickmott
C L Hicks
Highbury Law Centre
B S Hill
J M Hill
Mrs M E Hill

Mrs R M Hill
Hillingdon Community Law Centre
J F Hillman
C Hinchliffe
S L Hing
M H Hingorani
Mrs C Hoar
Mrs I E Hobby
Miss M A Hodges
E J Hogg
F E Hogwood
V W Hogwood
B Holden
J G Holland
R Holland
Holloway Law Centre
F L Holman
Mrs M Holmes
S E Holmes
H Holroyd
Mrs P Holt
A F Honeybun
Honor Oak Legal Advice Centre
H H Hood
A H Hoole
B Hooper
D Hope
Mrs K A Hopkins
L R Hopper
C F Horn
T J Horner
J V Horrill
H T Horsfield
Mrs B Horsley
Mrs E Horsman
Miss J S G Horten
W Horton
D Houghton
E H House
A G J Howard
J A Howard
D Howell
Miss M Howse-Crompton
F Howson
Hoxton Legal Advice Centre
E I Hubbard

27

C Hudson
B J Hughes
C R G Hughes
W T Hughes
Mrs E M Hull
Hull Legal Advice Centre
R W Humphries
A R Humphriss
L M Hunn
R J Hunt
J Hurman
A Hurst
Mrs C E Hustwaye
Chambers of Arthur E Hutchinson
His Honour Judge Hutchison
A E Hyams

D Ibbotson
L W Ibbott
Mrs N Imhof
Incorporated Law Society of Ireland
Incorporated Society of Valuers
   and Auctioneers
C W Indge
F R Inglis
Institute of Actuaries
Institute of Chartered Accountants·
   in Ireland
Institute of Judicial Administration
Institute of Plumbing
Institute of Statisticians
International Common Law
   Exchange Society
International Welfare Association
Mrs D D Irons
A B Irving
Islington Law Centre
Islington Legal Advice Centre

G Jackson
G P Jackson
K Jackson
K Jackson
P L Jackson
S J A Jackson

Sir Jack Jacob, QC, Senior Master,
   Queen's Bench Division
Mrs A A Jagger
R T Jago
A P James
B F James
W H James
Mrs G Jameson
Mrs E I Janes
Ms J Jardine
E J Jarmyn
R L Jeffries
R Jelley
Mrs R Jenkins
R E Jenkinson
J W Jennings
Ms E J Jensen (USA)
G J Jessup
H L D Jindal
Mrs A I Job
B John
J T Johns
D W Johnson
Professor E Johnson (USA)
Mrs H K Johnson
Mrs M Johnson
Mr and Mrs A J Johnston
B A Jolly
Mrs B Jones
C A Jones
Mrs D Jones
E Jones
F Jones
G Jones
G P Jones
His Honour Judge Jones
H N Jones
J Jones
J E Jones
Mrs R Jones
S Jones
T Jones
W Jones
Mrs C M Jonietz
H G Jordan
T E Jordan

28

S M Joseph
M D Jowett
Chambers of Edwin F Jowitt, QC
D F Joy
W Joy
W W Joynes
Judicial Council of California

E Kalibala
R Kasanof (USA)
H Kay
P Kay
H A Kaye
Miss J M M Kearvell
Dr N A Keen
R Kelk
Mrs J E Kellner-Stevens
Kennington Legal Advice Service
H K Kenny
Mr Justice Kerr
Mrs B Kerr
Mrs M Kerr
A Kerton
Ms C Kettle
R K Kewin
V A Khan
E Kindon
H King
R King
King's College, University of
   London
Kingsmead Legal Advice Centre
Councillor M Kingston
P M Kingston
C T Kirk
H Kirk
L G G Kirton
L Kirwin
Miss M G Kitley
Miss S Klein
H Kligerman
P Kneale
N D H Knight
B S Kohli
P V de Korda
P D Kornhauser

J S Korycki
Mrs S E Kriefman
H B Kuder Jnr (USA)
Mrs C M Kulawy
W Kuy

L & A Accident Repair Company
   Limited
Mrs J la Bouchardiere
Ms J Ladd
P Lamb
W Lamb
Lambeth Community Law Centre
Professor L F Lamerton
Land Registration and Information
   Service (Canada)
C B Lane (USA)
S A Latif
S A Latimer
A H Laughlin
Dr A E Laurence
Lavender Hill Legal Advice Centre
The Law Commission
Law Council of Australia
Law Foundation of New South
   Wales
Law Institute of Victoria
E Lawrence
F S Lawrence
G M Lawrence
Lawrence, Graham, Middleton and
   Lewis
J B Lawrence
T Lawrence
Mrs V Lawrence
J R Lawrenson
Law Society of Alberta
Law Society of Newfoundland
Law Society of New South Wales
Law Society of Saskatchewan
Law Society of South Australia
   Incorporated
Law Society of Upper Canada
R J Lawton
J M G Layton

H A Leal, QC, Deputy Attorney General of Ontario
W Leather
R B Leaver
Mrs E Lee
R L Lee
S Lee
Leeds Polytechnic
C H Lees
Legal and Civil Rights for Children Society
Legal Services Commission (Canada)
Legal Services Corporation (USA)
A Leggatt
Ms J Leggatt
Ms M Leicester
A Leigh
Dr L J S Lesley
H Levenson
R Leverington
Mrs R Levy
E J Lewis
J Lewis
S Lewis
T C Lewis
Lewisham Council for Community Relations
Lewisham Legal Advice Centre
C Leyman
A Licudi
Ms M A Lile
R Lill
Lincoln's Inn Treasury Office
C Lindsay
G Ling
Professor I M D Little (USA)
Miss J Livock
C F A Lloyd
D G Lloyd
D R Lloyd
Ms E Lloyd
F Lloyd
His Honour Judge Seys Llewellyn
His Honour Judge Lloyd-Jones
Lloyd's of London

Lloyds Aviation Underwriters
Lloyds Bank Limited
Ms D A Lobb
L Lochridge (USA)
F J Lodder
R A Lodge
London Council of Social Services
London Sports Car Centre
London Young Solicitors Group
L Long (USA)
R R Long
M J Longthorn
J D Lothian
Mrs C D Loundon
Mrs M A Lovett
G Lowndes
F J Lubbock
Charles Lucas and Miles
Mrs M E Lucy
J T Luff
L L Lukacs
L D Luke
W G Luscombe
Luton Legal Advice Centre
H Lydiate
D Lynn
T Lyons

D Maby
F McAllen
J S McAllister
C J McCalvey
Mrs G McCarthy
Mrs A L McClean
Mrs I M McConnell
M McConville
J H McDermott
J B Macdonald
A Macdonald Fraser
L McDonnell
H MacDougall
Miss A J McElhinney
M H McEwan
The Honourable W A McGullivray, Chief Justice of Alberta
Lord McGregor

30

T S McGuane
A A Machin
Ms M P McHugh
W B McIvor
F R Mackegg
James Mackie and Sons Limited
A W McKenzie
T McLaren
Mrs H McLaren
J McLaughlin
I E Maclean
J Maclean
I McManus
J McManus
Mr and Mrs D McNally
Mrs O L McNee
T D G MacNeece
A McNulty
K D McRobert
P C Madsen
G Maidment
Mrs Malin
Mrs J Mallett
F Mallinson
Manchester Arbitration Scheme for
    Small Claims
Manchester Law Centre
R Manning
J Mannion
J K Mansfield
Mrs A Mansley
H F Manson
N Marbrow
D Marcan
Mr Maricanday
F V Marine
D H Markes
L Marlowe
Mrs V M Marriott
D A Marsh (USA)
The Reverend S Marsh
S Marshall
Mrs V Marshall
Mrs E Marston
Mrs J Martin
T S Martin

Mary Ward Legal Advice Centre
H Maslen
M Massie Wildig
B C Masterson
Mrs R Mastrangelo
A A D Matthews
P Matthews
Mrs M Maxwell
J Maycock
Mrs V Mayers
G T Mayo
Mrs E M Meads
Medical Protection Society
M Melhuish
Mrs V Melia
J Mercer
W T Merritt
Metropolitan Police Solicitor's
    Department
Metson, Bradford and Clements
Metson Cross and Company
J Meunch (USA)
His Honour Judge Meurig Evans
C Meyer
E Middleton
Midland Bank Trust Company
    Limited
W Miles
S G Millar
E A C Millen
L Miller
Miss V J Miller
E Mills
MIND (National Association for
    Mental Health)
Ministry of Legal Affairs (Zambia)
W H Mirfin
K H Mirren
Mirror Group of Newspapers
Mrs A Misir
Mrs J Mitchell
R Mitchell
G Mogford
Monlough Food Production
    Company Limited
L S Montgomery

Mrs J Moodie
L W Mooney
Mrs N Moor
A D Moore
E H Moore
Mrs K M Moore
M Moore
Mrs E Morey
D S Morfey
E Morgan
Mrs G Morgan
G J Morgan
L B Morgan
M Morgan
Mrs R D Morgan
Ms R M Morgan
W J Morgan
Sir Godfrey Morley
J Morley
J Morley
Mrs L F Morley
A T Morris
Mrs B Morris
J A Morris
Dr P J Morris
Mrs R J Morrison
J Mortimer
J B Morthland (USA)
A M Morton-Jacobs
Mrs M W Munsey
J F Murphy
P A D Murphy
R J Murrison
W K Musoke
V E Myson

Sir Patrick Nairne
M A Narborough
National Association of Citizens
  Advice Bureaux, South Wales
  Area
National Centre for State Courts
  (USA)
National Farmers' Union
National Federation of Building
  Trades Employers

National League of Husbands
National Market Traders'
  Federation
National Union of Teachers
National Westminster Bank
  Limited
C A N Neal
J H Neal
M Neaum
Network Legal Advice Centre
A J Nevison
New Ash Green Village
  Association Limited
New Cross Legal Advice Centre
Newham Rights Centre
Ms D J Newman
H Newman
R Newman
R C Newman
D W Newmarch
G D Newmarch
M C Newsome
New South Wales Law Reform
  Commission
New Zealand Law Society
Mrs W A Newton
Professor B Niblett
H J Nicholas
Mrs J Nicholson
J P Nickolls
W Nightingale
G A Nix
Mrs A M Nixon
Miss T Nolan
Northern Ireland Office
North Lewisham Law Centre
Northolt Community
  Neighbourhood Legal Advice
  Centre
Norton Rose, Botterell and Roche
Mr and Mrs P A Norvell
Nottingham Law Centre
Nottingham People's Centre
Nottinghamshire Law Society/
  TOC H Advice Centre
Nucleus

Mrs G C W Nutt
L M Nyary

Miss M O'Brien
Mr Justice O'Connor
J O'Connor
Mrs K D O'Connor
H E Odd
Office of Fair Trading
S W Ogden
Hugh O'Kane and Company
  Limited
P F O'Keeffe
G Oldacre
Miss M Oliphant
P O'Mahoney
P O'Neill
Miss L A Ong
Ontario Law Reform Commission
A P Oodan
A Organ
R Orme
D L Orr (USA)
D F O'Sullivan
A J Oughan
Mrs F M Owen
T P Owen
Owen White and Catlin
Oxford Free Legal Advice Scheme
Oxford House Rights and Legal
  Advice Centre
Oxford University Law Society
Oxford University—Faculty of Law
Mrs L C Oxley
D Oxley

P Packer
Mrs M Padgen
Ms M K T Page
J R Paine
Mrs M Paintan
Mrs C M Palmer
H G Palmer
Mrs J E Palmer
D Pappin

D Parker
Mrs N Parker
F Parkes
G A E Parkes
S Parrianen
S A Parsonage
Mrs B D Parsons
L A Parsons
S G Parsons
Mr and Mrs Part
K Partington
M Partington
Mrs F M Partridge
Dr H R Patel
J H Patterson
L F Paul
Mrs K J Paull
Mrs R Pavey
F C Payne
Professor J C Payne (USA)
Mrs L Payne
Squadron Leader S Payne
Mr and Mrs Payne
L A Peake
His Honour Judge Pearce
His Honour Judge Pears
J Pearson
E W Pedley
J Pendlebury
J Penty
N E Penty
J C Percival
T C Peries
Ms C T Perkins
R O A Perkins
J W Perry (Australia)
Mr and Mrs A Peters
F D Peters
P Petrams
Ms S Petritz
G W W Pettman
Philip Conway Thomas and
  Company
Mrs J Philipson
C Phillips
Miss D F Phillips

D L Phillips
R Phillips
R E Phillips
Phoenix Assurance Company
    Limited
G A Pilborough
C D Pile
I Pinnock
Mrs N I Piper
G L B Pitt
R C Pitt
E W Plant
B T Plunkett
R Pobjoy
E L Podd
D Podmore
Police Federation of England and
    Wales
J H Ponder
J Poole
Mr and Mrs R Poole
D C Pooley
J Porter
J A Porter
M V Postins
Mrs R Postlethwaite
F K Potter
Reverend A L Poulton
J G Poust (USA)
Mrs L E Pottinton
N Powell
S Preston
L P Preuss
Price Commission
C F Price
C H Price
Ms E Price
Ms M E Price
P Price
R L Price
Mrs J Prideaux
Mr R D Pridgeon
Mrs R Priest
R Prigmore
V L Prince
Mr and Mrs P K Prior

L Prittard
Professional Organizations
    Committee (Toronto)
Ms D Proudman
Provincial Building Society
W Prowting
E Pulham
D E Pursey
A R P Purvis

S Quan
Miss J Quinn
Miss K Quinn
W Quinn

H P Rabbich
E G Rackstraw
Major R B Rafferty
F G Rainbow
G K Raine
Rance and Company
Miss P J Rankin
C R Ravenhill
J Rawlins
D L Ray
R B Ray
Mrs E B Raymond
J Raymond
Mrs T J Raynor
D Rea
Mrs R M Read
H Reed
Mrs V Reeks
M V C Rees
N Reeves
R W K Reeves
Mr and Mrs T J Reeves
Regional Office of Industrial
    Tribunals, Cardiff
Registry of Friendly Societies
C Reid
L Reid
Professor B J Reiter
Release
A S Renton
B Renwick

Ms M Reynolds
J Richards
J E Richards
M Richmond
Richmond Legal Advice Centre
Richmond Road Services Limited
Mrs R A Ricketts
A Riddington
J D Riddiough
R V Ridges
M Ridgway
J Ridsdale
The Honourable S H Rifkind (USA)
Mrs A M Rigby
Mrs C A Rigby
G W Riley
G W Riley
K Riley
J B Rimmer
M H Riordan
E C Rivers
Mrs P Robbins
H Roberts
Mrs J A Roberts
Mrs S Roberts
W J Roberts
Mrs P Robins
D G Robson
D J Robson
J Robson
R Robson
Commander R H S Rodgers
T W Roe
E C Rogers
H R Rogers
Mrs M Rogers
N J Rogers
P Rogers
Mrs E Rokas
T I Rollo
E Romilly
W E Roscher
M I Ross
A Rothwell
R G Rougier, QC
C J Rowe

Royal Automobile Club
Royal Bank of Scotland Limited
Royal British Legion
A D Royoe
Mrs S Ruddock
B S Russell
T Ryalls
T D Ryder

J A Sabourin
A Saliba
Saltley Action Centre—Birmingham
R H Sampson
W D Sampson (USA)
Mrs M Sanders
L Sanderson
E W Saunders (USA)
H Saunders
Judge R Sauve (Canada)
Mrs M B Savage
Mrs E Savill
A F Saville
G Scales
Mrs B M Scannell
D P Scannell
P H Scannell
T M Schroeder (USA)
Professor C J M Schuyt (Holland)
H L Schwab (USA)
M Schwartz (USA)
A Scott
A G Scott
E J Scott
F W Scott
Miss D Scott-Stevenson
G H Scriven
J Seaman
A J S De Segundo
Seldon, Ward and Nuttall
Major G R Sell
B Sellers
G G Selway
Major A J Sergeant
Ms K Sergeant
Mrs M Service
S I M Shah

Shanklin Legal Advice Centre
R Shanks
K Sharif
Mrs N Shattock
E Shawyer
Mrs A M Shayler
A R Shea
H T Shearing
Sheffield Free Legal Information
  Service
Sheffield Polytechnic
P F Sheils
Shelter National Housing Aid Trust
P J Shephard
S Shepherdson
D K Sheridan
K B Shillitoe
H Shindler
V Ship
J Shipley
Ms M Shire
Ms S Shopper
H Siddall
Mrs B Sieber
R D Siefman
G J Silk
S C Silkin, QC, MP
Ms J F Sillwood
Mr and Mrs J Simlett
P E Simmonds
A Simpson
L J Simpson
M E Simpson
W A Simpson
W E Simpson
Dr R Simpson-White
Sir Norman Skelhorne, QC
V R Skidmore
Mrs D Skillington
R C E Skolfield
Miss M Slegg
R T Sloan
Miss M P Small
A F Smallbone
Small Heath (Birmingham)
  Community Law Centre

J Smallpage
J W Smiles
A D Smillie
A Smith
A F Smith
A G Smith
A W Smith
B C Smith
B P Smith
Miss C M Smith
D Smith
D Smith
D F Smith
Mrs E Smith
Mrs I E Smith
J R Smith
M Smith
Miss M J Smith
R A Smith
T D Smith
Reverend P R Smythe
Mrs E J Sneddon
A S Soan
Social Science Research Council
Society of Immigrant Lawyers
D Sollars
R Somerville
R F Soul
Southampton Legal Advice Centre
E R F Southgate
South Glamorgan Institute of
  Higher Education
Southampton Duty Solicitor
  Scheme
B Southwell
South Wales Anti-Poverty Action
  Centre
Southwark Law Project
J H Spackman
R J Speechley
A S Spokes
W N Spurway
A H G Staines
J R Staines
A D Staite
N C Staley

H J L Stallard
A R Stancombe
J P Stanley, MP
S P Stanley
R H Stanway
Ms G Stark
G Startup
R T Steele
Steering Committee for One
  Parent Welfare
H G C Stephens
His Honour Judge Stephen
Mrs D Stephenson
H W Stephenson
J R Stephenson
W S Stepney
P M Stern (USA)
Mrs E Stevens
Mrs L Stevens
S C Stewart
Mrs W Stewart-David
Miss M St John
C Stock
F W Stockdale
Ms P J Stockham
St Paul's Legal Advice Centre
Stoke Newington Advice Group
  Service
E B Stone
L Stone
Mrs S Stone
D Stonebanks
Mrs M Stonehouse
R H Stoner
G S Stout (USA)
Mrs W Streen
Mrs A Street
Mrs B Street
Strover and Company
J T Stubley
T Studholme
F D Sullivàn
His Honour Judge Sunderland
Supreme Court of New South
  Wales
Sussex TV Rentals

E G Sutton
E H Sutton-Evans
B E Swain
Mrs G Swain
F J Swan
J Swan
Swedish Courts Administration
Swedish Savings Banks' Association
C Sweeney
N Sweeny
P G F Swift
Mrs E M Szmyrko

Mrs C Tait
Mrs S Tamlyn
Mrs B A D Tansley Witt
R Tatem
Taylor, Simpson and Mosley
Mr and Mrs A Taylor
Mrs F Taylor
F L Taylor
G A Taylor
H Taylor
Mrs L Taylor
Lewis W Taylor and Company
P M Taylor and Company
R H Taylor
W M Taylor
Mrs M E Tearle
D Tedman
Mr and Mrs J R Teggin
M I Telfer
Mrs S Temple-Smith
A T Terry
J A Tester
A G Thomas
B D Thomas
Ms C F Thomas
J Thomas
J Thomas
P Thomas
P C Thomas and Company
P E H Thomas
T H Thomas
Mrs V Thomas

A G Thompson
Master D R Thompson
Judge E Thompson (USA)
Mrs J Thompson
R Thompson
Mrs V Thompson
Mrs A Thorne
G W Thorne
Mrs S E Thornley
Professor G Thoran (USA)
J E Thorpe
Ms E Thurgood
M Thynne
Dr A Tibbitts
H O Tidball
F E Till
Mrs C R Timson
K Tingle
K M D Tolley
Mr and Mrs K M Tomlinson
J A Torrence
Tottenham Legal Advice Centre
Tower Hamlets Law Centre
Mrs V Townsend
Trafford Park Estates Limited
J P Traynor
A J Tremayne
D Tremayne
Trent Polytechnic
C E W Tribe
Mrs V Troth
D Trott
Mrs J Trotter
M T Troughear
A M V Trust
Tuck and Mann
R Tucker
M Tulip
Miss E J Turner
F R Turner
J F Turner
J F Turner
Mrs V M Turner
W G Turner
Ms Turpin
A Twitchings

R Uddin
Mrs J Uglow
F Uhlman
Professor W Ullman
C Unerman
United Kingdom Immigrants
  Advisory Service
University College, Cardiff
University House Legal Advice
  Bureau
University of Nottingham
R J Urowsky (USA)
J Urpeth
S J Uzzell

S Vague
Miss C I Van Dine (Canada)
Vauxhall Community Law Centre
Mrs O G Vernon
A G Vicary
F L Vicary
Victoria Law Foundation
F Vidler
R A Vine
J De Vries

S Wadiwala
A H Wadkins
T Wagg
Mrs L Wakefield
Mrs R G Wakeling
A Walker
A Walker
F E Walker
Mrs J Walker
R Walker
J Wall
C C Wallis
G C Wallis
J R Walsh
W L Walsh
J A Walsworth-Bell
J Walter
Mr Walters
Waltham Forest Aid Centre
A Walton

Mr and Mrs A Walton
A C Walton
L A Wanless
D Ward
Ms L Ware
R Wareing
D R Warltier
M Warman
A Warrick
J J Warrington
F Wastell
L Waterfall
Waterloo Legal Advice Centre
D C Watkins
A A Watts
F R J Watts
C A Watts
T E Waugh
S Waxman
A T Wealthy
L F Weatherall
R V B Webb
S A C Webb
K R Webber
C W Webster
Mrs J M Webster
Miss L P Weekes
C Weight
Mrs D Wells
R A Wells
Mrs G Welsh
J Welsh
Mrs E P J West
West London Law Society
West Hampstead Community Law
  Centre
Westminster City Council
D N Weston
M Weston
Mrs F M Westover
G Westrupp
Ms Weynes
Mrs S Whalley
Mrs A Wharton
A G Whatling
L Wheatley

Lord Wheatley
Mrs S Wheatley
J M Whetton
F C Whitaker
Mrs V I Whitbread
Mr and Mrs E White
L A White
S White
V S Whitehead
Whiteside and Knowles
Miss M Whitson-Fay
A M Whittaker
A Whittle
H Whitton
E Wickwar
Lord Wigoder
V Wijetunge (Sri Lanka)
E T Wild
A F Wilkinson
Mrs A Wilks
J Wilkinson
A Williams
Miss D Williams
D A Williams
D G Williams
E S Williams
F G Williams
I T Williams
J H Williams
J J Williams
K H Williams
R J Williams
R M Williams
T Williams
W Williams·
R A Williamson
S Williamson
Miss V J Williamson
R J Willicome
Mrs A Willmott
J A Willis
D H Wilson
Ms G I Wilson
J Wilson
J Wilson
T Wilson

Mrs N E Wilton
George Wimpey and Company
   Limited
A Wimpory
Miss M D Winch
J H Windsor
P Wise
R D Wise
Mrs J E Wiseman
A Wolf
G Wolf
G Woobey
D E Wood (U.S.A.)
E W Wood
F W Wood
Reverend G E Wood
J D T Woodall
Ms H Woodhouse
J W Woodley
J A Woods
J M Woods
B E Woody
J Woolf
Commander E D Woolley
Woolwich Legal Advice Centre
L M Worboys

Mrs G J C Wright
S G Wright
W Wright
Mrs M Wu
Mrs A A Wroe
T Wyatt
H Wyld
M H Wylde
P Wyndham Lawes
I Wynn-Jones

Mr C S Yakes
F Yeo
Mrs C Young
Mrs C L Young
Mrs F J Young

G A Young
H R Young
M Young
Dr W Young
Young Motherhood Limited

M R Zebaida
H Zys

LIST 3

The Commission's Consultants

Coopers & Lybrand, Chartered Accountants

Department of Finance, Northern Ireland

Office of Manpower Economics

Social and Community Planning Research

Mrs V Bell

P S C Lewis, Esq

E G Nugee, Esq, QC

T B F Ruoff, Esq., CB, CBE

L A White, Esq, MC

PART B

Surveys and Studies

Definitions of statistical and accounting terms

Statistical terms

The principal statistical terms used in the sections that follow are explained below.

The average is the arithmetic mean.

The median is the mid-point in a list arranged in order of magnitude. Median earnings indicates a level of earnings half way down the list with half of those surveyed earning more, and half less.

The upper quartile is the figure one-quarter of the way down the list, in order of descending magnitude. One-quarter of those responding to a survey of remuneration earn an amount equal to or greater than this.

The highest decile is the figure one-tenth of the way down the list, in order of descending magnitude. One-tenth of those responding to a remuneration survey earn an amount equal to or greater than this, and 90 per cent less.

Accounting terms

The principal accounting terms used in the following sections are set out below.

Gross fees represent the fee income (excluding VAT) before any deduction.

Gross income is the fee income plus other professional income, such as commission, and interest retained on clients' accounts.

Net profit is the gross income after deducting professional expenses. The figure is struck before making any charge or allowance for:

    the principal's own pension;

    interest on the principal's own capital investment;

    national insurance contributions;

    tax.

44

SECTION 1

Numbers of Barristers and Solicitors

Contents *paragraph*

Introduction

1.1 This section gives information about the number of barristers and solicitors in England and Wales and includes information about students and numbers entering the legal profession.

Numbers of lawyers

1.2 Table 1.1 below summarises, by category of employment, the number of lawyers (excluding students) in England and Wales in 1978. It includes only solicitors with practising certificates; no information is available of the total number of solicitors in commerce and industry and the Law Society consider there are a substantial number who do not hold practising certificates. Statistics are not kept of the numbers of barristers who are not in private practice. The figure in Table 1.1 of 3,000 is a broad estimate by the Senate of the number of barristers engaged in occupations involving legal matters.

TABLE 1.1

Numbers of lawyers in England and Wales in 1978

	Barristers	Solicitors with practising certificates
Private practice:		
principals	4,263	19,908
employed	—	9,031
Total	4,263	28,939
Employed other than in private practice	⎫	4,821
Abroad	⎬ 3,000	104

Source: Law Society and Senate.

1.3 Even with the qualifications mentioned in the last paragraph, Table 1.1 shows that while the great majority of lawyers are engaged in private practice a substantial number are engaged outside private practice—in commerce, finance, industry and government.

1.4 Against this background, we set out, in the following paragraphs, more detailed information of the numbers of students and the numbers of barristers and solicitors.

Numbers of law graduates

1.5   Table 1.2 shows the number of law graduates from 1967 to 1977.

TABLE 1.2
Numbers of law graduates in England and Wales, 1967–1977

Year	Law graduates from universities[1]	Law graduates with external degrees	Law graduates with CNAA[2] degrees	All law graduates
1967	1,306	250	—	1,556
1968	1,451	373	—	1,824
1969	1,521	457	39	2,017
1970	1,449	463	108	2,020
1971	1,584	425	126	2,135
1972	1,663	524	155	2,342
1973	1,706	490	231	2,427
1974	1,882	435	295	2,612
1975	1,973	375	435	2,783
1976	2,071	380	526	2,977
1977	2,327	103	689	3,119

[1] Universities of England and Wales.
[2] Council for National Academic Awards.
Source: Council for National Academic Awards.

1.6   The number of law graduates from universities almost doubled in this period, from 1,306 in 1967 to 2,327 in 1977. There was also a substantial increase over the period in the number of CNAA law degrees. These are awarded following degree courses approved by the Council for National Academic Awards at polytechnics and other non-university institutions.

Solicitors

Students

1.7   New applications for enrolment as students with the Law Society increased by six per cent per annum between 1971 and 1978. During this period the proportion of law graduates among student enrolments fluctuated between 58 per cent and 70 per cent. The detailed figures are shown in Table 1.3.

Articles

1.8   With very limited exceptions, before he can be admitted as a solicitor, a student must serve a period of articles, two years for graduates and five years for non-graduates. In 1978, 2,983 new articles were registered with the Law Society, of which 91 per cent were by graduates. A survey by the Association of Graduate Careers Advisory Services (AGCAS) among those who graduated in law in 1977 whose intention it was to seek articles, showed that nearly 80 per cent were successful in obtaining articles within one year of graduation. The vast majority of their articles were with solicitors in private practice: 91 per cent compared with 6 per cent in local government, 2 per cent in the magistrates' courts services and 1 per cent in industry and commerce.

TABLE 1.3

Applications for enrolment with the Law Society as students, 1971–1978

Year	Number	Percentage change on previous year	Percentage of enrolments who were law graduates
1971	2,721		58
1972	3,086	+13·4	61
1973	3,182	+ 3·1	64
1974	3,235	+ 1·7	70
1975	3,639	+12·5	not available
1976	3,950	+ 8·5	60
1977	4,120	+ 4·3	67
1978	3,979	− 3·5	63
Average increase per annum 1971–1978	—	6·0	—

Source: Law Society.

1.9   The AGCAS survey also showed that graduates seeking articles typically made a large number of applications: on average 29 applications were made which resulted in three interviews and one offer. However, just over one-third of graduate applications used personal contacts and made many fewer applications before finding articles.

1.10   The number of new articles registered with the Law Society during the period 1971 to 1978 is shown in Table 1.4.

TABLE 1.4

Numbers of new articles registered with the Law Society, 1970–1978

Year	Number	Percentage change on previous year
1970	1,739	
1971	1,856	+ 6·7
1972	1,914	+ 3·1
1973	2,423	+26·6
1974	2,481	+ 2·4
1975	2,412	− 2·8
1976	2,730	+13·2
1977	2,535	− 7·1
1978	2,983	+17·8
Average increase per annum 1970–1978	—	7·0

Source: Law Society.

1.11 While the increase in the number of articles registered over the nine-year period shown was, on average, 7 per cent per annum, there were significant variations from year to year as can be seen from Table 1.4. In December 1978 there were 8,766 persons serving under articles.

Admissions

1.12 Table 1.5 sets out the figures for admission to the Roll of solicitors during the period 1971 to 1978. The increase over this period was 5·5 per cent per annum.

TABLE 1.5

Numbers of admissions to the Roll of solicitors, 1971–1978

Year	Number	Percentage change on previous year
1971	1,682	
1972	1,713	+ 1·8
1973	1,768	+ 3·2
1974	1,849	+ 4·6
1975	2,203	+19·1
1976	2,164	− 1·8
1977	2,480	+14·6
1978	2,448	− 1·3
Average increase per annum 1971–1978	—	5·5

Source: Law Society.

Practising certificates

1.13 Before commencing to practise on his own account or in partnership, a solicitor must obtain a practising certificate from the Law Society, which is renewable annually. Many solicitors employed in commerce, finance and industry do not hold practising certificates.

1.14 Table 1.6 shows the number of practising certificates issued from 1963 to 1978. The first part of the table covers two five-year periods and the second part gives figures each year from 1974 to 1978. The average annual increase over the period was 3·5 per cent but the growth was more rapid between 1973 and 1978.

TABLE 1.6

Numbers of practising certificates, 1963–1978

Year	Number of practising certificates	Average increase per annum %
1963	20,269	
1968	22,787	2·4
1973	27,379	3·7
1974	28,741	5·0
1975	29,850	3·9
1976	31,250	4·7
1977	32,812	5·0
1978	33,864	3·2
Average increase per annum 1963–1978	—	3·5

Source: Law Society.

1.15 Table 1.7 shows the number of practising certificates issued in 1968 and in 1978 analysed between principals in private practice, assistant solicitors and consultants employed in private practice, and solicitors employed outside private practice who had taken out a practising certificate.

TABLE 1.7

Practising certificates issued, 1968 and 1978

	Number		Percentage increase 1968 to 1978 %
	1968	1978	
Solicitors in private practice:			
principals	15,900	19,908	25
assistant solicitors	3,474	7,645	120
consultants and others	386	1,386	259
Total	19,760	28,939	46
Employed other than in private practice	2,994	4,821	61
Abroad	33	104	215
Total practising certificates issued	22,787	33,864	49

Source: Law Society.

1.16   It can be seen from Table 1.7 that most solicitors with practising certificates are engaged in private practice. Over the ten-year period shown by the table, the number of practising certificates issued to solicitors in private practice increased by 9,179. The number of principals and the number of salaried assistant solicitors both increased by about 4,000; but this meant that the number of assistant solicitors more than doubled in the period whereas the number of self-employed principals increased by only 25 per cent. One reason for this is that the number of sole practitioners declined slightly over this period, suggesting that young solicitors were accepting appointments as salaried assistant solicitors rather than starting to practise on their own account.

Solicitors with practising certificates employed outside private practice
1.17   Table 1.8 shows that over half the solicitors with practising certificates employed outside private practice in 1978 were in local government, and that just over one-quarter were in industry and commerce. Of the solicitors employed in central government in 1978 (about 450) 258 took out practising certificates, a considerable increase over 1968 when there were about 400 solicitors in central government, of whom 47 had practising certificates.

TABLE 1.8

Solicitors with practising certificates employed outside private practice, 1968 and 1978

	1968		1978	
	Number	%	Number	%
Local government	1,721	57	2,520	52
Industry and commerce	745	25	1,238	26
Central government service	47	2	258	5
Other employment	481	16	805	17
Total	2,994	100	4,821	100

Source: Law Society.

Seniority and age of solicitors in private practice
1.18   The seniority of principals and assistant solicitors engaged in private practice in 1976, the latest year for which information is available, is shown in Table 1.9.

1.19   Table 1.9 shows that 48 per cent of all solicitors in private practice in 1976, as principals or employed in solicitors' firms, had been admitted as solicitors in the previous ten years. This was mainly because 87 per cent of assistant solicitors were admitted in this period; and over three-quarters of assistant solicitors in 1976 had been admitted as solicitors in the previous five years. The seniority structure of principals in private practice was much more evenly spread, as Table 1.9 shows.

51

TABLE 1.9

Seniority of solicitors employed in private practice in 1976

Years since admission as solicitor	Principals %	Assistant solicitors[2] %	All solicitors in private practice[3] %
Up to 5	11	77	31
6–10	20	10	17
11–15	14	2	10
16–20	12	2	9
21–25	11	1	8
26–30	12	1	9
More than 30	14	3	11
Not stated	6	2	5
Total	100	100[1]	100
Number	19,247	7,414	26,661

[1] In this table, and in some of those which follow, totals shown may not be equal to the sum of the constituent numbers, because of rounding.

[2] Includes salaried partners.

[3] Excludes consultants.

Source: Consultants' report on the Law Society's remuneration survey, Section 16.

1.20 The age distribution of solicitors engaged as self-employed principals in private practice is shown in Table 1.10. A tenth of solicitor principals were less than 31 years of age and 15 per cent were 61 years of age or more.

TABLE 1.10

Age of solicitors engaged as principals in private practice in 1976

Age group	Solicitors engaged as principals in private practice %
Under 31	10
31–40	34
41–50	23
51–60	18
61 and over	15
Total	100

Source: Consultants' report on the Law Society's remuneration survey, Section 16.

Barristers

Numbers of students entering the profession

1.21 A prospective barrister must first join one of the Inns of Court as a student. After passing his Bar examinations the student may be called to the Bar. The student barrister then does one year's pupillage with an established barrister, during the second half of which he may undertake fee-earning work. Table 1.11 shows the number of students domiciled in Great Britain admitted to the Inns of Court, the numbers called to the Bar and the number commencing practice (after pupillage) between 1965 and 1978.

TABLE 1.11
Numbers of student barristers, calls to the Bar and numbers starting practice, 1964–1978

Year ending in October	Number of student admissions[1] to Inns of Court	Called to the Bar[1]		Starting practice	
		number	percentage of students	number	percentage of those called to the Bar
1964	Not available	237		80[2]	
1965	Not available	283		138	
1966	699	236		129	
1967	931	247		206	
1968	759	246		139	
1964–68	—	1,249	—	692	55
1969	674	370		137	
1970	537	471		241	
1971	659	556		222	
1972	745	561		275	
1973	838	561		321	
1969–73	3,453	2,519	73	1,196	47
1974	840	529		299	
1975	1,023	663		354	
1976	827	628		382	
1977	616	654		326	
1978	596	677		285	
1974–78	3,902	3,151	81	1,646	52

[1] Students domiciled in Great Britain only.
[2] 1964 covers a nine-month period only.
Source: Senate.

1.22 Table 1.11 shows that in the last ten years about three-quarters of those admitted as students have been called to the Bar although the proportion was lower in the middle and late 1960's. Of those called to the Bar in the last fifteen years, about one half started in private practice.

Numbers of practising barristers

1.23 The numbers of barristers engaged in private practice in the years 1963 to 1978 is shown in Table 1.12. The first part of the table covers two five-year periods and the second part of the table gives annual figures for 1974 to 1978.

TABLE 1.12

Numbers of practising barristers, 1963–1978

Year (at October)	Number	Average annual increase %
1963	2,073	
1968	2,379	2·8
1973	3,137	5·7
1974	3,368	7·4
1975	3,646	8·3
1976	3,881	6·4
1977	4,076	5·0
1978	4,263	4·6
Average increase per annum 1963–78	—	4·9

Source: Senate.

1.24 It will be seen from Table 1.12 that, while the average annual increase in the number of practising barristers over the period 1963 to 1978 was just under 5 per cent, there was a higher rate of increase in the middle 1970's which fell back after 1976 to between 4 per cent and 5 per cent. While between 1963 and 1968 there was a net addition to the number of barristers in practice of only 306, in the next ten years there was a net addition to the number of barristers in practice of 1,884.

1.25 The increase in the numbers of practising barristers is the net figure of those starting to practise and the number ceasing to practise. Table 1.13 gives the details: the last three sections give the figures for five-year periods and in addition annual figures are given for 1974 to 1978.

TABLE 1.13

Barristers starting to practise and ceasing to practise, 1964–1978

Period	Number started practice	Number ceased practice		Net increase
		under ten years' seniority	over ten years' seniority	
1964–1968	692	183	203	306
1969–1973	1,196	101	337	758
1974–1978 (detailed below)	1,646	267	253	1,126
1974	299	38	30	231
1975	354	39	37	278
1976	382	41	106	235
1977	326	79	52	195
1978	285	70	28	187

Source: Senate.

1.26 It can be seen that while most of those ceasing to practise had been in practice for ten years or more, a substantial proportion had less than ten years at the Bar, particularly in the five years 1974 to 1978.

Seniority and age of barristers

1.27 The seniority of barristers in practice at October 1977, with juniors analysed by reference to the number of years in practice after completion of pupillage, is shown in Table 1.14.

TABLE 1.14

Seniority of barristers, October 1977

Seniority	Number	Percentage
QCs	384	9
Juniors:		
over 15 years	804	20
9–15 years	712	18
4–8 years	1,150	28
3 years or less	1,026	25
All juniors	3,692	91
All barristers	4,076	100

Source: Senate.

1.28 It will be noted from Table 1.14 that, at October 1977, one-quarter of barristers had been in practice for three years or less and over half had been in practice less than nine years.

1.29 The survey of remuneration carried out by the Bar in 1976–77 (see Section 18) provides information on the age structure of the profession at April 1976. The details are set out in Table 1.15.

TABLE 1.15

Proportion of barristers responding to the survey by age group, 1976

Age group (at April 1976)	All barristers %	QCs %	Juniors %
under 30	38	—	43
30–39	33	2	36
40–49	18	47	14
50–59	8	38	5
60 or over	3	13	2
All	100	100	100

Source: Consultants' report on the survey of income at the Bar 1976/77, Section 18.

1.30 Table 1.15 shows that in 1976 38 per cent of barristers were under 30 years of age and 71 per cent were under 40 years. Almost all of the QCs were in their 40's or 50's; it will be appreciated that many of the more senior and experienced barristers will have been given judicial appointments.

SECTION 2

The Social Background of Entrants to the Legal Profession

Contents *paragraph*

Introduction

2.1 This section sets out information concerning the parental occupation of entrants to the legal profession in comparison to that of other young people and to entrants to other professions.

2.2 There is no comprehensive information about the parental background of entrants to the legal profession. Neither the Senate nor the Law Society collects information about parental occupation on a regular basis. Among surveys of the legal profession which include information about parental background are those of D Harris ("The Legal Profession in England and Wales—a study of lawyers with special reference to solicitors, barristers and the higher judiciary", unpublished doctoral thesis, 1966) and D Podmore ("A Survey of West Midlands Solicitors", The Law Society's Gazette, 13th July 1977).

2.3 The Universities Statistical Record keeps detailed information about all university entrants including subject of study, parental occupation, and further education or first employment after graduation. From this it is possible to obtain information about intending lawyers and to make comparisons with entrants to other professions. Most of the information in this note is obtained from this source. However, this information relates only to university students, and therefore excludes entrants to the legal profession graduating from other institutions (mainly polytechnics), mature entrants and school leavers. In 1976 university graduates were estimated to include three-quarters of intending barristers and one half of intending solicitors. In both branches of the profession, therefore, university graduates were the largest single group of entrants.

2.4 Information has also been obtained from two of the Inns of Court about the parental background of student admissions. In order to analyse this information allocation to occupational groups was made by the Commission's secretariat on the basis of data concerning parental occupation provided from the records of the Inns.

Comparison with other young people
2.5 Table 2.1 deals separately with four broad groups of young people. Each group has been classified according to the occupation of the head of household (in the case of data from the General Household Survey), or the chief economic supporter (in the case of data from the Universities Statistical Record). In most cases this would be the father, so the description "father" has been used throughout, but this should not be taken to exclude cases where someone other than a father is the head of household or its chief economic support. The table sets out the proportion of young people in each group with fathers in professional and managerial occupations, the proportion of young people with fathers in manual occupations and the proportion with fathers in clerical or similar non-manual occupations, the forces and various unclassified occupations.

2.6 The various sources from which the information in Table 2.1 was obtained (set out in the footnotes to the table) used slightly different descriptions for the classes of parental occupation. One major difference is that in the socio-economic groupings used in the General Household Survey, most teachers and nurses are classified as being in the "intermediate" group of occupations, whereas in the Universities Statistical Record, they are classified as being in professional occupations.

2.7 The first line of Table 2.1 shows the proportions of all young people aged 16–19 grouped according to parental occupation. A comparison of these figures with those of young people continuing in full-time education shows that young people with fathers in a professional or managerial occupation are more likely than those with fathers in a manual occupation to stay at school after 16 and to continue in full-time education after the age of 19.

2.8 The second part of Table 2.1 shows the proportion of university entrants studying law or some other professional subject whose fathers have a manual occupation. The proportion of those studying law (16 per cent) is close to that of those studying professional subjects in general (15 per cent).

2.9 The third part of the table gives figures for university graduates who study for the examinations of the Bar or train to become solicitors. The table shows that a slightly lower proportion of graduates studying for the Bar examinations have fathers in a manual occupation.

2.10 The final part of Table 2.1 gives information concerning people admitted to the Bar provided by two of the four Inns of Court. The table shows that three-quarters or more of those admitted to Middle Temple and Gray's Inn had fathers in professional or managerial occupations.

TABLE 2.1

Occupation of the fathers of certain classes of young people

	Fathers' occupation		
	professional or managerial %	manual %	intermediate or other occupation %
All young people:			
aged 16–19[1]	21	66	13
aged 16–19 in full-time education[1]	32	50	18
aged 20–24 in full-time education[1]	50	30	20
University entrants: [2]			
studying professional subjects	58	15	27
studying law	54	16	30
University graduates: [2]			
studying for Bar exams	59	11	30
training to become solicitors[3]	56	15	29
Admissions to Bar: [4]			
Middle Temple	76	14	10
Gray's Inn[5]	77	8	16

Sources:

[1] Data from the General Household Survey (1974 and 1975). Parental occupation is classified according to the Registrar General's socio-economic grouping.

[2] Data from the Universities Statistical Record (1976 and 1977). Parental occupation is classified according to the Registrar General's Classification of Occupations 1966.

[3] Graduates stating they were entering articles or studying for the Law Society's examinations.

[4] Data supplied by the Inns and classified as far as possible according to the Registrar General's socio-economic groupings. Data from the Middle Temple relates to the first half of 1977 and from Gray's Inn to 1977 and 1978.

[5] The information given relates to 70 per cent of admissions. In the remaining 30 per cent of cases, either the father was deceased, or insufficient information was available about his occupation.

Relationship between parental occupation and graduate career

2.11 Table 2.2 sets out in the first column the percentage of those graduating from university in 1976 and 1977 whose fathers were engaged in selected professional occupations. 1·1 per cent of the fathers of all university graduates were solicitors in private practice, practising barristers or judges. The second column of the table sets out the percentages of university graduates entering the occupation in which their fathers were engaged. For example, of those university graduates taking up solicitors' articles, studying for the Law Society's examinations or studying for the Bar examinations, 5·2 per cent had fathers who were solicitors, barristers or judges.

TABLE 2.2

Professions chosen by graduates compared with fathers' professions, 1976 and 1977

Profession of father	Percentage of all university graduates with father in profession shown (1)	Number of university graduates entering profession of father (as shown) as a percentage of all university graduates entering that profession (2)	Ratio of column (2) to column (1) (3)
	%	%	
Solicitor/barrister/ judge	1·1	5·2[1]	5
Doctor	2·6	12·4	5
Dentist	0·4	4·4	11
Accountant	1·7	5·1	3
Architect/surveyor	1·5	7·1[2]	5

[1] This figure represents university graduates taking up solicitors' articles or studying for the Law Society's examinations and those studying for the Bar examinations.

[2] This figure relates only to university graduates intending to become architects.

Source: Universities Statistical Record.

2.12 If there were no link between careers chosen by graduates and their fathers' professions, the proportion of graduates intending to enter the legal profession whose fathers were lawyers or judges would be close to that for students as a whole, that is, around one per cent. Although the fathers of most graduates entering the legal profession were not lawyers or judges, there was some association between parental occupation and graduate career. The third column of Table 2.2 shows a comparison among professions of the association between choice of career and parental occupation. It is obtained by expressing the percentage of university graduates entering the same occupation as their fathers as a ratio of the percentage of all university graduates with fathers in that occupation. It can be seen that the extent of the association with parental occupation, shown in the third column of Table 2.2, is very similar for all the professions shown, other than dentistry. In the latter case there seems to be a stronger link between parental occupation and choice of career.

2.13 Table 2.3 gives the proportion of graduates taking up careers in the law whose fathers were in the legal profession. It shows that the proportion of Bar students with fathers in the legal profession is higher than that of student solicitors, but even in the case of Bar students the proportion is no more than 8·4 per cent.

TABLE 2.3

Proportion of university student lawyers with fathers in the legal profession, 1976 and 1977

Graduate career or vocational study	Percentage of university graduates with father in legal profession %
Bar examinations	8·4
Trainee solicitor	4·7
All entrants to the legal profession	5·2

Source: Universities Statistical Record.

2.14 In Tables 2.2 and 2.3 fathers classified as being in the legal profession include only lawyers in private practice and judges. Some students may have fathers who qualified as lawyers but did not practise, or who are employed as lawyers in commerce, industry or national or local government; others may have close relatives in the legal profession. There is no information from which to deduce the proportion of graduates whose fathers are not lawyers or judges but who have family or other connections with the legal profession.

Conclusions

2.15 The information set out in this section shows that graduates studying subjects leading to a professional career are likely to come from a professional or managerial background but that the law does not differ markedly in this respect from other professions. The great majority of students entering the legal profession are not lawyers' children.

SECTION 3

Law Centres and Legal Advice Centres

Introduction

3.1   Both law centres and legal advice centres provide legal services to the public. There is no clear distinction between their respective functions, although the following extracts from the Legal Action Group (LAG) directory of legal advice and law centres provides a useful description:

> Legal advice centres are staffed by volunteer lawyers (solicitors, barristers and articled clerks) and have limited opening hours. The centres are essentially for advice and usually offer only a limited amount, if any, of further assistance. There is no charge for the service . . . The telephone, where there is one, may be staffed only during advice sessions . . .
>
> Law centres employ full-time staff, including lawyers, and will handle a client's case from beginning to end, including representation in court or at a tribunal. The service is free unless the centre explains otherwise. Law centres vary in the services that they provide for individual clients.
>
> (a)   They are all restricted to acting for clients living (or sometimes working) within a limited geographical area round the centre.
>
> (b)   They all operate on a very broad restriction against acting for clients who can afford to pay solicitors' fees.
>
> (c)   They are restricted in the kind of work they undertake. This varies from centre to centre but most specialise in landlord/tenant, juvenile crimes and care cases, employment and welfare benefits.
>
> (d)   Some centres concentrate on group work and do little individual case work.
>
> All centres may be prepared to give preliminary advice to clients falling outside these categories . . .

Source: LAG directory of legal advice and law centres.

3.2   In 1978 there were 27 law centres and about 130 legal advice centres in England and Wales; the latter included those which are part of agencies which offer more general advice.

3.3   The Commission carried out a survey of law centres and legal advice centres in order to obtain information on their organisation and finance, and on the type of work undertaken. The surveys were conducted by questionnaire and the answers are set out in detail in the annexes to this section. The following paragraphs describe the principal results of the surveys: paragraphs 3.4 to 3.18 refer to law centres and paragraphs 3.19 to 3.35 refer to legal advice centres.

Law Centres

Survey of law centres

3.4 Information was obtained by way of questionnaires from all 27 law centres operating in 1978; annex 3.1 summarises the replies received. The survey was conducted in two stages: 19 questionnaires were completed in the second half of 1977 and in 1978 questionnaires were completed by a further eight law centres. Changes may therefore have taken place since the questionnaires were completed which are not reflected in the information given in this Section. Financial information provided by the law centres covered different accounting periods, as explained later, but the available information nevertheless gives an indication of their financial position.

Location and size

3.5 Table 3.1 shows, for the 27 law centres in the survey, their location and the number of full-time staff employed. It can be seen that over half the centres are in Greater London.

TABLE 3.1

Location and size of law centres

Location	Number of centres	Number of full-time staff[1]
Greater London	17	153
Manchester	1	12
Liverpool	1	3
Newcastle-upon-Tyne	1	6
Birmingham	3	23
Coventry	1	4
South Wales	2	14
Belfast	1	4
	27	219

[1] Lawyers and non-legal staff. In addition, some law centres employ part-time staff.

Foundation

3.6 Nearly half the 27 law centres were opened after the beginning of 1976. Some had not completed a full year's operation at the time the questionnaire was completed, and were therefore unable to answer certain questions.

3.7 The initiative in founding the law centres came from a wide variety of local individuals and organisations, including local councillors, citizens advice bureaux (CABx) and tenants' and residents' associations. Four law centres were opened as part of a community development project; these were projects established and financed by the Home Office for a limited period in the early 1970's to promote community work in certain areas.

3.8   Opposition to their establishment was mentioned by seven law centres, but three of these said that the objections were not serious. Two law centres said that they had experienced opposition since opening. While some law centres had undoubtedly received opposition to their establishment and operation—for example from the local council or local law society—the survey indicates that there was no widespread and serious opposition.

Status
3.9   The two most common forms of organisation adopted by the law centres were those of a charitable trust (nine) or a company limited by guarantee (eight). The other law centres said that they were unincorporated associations or had not decided on the form of organisation at the time of the survey.

3.10   Law centres were asked to estimate the population in their catchment area, that is the total population in the area they covered. Answers varied from a population size of 11,000 to 2 million; the median catchment area had a population of about 70–80,000. The four law centres set up as part of a community development project generally served smaller areas. Nine of the 27 law centres considered that they served an area with a population of 200,000 or more.

Management
3.11   All of the law centres had (or were in the process of forming) a management committee, although it appeared from the survey that there was sometimes no formal constitution governing its rôle. Membership of the committees usually included in addition to staff of the law centre, local councillors, representatives from the local law society, delegates from local organisations and individuals from the local community.

Staff
3.12   All law centres employed at least one full-time lawyer and a number of other full-time staff. Table 3.2 shows the numbers of lawyers employed in the 27 law centres, and Table 3.3 shows the numbers of other staff employed. Several centres which had opened shortly before completing the questionnaire did not have their full complement of staff.

TABLE 3.2

Numbers of lawyers employed in law centres

Number of lawyers	Number of law centres
1	4
2	9
3	6
4	5
5	3
Total	27

TABLE 3.3

Numbers of full-time staff, other than lawyers, employed in law centres

Number of full-time staff	Number of law centres
1	1
2	1
3	5
4	1
5	6
6–10	11
Over 10	2
Total	27

3.13   It will be seen from Tables 3.2 and 3.3 that the number of lawyers and other staff employed varied considerably. Half of the centres employed one or two lawyers and half between three and five lawyers. The majority of centres (17) employed between five and ten other staff, but only two employed more than ten. In addition to these full-time staff, most law centres were supported by part-time staff and volunteers, who may be lawyers who assist for only a few hours a week.

Type of work

3.14   The questionnaire asked law centres to give information about the number of cases handled in the last year, the number of files opened and other details of the type of work undertaken. The information relating to numbers of cases and files opened may not be comparable between law centres, because methods of recording will differ. The information cannot, therefore, be treated as precise but it gives an illustration of the type and volume of work undertaken.

3.15   Several law centres said that apart from legal advice and assistance given to individuals, their work included talks to local groups and schools on legal matters and assisting in campaigns, surveys and youth projects.

3.16   Most law centres said that, under the terms of the waivers from the Law Society, they did not take on cases involving conveyancing, commercial matters, divorce and other matrimonial business, probate and administration of estates, and criminal business involving adults over 21. Law centres also refer work to solicitors in private practice, usually where legal aid is available or where they take the view that the client can afford to pay a solicitor's fee.

Finance

3.17   The greater part of the financial requirements of law centres were met from three sources: Urban Aid (a government programme for financing community projects in urban areas—75 per cent of the finance is provided by central government and 25 per cent by local government); directly by the local authority;

or by the Lord Chancellor's department. Most law centres obtained some fee income from legal aid, which sometimes went to reimburse part of local authority grants. Table 3.4 analyses the sources of finance of law centres. The figures should be treated as approximate, because they do not all represent the same financial year, though most refer to 1976/77 or 1977/78, and because a number of law centres gave estimated figures.

TABLE 3.4

Sources of finance of law centres, 1976/77 or 1977/78

Source	Amount (£000's)	Percentage of total
Urban Aid	433	34
Local authority	441	34
Lord Chancellor's Department/ Northern Ireland Office	192	15
Community development project	8	1
Legal aid	119	9
Foundations, charities, donations	37	3
Miscellaneous	47	4
Total	1,277	100

3.18   In summary, 43 per cent of the funds of law centres were contributed by local authorities (including their contribution to Urban Aid) and 41 per cent by central government grants—by way of Urban Aid, the Lord Chancellor's Department, the Northern Ireland Office and the community development project. The remaining funds came from legal aid, donations and miscellaneous sources. The average cost of operating a law centre is estimated to be about £50,000 to £60,000 per annum in 1978/79 prices.

Legal Advice Centres

Survey of legal advice centres

3.19   In January 1977 questionnaires were sent to about 100 centres known to be providing legal advice and replies were received from 67 legal advice centres. The detailed results are set out in annex 3.2. We have shown together in annex 3.2 a number of legal advice centres which are part of the same organisation.

3.20   Our enquiry did not seek to cover all organisations offering legal advice on a local basis, but the survey gives a useful indication of the organisation, scale and activities of legal advice centres.

68

Location and size

3.21 Table 3.5 shows, for the 67 legal advice centres in the survey, their location and the number of paid staff employed.

TABLE 3.5

Location and size of legal advice centres

Location	Number of centres	Number of paid full-time staff	Number of paid part-time staff
Inner London	31	25[1]	22[1]
Outer London	9	27	12
Rest of South East	4	3	5
South West	7	0	0
West Midlands	5	4	0
East Midlands	4	1	0
East Anglia	3	0	4
Yorkshire and Humberside	4	2	3
	67	62	46

[1] One Inner London advice centre did not specify the number of staff.

Foundation

3.22 Fifty-two of the 67 centres in the survey had been opened since the beginning of 1970; the most active year was 1974 when a total of 12 were opened, eight in London and four outside London. The oldest is Cambridge House, opened in 1894. No others were established until Springfield (1934), followed by Friendship House (1937), University House (1941) and Mary Ward (1942).

3.23 In 55 of the 67 centres in the survey, the initiative in founding the centres came from local individuals or organisations. Local authorities were responsible for founding 13 centres; the local law society was mentioned as one of the founders by four centres; and five centres were founded by the local community relations council. Some centres mentioned more than one body responsible for their foundation.

3.24 Two of the 67 centres mentioned some opposition to their establishment, but no serious opposition was encountered.

Status

3.25 Of the 67 centres in the survey, 29 were independent legal advice centres; 20 were part of agencies which also provide advice on non-legal problems, many of them being general advice or information centres such as a citizens advice bureau (CAB); the remaining 18 were part of some other organisation as Table 3.6 shows.

TABLE 3.6

Status of legal advice centres

	Number
Independent legal advice centre	29
Run by CABx	4
Part of other general advice or information centre	16
Part of community centre	7
Run by local authority, community relations council or church	11
	67

Catchment area

3.26 Legal advice centres were asked to estimate the population in their catchment area, that is the total population in the area they covered. Answers varied from a population of 10,000 each at Balsall Heath and East Greenwich to an estimated 9 million at Mary Ward. The median catchment area served had a population of 70,000.

Management

3.27 Over half of the legal advice centres in the survey were administered by management, advisory or planning committees of various kinds. In general the members were appointed annually from among the advisers or workers in the centre, or from local individuals interested in participating in the work of the centre. For the other legal advice centres, a quarter were run by the parent organisation, and the rest had informal meetings of individuals involved as and when necessary, or had no management committee at all.

3.28 Local law societies appeared to take little active part in the running of the legal advice centres. In the 67 legal advice centres in the survey, 43 said that their local law society was not involved at all. In the remainder there were informal links with the local law societies, for example through membership of the management committee. Two local law societies provided legal advisers or secretarial services to the centre.

Staff

3.29 The legal advice centres rely heavily on part-time and volunteer lawyers and non-legal staff. Only four centres in the survey employed a full-time lawyer; these were the larger centres of Mary Ward, Cambridge House, Haringey and Southend. Some centres used a large number of volunteer lawyers, for example there were 53 at Hull, 50 at Nottingham and 40 at Southampton; centres with more than ten volunteer lawyers were quite common.

A few centres said that they had difficulty in finding sufficient lawyers to meet their requirements.

Type of work

3.30 The smaller centres giving legal advice were usually open for one or two evenings a week; the larger general agencies opened five days a week, with specialist legal advice being available for a few hours of that time. Three advice centres, Southend, Mary Ward and Cambridge House, were open for legal advice for at least part of every working day.

3.31 Legal advice centres were asked to give the number of cases handled in a year. The answers can only give an approximate guide to the volume of work undertaken, because cases will vary in size and complexity and because the centres do not use a consistent definition for a "case". For example, some centres included non-legal work in their answers and some centres included all enquiries as a case, whereas others did not. Nevertheless it is apparent that there was considerable diversity between the centres in their caseloads, reflecting the varied nature of the centres, from 50 cases at the Kingsmead advice bureau in Hackney to over 8,000 cases at Waltham Forest.

3.32 Sixty-three out of the 67 centres in the survey said that other persons and agencies referred work to them. Table 3.7 shows the number of centres who said that work was referred to them from the various agencies shown in the table.

TABLE 3.7

Source of referrals to legal advice centres

Source of referral	Number of legal advice centres
Social services or related department	46
Citizens advice bureaux	42
Local groups	38
Individuals	24
Police	20
Local press/radio	16
Consumer advice agencies	10
Other	5

3.33 Forty-six of the 67 centres in the survey said that they would undertake all classes of work. Fifteen centres said that if they took the view that a client clearly had the means to obtain advice privately, they would refer the client to a solicitor. A further 18 centres said that they would immediately refer to a solicitor cases which involved litigation.

71

3.34   All but one of the centres said that, where appropriate, they referred clients to solicitors. This usually occurred where the case involved representation in court or litigation. Other classes of work referred to solicitors included matrimonial, criminal and conveyancing cases, and other cases where legal aid was available. In choosing a solicitor, 33 centres used the legal aid referral lists prepared by the Law Society. A further 23 had prepared their own list of local solicitors who were willing to undertake the work. Several centres gave their clients a choice of solicitor from the lists available.

Finance

3.35   The majority of legal advice centres had small budgets, usually less than £500 per annum, and relied almost entirely on volunteer help and free or subsidised accommodation. Thirteen centres had running costs in excess of £10,000 and these were financed either by the local authority, from Urban Aid, or by donations from charitable trusts; all of these centres employed full-time staff. In one or two cases the costs shown in annex 3.2 appear high, because the costs of the parent organisation have been given, and the cost of the legal advice section is not separately available.

LAW CENTRE AND LEGAL ADVICE CENTRES

ANNEX 3.1 AND 3.2

ANNEX 3.1

Law centres—detailed answers to questionnaire

(paragraph 3.4)

Area	Greater London			
Borough/Town	Brent	Camden		Hackney
Centre[1]	Brent CLC	Camden CLC	West Hampstead CLC	Hackney Advice Bureau and LC
Opening date	1971	1973	1975	1976
Organisation	Company limited by guarantee	Charitable trust	Charitable trust	Not decided
Initiators: Individuals (Ind) Local authority (LA) Local law society (LLS) Local groups (LG) National organisations (NO)	Ind LG	 LG	Ind	 LA LLS LG
Opposition to establishment of law centre	None	Legal profession, local law society	None	None
Catchment population ('000's)	250	150	40	200
Management committee: Size Membership: Individuals (Ind) Local authority (LA) Local law society (LLS) Local groups (LG) User groups (UG) Social services (SS) CAB Community development project (CDP) Other	12–15 UG	21 Ind LA LLS LG SS CAB Other	14 Ind LA LLS LG SS CAB	Not decided
Number of paid staff: Lawyers: full-time	4	4	2	2
Other workers: full-time part-time	3 0	5 5	3 0	3 1
Number of volunteers	Some	7	1	Occasionally
Number of cases[2] per annum	5,000	6,198	4,218	1,000
Files opened per year	700	970	380	700
Advice and assistance to individuals as % of caseload	40%	Not known	Over 50%	Over 50%
Annual budget (£'000s) year ending in	57 1979	67·8 1976	29.6 1977	48 1977
Source of funds as % of total budget: Community development project Lord Chancellor's Department Urban Aid[3] Local authority Foundations, charities, donations Legal aid Other funding agencies Miscellaneous	 .. .. 95 5	 .. .. .. 78 1 19 3 ..	 .. .. .. 94 1 4	 .. .. .. 92 .. 8 .. ..

[1] LC=law centre; CLC=community law centre.

[2] The definition and type of cases vary considerably; the answers therefore may not be comparable.

[3] Now Urban Programme funded by the Department of the Environment.

[4] Centre open for too short a time for workload to be estimated.

[5] Amalgamation of original two law centres founded in 1973 into existing law centre took place in 1976.

[6] Money from legal aid used to reduce contribution from other source.

ns=not stated.

	Greater London				
Haringey	Hillingdon	Islington	Kensington & Chelsea	Lambeth	Lewisham
Tottenham LC	Hillingdon CLC	North Islington LC	North Kensington Neighbourhood LC	Lambeth CLC	North Lewisham LC
1976	1975	1973	1970	1974	1978
Company limited by guarantee	Charitable trust	Company limited by guarantee	Charitable trust	Unincorporated association	Not decided
	LA	LA	Ind	Ind LA	Ind
LG	LG	LG	LG	NO	LG
None	Law Society, local law society	None	None	None	None
70	235	90	70	300	70
20	19	11	Not specified	18	17
Ind LA LLS	Ind LA LLS SS CAB Other	LA LLS LG	Ind LLS LG CAB	Ind LA LLS UG CAB Other	LA LLS LG CAB Other
Other					
3	2	4	4	5	2
6	5	6	11	11	3
1	2	0	2	1	0
0	0	2	About 20	5	0
670	1,300	5,500	Not known	12,000	Not known[4]
310	500	1,000	900	1,000	Not known[4]
50%	70%	About 50%	Not known	About 90%	Not known[4]
59·5 1977	35 1977	55 1977	72·5 1978	83 1977	55 1978
..	..	..	..	..	..
87	..	..	83	..	91
..	100	82	..	87	..
13	..	18	17	13	9
..	..	..	..	..	..
..	..	..	j	..	..

Law centres—detailed answers to questionnaire *(continued)*

Area	Greater London			
Borough/Town	Newham	Southwark	Tower Hamlets	
Centre[1]	Newham Rights Centre	Southwark Law Project	Tower Hamlets LC	Balham LC
Opening date	1973	1976	1976[5]	1974
Organisation	Company limited by guarantee	Company limited by guarantee	Unincorporated association	Unincorporated association
Initiators: Individuals (Ind) Local authority (LA) Local law society (LLS) Local groups (LG) National organisations (NO	NO	LG	LG	LG
Opposition to establishment of law centre	None	None	None	None
Catchment population ('000's)	250	70	150	40
Management committee: Size Membership: Individuals (Ind) Local authority (LA) Local law society (LLS) Local groups (LG) User groups (UG) Social services (SS) CAB Community development project (CDP) Other	15 LG	8 Ind LA LG	12 Ind LG	Not specified LA LLS LG
Number of paid staff: Lawyers: full-time	2	4	5	3
Other workers: full-time part-time	6 3	5 0	6 0	7 0
Number of volunteers	Over 40	Occasionally	24	Over 30
Number of cases[2] per annum	808	Not known[4]	2,000	7,160
Files opened per year	Not known	Not known[4]	900	867
Advice and assistance to individuals as % of caseload	Not known	Not known[4]	75%	88%
Annual budget (£'000's) year ending in	46·4 1977	38·5 1977	59·9 1977	53·3 1976
Source of funds as % of total budget: Community development project Lord Chancellor's Department Urban Aid[3] Local authority Foundations, charities, donations Legal aid Other funding agencies Miscellaneous	43 .. .. 47 3 .. 7	.. .. 89 .. .. 11	71 .. .. 7 23	.. .. 94 .. 5 .. 1

[1] LC=law centre; CLC=community law centre.

[2] The definition and type of cases vary considerably; the answers therefore may not be comparable.

[3] Now Urban Programme funded by the Department of the Environment.

[4] Centre open for too short a time for workload to be estimated.

[5] Amalgamation of original two law centres founded in 1973 into existing law centre took place in 1976.

[6] Money from legal aid used to reduce contribution from other source.

ns—not stated.

Greater London			Rest of England		
Wandsworth		Westminster	Manchester	Liverpool	Newcastle-upon-Tyne
Battersea LC	Garratt Lane LC	Paddington LC	Manchester LC	Vauxhall Law & Information Centre	Benwell Community Law Project
1978	1977	1973	1976	1973	1974
Charitable trust	Charitable trust	Company limited by guarantee	Trust	Other	Unincorporated association
	LA		Ind		
LG	LG	LG		LG	LG
None	Not known	Local law society	Not serious	None	None
70	45–50	65–80	500	15	10–20
31	Not specified	21	16	Not specified	11
Ind LA LLS LG CAB Other	LA LLS LG	LA LLS UG SS CAB Other	Ind LA LLS LG CAB	LLS	Ind LA LLS LG CDP
3	3	3	5	2	1
7	6	5	7	1	5
0	0	0	0	1	0
11	Several	Over 10	Some	Occasionally	0
About 2,000	Not known[4]	3,600	13,000	1,200	136
Not known	Not known[4]	500	Not known	690	136
Not known	Not known[4]	70–90%	67%	70%	60%
78·8 1979	66 1978	44·7 1977	52·2 1979	19·7 1977	7·8 1977
..	..	..	..	..	97
..	100	..	92	90[s]	..
97	..	83	..	..	..
3	..	17	8	10[s]	~3
..	..	..	..	..	..

Law centres—detailed answers to questionnaire (*continued*)

Area	Rest of England			
Borough/ Town	Birmingham			Coventry
Centre[1]	Handsworth LC	Saltley Action Centre	Small Heath CLC	Coventry Legal & Income Rights Service
Opening date	1976	1976	1977	1975
Organisation	Not specified	Company limited by guarantee	Charitable trust	Charitable trust
Initiators: Individuals (Ind) Local authority (LA) Local law society (LLS) Local groups (LG) National organisations (NO)	LG	LG	LG	LG
Opposition to establishment of law centre	None	None	None	None
Catchment population ('000's)	84	60	45	334
Management committee: Size Membership: Individuals (Ind) Local authority (LA) Local law society (LLS) Local groups (LG) User groups (UG) Social services (SS) CAB Community development project (CDP) Other	Not specified LG	Not specified Ind LLS LG	16–20 Ind LA LLS LG SS Other	12 LA LLS LG Other
Number of paid staff: Lawyers: full-time	2	2	3	1
Other workers: full-time part-time	4 1	6 0	6 0	3 0
Number of volunteers	3	Some	7	2
Number of cases[2] per annum	3,206	4,477	1,684	885
Files opened per year	500	Not known	1,131	500
Advice and assistance to individuals as % of caseload	Most	Most	Not known	75%
Annual budget (£'000's) year ending in	42 ns	41·8 1978	47 ns	26·2 1978
Source of funds as % of total budget: Community development project Lord Chancellor's Department Urban Aid[3] Local authority Foundations, charities, donations Legal aid Other funding agencies Miscellaneous	.. .. 91[6] .. .. 9[6]	.. 41 15 .. 22 12 .. 11	.. .. 89 .. .. 11	.. .. 94 .. .. 6 .. ..

[1] LC=law centre; CLC=community law centre.

[2] The definition and type of cases vary considerably; the answers therefore may not be comparable.

[3] Now Urban Programme funded by the Department of the Environment.

[4] Centre open for too short a time for workload to be estimated.

[5] Amalgamation of original two law centres founded in 1973 into existing law centre took place in 1976.

[6] Money from legal aid used to reduce contribution from other source.

ns=not stated.

	Wales		Northern Ireland
	Merthyr Tydfil	Cardiff	Belfast
	South Wales Anti-Poverty Action Centre	Adamsdown Community & Advice Centre	Belfast CLC
	1976	1972	1977
	Company limited by guarantee	Charitable trust	Not decided
	LG	LG	LG
	Not serious	Not serious	Legal profession, local law society, Northern Ireland Office
	2,000	11	400
	Not specified	12	22
		Ind	
	LG		LLS LG
			CAB
	1	1	2
	5	7	2
	0	2	0
	0	0	0
	Not known[4]	900	Not known[4]
	Not known[4]	475	Not known[4]
	Not known[4]	About 50%	Not known[4]
	34	26·7	30
	1977	1977	1978
	..	86	100
	..	..	..
	..	..	..
	..	4	..
	..	9	..
	100	..	..
	..	..	..

ANNEX 3.2

Legal advice centres—detailed answers to questionnaire
(a) Greater London
(paragraph 3.19)

Borough	Camden	Ealing	Greenwich		
Centre	Mary Ward	Northolt	East Greenwich	Woolwich	CRE Advice Service
Opening date	1942	1974	1976	1970	1966
Organisation	Part of community centre	Part of community centre	Independent legal advice centre	Independent legal advice centre	Run by CRE
Initiators: Individuals (Ind) Local authority (LA) Local law society (LLS) Local groups (LG) National organisations (NO) Not stated (ns)	LG	Ind LG	Ind	Ind LG	LA LG NO
Catchment population ('000's)	9,000	ns	10	ns	206
Management committee membership	Individuals, users	Informal management	Advice centre workers	Informal management	Parent organisation
Weekly opening hours	17	1½	1½	2½	41½
Hours lawyer available	17	1½	1½	2¾	1½
Number of paid staff: Lawyers: full-time part-time	1 0	0 0	0 0	0 0	0 0
Other workers: full-time part-time	2 1	0 0	0 0	0 1	0 0
Number of volunteers: lawyers others	10 0	1 5	4 2	6 2	2 1
Number of cases per annum[1]	1,800	350	200	550	206
Legal advice as % of cases handled (where advice given by generalist agency)	—	—	—	—	20
Source of referrals from outside organisation: CAB Social services (SS) Police, prisons, courts (Pol) Local radio and newspapers (Rad) Local groups (LG) Consumer advice agencies (CA) Individuals (Ind) Other	CAB SS Pol Rad LG CA Ind Other	SS LG	CAB SS	CAB SS Ind	SS LG Ind
Annual budget (£'000's) year ending in	33 1976	0 ns	0·3 1970	0·2 1976	0·1 1976
Source of funds as % of total budget: Urban Aid[4] Local authority Foundations, donations, charities Legal aid Other	.. 20 20 60 ..	.. ..	.. .. 100	50 .. 40 10 ..	 100

[1] The definition and type of cases vary considerably; the answers therefore may not be comparable.

[2] Cost of community centre.

[3] Amounts not given.

[4] Now Urban Programme funded by the Department of the Environment.

ns = not stated.

Hoxton (Hackney)	Kingsmead (Hackney)	Stoke Newington (Hackney)	Conningham Road (Hammersmith)	Wood Green (Haringey LA advice bureaux)	Tottenham (Haringey LA advice bureaux)	Hornsey (Haringey LA advice bureaux)	Turnpike Lane (Haringey LA advice bureaux)	Tottenham (Haringey)
1976	1976	1969	1973	Before 1965	1949	Before 1965	1975	1969
Run by LAG	Run by LAG	Part of generalist advice centre	Local authority advice centre	Local authority advice centres				Independent legal advice centre
LG	LG	LG	LA LLS	LA				Ind LG
20	ns	220	ns	230				ns
Parent organisation	Parent organisation	Users, advice centre	None	Parent organisation				Parent body
1½	1	2	42½	26½	26	25	25½	5
1½	1	2	8½	5	6	5	5	5
0	0	0	0	3				0
0	0	0	0	2				0
0	0	0	10	9				0
0	0	0	0	8				0
5	6	8	22	16				6
3	0	8	9	Insignificant				2
250	50	400	7,864	36,600				600
90	—	70	ns	ns				50
	SS	CAB SS		SS				SS
LG	LG		LG	LG				
Ind		Ind	Ind	Ind				
0·05	0	0·2	45	79				0·5
1976	ns	ns	1977	ns				ns
..	..	..	100				100	30
				100	100	100		..
ns	..	..	..					70
..	..	..	..	..	..	..	..	..
ns	..	..	..	..	..	..	..	

Legal advice centres—detailed answers to questionnaire (*continued*)
(a) Greater London

Borough	Islington				Kensington & Chelsea
Centre	Caledonian Road	Highbury	Holloway	Islington	Nucleus
Opening date	1969	1975	1971	1967	1974
Organisation	Independent legal advice centre	Independent legal advice centre	Independent legal advice centre	Independent legal advice centre	Part of generalist advice centre
Initiators: Individuals (Ind)	Ind	Ind	Ind	Ind	
Local authority (LA)					
Local law society (LLS)					
Local groups (LG)			LG	LG	
National organisations (NO)					NO
Not stated (ns)					
Catchment population ('000's)	ns	ns	ns	ns	68
Management committee membership	Advice centre workers	None	Advice centre workers	Parent body	Parent body
Weekly opening hours	1½	2	1½	7½	39
Hours lawyer available	1½	2	1½	7½	2
Number of paid staff:					
Lawyers: full-time		0	0	0	0
part-time	0	0	0	0	0
Other workers: full-time	0	0	1	0	0
part-time	0	0	0	0	0
Number of volunteers: lawyers	4	2	4	25	4
others	4	1	6	3	3
Number of cases per annum[1]	180	400	300	1,000	400
Legal advice as % of cases handled (where advice given by generalist agency)	—	—	—	—	5
Source of referrals from outside organisation:					
CAB			CAB	CAB	CAB
Social services (SS)	SS	SS	SS	SS	SS
Police, prisons, courts (Pol)			Pol		
Local radio and newspapers (Rad)					
Local groups (LG)			LG		
Consumer advice agencies (CA)					
Individuals (Ind)				Other	Other
Other					
Annual budget (£'000's)	0	ns	3·8	0·2	1·1
year ending in	ns	ns	ns	1976	1977
Source of funds as % of total budget:					
Urban Aid[4]	..		..	..	..
Local authority	..	100	..	90	100
Foundations, donations, charities	..	..	ns	..	..
Legal aid	..	..	..	10	..
Other	..	..	ns	..	..

[1] The definition and type of cases vary considerably; the answers therefore may not be comparable.

[2] Cost of community centre.

[3] Amounts not given.

[4] Now Urban Programme funded by the Department of the Environment.

ns=not stated.

Legal advice centres—detailed answers to questionnaire (continued)

(a) Greater London

	Lambeth						Lewisham	
	Brixton	Centre '70	Clapham	Friendship House	Kennington Road	Waterloo	Downham	Honor Oak
	1966	1970	1975	1937	1972	1972	1974	1974
	Part of generalist advice centre	Part of community centre	Part of community centre	Church	Independent legal advice centre	Part of generalist advice centre	Part of CAB	Part of CAB
	Ind	Ind			Ind	Ind		Ind
		LG	LG	NO		LG	LG	
	ns	ns	65	ns	ns	15	100	50
	Individuals	Individuals, local authority	Parent body	None	Informal management	Users	Parent body	Parent body
	20	28	1½	1½	2	35	2	2
	5	1½	1½	1½	2	2¼	2	2
	0	0	0	0	0	0	0	0
	0	0	0	0	0	0	0	0
	2	1	0	0	0	0	0	0
	1	4	0	0	0	0	0	0
	9	6	4	6	8	7	4	3
	5	0	0	5	2	6	3	1
	4,800	3,129	200	120	750	1,000	526	414
	ns	ns	ns	ns	—	30	—	
	CAB SS Pol Rad LG CA Ind Other	SS LG Ind	CAB SS Pol Ind	CAB Ind	CAB SS LG Ind	CAB SS LG Ind	CAB SS Pol LG Ind	CAB SS Pol LG
	11	20[2]	0·3	ns	0·3	0·6	0·2	0·2
	1978	1976	ns	ns	ns	ns	ns	ns
			100					
	100	43	..	..	..	..	100	100
	..	11	..	..	100	ns	..	..
	..	24	..	..	..	..	..	..
	..	22	..	..	..	ns	..	..

¹ The definition and type of case vary considerably; the answers therefore may not be comparable.

² Cost of centre usually shared.

³ Advocacy not taken.

⁴ Urban Programme funded by the Department of the Environment.

⁵ was not stated.

Legal advice centres—detailed answers to questionnaire (*continued*)
(a) Greater London

Borough	Lewisham		Newham	Southwark	
Centre	Lewisham CRE	New Cross	Canning Town	Bellenden	Cambridge House
Opening date	1973	1974	1974	1973	1894
Organisation	Run by CRE	Part of generalist advice centre	Part of generalist advice centre	Part of generalist advice centre	Part of community centre
Initiators: Individuals (Ind) Local authority (LA) Local law society (LLS) Local groups (LG) National organisations (NO) Not stated (ns)	LG	Ind LG	LG	Ind LA	ns
Catchment population ('000's)	238	300	43	20	2,250
Management committee membership	Parent body	None	Users, local authority	Advice centre workers	Parent body
Weekly opening hours	2	2	16	6	18½
Hours lawyer available	2	2	1	6	18½
Number of paid staff: Lawyers: full-time	ns	0	0	0	2
part-time	ns	0	0	0	0
Other workers: full-time	ns	0	3	0	0
part-time	ns	2	0	0	7
Number of volunteers: lawyers	ns	4	2	5	1
others	ns	0	0	15	6
Number of cases per annum[1]	250	1,400	ns	450	1,402
Legal advice as % of cases handled (where advice given by generalist agency)	15	—	ns	60	—
Source of referrals from outside organisation: CAB Social services (SS) Police, prisons, courts (Pol) Local radio and newspapers (Rad) Local groups (LG) Consumer advice agencies (CA) Individuals (Ind) Other	LG Ind	Ind	LG	SS LG Ind	CAB SS Pol LG Ind
Annual budget (£'000's)	ns	0·5	20	0·4	15
year ending in	ns	ns	ns	ns	1975
Source of funds as % of total budget: Urban Aid[4]	..	..	100	..	40
Local authority	..	..	..	100	16
Foundations donations, charities	..	..	..	..	30
Legal aid	..	..	..	..	
Other	..	100	..	..	14

[1] The definition and type of cases vary considerably; the answers therefore may not be comparable.

[2] Cost of community centre.

[3] Amounts not given.

[4] Now Urban Programme funded by the Department of the Environment.

ns=not stated

	Tower Hamlets		Waltham Forest	Wandsworth		Westminster	
	Oxford House	University House	Waltham Forest	Battersea	Lavender Hill	Community House	Pimlico
	1973	1941	1975	1974	1972	1974	1973
	Part of community centre	Independent legal advice centre	Part of generalist advice centre	Part of generalist advice centre	Part of CRE	Part of community centre	Part of generalist advice centre
	Ind	Ind LG	LA	Ind	LG	LG	Ind
	80	500	235	30	75	ns	ns
	Informal management	Parent body, advice centre workers	None	Local authority, users, advice centre workers	Local law society, CAB, users, individuals	Social services, users	Parent body
	14	28	49	4	2	37	27
	4	4	2	4	2	2	1½
	0 0	0 0	0 0	0 0	0 0	0 0	0 0
	0 4	1 1	12 0	0 0	0 0	1 1	4 0
	5 4	8 0	1 0	3 1	6 1	8 0	8 0
	1,000	2,000	8,100	300	250	200	238
	50	—	45	95	—	ns	15
	CAB	CAB SS Pol CA Ind	SS LG Ind	LG	CAB SS Other	CAB LG	CAB SS LG Ind
	5 ns	5 ns	58 ns	0·1 1978	No separate budget	19[2] 1976	No separate budget
	ns[3] ns[3] ns[3]	.. 50 20 30 ..	.. 100	.. 100		.. 80 20	

Legal Advice centres—detailed answers to questionnaire

(b) Outside London
(paragraph 3.19)

Town	Birmingham			
Centre	Balsall Heath	Campus	Dudley Road	Lane
Opening date	1973	1975	1975	1970
Organisation	Part of generalist advice centre	Part of generalist advice centre	Part of generalist advice centre	Part of generalist advice centre
Initiators: Individuals (Ind) Local authority (LA) Local law society (LLS) Local groups (LG) National organisations (NO) Not stated (ns)	Ind LG	Ind	Ind	Ind
Catchment population ('000's)	10	8	ns	ns
Management committee membership	Individuals, advice centre workers	Students	Students	Individuals
Weekly opening hours	35	4	2	40
Hours lawyer available	4	4	2	2
Number of paid staff: Lawyers: full-time part-time	0 0	0 0	0 0	0 0
Other workers: full-time part-time	1 0	0 0	0 0	3 0
Number of volunteers: lawyers others	6 0	8 100	8 20	4 1
Number of cases per annum[1]	1,000	150	400	290
Legal advice as % of cases handled (where advice given by generalist agency)	45	ns	ns	ns
Source of referrals from outside organisation: CAB Social services (SS) Police, prisons, courts (Pol) Local radio and newspapers (Rad) Local groups (LG) Consumer advice agencies (CA) Individuals (Ind) Others	ns	None	ns	LG
Annual budget (£'000s) year ending in	0·9 1977	0·2 1976	ns ns	ns ns
Source of funds as % of total budget: Urban Aid[4] Local authority Foundations, donations, charities Legal aid Other	60 .. 40	 100	.. ns ns	100 .. ..

[1] The definition and type of cases vary considerably; the answers therefore may not be comparable.

[2] Figures relate to CAB as a whole.

[3] Proportion of entire CAB caseload.

[4] Now Urban Programme funded by the Department of the Environment.

ns = not stated.

Bristol						
Association of Bristol Advice Centres						
St. Pauls	South Bristol	Southmead	Easton	Kingswood	Avonmouth	East Bristol
1972	1974	1975	1976	1976	1976	1975
Independent legal advice centres						
Ind						
LG						
420						
Advice centre workers						
4	2	4	2	2	2	4
4	2	4	2	2	2	4
			0			
			0			
			0			
			0			
			72			
			0			
560	230	660	140	440	ns	ns
			—			
			CAB			
			SS			
			Pol			
			Rad			
			LG			
			0·3			
			1977			
			..			
			100			
			..			
			..			

Legal advice centres—detailed answers to questionnaire (*continued*)

(b) Outside London

Town	Cambridge			Cheltenham	Hull
Centre	Cambridge Law Surgery			Contact	Hull CAB
	Arbury	Cambridge CAB	East Barnwell		
Opening date	1973	1970	1974	ns	1974
Organisation	Independent legal advice centres			Part of generalist advice centre	Run by CAB
Initiators: Individuals (Ind) Local authority (LA) Local law society (LLS) Local groups (LG) National organisations (NO) Not stated (ns)	LG			Ind LA	LLS LG
Catchment population ('000's)	22	100–250	17	80	430
Management committee membership	Advice centre workers			Parent body	CAB
Weekly opening hours	1½	5¼	1½	1	4
Hours lawyer available	1½	5½	1½	1	4
Number of paid staff: Lawyers: full-time part-time		0 3		0 0	0 0
Other workers: full-time part-time		0 1		0 0	2[2] 2[2]
Number of volunteers: lawyers others	 1	40 27	 1	11 0	53[2] 33
Number of cases per annum[1]	157	986	66	140	742
Legal advice as % of cases handled (where advice given by generalist agency)	—			36	4[3]
Source of referrals from outside organisation: CAB Social services (SS) Police, prison, courts (Pol) Local radio and newspapers (Rad) Local groups (LG) Consumer advice agencies (CA) Individuals (Ind) Others		CAB SS LG		CAB SS	CAB
Annual budget (£'000s) year ending in		4·8 1976		0 ns	0·5 1977
Source of funds as % of total budget: Urban aid[4] Local authority Foundations donations, charities Legal aid Other		.. .. 2 56 42		.. ..	.. 100 .. .. ..

[1] The definition and type of cases vary considerably; the answers therefore may not be comparable.

[2] Figures relate to CAB as a whole.

[3] Proportion of entire CAB caseload.

[4] Now Urban Programme funded by the Department of the Environment.

ns=not stated.

88

Leicester	Luton	Nottingham		Shanklin	Sheffield		
					Free Legal Information Service		
Leicester	Luton	Nottingham Law Society/ Toc H	People's Centre	Shanklin	City Centre	Chaucer	CAB
1973	1975	1965	1974	1973	1972	1972	1973
Independent legal advice centre	Independent legal advice centre	Independent legal advice centre	Part of generalist advice centre	Independent legal advice centre	Independent legal advice centres		
Ind LG	LG	LLS LG	LG NO	Ind LLS	LA		
300	180	500	581	20	500	50	50
advice centre workers	None	None	Users, advice centre workers	None	Advice centre workers		
2	4	4	50	1¼	2	2	1½
2	4	4	3	1¼	2	2	1¼
0 0	0 0	0 0	0 0	0 0	0 1		
0 0	0 2	0 2	1 0	0 0	0 0		
38 10	16 0	50 0	4 11	4 0	55 15		
700	1,344	1,500	4,160	170	680	300	380
—	—	—	12	—	—		
CAB Rad LG CA	CAB SS Pol CA Ind	CAB SS Pol Rad	SS Pol Rad	SS Pol CA	CAB Rad CA		
0·1 1976	0·3 1977	0 ns	4·8 ns	0·1 ns	1·5 ns		
.. .. 100	.. 100	.. ..	.. .. ns .. ns	.. .. 100	.. 67 33		

Legal advice centres—detailed answers to questionnaire (*continued*)

(b) Outside London

	Southampton	Southend	Stoke-on-Trent
Town	Southampton	Southend	Stoke-on-Trent
Centre	Southampton CRE	Southend CAB	Stoke-on-Trent
Opening date	1971	1976	1973
Organisation	Run by CRE	Part of CAB	Independent legal advice centre
Initiators: Individuals (Ind) Local authority (LA) Local law society (LLS) Local groups (LG) National organisations (NO) Not stated (ns)	Ind LG	LA LG	Ind
Catchment population ('000's)	215	250	500
Management committee membership	Informal	Local organisations, local authority, volunteers	Local law society, CAB, social services, individuals
Weekly opening hours	1	34	6
Hours lawyer available	1	34	6
Number of paid staff: Lawyers: full-time part-time	0 0	1 0	0 0
Other workers: full-time part-time	0 3	2[2] 0	0 0
Number of volunteers: lawyers others	40 0	36[2] 45[2]	24 4
Number of cases per annum[1]	125	1,350	1,000
Legal advice as % of cases handled (where advice given by generalist agency)	100	10[3]	—
Source of referrals from outside organisation: CAB Social services (SS) Police, prison, courts (Pol) Local radio and newspapers (Rad) Local groups (LG) Consumer advice agencies (CA) Individuals (Ind) Others	CAB	CAB	CAB SS Rad LG CA
Annual budget (£'000s) year ending in	0·2 ns	22[2] 1977	0·2 1976
Source of funds as % of total budget: Urban aid[4] Local authority Foundations donations, charities Legal aid Other	100	.. 46 54	.. 100 .. .. ..

[1] The definition and type of cases vary considerably; the answers therefore may not be comparable.

[2] Figures relate to CAB as a whole.

[3] Proportion of entire CAB caseload.

[4] Now Urban Programme funded by the Department of the Environment.

ns = not stated.

SECTION 4

Representation at Certain Tribunals

Introduction

4.1 The Commission made enquiries of the extent to which people appearing before certain tribunals in England and Wales were represented and the nature of the representation. The Commission also wished to consider the relationship between representation and outcome but, as noted later in this Section, the necessary information in many cases was not available. Where information was provided it has been set out in this Section but two points should be borne in mind in interpreting this information. First, it was not practicable to obtain information on the complexity of cases, and representation was more likely to have been obtained for the most difficult cases. Second, information could not be obtained on the detailed nature and strength of cases presented to the tribunals.

4.2 In this Section we summarise the results of the enquiries and refer, where appropriate, to research done by others. The term representation in this Section is only used to describe the position where a person is represented by a third party. Where a person attends in person at a tribunal, to present his own case, it is described as personal attendance.

Tribunals considered

4.3 Table 4.1 below lists the six tribunals considered in this Section, the numbers of each tribunal in England and Wales, and the government department responsible for their supervision.

4.4 The first five tribunals in Table 4.1 have a high volume of cases which are broadly concerned with social, employment or welfare matters. Only in the last mentioned tribunal is the liberty of the appellant at issue—in this case the right to enter or remain in the country.

4.5 Tribunals typically have three members, a chairman and two others. However, immigration adjudicators sit alone and the membership of Rent Assessment Committees and Rent Tribunals can vary from one to three members. Most of the tribunals have legally qualified chairmen. As an exception, only 6 per cent of the chairmen of the Supplementary Benefit Appeals Tribunals are legally qualified. The Department of Health and Social Security has stated the intention of appointing more legally qualified chairmen to these tribunals when vacancies arise, though legal qualifications will not be made a condition of appointment. Apart from the chairmen, few of the other members of tribunals are legally qualified.

4.6 In the following paragraphs of this section we give, for each of the tribunals shown in Table 4.1, the information we have been able to obtain concerning representation.

TABLE 4.1

Tribunals considered by the Commission

Tribunal	Number of tribunals (1977)	Supervising department	Reference to paragraph in this section
Rent Assessment Committees and Rent Tribunals	1	Department of the Environment	4.7
Supplementary Benefit Appeals Tribunals	124	Department of Health and Social Security	4.12
National Insurance Local Tribunals	156	Department of Health and Social Security	4.17
Industrial Tribunals	2	Department of Employment	4.20
Medical Appeal Tribunals	12	Department of Health and Social Security	4.24
Immigration adjudicators and Immigration Appeals Tribunal	3	Home Office	4.27

[1] Rent Assessment Committees are appointed *ad hoc* from 16 regional rent panels. There were 53 Rent Tribunals in 1977.

[2] In 1977 Industrial Tribunals sat in 74 centres in England and Wales.

[3] At 31 December 1977 there were 20 full-time and 37 part-time adjudicators. There was one Immigration Appeals Tribunal which could sit in five divisions.

Rent Assessment Committees and Rent Tribunals

4.7   Rent Assessment Committees are appellate bodies who hear objections to "fair" rents determined by rent officers. Rent Tribunals hear cases at first instance involving questions of valuation and security of tenure. Although these two bodies have separate functions, their administration has largely been integrated. In 1976 Rent Assessment Committees dealt with about 12,200 cases and Rent Tribunals dealt with about 6,500 cases.

4.8   The incidence of representation of applicants by lawyers, surveyors and estate agents at Rent Assessment Committees and Rent Tribunals in 1976 is shown in Table 4.2. Information is not available to distinguish the numbers of people with some other type of representative from those who attended in person without representation; they are therefore shown together in Table 4.2.

4.9   Table 4.2 shows that 16 per cent of landlords had legal representation and nearly one-quarter were represented by a surveyor or estate agent. Only 9 per cent of tenants were represented at these hearings by a lawyer, surveyor or estate agent. However, there could be a substantial proportion of tenants with some other type of representative; 52 per cent of tenants attended personally or had some other type of representative.

TABLE 4.2

**Rent Assessment Committees and Rent Tribunals in England:
representation and personal attendance in 1976**

Nature of representation or personal attendance	Landlords %	Tenants %
Legal	16	5
Surveyor/estate agent	23	4
Other representation or personal attendance without representation	36	52
Written submissions made without personal attendance	17	15
No representation or personal attendance	8	24
Total	100	100

Source: Department of the Environment.

4.10   The Rent Assessment Committees and tribunals sit throughout the country hearing local cases. Almost two-thirds of the 1976 cases were dealt with in London; no other area accounted for more than 5 per cent of the number of cases. Table 4.2 shows that in England 92 per cent of landlords were represented at, or personally attended, hearings, compared with 76 per cent of tenants. In London 96 per cent of landlords were represented at or personally attended hearings compared with 78 per cent of tenants. But while the extent of representation or personal attendance was therefore higher in London than in the rest of the country, the proportion legally represented was in fact about the same in London as that shown for England as a whole in Table 4.2.

4.11   The degree of representation and personal attendance was particularly low in the areas covered by the Northern and Eastern Rent Assessment Panels. In the north, 52 per cent of landlords and 41 per cent of tenants were represented at or personally attended hearings. In the east, the figures were 60 per cent for landlords and 38 per cent for tenants.

Supplementary Benefit Appeals Tribunals
4.12   Supplementary Benefit Appeals Tribunals hear appeals against decisions by the local office of the Supplementary Benefit Commission. In 1977, 63,943

appeals were heard by 124 tribunals. Nearly 63,000 of these appeals related to supplementary benefit matters, and the remainder (about 1,000) concerned Family Income Supplement payments.

4.13   Table 4.3 shows the extent to which appellants were represented by a third party at supplementary benefit appeal hearings.

TABLE 4.3

Supplementary benefit appeals:
representation at hearings in 1977

Nature of representation	Proportion of appellants %
Legal	1
Trade union, claimants' union or voluntary organisation representative	4
Social or welfare worker	4
Friend or relative	15
Represented by third party	23
Not represented by third party: personal attendance	28
not attending	49
Total	100

[1] Less than 1 per cent.
Source: Department of Health and Social Security.

4.14   It can be seen from Table 4.3 that legal representation was very low and that over three-quarters of the appellants were not represented by a third party. Most of those represented at these hearings also attended in person. But a majority of the unrepresented appellants did not personally attend the hearing, so that about half the appellants were neither represented by a third party nor attended the hearing in person.

4.15   In supplementary benefit appeals a decision favourable to the appellant was reached by the tribunals in 19 per cent of cases; Table 4.4 shows that the percentage of favourable decisions reached was highest in those cases where the appellant was represented by a third party. Where the appellant was unrepresented by a third party, the percentage of favourable decisions was higher in cases where the appellant attended in person.

95

TABLE 4.4

Supplementary benefit appeals: outcome of appeals in 1977

Representation and attendance	Favourable decision %
Representation by third party, appellant personally attending	37
Representation by third party, appellant not personally attending	34
All appellants represented by third party	36
Attendance by appellant without representation by third party	26
No representation or attendance in person by appellant	7
All those not represented by third party	14
All appellants	19

Source: Department of Health and Social Security.

4.16 Table 4.5 shows, for those supplementary benefit appeals where the appellant was represented by a third party at a hearing, the proportion of decisions favourable to the appellant analysed according to the type of representative.

TABLE 4.5

Supplementary benefit appeals: outcome of appeals in 1977 related to type of representative

Type of representative	Favourable decision %
Legal	37
Trade union or voluntary organisation representative	41
Social or welfare worker	51
Friend or relative	32
All appellants represented by third party	36

Source: Department of Health and Social Security.

National Insurance Local Tribunals

4.17 National Insurance Local Tribunals decide cases referred to them by insurance officers and hear appeals from claimants against decisions of insurance officers. In 1977 they dealt with 34,825 appeals, covering mainly unemployment, sickness and invalidity benefits.

4.18 Information is not collected by the Department of Health and Social Security in respect of representation or attendance at National Insurance Local Tribunals. However, information is available from a sample of 96 cases heard in 1973, which were recorded as part of a wider study on administrative tribunals conducted by the Legal Advice Research Unit. The findings are set out in Table 4.6.

TABLE 4.6
National Insurance Local Tribunals:
outcome of sample of appeals in 1973

Representation and personal attendance	Number of appellants	Successful appeal
Represented by third party (all appellants attend in person)	13	3
Not represented by third party:		
personal attendance by appellant	30	8
no personal attendance by appellant	53	4
Total	96	15

Source: Frost and Howard, *Representation and Administrative Tribunals* (Routledge & Kegan Paul, 1977).

4.19 Table 4.6 shows that only a small proportion of the appellants were represented by a third party; 53 of the 96 appellants neither attended nor were represented by a third party. However, no general observations can be made by reference to the outcome of these appeals in view of the small sample of cases.

Industrial Tribunals

4.20 Industrial Tribunals hear applications and appeals relating to redundancy payments, unfair dismissal and discrimination. In 1977, Industrial Tribunals sat at 74 centres in England and Wales and disposed of a total of 39,839 cases. Of these, 17,329 cases (43 per cent) were heard, the other cases being disposed of without a hearing.

4.21 The Central Office of the Industrial Tribunals (England and Wales) collected information about the incidence and nature of representation at the 1,543 cases dealt with by Industrial Tribunals during a four-week period in

October 1977. The results are shown in Tables 4.7 and 4.8. Further statistics collected in October 1978 were similar in all respects to the 1977 figures apart from a very slight increase in the proportion of respondents who were legally represented.

4.22 Table 4.7 shows that applicants were represented by a third party in 57 per cent of cases and respondents (usually an employer) in 59 per cent of cases. The applicant's representative was usually a lawyer or a trade union representative. The respondent's representative was usually a lawyer.

TABLE 4.7

Industrial Tribunals: incidence of representation in the period 3–28 October 1977

Nature of representation	Applicants %	Respondents %
Legal	33	49
Trade union/employers' organisation	16	7
Other third party representation	8	4
Represented by third party	57	59[1]
Not represented by third party	43	41
Total	100	100[1]

[1]In this column the total shown is not equal to the sum of the constituent numbers because of rounding.
Source: Central Office of the Industrial Tribunals (England and Wales).

4.23 Table 4.8 shows that only one side was represented by a third party in 38 per cent of cases and that both sides were represented in 39 per cent of cases.

TABLE 4.8

Industrial Tribunals: extent of representation by a third party in the period 3–28 October 1977

Extent of representation by third party	Applicants %	Respondents %
Both sides represented	39	39
Applicant only represented	18	—
Respondent only represented	—	20
Total represented by third party	57	59

Source: Central Office of the Industrial Tribunals (England and Wales).

Medical Appeal Tribunals

4.24 Medical Appeal Tribunals are concerned with claimants' appeals and references by the Secretary of State for Social Services from assessments of disablement arising from industrial accidents and diseases. Claimants have a statutory right of appeal except in cases where disablement has been assessed provisionally and less than two years has elapsed since the claimant was first examined by a medical board. In these cases, however, where it seems that injustice may have been done, the Secretary of State may refer a decision by a medical board directly to the tribunal. In 1977 20 per cent of the cases dealt with by the tribunals were referred in this way. There are 12 Medical Appeal Tribunals in England and Wales sitting at 22 centres and in 1977 they disposed of 13,432 cases.

4.25 No statistical records are kept by the Department of Health and Social Security on the incidence of representation and attendance at Medical Appeals Tribunals. However, the Department analysed for the Commission a sample of 100 cases dealt with in 1976.

4.26 Table 4.9 shows that 56 appellants were represented by a third party at the 100 hearings in the sample, nine by a legal representative, 44 by a trade union representative and three by a friend or relative. A further 36 appellants attended alone and eight were neither represented by a third party nor attended in person. The table also shows the cases where the assessment was improved, unchanged or reduced. One cannot conclude from this sample of cases whether the outcome was related to representation or personal attendance.

TABLE 4.9

Medical Appeal Tribunals: outcome of appeal related to representation and attendance at sample of 100 cases in 1976

Nature of representation or personal attendance	Outcome to appellant			
	improved assessment	no change	reduced assessment	total
Legal	4	4	1	9
Trade union	19	21	4	44
Friend or relative	1	1	1	3
Attended alone	12	13	11	36
Neither represented nor attended in person	4	2	2	8
Total	40	41	19	100

Source: Sample of cases analysed by the Department of Health and Social Security in 1976.

Immigration adjudicators and Immigration Appeals Tribunal

4.27 Appeals against decisions by the Home Secretary regarding admission to, permission to remain in and removal from, the United Kingdom of certain categories of Commonwealth citizens and aliens are (with a few exceptions involving deportation proceedings) in the first instance made to adjudicators who sit alone. From an adjudicator there is, in a few cases, a further right of appeal to the Immigration Appeals Tribunal. In all other cases, however, an appeal is only with the leave of the adjudicator or of the tribunal. Appellants are in many cases represented by either the United Kingdom Immigrants Advisory Service (UKIAS), the Joint Council for the Welfare of Immigrants (JCWI), other voluntary bodies, or High Commissioners' legal advisers.

4.28 In 1976 12,407 appellants were dealt with by adjudicators; the outcome of the hearings is shown in Table 4.10.

TABLE 4.10

**Immigration adjudication: outcome of cases heard
by adjudicators in 1976**

Outcome	Number of appeals	% of total
Appeal allowed	1,297	10
Appeal dismissed	7,126	57
Appeal withdrawn	3,302	27
No jurisdiction	682	6
All adjudicator appeals	12,407	100

Source: Immigration appellate authorities.

4.29 Statistics of representation at these cases are not normally recorded. However, during February 1977, special records were maintained by the immigration appellate authorities of the cases dealt with in that month by adjudicators. There were 720 cases, of which 288 were determined or withdrawn before the hearing and 432 went to a hearing.

4.30 Table 4.11 shows the forms of representation and attendance at the 432 adjudication hearings in February 1977. Separate figures on attendance in person are not given; about 50 per cent of cases concern persons living abroad who would be unable to attend a hearing. Appellants are made aware at the outset of the services available from UKIAS and can nominate a representative to act on their behalf.

TABLE 4.11

**Immigration adjudication: cases heard by adjudicators
during February 1977**

Nature of representation by third party and attendance in person	Appeals	
	number	%
UKIAS	251	58
JCWI	25	6
Solicitor or counsel	74	17
Sponsor in UK (including other organisations) or appellants in person without third party representative	82	19
Total	432	100

Source: Sample of cases analysed by the immigration appellate authorities in February 1977.

4.31 No similar figures on representation or outcome are available for cases heard by the Immigration Appeals Tribunal.

Conclusion concerning representation at tribunals

4.32 It will be seen from the foregoing paragraphs that the Commission obtained, with the assistance of the supervisory government departments or the authorities concerned, information of the extent to which people were represented by a third party or personally attended before certain tribunals. Information comparing the outcome of hearings with the extent of representation was also obtained in some instances. While the limited information available gives some support to the view that a favourable outcome is more likely to be achieved when the appellant or respondent is represented and attends the hearing, the available data is insufficient for firm conclusions to be drawn. In any event, it is not possible to assess the effectiveness of the different types of representation without also considering the complexity and reasonableness of the cause of action.

TABLE 4.1?

Immigration Adjudication cases heard by adjudicators
during February 1977

Nature of representation by third party and attendance in person	Appeal	
	number	%
UKIAS	231	56
JCWI	25	6
Solicitor or counsel	74	17
Sponsor in UK (including other organisations) or appellants in person without third party representative	82	19
Total	432	100

Source: Sample of cases analysed by the immigration appellate authorities in February 1977.

4.31 No similar figures on representation or outcome are available for cases heard by the Immigration Appeals Tribunal.

Conclusion concerning representation at tribunals

4.32 It will be seen from the foregoing paragraphs that the Commission obtained, with the assistance of the supervisory government departments or the authorities concerned, information of the extent to which people were represented by a third party or personally attended before certain tribunals. Information comparing the outcome of hearings with the extent of representation was also obtained in some instances. While the limited information available gives some support to the view that a favourable outcome is more likely to be achieved when the appellant or respondent is represented and attends the hearing, the available data is insufficient for firm conclusions to be drawn. In any event, it is not possible to assess the effectiveness of the different types of representation without also considering the complexity and reasonableness of the cause of action.

SECTION 5

Recent Trends in the Volume and Value of Conveyancing

Contents

Introduction

5.1 Section 16 of this volume gives the consultants' report on the Law Society remuneration survey, which provides information from the accounts of solicitors ending in 1974, 1975 and 1976. Section 6 gives the results of a survey by the Commission among solicitors' firms in November 1978 concerning charges for domestic conveyancing. Both of these surveys show that conveyancing is the most important source of income for firms of solicitors, accounting on average for about half of their fee income. This section summarises the various published statistics concerning the volume and value of transactions in land and buildings over the years 1973 to 1977: the purpose is to examine whether the years covered by the surveys were typical in this respect and to examine trends subsequent to these surveys.

Sources of information

5.2 Comprehensive records are not kept of the number and value of property transactions, although the Inland Revenue has published estimates based on information supplied for stamp duty purposes. Information taken from these estimates is given at annexes 5.1 to 5.3. In addition, the Inland Revenue has carried out a survey of property transactions in one week at the end of each year, 1973 to 1977, from which it calculates and publishes data on the volume and value of transactions; the data obtained from the one week survey is grossed-up by the Inland Revenue to give estimates covering one month at the end of each year. Information available from these surveys is given at annexes 5.4 to 5.6.

Annual trends in number and value of transactions, 1973 to 1977

5.3 Annex 5.1 shows that the value of all sales of land and buildings in England and Wales fell substantially in 1974 and recovered in 1975. From 1975 to 1978 the value of transactions increased by over half, from just over £12,000 million in 1975 to just under £19,000 million in 1978.

5.4 In relation to the conveyancing fee income of solicitors, it is important to consider mainly the changes in the volume and value of domestic or residential property transactions rather than all transactions in land and buildings. In its report No. 54, the National Board for Prices and Incomes showed that the conveyancing fee income of solicitors was mainly derived from the conveyance of private dwelling-houses; the conveyance of other property accounted for less than 10 per cent of all conveyancing fee income in 1966. More recent figures are not available.

5.5 Separate figures for sales of residential property are only available from the fourth quarter of 1976, which are set out in annex 5.2. However, in giving figures for 1976 and the first three-quarters of 1977, the Inland Revenue estimated that individual sales above £30,000 mainly represent non-residential property; the figures excluding these sales are given at annex 5.1. The trends indicated by the figures in annexes 5.1 and 5.2 are:—

(a) From 1975 to 1977 an increase in the total sales value of all property of some 20 per cent and a corresponding increase in the total sales value of residential property of some 11 per cent.

(b) From 1977 to 1978 an increase in the total sales value of all property of some 29 per cent and an increase in the sales value of residential property of 26 per cent.

5.6 In summary, the figures indicate a fall in the total sales value of properties in 1974 over the previous year of 17 per cent; separate figures for residential property are not available for this year, but as we note later (paragraph 5.10), it is estimated that the total sales value of residential property increased throughout the period and that the fall in 1974 can be attributed to a fall in sales of other property. The total sales value of properties increased from 1975 with a higher rate of increase from 1977 to 1978.

Seasonal pattern of sales

5.7 Annex 5.3 shows the sales for 1973 to 1978 analysed by quarters. The figures reflect increases in house prices as well as changes in the number of transactions. However, the point to note is that the value of sales in the first quarter of each year was always lower than in the fourth quarter of the preceding year. The data show a definite seasonality in the total value of transactions.

Estimates from Inland Revenue surveys

5.8 Annexes 5.4 to 5.6 give information of the volume and value of transactions in October 1973 and 1974 and November 1975, 1976 and 1977, based on surveys by the Inland Revenue. Although the figures represent transactions in only one month of each year, they are useful in that detailed information is given of the types of transaction; and while it is not possible to say if the monthly figures are representative of each year, it is reasonable to assume that they indicate the general trend.

5.9 Annex 5.4 analyses the monthly figures of the number and value of sales between residential and non-residential properties. The Inland Revenue stated that non-residential properties comprise a great variety of types, such as agricultural land, building land, offices, factories and shops; and that a large proportion of the value lies within a relatively few large transactions.

5.10 Annex 5.4 shows that the fall in the total value of transactions from October 1973 to October 1974 was wholly due to a fall in the total value of non-residential transactions. From October 1973 to November 1977, the value of transactions in residential property increased each year. There was, however, a fall in the number of residential transactions in 1974; the figures are summarised in Table 5.1.

TABLE 5.1

Sales of residential properties in England and Wales, 1973 to 1977

Survey month	Number		Value	
	thousands	index	£ million	index
October 1973	93	100	760	100
October 1974	84	90	786	103
November 1975	90	97	879	116
November 1976	98	105	1,021	134
November 1977	109	117	1,286	169

Source: Inland Revenue survey published in "Economic Trends", March 1979.

5.11 Further analysis of the value of sales is given at annex 5.5, which gives separate figures for sales by individuals, property companies and other companies or organisations. Annex 5.6 gives a similar analysis for purchases of property; the figures differ from the sales figures because individuals were net purchasers of property from the other two sectors in each of the survey months. Table 5.2 summarises the sales and purchases of residential property by individuals.

TABLE 5.2

Sales and purchases of residential property by individuals, 1973 to 1977

Survey month	Sales		Purchases	
	£ million	increase on previous year %	£ million	increase on previous year %
October 1973	592	—	674	—
October 1974	610	3·0	710	5·3
November 1975	718	17·7	833	17·3
November 1976	829	15·5	974	16·9
November 1977	1,048	26·4	1,236	26·9

Source: Inland Revenue survey published in "Economic Trends", March, 1979.

5.12 Table 5.2 shows that the value of property transactions by individuals increased in each of the survey months from 1973 to 1978: there was only a small increase from 1973 to 1974 and a substantially larger increase from 1976 to 1977.

5.13 Much of the increase in the total value of transactions shown by Tables 5.1 and 5.2 can be accounted for by increased house prices. Annex 5.7 sets out information on the trend in average house prices from 1970 to 1977, and the change in the general index of retail prices over the same period. It can be seen from this that the average price of houses increased from 1970 to 1973 at a greater rate than the increase in general retail prices; but from 1973 to 1977 the increase in house prices was much less than the increase in general retail prices. The 1978 figures presently available indicate a substantial increase in average house prices.

5.14 Annex 5.8 sets out information on the number and amount of building society advances from 1970 to 1978. It shows that the number and value of advances fell between 1972 and 1974 but increased each year thereafter. There was a particularly large increase in the total amount of advances from 1974 to 1975 and from 1977 to 1978.

Comparisons with remuneration survey and conveyancing survey

5.15 The Law Society remuneration survey obtained information on the revenue costs and profits of solicitors shown by their accounts for accounting years ending in 1974, 1975 and 1976. The accounting year-end dates of firms were spread throughout each year, with the figures for 1976 weighted towards the first half of the year. There will be a delay between the date work is carried out and the date it appears in the accounts of solicitors. Given these factors it is reasonable to assume that the figures given earlier in this Section in respect of the number of property transactions in 1976 are only partly reflected in the remuneration survey results for 1976.

TABLE 5.3

Percentage of gross fee income derived from conveyancing

Size of firm by number of principals	Remuneration survey[1] (1975/76) %	Conveyancing survey[2] (1977) %
Sole practitioners	60	60
2 partners	56	54
3/4 partners	53	54
5/9 partners	48	49
10 or more partners	32	34

Source: [1] Consultants' report on the Law Society's remuneration survey, Section 16

[2] Survey of charges for domestic conveyancing, Section 6.

5.16 The survey of charges for domestic property conveyancing carried out by the Commission at the end of 1978 gives information on the percentage of total gross fee income of firms derived from conveyancing for accounting years ending in 1977; these figures can be compared with the results of the remuneration survey, which gives information for accounting years ending in 1975 (mainly at the end of the year) or 1976, as shown in Table 5.3.

5.17 It should be noted that the information in both surveys is partly based on estimates; the figures from the conveyancing survey are averages based on broad estimates by industrial respondents. Nevertheless there is little difference between the two surveys for the proportion of solicitors' fee income derived from conveyancing.

Conclusions

5.18 From the figures given in this section, the fall in the total value of property sales in 1974 can be attributed to a substantial fall in the total value of sales of non-residential property. However, while the total value of residential property sales increased throughout the period 1973 to 1977, the figures indicate that there was a fall in the number of residential property sales in 1974.

5.19 There was an increase in the total number and value of property sales from 1975 to 1978, with the greatest increase arising from 1977 to 1978. It is therefore reasonable to expect the gross fee income of solicitors from conveyancing to have increased after the periods covered by the remuneration survey.

5.20 While gross fee income may thus have increased, there are a number of other factors which will have affected the net profit levels of solicitors, for which information is not available without further detailed surveys of remuneration. In particular the effect of increased gross fee income will be reduced by increases in overheads; and the net profits of individual solicitors will be affected by changes in the size of the profession, that is, the number of solicitors in the profession undertaking the work. We also do not have information on the movement in other important elements in the profession's gross fee income.

5.21 Information is not available, and cannot be deduced from the figures on the volume and value of property transactions given in this section, of how the net profit levels of solicitors have changed since 1976 in relation to levels of remuneration in other occupations or in relation to changes in general price levels.

ANNEX 5.1

Sales of land and buildings in England and Wales, 1973 to 1978
(paragraph 5.3)

	All properties		Excluding sales above £30,000	
	£ million	index	£ million	index
1973	11,920	97	—	—
1974	9,930	81	—	—
1975	12,270	100	10,000	100
1976	13,410	109	10,270	103
1977	14,760	120	11,110	111
1978	18,990	155	13,150	132

Source: Inland Revenue estimates based on stamp duty data, published in "Economic Trends", March 1979.

ANNEX 5.2

Sales of residential property in England and Wales, 1976 to 1978
(paragraph 5.5)

Year and quarter		£ million	Index (1976 Qtr. 4 = 100)
1976	4	2,900	100
1977	1	2,420	83
	2	2,850	98
	3	3,350	116
	4	3,530	122
		12,150	
1978	1	3,470	120
	2	3,750	129
	3	4,010	138
	4	4,020	139
		15,250	

Source: Inland Revenue survey published in "Economic Trends", March 1979.

ANNEX 5.3

Sales of land and buildings in England and Wales:
estimates of quarterly transactions, 1973 to 1978
(paragraph 5.7)

Year and quarter		All properties	Excluding sales above £30,000
		£ million	£ million
1973	1	2,860	—
	2	3,000	—
	3	3,050	—
	4	3,010	—
1974	1	2,430	—
	2	2,360	—
	3	2,430	—
	4	2,700	2,150
1975	1	2,530	2,060
	2	3,070	2,520
	3	3,310	2,740
	4	3,360	2,690
1976	1	2,890	2,250
	2	3,260	2,540
	3	3,710	2,760
	4	3,540	2,700
1977	1	2,950	2,280
	2	3,450	2,680
	3	4,030	3,030
	4	4,320	3,110
1978	1	4,280	2,980
	2	4,590	3,310
	3	4,900	3,410
	4	5,210	3,430

Source: Inland Revenue estimates based on stamp duty data, published in "Economic Trends", February 1978 and March 1979.

ANNEX 5.4

**Sales of land and buildings in England and Wales:
all sales in month of survey, 1973 to 1977**
(paragraph 5.9)

Survey month	Number (thousands)			Value (£ million)		
	residential	non-residential	total	residential	non-residential	total
October 1973	93	16	109	760	365	1,125
October 1974	84	13	97	786	180	967
November 1975	90	13	103	879	156	1,035
November 1976	98	15	113	1,021	194	1,214
November 1977	109	16	125	1,286	296	1,582

Source: Inland Revenue survey published in "Economic Trends", March 1979.

ANNEX 5.5

**Sales of land and buildings in England and Wales:
analysis of sales in month of survey, 1973 to 1977**
(paragraph 5.11)

Survey month and sector	Residential	Non-residential	Total
	£ million	£ million	£ million
October 1973:			
individuals	592	145	737
property companies	99	70	169
others[1]	69	150	219
Total	760	365	1,125
October 1974:			
individuals	610	61	671
property companies	157	52	209
others[1]	19	67	86
Total	786	180	966
November 1975:			
individuals	718	51	769
property companies	131	42	173
others[1]	30	63	93
Total	879	156	1,035
November 1976:			
individuals	829	61	890
property companies	145	65	210
others[1]	47	68	115
Total	1,021	194	1,215
November 1977:			
individuals	1,048	95	1,143
property companies	162	93	255
others[1]	76	108	184
Total	1,286	296	1,582

[1] Includes companies other than property companies, local authorities, central government, nationalised industries, banks and insurance companies.

Source: Inland Revenue survey published in "Economic Trends", March 1979.

ANNEX 5.6

**Purchases of land and buildings in England and Wales:
analysis of purchases in month of survey, 1973 to 1977**
(paragraph 5.11)

Survey month and sector	Residential	Non-residential	Total
	£ million	£ million	£ million
October 1973:			
individuals	674	92	766
property companies	33	100	133
others[1]	53	173	226
Total	760	365	1,125
October 1974:			
individuals	710	53	763
property companies	18	28	46
others[1]	58	99	157
Total	786	180	966
November 1975:			
individuals	833	47	880
property companies	13	26	39
others[1]	33	83	116
Total	879	156	1,035
November 1976:			
individuals	974	55	1,029
property companies	17	35	52
others[1]	30	104	134
Total	1,021	194	1,215
November 1977:			
individuals	1,236	82	1,318
property companies	21	56	77
others[1]	29	158	187
Total	1,286	296	1,582

[1] Includes companies other than property companies, local authorities, central government, nationalised industries, banks and insurance companies.

Source: Inland Revenue survey published in "Economic Trends", March, 1979.

ANNEX 5.7

Average house prices, 1970 to 1977
(paragraph 5.13)

Average for year	£[1]	Index (1973 = 100)	Retail price index[2] (1973 = 100)
1970	5,000	50	78
1971	5,650	56	86
1972	7,420	74	92
1973	10,020	100	100
1974	11,100	111	116
1975	11,945	119	144
1976	12,759	127	168
1977	13,712	137	195

Sources: [1]House prices at mortgage completion, the Building Societies Association, "BSA Bulletin", January 1979.
[2]Department of Employment, general index of retail prices, average for calendar year.

ANNEX 5.8

Building society advances, 1970 to 1978
(paragraph 5.14)

Year	Number (thousands)	Value (£ million)
1970	544	2,021
1971	660	2,758
1972	690	1,649
1973	551	1,540
1974	438	1,950
1975	652	1,965
1976	717	1,117
1977	738	1,889
1978	804	1,734

Source: The Building Societies Association, "BSA Bulletin", January 1979.

SECTION 6

Charges for Domestic Conveyancing

Contents

Introduction

6.1 Chapter 21 of Volume I refers to conveyancing charges. In considering the matter of conveyancing as a whole the Commission decided that it was necessary to establish the level of charges made for domestic conveyancing and the amount of time spent upon this activity. This section summarises the results of a survey conducted by the Commission in November 1978 among 20 per cent of firms of solicitors in private practice. The overall response to the survey was 60 per cent, which is satisfactory. Further information relating to the nature of the survey is set out in annex 6.1.

TABLE 6.1

Percentage of total gross fee income derived from conveyancing: by size of firm

Percentage of gross fee income from conveyancing of all types	Size of firm					
	Sole prac-titioner %	2 partners %	3–4 partners %	5–9 partners %	10 or more partners %	All firms %
Up to 20%	5	7	3	2	24	5
21–40%	8	10	8	21	35	12
41–60%	33	41	55	54	30	43
61–80%	36	36	30	21	8	30
81–100%	17	4	3	1	0	7
Not stated	1	3	1	1	3	2
Total %	100	100[1]	100	100	100	100[1]
Average %	60	54	54	49	34	—
Number of firms	241	160	207	112	37	768

[1]In this table, and in some of those which follow, totals shown may not be equal to the sum of the constituent numbers, because of rounding.

117

Importance of conveyancing income

6.2   The percentage of total gross fee income derived from conveyancing of all types is set out in Table 6.1 related to the size of firm as measured by the number of profit-sharing partners. This demonstrates the extent to which firms depend on income from conveyancing. While the sole practitioner is most dependent on conveyancing, deriving, on average, 60 per cent of his income from this source, even the larger firms with ten or more partners derive one-third of their income from conveyancing.

Nature of conveyancing transactions

6.3   The nature of the conveyancing transactions dealt with by the bills upon which the survey was based is set out in Table 6.2.

TABLE 6.2
Nature of conveyancing transactions in the survey

Nature of transaction	Percentage of bills in survey %
Sale of residential property (freehold or leasehold) for owner-occupation	47
Purchase of residential property (freehold or leasehold) for owner-occupation	49
Purchase by sitting tenants of local authority houses or flats	1
Purchase of the freehold reversion in property held on leasehold	1
Conveyance or assignment of interests of joint tenants or tenants in common among themselves	1
Conveyance by way of gift, or not for full consideration	1
Total	100

6.4   Table 6.2 shows that bills involving the sale or purchase of residential property for owner-occupation account for 96 per cent of domestic conveyancing transactions and the remainder of this section concentrates upon these types of transactions.

6.5   Certain characteristics of the sales and purchases of residential property for owner-occupation are set out in Table 6.3.

TABLE 6.3

Characteristics of transactions involving residential property

Characteristic	Sales %	Purchases %
Same solicitor acted for both parties	5	5
Solicitor acted for mortgagee and/or mortgagor	36	73
Title was freehold	84	83
Title was registered before transaction	42	43

6.6   It should be noted that the same solicitor acted for both parties in only 5 per cent of the conveyances and that the majority of transactions involved properties where the title was freehold.

Total amount of bill for a conveyance

6.7   The average total amount of the bill for a conveyance is set out in Table 6.4. The major part of the bill for sales relates to work concerning the transfer of the property, but in purchases, disbursements (which include the payment of land registry fees, stamp duty and search fees) are almost equal to the transfer charge. The costs of disbursements are shown in more detail in Table 6.13.

TABLE 6.4

Average amount of bill for a conveyance

Item	Average amount for conveyance	
	Sales £	Purchases £
Transfer	154	153
Mortgage work	2	22
VAT	13	14
Disbursements	15	148
Total	184	337

The average charge for mortgage work is based on the information given in all the bills but in 80 per cent of sales there were no mortgages so that the average figure given above is misleading. Table 6.6 shows the charges made only on those bills to which mortgage work applied.

119

Factors in the nature of the conveyance affecting the transfer charges

Price of property

6.8   Table 6.5 shows that the charge made for the transfer of a property varied by reference to the price of the property. The amount charged also varied by reason of other factors, such as the amount of mortgage, the nature of the title (whether registered or not), and the geographical location: these are discussed in paragraphs 6.9 to 6.12.

TABLE 6.5
Average charge for transfer: by price of property

Price of property (£'000's)	Average charge for transfer	
	Sales £	Purchases £
Up to 5	74	76
5–10	110	108
10–15	134	131
15–20	159	160
20–30	200	199
over 30	322	309
All bills	154	153

Mortgages

6.9   The average amount charged for mortgage work increased according to the amount of the mortgage involved, as can be seen from Table 6.6.

TABLE 6.6
Average charge for mortgage work: by amount of mortgage

Amount of mortgage (£'000's)	Average charge for mortgage work	
	Sales £	Purchases £
Up to 3	12	18
3– 5	12	25
5–10	18	34
10–15	25	39
15–20	31	46
Over 20	58	57
All bills in which a charge was made for mortgage work	14	36

Nature of title

6.10 The information provided showed that where the prices of the properties were the same there was no discernible difference between the charges made, whether the property was freehold or leasehold.

Registration of property

6.11 Differences in charges arise between registered and unregistered titles. Table 6.7 shows that the average charge for transfer is less when the property has been previously registered, although in some cases registration during transfer may cause the charge to equal or slightly exceed that for an unregistered property.

TABLE 6.7

Average charge for transfer: by degree of registration and price of property

Degree of registration	Average charge for transfer (£)					
	Price of property (£'000's)					
	0–5	5–10	10–15	15–20	20–30	Over 30
Sales:						
Previously registered	77	103	127	153	190	304
Registered during transfer	71	112	140	165	212	333
Unregistered before or after transfer	77	114	140	164	210	342
All bills	74	110	134	159	200	322
Purchases:						
Previously registered	76	100	121	153	187	296
Registered during transfer	74	115	139	168	213	310
Unregistered before and after transfer	78	110	137	166	211	328
All bills	76	108	131	160	199	309

Geographical location

6.12 Table 6.8 shows the variations in the charges when analysed on a geographical basis and by reference to the price of the properties.

121

TABLE 6.8

Average charge for transfer: by geographical location and price of property

Area	Average charge for transfer (£)					
	Price of property (£'000's)					
	0–5	5–10	10–15	15–20	20–30	Over 30
Sales:						
Greater London	87	119	140	168	210	360
Rest of South East	117	117	135	158	200	307
North West & W. Midlands	73	107	131	158	182	292
East Anglia	92	119	130	145	211	280
South West	78	132	143	165	206	311
North	71	107	134	156	209	318
Yorkshire, Humberside, E. Midlands	66	103	131	154	189	309
Wales	74	109	140	143	186	438
All bills involving sales	74	110	134	159	200	322
Purchases:						
Greater London	75	138	140	163	204	339
Rest of South East	76	115	133	154	199	313
North West & W. Midlands	74	108	132	154	193	267
East Anglia	70	106	125	160	195	294
South West	116	118	136	163	203	294
North	70	103	122	161	198	289
Yorkshire, Humberside, E. Midlands	73	101	128	162	201	282
Wales	74	108	124	171	212	301
All bills involving purchases	76	108	131	160	199	309

Factors in the nature of the firm of solicitors affecting the transfer charges

Gross fees derived from all types of conveyancing

6.13   Table 6.9 shows that transfer charges tend to decline slightly as the percentage of gross fee income received by solicitors' firms in respect of conveyancing work increases. Firms who received 20 per cent or less of their gross fee income from conveyancing work made a relatively higher charge for properties over £30,000.

TABLE 6.9

Average charge for transfer: by percentage of fee income and price of property

| Percentage of fee income from all types of conveyancing | Average charge for transfer (£) | | | | | |
| | price of property (£'000's) | | | | | |
	0–5	5–10	10–15	15–20	20–30	Over 30
Sales:						
up to 20%	78	117	141	187	222	481
21–40%	75	115	128	169	207	348
41—60%	74	111	135	159	201	305
61–80%	71	108	133	157	192	303
81–100%	81	108	141	151	196	279
All bills	74	110	134	159	200	322
Purchases:						
up to 20%	66	106	165	179	209	412
21–40%	68	111	127	154	213	321
41–60%	79	110	132	162	198	307
61–80%	73	105	128	156	199	273
81–100%	83	112	139	154	200	255
All bills	76	108	131	160	199	309

Size of the firm

6.14   Table 6.10 shows the charges made analysed by reference to the price of the property and the size of the firm. The amounts charged show a slight, but not significant, variation with the size of the firm.

TABLE 6.10

Average charge for transfer: by number of partners
and price of property

Number of partners	Average charge for transfer (£)					
	price of property (£'000's)					
	0–5	5–10	10–15	15–20	20–30	Over 30
Sales:						
1	70	105	131	159	199	298
2	63	109	135	154	200	316
3–4	80	108	136	164	200	332
5–9	80	117	137	157	196	297
10 or more	82	112	128	160	207	369
All bills	74	110	134	159	200	322
Purchases:						
1	73	113	134	157	199	308
2	76	108	125	167	203	306
3–4	74	107	131	158	196	308
5–9	77	109	133	159	203	298
10 or more	83	107	132	157	200	324
All bills	76	108	131	160	199	309

Special factors affecting the transfer charge

6.15   Solicitors were asked to specify which special factors, if any, involved in the conveyancing transaction had affected the charge made by their firm to the client. Overall, 60 per cent of bills involved special factors; 57 per cent of sales and 62 per cent of purchases. Since more than one special factor might be involved in a given transaction, the totals of special factors in Table 6.11 add to more than 100 per cent.

Average cost of a conveyance

Transfer charges

6.16   As pointed out in paragraph 6.8 a number of factors affect the transfer charges made by solicitors for conveyancing transactions. Table 6.12 shows the average charge for the transfer of a typical property in which the title is freehold and registered before the transaction.

TABLE 6.11

Special factors affecting the transfer charges

Special factor	Sales %	Purchases %
Work on arranging mortgage	2	16
Previous work on unsuccessful conveyancing transactions	16	12
Planning matters	3	7
Building estate development	4	7
Recent dealing with same title	5	2
Work containing a charitable element	1	1
Work on matters ancillary to transactions not separately billed	22	20
Other factors	26	27
Transactions in which there were special factors	57	62
No special factors	43	38
Total number of transactions	4,111	4,309

TABLE 6.12

Average charge for transfer in a typical conveyance: by price of property

Price of property (£'000's)	Charge for transfer	
	sales £	purchases £
Up to 5	78	77
5–10	101	96
10–15	124	119
15–20	151	151
20–30	190	181
Over 30	297	288
All bills	160	151

Disbursements

6.17 As shown in Table 6.4 the average total amounts of disbursements were £15 in transactions involving a sale and £148 in transactions involving a purchase. The latter amount is analysed in Table 6.13.

TABLE 6.13

Average amount of disbursements: purchases only

Nature of disbursement	Average disbursements[1] £
Land Registry	25
Stamp duty	113
Search fees	8
Other disbursements	2
Total disbursements	148

[1]In a few transactions the amount of a particular disbursement was not recorded. Hence the average figures for disbursements are calculated from slightly different bases and constituent parts do not sum to the total shown.

6.18 The most important single disbursement cost is stamp duty which is related to the price of the property. The stamp duty currently payable for various purchase prices of properties up to £50,000 is set out in Table 6.14.

TABLE 6.14

Stamp duty payable

Purchase price of property £	Stamp duty £
Up to 15,000	Nil
15,050	75·25
16,050	80·25
17,050	85·25
18,050	90·25
19,050	95·25
20,050	200·50
23,050	230·50
25,050	375·75
27,050	405·75
30,050	601·00
35,050	701·00
40,050	801·00
45,050	901·00
50,000	1,000·00

Factors affecting time spent on conveyancing

Price of property

6.19   Table 6.15 sets out the average hours spent by all fee-earners on a conveyancing transaction compared with the price of the related properties, and shows that whilst the hours spent on sales and purchases are similar for different price ranges, the hours spent increase as the price of the property increases.

TABLE 6.15

Average hours spent by all fee-earners on a conveyancing transaction:
by price of property

Price of property (£'000's)	Average hours of all fee-earners	
	sales	purchases
Up to 5	4·2	4·9
5–10	5·3	6·0
10–15	5·9	6·5
15–20	6·5	7·0
20–30	7·0	7·5
More than 30	9·7	9·7
All bills	6·2	6·8

TABLE 6.16

Average hours spent by all fee-earners on a conveyancing transaction:
by price of property (actual and estimated figures)

Price of property (£'000's)	Average hours of all fee-earners			
	sales		purchases	
	actual	estimated	actual	estimated
Up to 5	5·5	6·0	5·6	4·6
5–10	5·7	5·2	6·7	5·8
10–15	6·1	5·8	7·1	6·3
15–20	6·3	6·6	7·7	6·7
20–30	6·9	7·0	8·2	7·4
More than 30	12·1	8·8	11·0	9·1
All bills	6·9	6·0	7·7	6·5
Number of bills	925	3,007	1,036	3,048

127

6.20 Many firms do not keep records which would enable them to provide exact figures on the hours spent in a particular transaction, and so in approximately 75 per cent of the returns the information relating to time spent on a conveyance was estimated. Table 6.16 shows that the differences between actual and estimated figures are relatively slight and that, overall, firms lacking actual figures tended to under-estimate the amount of time spent on the conveyance. As regards the figures relating to actual hours, there is a similar tendency for the hours spent on the transaction to increase with the price of the property.

Geographical location

6.21 Table 6.17 shows that the average total hours spent on a conveyance by all fee-earners varies according to the geographical location of the principal office of the firm. In general the relationship between sales and purchases follows the geographical location.

TABLE 6.17

Average hours spent by all fee-earners on a conveyancing transaction: by geographical location

Region	Average hours of all fee-earners	
	sales	purchases
Greater London	8·0	8·1
Rest of South East	6·7	7·4
North West & W. Midlands	5·4	6·2
East Anglia	6·0	6·4
South West	7·0	7·0
North	5·6	6·1
Yorkshire, Humberside, E. Midlands	5·2	6·2
Wales	6·3	7·2
All bills	6·2	6·8

Income derived from conveyancing of all types

6.22 As Table 6.18 shows, the average total hours spent on a conveyancing transaction by all fee-earners declines as the percentage of gross fee income arising from all types of conveyancing increases, except in those practices earning more than 80 per cent of income from this activity.

128

TABLE 6.18

Average total hours spent by all fee-earners on a conveyancing transaction: by percentage of gross fee income derived from conveyancing of all types

Percentage of income derived from conveyancing of all types	Average total hours of all fee-earners	
	sales	purchases
Up to 20%	10·3	10·0
21–40%	6·8	7·5
41–60%	5·9	6·7
61–80%	6·0	6·3
81–100%	7·4	8·1
All bills	6·2	6·8

Partners' hours

6.23   Solicitors were asked to indicate the number of hours spent on a conveyance by each type of fee-earner; namely, profit-sharing partners, salaried partners and assistance solicitors, trainee solicitors and other fee-earners including legal executives. The percentage of the total time involved in the conveyance which was spent by each type of fee-earner is set out in Table 6.19.

TABLE 6.19

Time spent on a conveyancing transaction: by different classes of fee-earner

Status of fee earner	Percentage of total time on conveyance	
	sales %	purchases %
Profit-sharing partners	57	55
Salaried partners and assistant solicitors	14	14
Trainee solicitors	3	4
Other fee-earners	26	27
Total	100	100
Average total hours per conveyance	6·2	6·8

129

6.24   The survey showed that, of the total hours spent, profit-sharing partners' time represented 57 per cent of the total in the case of sales and 55 per cent in the case of purchases. Table 6.20 analyses in further detail the time spent by partners. It shows that, of the total hours spent on each case, all of it was partners' time in respect of 42 per cent of sales and 45 per cent of purchases. In 29 per cent of cases no profit-sharing partners' time was involved. In the remaining cases the work was spread between partners and other categories of fee-earners.

TABLE 6.20
Profit-sharing partners' time involved in conveyancing transactions

Partners' time spent	Percentage of bills included in the survey	
	sales %	purchases %
No partners' time	29	29
Some partners' time spent	23	26
All partners' time	45	42
Not stated	2	3
Total	100	100

TABLE 6.21
Conveyances in which none of the work was handled by profit-sharing partners

Time spent by	Sales %	Purchases %
Assistant solicitors or salaried partners	39	37
Trainee solicitors	6	6
Other fee-earners	55	57
Total time	100	100

6.25   Table 6.21 sets out an analysis of the time spent on the 29 per cent of the bills shown in Table 6.20 as not handled by partners. The majority of the time was spent on a conveyance by "other fee-earners" such as legal executives, but over one-third of the time was spent by salaried partners or assistant solicitors. It can be deduced from Tables 6.20 and 6.21 that, of the conveyances reported on in the survey, no time was recorded as spent on the conveyance by qualified solicitors in 18 per cent of cases.

Charges made and time spent by the solicitor

6.26 The charge made for the transfer of the property is directly related to the time involved in the conveyance, as shown in Table 6.22.

TABLE 6.22

Average charge for transfer: by hours spent

Total hours spent on transaction	Average charge for transfer	
	sales £	purchases £
Up to 4	123	117
5–8	157	154
9–12	199	181
13–16	244	233
17–20	302	251
Over 20	376	366
All bills	154	153

TABLE 6.23

Average transfer charge per hour: by price of property

Price of property (£'000's)	Average transfer charge per hour	
	sales £	purchases £
Up to 5	17·6	15·5
5–10	20·8	18·0
10–15	22·7	20·2
15–20	24·5	22·9
20–30	28·6	26·5
More than 30	33·2	31·9
All bills	24·8	22·5

Transfer charge per hour

6.27 Table 6.23 shows the average charge per hour arrived at by dividing the total average hours spent into the average transfer charge. The hourly charge

131

is lower for properties in the lower price ranges. The rates charged for a transaction involving a sale of a property are in all cases slightly higher than the rates charged for a purchase of a property.

Charge for a typical conveyance

6.28 The average charge for a "typical" conveyance of a freehold property in the £10,000–£15,000 range registered prior to the transaction varied with the time spent on the conveyance as shown in Table 6.24.

TABLE 6.24

Average charge for a transfer of a property in the £10,000–£15,000 price range in a typical conveyance: by time spent on the transaction

Total hours spent on transaction	Sales		Purchases	
	average charge £	percentage of bills	average charge £	percentage of bills
Up to 4	117	40	113	31
5–8	131	50	121	52
9–12	138	8	130	13
13–16	sample		sample	
17–20	too	2	too	3
Over 20	small		small	
All bills	124	100	119	100
Number of bills	243	—	309	—

Summary of main results

Nature of transactions

6.29 Almost all (96 per cent) of the transactions reported involved the sale or purchase of freehold or leasehold residential property for owner-occupation. Of such transactions, the title was freehold in over 80 per cent of cases and registered before the transaction in over 40 per cent of cases. Mortgage work (for which a charge was made) was involved in two-thirds of the purchases but only in 20 per cent of the sales. The same solicitor acted for both buyer and seller in only 5 per cent of the transactions reported but it was very common for the same solicitor to act for both mortgagor and mortgagee. In about 60 per cent of cases special factors which affected the amount charged were reported. Of those identified, work on ancillary matters not separately billed, previous work on unsuccessful conveyancing transactions and work on arranging a mortgage for prospective purchasers were the most common.

Level of charges

6.30 The average transfer charge (excluding mortgage work and VAT) emerged as almost identical for sales and purchases at £153. Disbursements added £15 to this figure in the case of sales but a further £148 (mainly stamp duty) in the case of purchases. Where mortgage work was involved it increased buying costs by an average of £36 and selling costs by an average of £14.

6.31 There was considerable variation in the size of the transfer charge around the average of £153. Both for sales and purchases, approximately 23 per cent of these charges came to less than £100 and 16 per cent amounted to more than £200. The factors which explain this variation relate to both the characteristics of the transaction and the nature of the firm handling it, and it would be imprudent to draw definite conclusions about some of them from the survey without extensive further statistical analysis. The price of the property involved and the amount of time spent on the work appear to be the most important. Properties costing £20,000–£30,000 cost on average £65 more to transfer than cheaper properties in the price range £10,000–£15,000. Although more time was spent on transferring more expensive property this did not fully account for the higher charges since the charge per hour was also higher for such property.

6.32 Among other factors which were considered as possibly affecting the level of transfer charges were whether the property was freehold or leasehold, whether it was registered or unregistered, the size of the firm of solicitors as measured by the number of its partners, the degree to which the firm relied on conveyancing work and the geographical location of the firm's principal office.

6.33 No differences emerged between the charge made for transferring property of similar price whether it was freehold or leasehold.

6.34 The charge for transferring unregistered property was higher than that made for transferring registered property of the same price, both for sales and purchases. Again the additional cost varied with the price of the property, unregistered property in each price range costing around 10 per cent more to transfer. In a number of cases the property was registered during the transaction; on average the charge in such cases was about the same as that made for property which remained unregistered.

6.35 The analysis by geographical location of the firms' principal offices does not establish any strong and consistent variations in charges even when transactions in properties of the same price class are compared, although such variations may be obscured by other factors and more detailed study would be required before concluding whether regional variations exist.

6.36 The size of the firm of solicitors handling the transaction appeared to have little consistent effect on transfer charges, but the contribution which conveyancing made to the firm's gross fee income did appear to have an effect. Charges were higher for each price category, and especially for transferring more expensive properties, where the firm derived less than 20 per cent of its fee income from conveyancing. This is partly a reflection of time spent as noted in paragraph 6.43 below.

Time spent

6.37 The overall time spent per conveyance by all fee-earning members of reporting firms was 6·2 hours for sales and 6·8 hours for purchases, partners' time on average accounting for about half of the total time in each case.

6.38 In just over three-quarters of the cases reported the information on the number of hours spent by the firm was estimated and not based on actual records. When the returns based on actual records were analysed separately the average time spent was 6·9 hours for a sale and 7·7 hours for a purchase, that is the time spent was shown to be slightly higher where actual records were kept than where estimates were made.

6.39 The fact that slightly less time, on average, was spent on a sale than on a purchase also emerges when each price category of property is examined separately. The absolute average transfer charge was virtually identical but there was a higher rate per hour for sales than for purchases.

6.40 More time was spent on transferring more expensive properties, the average on a purchase of a £10,000–£15,000 property being just over six hours compared with just over 7½ hours on a property costing between £20,000 and £30,000.

6.41 On average, firms which derived less than 20 per cent of their gross fees from all types of conveyancing spent much more time per conveyance than did other firms. Only 5 per cent of firms included in the survey, however, derived less than 20 per cent of their total gross income from conveyancing.

6.42 In over 40 per cent of the cases reported all the work was carried out by a profit-sharing partner of the firm, and profit-sharing partners handled some of the work in 70 per cent of the conveyances. In 18 per cent of the conveyances, however, no time was recorded as spent by qualified solicitors.

Transfer charge per hour

6.43 The overall average rate per hour was £24·80 for sales and £22·50 for purchases. This varied markedly by price of property, the average rate for purchases between £10,000 and £15,000 being £20·20 per hour as opposed to £26·50 per hour for properties costing £20,000–£30,000.

Importance of conveyancing income

6.44 The average proportion of gross fee income derived from all types of conveyancing ranged from an average of 60 per cent among sole practitioners (241 firms) to 34 per cent for firms with ten or more partners (37 firms).

ANNEX 6.1

Nature of the survey
(paragraph 6.1)

Method

A.6.1.1 The survey was conducted by means of a postal questionnaire which consisted of two parts: sheet A which contained information relating to the firm, and sheet B which contained information relating to charges, and was completed for each bill rendered during the transaction. The Law Society was consulted throughout on the design and content of the questionnaire.

A.6.1.2 The questionnaires were sent to a random 20 per cent sample of firms of solicitors by the London Insurance Brokers. The sample was obtained by taking every fifth firm on the list of solicitors maintained by them for the purposes of the Law Society's compulsory indemnity insurance scheme.

A.6.1.3 The questionnaires were distributed to 1,287 firms on 22 November 1978 who were asked for details of bills rendered in relation to domestic conveyancing transactions during the two-week period ending 11 November 1978. Questionnaires were requested to be returned by 16 December 1978. On 16 December, a reminder letter was sent to all firms included in the sample. The final date for return of the questionnaires was 2 January 1979, upon which date data processing began and was completed by 23 January 1979.

Response rate

A.6.1.4 Returns were received from 779 firms, of which 768 returns were usable. This represents a response rate of 60 per cent which is considered to be satisfactory in view of the relatively short period allowed for the questionnaire to be completed and the detailed nature of the information requested.

Number of partners

A.6.1.5 The response by size of firm, as measured by the number of profit-sharing partners, is set out in Table A.6.1.1.

TABLE A.6.1.1

Size of firm by number of profit-sharing partners

Number of partners	Number of firms in sample	Number responding	Response rate %
1	441	241	55
2	322	160	50
3–4	297	207	70
5–9	172	112	65
10 or more	55	37	67
Not stated	—	11	—
All firms	1,287	768	60

Income arising from conveyancing

A.6.1.6 Table A.6.1.2 analyses the respondents to the questionnaire by percentage of fee income arising from all types of conveyancing in both this survey and the Law Society's remuneration survey and shows that, for example, three-quarters of the respondents earned between 41 per cent and 80 per cent of their gross fees from conveyancing.

TABLE A.6.1.2

Distribution of firms: by percentage of gross fee income earned from all types of conveyancing

Percentage of total gross fee income from all types of conveyancing	Percentage of firms responding to	
	conveyancing survey %	Law Society's remuneration survey[1] %
Up to 20%	5	4
21–40%	12	12
41–60%	44	41
61–80%	31	34
81–100%	8	9
Total	100	100
Number of firms	768	1,377

[1]Consultants' report on the Law Society's remuneration survey, Section 16.

Size of firm

A.6.1.7　The distribution of firms in the survey by number of partners is set out in Table A.6.1.3 and can be seen to follow the patterns of distribution found in the London Insurance Brokers' records for 1976 and the Law Society's remuneration survey.

TABLE A.6.1.3

Distribution of firms: by size of firm

Number of partners	Conveyancing survey (1978) %	LIB[1] (1976) %	Law Society's remuneration survey (1976)[2] %
1	31	32	28
2	21	26	24
3–4	27	24	27
5–9	15	14	17
10 or more	5	3	4
Not stated	1	—	—
All firms	100	100	100
Number of firms	768	6,421	4,230

[1] London Insurance Brokers.

[2] Consultants' report on the Law Society's remuneration survey, Section 16.

Geographical distribution

A.6.1.8   The distribution of response is aiso measured against the geographical distribution of the principal office of the firms included in the sample in Table A.6.1.4.

TABLE A.6.1.4

Geographical distribution of firms

Region	Conveyancing survey %	Law Society's remuneration survey[1] %
Greater London	22	18
Rest of South East	16	22
North West & W. Midlands	22	21
East Anglia	3	3
South West	10	10
North	6	5
Yorkshire, Humberside & E. Midlands	14	14
Wales	6	6
Not stated	1	1
All firms	100	100
Number of firms	768	4,230

[1] Consultants' report on the Law Society's remuneration survey, Section 16.

General information

A.6.1.9   Information was obtained from 768 firms, in respect of 8,902 bills rendered for domestic conveyancing transactions. (Certain types of transaction to be included are set out in note 3 attached to the questionnaire, annex 6.2.) This gives an overall average of 11·5 bills per firm. Forty-four firms, however, rendered a nil return, with the result that the average number of bills for those firms which rendered them during the relevant period was 12.

Bills analysis

A.6.1.10   Firms were asked to provide details of all bills rendered during the prescribed period in respect of domestic conveyancing transactions. The number of bills in respect of which information was provided by a single firm ranged from 0 to 310. The distribution is shown below, related to the percentage of conveyancing fee income to total income.

TABLE A.6.1.5

Distribution of bills: by percentage of gross fee income from conveyancing

Number of bills from firms	Percentage of gross fee income from conveyancing					All firms
	Up to 20%	21–40%	41–60%	61–80%	81–100%	
0	34	7	3	4	5	6
1– 5	34	35	24	24	37	27
6–10	15	25	25	29	26	26
11–20	10	16	28	27	29	25
21–50	7	17	18	12	2	14
Over 50	0	0	2	2	0	1
Total	100	100	100	100	100	100
Number of firms	41	89	330	233	57	768

A.6.1.11 The distribution of bills rendered per firm is set out in Table A.6.1.6.

TABLE A.6.1.6

Distribution of bills by firm

Number of bills from firms	Number of firms	Percentage of firms	Percentage of bills
0	44	6	0
1– 5	209	27	7
6–10	196	26	17
11–20	192	25	31
21–50	110	14	37
More than 50	13	1	8
Not stated	4	1	—
All firms	768	100	100

A.6.1.12 Table A.6.1.7 shows the number of bills rendered according to the size of firm, measured by the number of profit-sharing partners.

TABLE A.6.1.7

Distribution of bills: by size of firm

Number of partners	Number of bills						Average number of bills
	0	1–5	6–10	11–20	21–50	50+	
1	30	119	60	28	4	0	5
2	6	49	55	41	8	1	9
3–4	7	29	60	74	35	1	13
5–9	1	9	14	36	48	3	21
10 or more	0	1	3	12	13	8	35
Not stated	2	2	4	1	2	—	—
All firms	46	209	196	192	110	13	12

A.6.1.13 Table A.6.1.8 shows that the distribution of bills related to the amounts charged for sales and purchases of property respectively are similar.

TABLE A.6.1.8

Distribution of transfer charges: by number of bills

Charge for transfer of property £	Sales		Purchases	
	number of bills	%	number of bills	%
0– 50	137	3	128	3
51–100	827	20	823	19
101–150	1,481	36	1,551	36
151–200	937	23	920	21
201–300	455	11	504	12
Over 300	189	5	172	4
Not stated	85	2	211	5
All bills	4,111	100	4,309	100
Average (£)	154	—	153	—
Median (£)	140	—	140	—
Lower quartile (£)	105	—	106	—
Upper quartile (£)	180	—	179	—

Time spent on conveyancing

A.6.1.14 Solicitors were asked to indicate either the number of hours spent on the conveyance by each type of fee-earner (profit-sharing partners, salaried partners or assistant solicitors, trainee solicitors, other fee-earners) or if this information was not available, to give the percentage of total time spent by each type of fee-earner. Many firms found it difficult to give exact figures for the number of hours spent by each fee-earner, preferring to give a percentage figure, and to estimate this if necessary. The comparison below of actual and estimated figures for the distribution of hours between the various types of fee-earner demonstrates that the estimated figures are very similar to those from actual records.

TABLE A.6.1.9

Time spent on conveyancing

Status of fee-earner	Percentage of time			
	sales		purchases	
	actual %	estimated %	actual %	estimated %
Partners	55	58	53	56
Assistant solicitors	15	14	15	13
Trainee solicitors	4	3	6	3
Other fee earners	26	26	25	27
Total	100	100	100	100
Number of bills	925	3,007	1,036	3,048

A.6.1.15 Comparisons have been made of the figures given for time according to whether they were actual or estimated. It appears that the total time involved was slightly greater in those bills where the information was taken from actual records as can be seen from Table A.6.1.10.

TABLE A.6.1.10

Comparison of actual with estimated hours

	Total number of hours involved	
	actual	estimated
Sales	6·9	6·0
Purchases	7·7	6·5

A.6.1.16 The distribution of hours over total bills was broadly similar for estimated and actual hours and suggests that the estimated figures are sufficiently reliable to be aggregated with the figures from actual records.

ANNEX 6.2

Survey questionnaire

(paragraph 6.3)

THE ROYAL COMMISSION ON LEGAL SERVICES

SURVEY OF DOMESTIC CONVEYANCING CHARGES

	FOR OFFICE USE
SHEET A—INFORMATION RELATING TO YOUR FIRM	

The information should be correct as at 11th November, 1978. If your firm has more than one office in England and Wales, the records should be amalgamated for the purpose of this survey. Information from all offices should be returned together in the envelope provided.

A1. Where is the principal office of your firm located? (SEE NOTE 1)
PLEASE TICK ONE BOX

Greater London ☐ 1   South West ☐ 5

Rest of South East ☐ 2   The North ☐ 6

North West & West Midlands ☐ 3   Yorkshire, Humberside & East Midlands ☐ 7

East Anglia ☐ 4   Wales ☐ 8

(12)

A2. How many profit-sharing partners are there?

PLEASE WRITE IN .... partners.   (13–14)

A3. How many other fee-earners are there? (SEE NOTE 2)

PLEASE WRITE IN .... other fee-earners.   (15–16)

A4. What percentage of the total gross fee income in the accounting year ended in 1977 was from conveyancing of all types?

PLEASE TICK ONE BOX   0% ☐ 1

1–20% ☐ 2

21–40% ☐ 3

41–60% ☐ 4   (17)

61–80% ☐ 5

81–100% ☐ 6

Please indicate whether the percentage is actual or estimated.

Actual ☐ 1   (18)

Estimated ☐ 2

PLEASE TURN OVER

A5.   How many bills were rendered by the firm during the fortnight ending 11th November, 1978 in respect of completed domestic conveyancing transactions? (SEE NOTE 3)

PLEASE WRITE IN .... bills.

(19–21)

IF THE FIRM ACTED FOR A CLIENT IN RESPECT OF A CONCURRENT SALE AND PURCHASE, PLEASE COUNT THE RESULTANT CHARGE AS TWO BILLS.

PLEASE COMPLETE ONE SHEET B FOR EACH OF THE BILLS RENDERED DURING THE PERIOD.

PLEASE READ NOTES BEFORE COMPLETING THIS FORM	FOR OFFICE USE
SHEET B—INFORMATION RELATING TO BILLS RENDERED IN THE TWO-WEEK PERIOD ENDING 11th NOVEMBER 1978 IN RESPECT OF DOMESTIC CONVEYANCING TRANSACTIONS AS DEFINED IN NOTES.	P.540 (1–3) Record No. (4–7) Card 2 (8)
IF YOU WERE INSTRUCTED BY A CLIENT ON BOTH HIS SALE AND PURCHASE, PLEASE TREAT AS TWO TRANSACTIONS AND COMPLETE SEPARATE SHEETS.	(9–11)

B1. Specify the type of transaction by indicating the letter of the sub-paragraph in Note 3.

PLEASE WRITE IN LETTER

☐ (12)

B2. Did you act for both vendor and purchaser in this transaction?

PLEASE TICK ONE BOX Yes ☐ 1 (13)

No ☐ 2

B3. Did you also act for:
PLEASE TICK ONE BOX

the mortgagor ☐ 1 both mortgagor and mortgagee ☐ 3 (14)

the mortgagee ☐ 2 OR: neither? ☐ 4

B4. Was the title:

SEE NOTE 4. freehold ☐ 1 (15)

PLEASE TICK ONE BOX OR: leasehold? ☐ 2

B5. Was the title:

PLEASE TICK ONE BOX already registered ☐ 1

registered during the transaction ☐ 2 (16)

OR: unregistered before and after the transaction ☐ 3

B6. What was the price of the property?

PLEASE WRITE IN £.. (17-19)

B7. What was the amount of the mortgage?

PLEASE WRITE IN £.. (20–22)

B8. What charge (to the nearest £) was made to the client for:

PLEASE WRITE IN The transfer of the property £ .... (23–25)

The mortgage work £ .... (26–28)

VAT £ .... (29–31)

total disbursements (see below) £ .... (32–34)

TOTAL CHARGE £ .... (35-37)

| PLEASE TURN OVER |

	FOR OFFICE USE

Please itemise the disbursements:

Land Registry Fees £ .... (38–40)

Stamp Duties £ .... (41–43)

Search Fees £ .... (44–46)

Others £ .... (47–49)

TOTAL DISBURSEMENTS £

B9.   Please indicate below any special factors which affected the charges as set out in B8.

PLEASE TICK AS MANY AS APPLY

work on arranging the mortgage ☐ 1   recent dealing with the same title ☐ 5

previous work on unsuccessful conveyancing transactions ☐ 2   work containing a charitable element ☐ 6

planning matters ☐ 3   work on matters ancillary to the conveyancing transaction which were not separately billed ☐ 7

building estate development ☐ 4

(50)

any of the factors listed in the Remuneration Order 1972 which apply   (51)
(specify) ....

....

Others (specify)...

No special factors ☐

B10.   If possible, please indicate in column (a) below the total number of hours (in accordance with Note 5) spent on the transaction by fee earners.

Please give the best estimate if exact figures are not available.

If you cannot complete column (a), please indicate in column (b) what percentage of the total time involved was spent by each category of fee earner on the whole transaction.

COMPLETE ONLY ONE COLUMN

	(a) No. of hours spent (See Note 5)	(b) % of total time	
Profit sharing Partners			(52–56)
Salaried Partners or Asst. Solicitors			(57–61)
Articled clerks			(62–66)
Other fee earners			(67–71)
Total		100%	(72–74)

B11.   Please indicate whether the information in B10 is actual (i.e., taken
from time records) or estimated.

PLEASE TICK ONE BOX

Actual ☐ 1   (75)

Estimated ☐ 2

ALL COMPLETED B SHEETS FOR OFFICES OF YOUR
FIRM SHOULD BE RETURNED THROUGH THE FIRM'S
PRINCIPAL OFFICE.

IF YOU HAVE INSUFFICIENT B SHEETS, WE WOULD
BE GRATEFUL IF YOU WOULD PHOTOCOPY MORE.

NOTES

1. (Question A1) Regions are to include the following counties:

Greater London:	GLC area.
Rest of South East:	Bedfordshire, Buckinghamshire, Hertfordshire, Essex, Kent, West Sussex, East Sussex, Surrey, Hampshire, Isle of Wight, Berkshire, Oxfordshire.
NW & W Midlands:	Lancashire, Greater Manchester, Merseyside, Cheshire, Salop, Staffordshire, West Midlands, Hereford and Worcester, Warwickshire.
East Anglia:	Norfolk, Cambridgeshire, Suffolk.
South West:	Gloucestershire, Avon, Wiltshire, Somerset, Dorset, Devon, Cornwall.
The North:	Northumberland, Cumbria, Durham, Cleveland, Tyne and Wear.
Yorkshire, Humberside and E Midlands:	North Yorkshire, West Yorkshire, South Yorkshire, Humberside, Derbyshire, Nottinghamshire, Lincolnshire, Leicestershire, Northamptonshire.
Wales:	Clwyd, Gwynedd, Powys, Dyfed, West Glamorgan, Mid-Glamorgan, Gwent, South Glamorgan.

2. (Question A3) This should include salaried partners, assistant solicitors, legal executives, articled clerks and any other fee-earning staff. Part-time fee-earners should be counted as one half unless a more accurate fraction is available.

3. (Question A5 and Part B) The purpose of this enquiry is to obtain information about domestic conveyancing transactions conducted for private individuals, other than those which did not lead to a completed transaction. Answers given in respect of Question A5 and in Part B should therefore cover the following types of transaction:

    A. the sale of residential property (whether freehold or leasehold) for owner occupation;

    B. the purchase of residential property (whether freehold or leasehold) for owner occupation;

    C. purchase by sitting tenants of local authority houses or flats;

    D. purchase of the freehold reversion in property held on long leasehold;

    E. conveyance or assignment of interests of joint tenants or tenants in common among themselves (e.g. conveyance by husband to himself and his wife);

    F. conveyance by way of gift, or not for full consideration.

Please use one and only one of the letters A–F above in answering Question B1.

4. (Question B4) "Leasehold" means residential property sold by way of, or held under long lease at a ground rent.

5. (Question B10) Including where appropriate time spent (*inter alia*) on:

    attendance on client or any other person
    preparing letters and perusing letters received
    telephone calls
    preparation of documents
    perusal of documents received
    supervision.

SECTION 7

Conveyancing: International Comparisons

Contents *paragraph*

Introduction

7.1 The purpose of this study was to obtain comparative information about the procedures for transferring ownership of land in this country and overseas, the functions of lawyers and non-lawyers and the duration and cost of the transaction. Enquiries were also made about the use of computerised data retrieval systems in conveyancing.

7.2 Conveyancing procedure in England and Wales is described in Volume I, Chapter 21. Procedure in Northern Ireland differs in some respects and is described in annex 7.1 to this Section. This paper contains the results of enquiries in Scotland and abroad.

7.3 It is accepted that variations between one country and another in economic, social and other ways make it difficult to draw direct conclusions from comparative studies of this kind. The information obtained was, however, requested by the Commission for the purpose of its work on conveyancing and is reproduced here as being of some general interest.

7.4 Our consultees (listed in annex 7.2) were sent a description of a typical domestic conveyancing transaction, together with an outline showing the basic steps in conveyancing in England and Wales, and were asked to describe how such a transaction would be conducted in their country or jurisdiction.

7.5 The transaction specified involved the transfer of a suburban house with three bedrooms, two reception rooms, bathroom, kitchen, garage and small garden. The example assumed that the vendor had purchased it by means of a loan, secured on the property, which had not been paid off, and that he wished to move to a similar property in another town in the same area. The consultees were asked to assume that the property was freehold, or the nearest equivalent under their law. They were asked to describe:—

(a) the arrangements the owner would make to bargain for and acquire the property to which he wished to move and to raise the necessary money;
(b) what would happen during these transactions and who would be expected to handle each stage;
(c) how long each stage would probably take and the likely cost of each service involved;
(d) what would be the likely cost of the sale of his home; and
(e) measures taken or pending to introduce computerisation into the process of property transfer.

7.6 Replies were received from the following jurisdictions:—
(a) Northern Ireland
(b) Scotland
(c) Sweden
(d) Australia – New South Wales
             – South Australia
             – Victoria
(e) New Zealand
(f) Canada   – Ontario

(g) USA   – California
            – Illinois
            – Missouri
            – New York
            – Texas

Comparisons of conveyancing procedures

7.7 Summaries of the information given by our consultees relating to conveyancing procedures in their jurisdictions are set out in annex 7.1. As the summaries show, certain steps appeared to be fundamental to the transfer of property and occurred in conveyancing transactions in all the jurisdictions consulted. There is, for example, always a contract to transfer based on offer and acceptance, and there is invariably some time-lag between contract and completion of the transaction to enable matters relating to title and finance to be resolved. There is always some means of establishing title and of investigating various ancillary matters relating to use of property.

7.8 There are also wide variations in procedure among the jurisdictions consulted. These can be divided into four main categories:—
(a) the method by which title is recorded and deduced;
(b) the means by which ancillary matters are investigated;
(c) the stage at which a contract becomes binding;
(d) the varying services provided by experts such as lawyers and estate agents.

The manner in which title is recorded and deduced
7.9 Registration of title has been introduced in a number of countries. It simplifies the task of proving title by removing the need to trace it back over many years. It should thus simplify transactions and reduce cost. In England and Wales in 1978–79 a little over 50 per cent of all transactions involved land already registered, and 25 per cent land that was registered for the first time. In New Zealand all land available to purchasers is registered, and in the three Australian states covered by our enquiry a very large proportion (in South Australia, for example, over 90 per cent) is registered under a system of land registration first introduced in South Australia in the nineteenth century by Sir Robert Torrens.

7.10 In some countries, as in England and Wales, the difficulty of proving title to unregistered land has been reduced by the introduction of a statutory limitation on the period for which a good root of title may be required.

7.11 In the USA a relatively small proportion of titles are registered. Legal title, if unregistered, must often be deduced from an original Crown or state grant. As a practical means of simplifying conveyancing and keeping down costs there has developed a system of insurance to provide monetary compensation if the purchased title is invalid or if there is a defect in the title within the scope of the policy. Title insurance companies frequently maintain private registers of title, the cost of which forms part of their overhead expenses paid out of premium income.

The way in which ancillary matters are investigated

7.12   In any jurisdiction, a purchaser or his mortgagee will wish to investigate the physical condition of the property and any local developments which might impinge upon his use of it. The mortgagee will generally require a survey, as will the purchaser for his own protection. Local conditions affect the matters investigated; for example in New York and Texas it is customary to arrange a termite inspection, in parts of England and Wales a survey for woodworm. In addition, there may be a number of matters affecting the property which can only be discovered by searching local records. These relate, for example, to orders made under building or health regulations, area zoning, planning consents, road construction proposals, local land charges, and compulsory purchase orders. Such enquiries are generally carried out before contracts are exchanged, although in some areas, for example New South Wales, the usual form of contract allows for enquiries to be made of the various statutory authorities after exchange of contracts. The length of time taken by such enquiries varies from country to country: in New Zealand, for example, some authorities will answer telephone enquiries; in New South Wales enquiries take about four weeks; in England and Wales they vary in most cases between five days and five weeks.

7.13   In a number of places steps have been taken to ensure that information relating to ancillary matters is recorded in an easily retrievable form. For example:—

(a)   In South Australia all developers must submit a site plan to the registration and planning authorities and to all utility undertakings and when this has been approved no developments on the ground may depart from the approved plan without permission. The plan gives details of all easements over the land.

(b)   In Northern Ireland there is a register which shows such things as statutory charges and public health and building notices. This is kept at the Land Registry and is entirely separate from the register of titles.

(c)   In Sweden, the data bank in the county of Uppsala contains a wide range of computerised information about land ownership and use. This is in two parts, reflecting the division of responsibility between the title register and local authority register for recording information. A search against any address of property should reveal all registered information which the conveyancer will need. This system is described in greater detail in paragraphs 7.32 and 7.33.

The stage at which the contract becomes binding

7.14   In England and Wales contracts, when exchanged, create a binding and unconditional commitment to complete the transaction. The financial penalties for breach may be heavy. For this reason, before contract there is a stage in which searches and surveys are carried out and finance is arranged. Before exchange of contracts, either party is free to repudiate the agreement without penalty.

7.15 In certain of the jurisdictions mentioned, contracts are exchanged at a much earlier stage but may be conditional on specific matters, for example:—
(a) the purchaser obtaining a mortgage (Northern Ireland, New Zealand, South Australia, Victoria, Missouri, Illinois, New York and Texas);
(b) local searches not revealing any matters which adversely affect the land (Northern Ireland);
(c) a satisfactory survey report (Illinois);
(d) the sale of the purchaser's own house (South Australia).

7.16 In Victoria and New York the vendor and purchaser may enter into an agreement to transfer the property conditional on the purchaser obtaining a mortgage. In South Australia the contract, as well as being conditional, is subject to a two-day cooling-off period in which the purchaser may repudiate without penalty.

7.17 In contrast to the examples quoted above of conditional contracts and agreements, Scotland has a system whereby the acceptance in writing by a vendor of a written offer constitutes a contract binding upon both parties. Such contracts may be subject to conditions relating, for example, to the purchaser's freedom to use the property for some specified purpose, but are not, as a rule, conditional upon a satisfactory survey report being received by the purchaser.

The role of lawyers and others in the conveyancing process

7.18 In the jurisdictions consulted, the functions of lawyers, land brokers, estate agents, institutional mortgagees or title insurers vary considerably.

7.19 In England and Wales the parties are normally introduced through an estate agent. Thereafter solicitors usually act on behalf of the parties. Lawyers are employed in the same way for conveyancing work in Northern Ireland, Scotland, New York and New Zealand.

7.20 In South Australia most conveyancing work is carried out by brokers trained in land law while in Victoria and New South Wales where most of the land is registered under the same system as in South Australia, solicitors carry out most of the work when the parties have been introduced by agents.

7.21 In Ontario and Illinois the purchaser rarely consults a lawyer until after he has signed the binding contract, which is prepared by an estate agent.

This contrasts with the practice in Scotland where solicitors usually handle what in England and Wales is at present regarded as estate agents' work, for example advertising the property for sale.

7.22   In California, Missouri and Texas lawyers are rarely employed for conveyancing. In these three states the contracts are in standard form and are drawn up by estate agents, although they may be amended by a lawyer where one is employed. Estate agents, with mortgagees and the title insurance companies, usually handle all stages of the transaction.

7.23   In South Australia property transfers may be handled by lawyers or by specialist conveyancers/land brokers. Land brokers qualify by examination in property and contract law and conveyancing procedures. They are controlled by statutory rules under the general supervision of a government licensing authority. Both land brokers and estate agents are required to deposit clients' money in a trust account, the income from which is used to finance a compensation fund to protect clients who suffer financial loss through fiduciary default by a principal or employee. Conveyancing fees, whether charged by a broker or by a solicitor, are governed by a statutory scale.

7.24   In Sweden a comprehensive service is offered by the Swedish Savings Banks' Association's estate agency, the largest in Sweden, which may handle all the stages of the transfer from advising the vendor about marketing his property to arranging for the registration of the purchaser's title, and whose facilities include an insurance scheme (launched in 1975) covering vendors and their purchasers against the financial consequences of defects or deficiencies in the property not previously known to the vendor.

Comparison of conveyancing costs

7.25   Comprehensive information about costs was provided by consultees in only six of the jurisdictions consulted. This and similar information relating to England and Wales is summarised in Tables 7.1 and 7.2. The information obtained from our consultees related to 1977, and the figures are based on assumptions as to the price of a typical property and the size of the associated mortgage. The amount of major items of cost (lawyers' and estate agents' fees, mortgage work, and taxes) is dependent on these assumptions.

7.26   Direct comparisons between jurisdictions cannot easily be made because their procedures are not the same and lawyers and non-lawyers have different functions. Examples of these variations are to be found in paragraphs 7.18 to 7.24.

7.27   For the reasons stated above, only the most general of conclusions may be drawn from the available information. However, limited comparisons may

TABLE 7.1
Cost of a typical purchase in 1977

Jurisdiction	England and Wales[1]			Australia—					New Zealand	Canada—Ontario	USA—New York City	
				New South Wales		South Australia	Victoria					
Status of title	previously registered	first registration	un-registered	registered	un-registered	registered	registered	un-registered	registered	registered	previously investigated	not investigated
1 Price of typical dwelling	£18,000	£14,500[2]	£15,800	$35,000	$35,000	$35,000	$55,000	$55,000	$30,000	$59,000	$100,000	$100,000
2 Amount of mortgage	£11,100	£9,200	£10,000	$26,250	$26,250	$25,000	$33,100	$34,100	$15,000	$30,000	$75,000	$75,000
3 Cost of purchase (see serial 5 for % breakdown)	£530	£442	£441	$1,370	$1,862	$1,113	$2,720	$3,039	$670	$1,129	$2,947	$3,121
4 Cost (serial 3) as percentage of price (serial 1)	2·9%	3·0%	2·8%	3·9%	5·3%	3·2%	4·9%	5·5%	2·2%	1·9%	2·9%	3·1%
5 Cost of purchase	%	%	%	%	%	%	%	%	%	%	%	%
legal services including searches:												
lawyer	30	36	38	38[3]	51[3]	14[4]	30	37	26[6]	31	34	32
non-lawyer	7	8	9								17[5]	16[6]
mortgagee's fees:												
legal work	6[5]	7[5]	7[5]				12	15	17[5]	22	12	11
other charges	21	18	20[8]	8	6	10	4	3	9	9	4	4
surveys:												
for mortgagee	8[8]	5[8]		3	2	3	4	8	3	13	1	6
for purchaser	28	24	25	41	30	73	50	44	45	2	1	1
registration authority's fees[7]	1	1	1	10	11					22	31	29
taxes												
other costs												
Total	100[9]	100[9]	100	100	100	100	100	100[9]	100	100	100	100[9]

[1] Figures for England and Wales related to 1978 and, with the exception of the survey costs, are averages taken from the survey of conveyancing costs described in Section 6. The cost of the purchasers' surveys are estimated.
[2] Average figure that takes account of newly completed properties purchased for the first time.
[3] Includes cost of work for mortgagee as well as mortgagor.
[4] Work may be done by a lawyer or a land broker: the same statutory scales apply in either instance.
[5] Scale fees.
[6] Title insurance premiums: insurer undertakes or commissions searches.
[7] Cost of registering title or mortgage or both, as appropriate.
[8] Greater than zero, but less than 0·5 per cent.
[9] Percentages do not add to 100 due to rounding.

155

TABLE 7.2

Cost of a typical sale in 1977

Jurisdiction	England and Wales[1]			Australia—					New Zealand	Canada—Ontario	USA—New York City
				New South Wales		South Australia	Victoria				
Status of title	previously registered	first registration	unregistered	registered	unregistered	registered	registered	unregistered	registered	registered	—
1 Price of typical dwelling	£18,000	£12,100	£15,800	$35,000	$35,000	$35,000	$35,000	$35,000	$30,000	$59,000	$100,000
2 Cost of sale (see serial 4 for % breakdown)	£545	£403	£507	$1,689	$1,918	$1,311	$1,620	$1,778	$904	$4,040	$8,008
3 Cost (serial 2) as percentage of price (serial 1)	3·0%	3·3%	3·2%	4·8%	5·5%	3·7%	4·6%	5·1%	3·0%	6·8%	8·0%
4 Cost of sale:	%	%	%	%	%	%	%	%	%	%	%
estate agents' fees	66	60	62	80	70	93	75	68	86	88	75
lawyers' fees	29	34	31	18[3]	27	3[3]	18	26	12[3]	12	12
mortgagee's fees: legal work	1	[4]	[4]			2	6	5			[4]
other charges		3	3			[4]	[4]	[4]			12
taxes	2	3		2	3	1	1	[4]	2	1	
other costs	2	2	3			1	1		2	1	
Total	100	100[5]	100[5]	100	100	100[5]	100	100[5]	100	100[5]	100[5]

[1] Figures for England and Wales relate to 1978 and, with the exception of estate agents' fees, are averages taken from the survey of conveyancing charges described in Section 6. Estate agents' fees have been calculated at 2 per cent of selling price.
[2] Work may be done by a lawyer or a land broker: the same statutory scales apply in either instance.
[3] Scale fee.
[4] Greater than zero, but less than 0·5 per cent.
[5] Percentages do not add to 100 due to rounding.

be made of the total cost of sales or purchases when expressed as proportions of the price of the properties. The relative amounts of the component items of cost may also be considered. Certain features appear common to all or most jurisdictions:—

(a) it costs more to transfer an unregistered than a registered title;
(b) the most substantial costs borne by purchasers are lawyers' fees and taxes, the latter being usually the larger;
(c) the biggest cost borne by vendors is estate agents' fees;
(d) the cost of selling a family house of the kind selected as an example is more expensive than buying a similar house; in Ontario and New York City the difference is particularly great.

7.28 In order to express in common terms the costs of buying and selling in the different jurisdictions these costs have been divided by the appropriate average hourly industrial wages. The results, set out in Table 7.3, show the number of hours a typical industrial worker would have to work to earn (gross) an amount equal to the cost of selling one house and buying another.

TABLE 7.3
Time taken to earn cost of typical purchase and sale

Jurisdiction	Status of title	Cost		Average industrial earnings[1] per hour	Time in hours		
		purchase	sale		purchase	sale	Both purchase and sale
England and Wales[2]	Previously registered[3]	£530	£545	£1·90	279	287	566
	First registration [3] [4]	£442	£403		232	212	444
	Unregistered[3]	£441	£507		232	266	498
Australia— New South Wales	Registered	$1,370	$1,689	$5·43[6]	252	316	568
	Unregistered	$1,862	$1,918		343	353	696
South Australia	Unregistered[5] Registered	$1,113	$1,311	$5·18[6]	214	253	467
Victoria	Registered[4]	$2,720	$1,620	$5·48[6]	496	296	792
	Unregistered[4]	$3,039	$1,778		554	324	878
New Zealand	Registered	$670	$ 904	$3·36	199	269	468
Canada—Ontario	Registered	$1,129	$4,040	$6·65	169	608	777
USA—New York City	Previously investigated	$2,947	$8,008	$5·26	560	1,522	2,082
	Not investigated	$3,121			593		2,115

[1] Source: Department of Employment.
[2] Figures for England and Wales relate to 1978.
[3] The costs of purchase and sale in England and Wales are based largely on the results of the survey of conveyancing charges described in Section 6. The average price of registered property involved in transactions covered by the survey was higher than that of unregistered property similarly involved, which in turn was higher than that of property registered for the first time (see Tables 7.1 and 7.2).
[4] Figures relate to sale and purchase of houses of different prices (see Tables 7.1 and 7.2).
[5] Figures not obtained.
[6] Average weekly earnings divided by average weekly hours worked.

157

Time taken by conveyancing transactions

7.29 The information received from consultees as to the duration of the typical conveyancing transaction was incomplete in most cases. Where the total time taken by the transaction was given it is shown in Table 7.4.

TABLE 7.4
Duration of conveyancing transactions

Jurisdiction	Estimated duration in weeks
England and Wales	8–12[1]
New York	5–8
New Zealand	$4\frac{1}{2}$–$8\frac{1}{2}$
Scotland	6–9
Texas	6–13
Victoria	7–13

[1]Median category from results of the National Board for Prices and Incomes conveyancing survey, 1970 (NBPI Report No. 164, Cmnd 4624).

Computerisation of information required by conveyancers

7.30 Consultees were asked for information about developments in the use of computers for storing and retrieving information relevant to land transactions.

7.31 The growth in legislation concerning land use, local authority charges on property, health and building regulations and conservation measures has meant that, even in countries where investigation of legal title is aided by registration, the conveyancer may have to spend considerable time obtaining information about the property from a number of different sources. Various attempts, some of which are described in the paragraphs that follow, have been made to apply the advantages of computerisation to this task.

Sweden

7.32 In the county of Uppsala in Sweden a computerised land data bank system replaced manual registers in 1976. Uppsala contains some 100,000 property units (about 0·3 per cent of all units in Sweden) but it is planned to extend the system to certain other major urban areas until its capacity is fully utilised. The data bank will then hold details of approximately 30 per cent of Sweden's property units. The data bank is operated by the Central Board for Real Estate Data, which is responsible to the Ministry of Justice, and is in two parts.

158

(a) The land register which contains details of:—

   (i) legal title;

   (ii) leasehold rights;

   (iii) mortgages; and

   (iv) various items of additional data (for example tax information).

Information about the owner, such as marital status and address, is obtained and up-dated automatically from registers maintained by other authorities.

(b) The property register comprises six sub-registers:—

   (i) the main register concerned with the identification of properties by administrative area (size and position are given with locational references and rights and restrictions affecting the property are also listed);

   (ii) the coordinate register, which records the location of properties by a coordinated system which covers the entire county;

   (iii) the plan register, which records official plans concerned with, for example, statutory regulations and prohibitions governing the use of land and surveys dealing with road costs.

   (iv) the block register, concerned with plans and regulations involving blocks of housing and area and street expenses;

   (v) the address register (for access using the property's postal address); and

   (vi) the institutional establishments register.

When certain of the information held in the main register is changed the system ensures that other registers are amended as appropriate. Similarly, the fact that a property is affected by a plan recorded in the plan register is automatically noted in the main register.

7.33 Contrary to usage in the United Kingdom information stored in the data bank is public and any terminal connected to the system gives direct access to the information.

Canada

7.34 In the Maritime Provinces of Canada the introduction of compulsory registration of title was synchronised with the creation of a national grid, with a view to the creation of a land data bank, based on the unique reference number of each parcel identified by means of the new grid coordinates. This system, which was inaugurated in 1973, provided for the following developments.

(a) It initiated a detailed land survey with new coordinates integrated into the existing national grid.

(b) It facilitated the production of small scale cadastral maps in which each identified parcel of land is given a unique reference number; compatible maps may also be prepared to show the presence of, for example, supply lines and water mains. The unique cadastral reference is used as the data base for existing and potential files (required for legal, demographical, sociological and geographical purposes) containing information about individual parcels or groups of plots.

(c) It facilitated the compulsory registration of land. The description of each plot is based on the unique cadastral reference based on the new grid coordinates. In the event of conflict these measurements take precedence over any structures on the ground.

(d) It enabled the title registration system to be fully computerised to allow easy access by visual display unit or print-out facilities for the purpose of dealing in land. Basic information (such as reference numbers, boundaries location and easements) are recorded permanently while transitory information (for example ownership and encumbrances on title such as mortgages) are deleted from the record at the conclusion of the relevant transaction.

England and Wales

7.35 In England and Wales the index to the registers of the Land Charges Department of the Land Registry was computerised in 1974. The registers, which hold against the name of the landowner details of charges affecting unregistered land, are five in number and are concerned with:—

(a) land charges, particularly restrictive covenants, estate contracts, right of occupation of the matrimonial home, and those financial charges that are not protected by the deposit of the mortgagor's title deeds;

(b) pending land actions and petitions in bankruptcy;

(c) writs and orders affecting land;

(d) deeds of arrangements affecting land; and

(e) annuities.

7.36 Prior to computerisation, searches of the index to the registers could take ten days or more in busy periods. Under the present system, the majority of applications for searches are made through the post and are completed within one or two days. Applications can be made by telephone or telex. Replies to telephone enquiries are given immediately by an operator using a visual display unit to interrogate the computer records. The reply is subsequently confirmed by a printed certificate of the result of the search which is sent to the applicant by post.

7.37 The number of subsisting registrations on these registers was estimated to be about 5 million at the end of March 1979 and during 1978–79 searches were made against 4·3 million names.

7.38   At the end of March 1979 there were approximately 6·3 million registered titles. A recent study into the feasibility of applying computer techniques to the registration of title concluded that computerisation could produce considerable practical and economic benefits. A pilot study is in progress, using the land charges computer.

7.39   There has been, since late 1977, a computerised system of indexing the names of proprietors of registered land and of registered charges.

Conveyancing procedures in the jurisdictions consulted

(paragraph 7.7)

A.7.1.1 This annex contains a brief description of the main features of a typical conveyancing transaction of domestic property in each of the jurisdictions consulted, based on the detailed information provided by the consultees. For ease of comparison, a short summary of such a transaction in England and Wales is set out first. A fuller description is given in Volume I, between paragraphs 21.12 and 21.20.

England and Wales

A.7.1.2 The vendor and purchaser enter into a preliminary agreement to transfer. This is normally made through the vendor's estate agent and is not legally binding.

A.7.1.3 Draft contracts are drawn up (normally through solicitors). The purchaser then:—

(a) applies for a building society mortgage;

(b) makes enquiries and searches of the local authority (normally through his solicitor) about the property (for example about building regulations, planning consents and local land charges);

(c) may instruct a private surveyor to examine the property;

(d) makes enquiries of the vendor (through solicitors) about legal matters affecting the use of the property;

(e) discusses details of the draft contract, financial arrangements and results of enquiries with his solicitor.

A.7.1.4 Legally binding contracts are signed and exchanged. The purchaser pays a 10 per cent deposit (normally to the vendor's solicitor as agent of the vendor). Property insurance is arranged to run from the date of exchange.

A.7.1.5 The vendor's solicitor supplies the abstract of title (if the land is unregistered) or a copy of the register filed plan and authority to inspect the Land Register (if the land is registered).

A.7.1.6 The draft conveyance is prepared by the purchaser's solicitor and approved by the vendor's solicitor. Mortgage arrangements are finalised with the building society.

A.7.1.7 Final searches are made by the purchaser's solicitor of the Land Register (if the property is registered) or the Land Charges Register (if the property is not registered).

A.7.1.8 On completion the balance of the purchase money is paid. The purchaser receives the keys, transfer and title deeds.

A.7.1.9 After completion the new title is registered (if the property is in an area of compulsory registration), and the purchaser complies with the tax regulations by paying stamp duty if the purchase price of the property is above £15,000.

Northern Ireland

A.7.1.10 The contract is drafted by the vendor's solicitor who forwards it to the vendor's estate agent.

A.7.1.11 The purchaser's solicitor (exceptionally in north Antrim, the vendor's solicitor) requests copies of property certificates from, as appropriate:—

(a) Department of the Environment;

(b) Northern Ireland Housing Executive;

(c) local council.

This is the equivalent of the local authority searches in England and Wales. The purchaser's solicitor (vendor's solicitor in north Antrim) also makes a search of the statutory charges register.

A.7.1.12 When a subject to contract offer is made the title deeds (and in north Antrim the property certificates and results of the statutory charges register search) are forwarded to the purchaser's solicitor.

A.7.1.13 The purchaser's solicitor makes bankruptcy searches and checks entries in the judgments enforcements register. He then inserts any special conditions (examples are given in paragraph A.7.1.14 below) and makes pre-contract enquiries.

A.7.1.14 The deposit and the contract are forwarded to the vendor's solicitor and the contract is executed by the vendor. The contract may be conditional on:—

(a) the purchaser obtaining a building society mortgage for a specified sum "without retentions or onerous conditions";

(b) the granting of planning permission;

(c) the property not being adversely affected by any matter in the local council property certificate;

(d) the roads and footpaths bounding the property being maintained by the local authority and there being no road charges affecting the premises.

A.7.1.15 The purchaser's solicitor submits requisitions on title and the draft conveyance to the vendor's solicitor. When requisitions have been answered satisfactorily and the conveyance settled, the purchaser's solicitor will submit a title report to the mortgagee and mortgage arrangements will be finalised.

A.7.1.16 After completion the purchaser's solicitor registers the conveyance and the purchaser's mortgage (if the property is registered). If the property is unregistered the deeds are recorded.

Scotland

A.7.1.17 In the past, virtually all domestic property in Scotland was sold through solicitors. Solicitors still deal with most transactions, but there has in recent years been an increasing tendency for the sale of domestic property to be handled by chartered surveyors, property and estate agents or insurance brokers. The summary that follows, which is based on the evidence of the Council of the Law Society in Scotland to the Royal Commission on Legal Services in Scotland, assumes that there are solicitors acting for both vendor and purchaser.

A.7.1.18 The vendor's solicitor advertises the property in the press and/or through the local solicitors' property centre. Such centres, which now cover most of the urban areas of Scotland, are a source of information for the public about domestic property for sale in the area. Sales may be arranged in a number of ways, but by far the most common is by postal bids culminating in missives of sale. These are the letters by which the purchaser or his solicitor makes an offer for the property and the acceptance by the vendor or his solicitor. The offer and acceptance constitute a binding contract which sets out details of the property, the date on which entry is to be given, the price payable and any other relevant information or intentions.

A.7.1.19 Before this stage is reached the vendor's solicitor must satisfy himself that his client has a marketable title since the missives will include an obligation to deliver a valid and marketable title and the purchaser's solicitor advises his client as to the terms of his offer (for example the amount and the proposed date of entry) and, when necessary, negotiates a loan on his behalf.

A.7.1.20 When formal missives have been concluded, the vendor's solicitor supplies his client's title deed to the purchaser's solicitor for his inspection. These will normally include a search for 20 years against the property which will give brief details of all the recorded documents affecting the property. This information is obtained from the Register of Sasines, a public register of all deeds and encumbrances affecting real property. The purchaser's solicitor arranges insurance, prepares the conveyance and agrees it with the vendor's solicitor.

A.7.1.21 The date of entry and the date of settlement may be the same but the latter may be postponed. Shortly before settlement the vendor's solicitor produces an up-to-date search of the Register of Sasines, to reveal any mortgages or other encumbrances to which the property has become liable during the ownership of the vendor. Mortgages will normally already have been disclosed and arrangements made for their discharge. Should a major encumbrance come to light in the examination of the title or search, such as to bring into question the title offered for sale, the contract would be invalidated and the vendor become liable for the costs incurred by the purchaser up to that date. At settlement the vendor's solicitor gives a personal guarantee to the purchaser against the risk of a very recent mortgage or encumbrance having been registered between the date to which the Register of Sasines is currently complete and the date of settlement.

A.7.1.22 The solicitors for both parties being satisfied that all deeds and encumbrances are known and accepted, and that they truly reflect the terms of the missives, settlement takes place on the date specified in the missives. The interval between missives and settlement is usually about four to six weeks. Immediately after settlement the purchaser's solicitor arranges to have the conveyance stamped and recorded in the Register of Sasines. The vendor's solicitor notifies the local authority of the change of ownership.

Sweden

A.7.1.23 In the description below both sale and purchase are undertaken by real estate brokers. No information is available as to the proportion of conveyances completed by lawyers in Sweden.

A.7.1.24 The vendor discusses the conduct of the sale with the estate agent who advises him. The agent then:—

(a) investigates the vendor's title;

(b) obtains details of financial charges on the property and other encumbrances;

(c) checks compliance with planning permission;

(d) inspects the property and checks whether a new title plan needs to be prepared.

A.7.1.25 The agent prepares the contract which is usually conditional on the vendor's purchase and the purchaser's sale. Neither party is legally obliged until the contract is signed. After it has been executed the agent:—

(a) obtains a title certificate;

(b) obtains a tax assessment certificate;

(c) arranges the lender's valuation;

(d) arranges a completion date;

(e) calculates the final financial settlement; and

(f) contacts the electricity and water companies to book a final meter reading.

A.7.1.26 After completion the lender arranges for the registration of the purchaser's title (which is combined with the payment of purchase tax).

New South Wales

A.7.1.27 The description below is of the transfer of registered title under the Torrens system of land registration. Other titles are more complex to investigate.

A.7.1.28 The vendor and purchaser are generally introduced through an estate agent. Once the price is agreed the vendor's solicitor is instructed to prepare a contract. The purchaser is usually represented by a separate solicitor.

A.7.1.29 The vendor's solicitor prepares the draft contract and submits it to the purchaser's solicitor; it usually includes a zoning certificate (showing existing town planning applicable to the property), a drainage diagram and often a survey certificate, all forming part of the basis of the contractual arrangements.

A.7.1.30 The purchaser's solicitor will discuss the contract and finance with his client and make any necessary mortgage arrangements. He will also order a search of the title register and may need to obtain a certificate of compliance with local ordinances from the local municipal council and a survey certificate.

A.7.1.31 Exchange of contracts occurs, creating obligations on the part of both vendor and purchaser. A deposit, usually of 10 per cent of the purchase price, is paid at this stage. Enquiries are made by the purchaser's solicitor from the various statutory authorities with regard to such matters as planning proposals and outstanding dues, which may constitute a charge upon the land.

A.7.1.32 After exchange of contracts, the vendor's solicitor makes arrangements for the redemption of any mortgage on the property to be effective at the time of settlement. The vendor's solicitor also provides brief particulars of the title to the purchaser's solicitor. The purchaser's solicitor has a limited time to make requisitions on title which must be answered. The purchaser's solicitor checks the survey of the land; he also makes a search of the register of titles and ensures from the answers to his enquiries from the vendor's solicitor and from the various statutory bodies that there is no impediment to the purchase and that dues can be adjusted on settlement. He submits a stamped transfer document to the vendor's solicitor to be completed and kept in readiness for the date of completion. The purchaser's solicitor obtains the execution of any mortgage for the provision of finance, has the document stamped and has the document, together with replies to the enquiries from the mortgagee, forwarded to the mortgagee's solicitor.

A.7.1.33 Settlement (completion): the agreed balance of purchase price is paid in return for the fully executed transfer, the title deeds, a duly executed discharge of vendor's mortgage on the property, keys and letters of attornment to tenants where applicable. Finally the documents are lodged for registration on the Torrens register by the purchaser's solicitor, or by the mortgagee's solicitor if there is a mortgage.

South Australia

A.7.1.34 A licensed estate agent drafts the contract, which must be in a statutory form and to which will be added details of any of the following matters which affect the land:—

(a) easements;

(b) restrictive covenants to which the land is servient;

(c) liens;

(d) leases, tenancy agreements or licences;

(e) planning and health notices;

(f) compulsory acquisition orders;

(g) land tax demands; and

(h) details of any sale within a period of twelve months of the date of the contract.

A.7.1.35 The purchaser has a two-day cooling-off period within which he may repudiate the contract without penalty. At this stage he pays a maximum deposit of $25. The contract is binding after the cooling-off period of two working days has expired, but is usually conditional on the purchaser:—

(a) obtaining a mortgage; and

(b) selling his own property.

Such contracts usually work because the agent advises the vendor to accept an offer from a client who should be able to obtain a reasonable loan and then assists the purchaser to obtain a mortgage. The estate agent holds the deposit (increased to, say, 10 per cent).

A.7.1.36 The purchaser normally instructs a land broker to prepare the transfer, investigate title and check the search results annexed to the contract. Except for the specialist solicitors' firms who handle commercial and industrial conveyancing, most of this work is undertaken by brokers. In South Australia 90 per cent of titles are registered under the Torrens system. The title to unregistered property must be deduced from title deeds, which may be done either by a solicitor or a land broker.

A.7.1.37 The estate agent usually assists the purchaser to obtain a mortgage, while the lender's solicitor or broker prepares the mortgage deed. Completion is usually handled by the broker or solicitor (paid by the purchaser but effectively acting for both parties). He will receive a mortgage discharge from an agent of the vendor's mortgagee, calculate apportionments and pay disbursements. Also he is responsible for the payment of stamp duty and the registration (in a Torrens case) of the transfer and mortgage.

Victoria

A.7.1.38 The purchaser signs a sale note on a statutory form (this can be a binding contract but is usually conditional on the purchaser raising a mortgage) at the estate agent's office and pays a deposit.

166

A.7.1.39 The vendor's solicitor drafts a formal contract using one of two standard forms, which will contain more details including encumbrances over the land. Solicitors acting for the parties settle the formal contract after the purchaser's solicitor has:—

(a) investigated the title (either Torrens or unregistered);

(b) made local searches in respect of any unpaid rates and taxes;

(c) checked land use regulations affecting the property;

(d) had the plot boundaries checked; and

(e) made enquiries of the Housing Commission and road authority to check that the property is free of encumbrances.

The contract is executed and by this time the purchaser will have paid a deposit of 10 per cent.

A.7.1.40 Requisitions on title are set within 14 days to determine whether there are any title defects not revealed by the searches or contract. If any such defects are revealed the vendor must put them right or the purchaser may terminate the contract.

A.7.1.41 The mortgagee's solicitor prepares the mortgage deed. If a mortgage is to be discharged, completion takes place at the office of the vendor's mortgagee's solicitor.

A.7.1.42 The purchaser's mortgagee's solicitor is responsible for the payment of stamp duty and the registration of the executed deeds or, in any unregistered transaction, recording the deeds.

New Zealand

A.7.1.43 Using the services of a land agent the parties reach agreement as to the price and dates of settlement and possession. Either the agent prepares a conditional agreement or one of the parties' solicitor prepares such an agreement. A contract agreement may be conditional on some of the following matters:—

(a) the purchaser obtaining finance;

(b) the property complying with planning requirements;

(c) the approval of the purchaser's solicitor.

A.7.1.44 The land agent usually receives the deposit, which is held in a trust account for ten days and then forwarded to the vendor's solicitor less the amount of his fees.

A.7.1.45 The purchaser's solicitor:—

(a) orders a title search (all land available to purchasers in New Zealand is registered) and makes enquiries of the local authority about possible requisitions and town planning requirements;

(b) obtains details of current insurance of the property from the vendor's solicitor;

(c) arranges a mortgage valuation.

A.7.1.46 The purchaser usually makes his own mortgage arrangements but if he has had no previous contact with institutional lenders the solicitor will probably also prepare and lodge his loan application and may sometimes arrange the mortgage himself.

A.7.1.47 If the results of searches and enquiries are satisfactory the purchaser's solicitor:—

(a) confirms the agreement as unconditional;

(b) arranges to obtain mortgage funds (he will usually act for the mortgagee);

(c) prepares the transfer and mortgage; and

(d) attends upon settlement (completion) at the vendor's solicitor's office.

After settlement the purchaser's solicitor attends to the registration of the transfer and mortgage, and the payment of taxes.

Ontario

A.7.1.48   The parties usually enter into a binding contract prepared by an estate agent. The purchaser rarely consults a lawyer until after signing an agreement, therefore the assistance the lawyer can give will be limited by the terms of the contract. Also the purchaser will usually make the mortgage arrangements himself, but his solicitor may frequently be instructed to act for the mortgagee. The purchaser's solicitor will:—

(a)   discuss matters such as the tax position, joint ownership and property insurance with his client;

(b)   search the title, preparing enrolment of title and requisition which must be submitted within 21 days;

(c)   check survey results for any encroachments;

(d)   make searches connected with municipal business, bye-laws, work orders, utilities, corporation tax debts, executions (court judgments);

(e)   check the draft transfer deed.

Before completion he will make a final search of the register of titles.

A.7.1.49   The vendor's solicitor drafts the deed and survey requisitions and makes arrangements for the discharge of his client's mortgage.

A.7.1.50   After completion both solicitors are involved in the transfer of the property insurance and between them notify a tax authority and the local authority of the transfer. The purchaser's solicitor registers the new title.

California

A.7.1.51   A licensed estate agent (who is licensed by the state and is required to have some knowledge of real estate law) prepares a contract on a standard form, amended as appropriate. Usually only the vendor retains an agent, although the agent may effectively work for both parties. The contract and the arrangement of the mortgage loan, which is also undertaken by the agent, are conditional on the issue of a title insurance policy.

A.7.1.52   Public land title records are indexed on a grantor-grantee basis in each county, but title insurance companies maintain records of the current status of properties in the most populous areas. Some of these insurance records are computerised, but, even with a manual system, only a short time is required to up-date the records relating to a property which is to be sold.

A.7.1.53   Mortgage deeds are prepared by the lending institution's non-legal staff.

A.7.1.54   The title insurance company prepares the transfer deed and attends to:—

(a)   recording the transfer, discharge of the vendor's mortgage and grant of the purchaser's mortgage;

(b)   the discharge of the repaid mortgage;

(c)   the payment of fees (for example estate agent's commission);

(d)   the disbursement of purchase money after deducting tax appropriations.

Illinois

A.7.1.55   The purchaser's offer, usually set out on a form prepared by the local real estate agents' association or by a title insurance company and completed with the assistance of the vendor's estate agent, is conveyed to the vendor by the agent. If the vendor is dissatisfied he will make a written counter-offer. When agreement has been reached on price and terms, the estate agent prepares a contract incorporating these, which the purchaser must accept or reject within a specified period (usually about two days). The contract is usually conditional on:—

(a) the availability of finance within a specified period (alternatively the vendor can provide a mortgage in lieu of the purchase money);

(b) a satisfactory survey report; and

(c) a commitment by a title insurance company to insure the title.

The estate agent holds the deposit (usually 10 per cent).

A.7.1.56 The purchaser instructs an attorney to review the contract and prepare for completion. He will review an insurance company report on the title and settle any matters arising from this or revealed by the survey, settle apportionments and advise his client about the mortgage offer. The vendor's attorney will answer all questions arising from the title report, order a new survey or the up-dating of an old one, draft the transfer deed and completion statement.

A.7.1.57 The purchaser's mortgagee will arrange for the preparation of a mortgage deed either by his own staff or an attorney (this will be recorded prior to completion). The purchaser's attorney or mortgagee will record the transfer deed. When the vendor's mortgage has been discharged after completion the purchaser's mortgagee will have the discharge recorded and the title insurance company will then issue its title policies.

Missouri

A.7.1.58 An estate agent acting for the vendor prepares a contract. In perhaps 5 per cent of transactions either or both parties have this examined by an attorney, or employ an attorney to deal with other aspects of the transaction. The contract is usually conditional on the purchaser being able to raise a loan for 60–80 per cent of the purchase price. The purchaser applies to a "savings and loan association" or a mortgage broker applies for mortgage loan.

A.7.1.59 Title is investigated by either:—

(a) a lawyer examining an abstract of title on behalf of the lender (the purchaser will rely on this examination); or

(b) a title insurance company issuing a report which gives details of the legal title, unpaid mortgages, unpaid taxes, easements for public utilities, and private building restrictions. Compliance with building codes and zoning ordinances is rarely investigated.

A.7.1.60 The preparation of documents and arrangements for completion in most cases is handled by the employees of the estate agent or mortgagee. In nearly all cases printed forms are used, which can be safely completed by experienced non-qualified staff. If a corporate lawyer is employed on this work no charge is made for his services.

New York

A.7.1.61 The purchaser may enter into:—

(a) a pre-contract agreement to buy (not usually binding—but it may fix the estate agent's commission);

(b) "a binder", which is theoretically an option but in practice might be enforceable as a contract.

A.7.1.62 The purchaser's lawyer will:—

(a) obtain information about the title to the property from the vendor's lawyer (these enquiries cover details such as existing mortgages, compliance with local ordinances and encumbrances); and

(b) agree the form of the contract.
The purchaser will apply for a loan.

A.7.1.63   The vendor's lawyer receives 10 per cent deposit on exchange of contracts. The contract may be conditional on the availability of a loan; if there is a chain of transactions, the date for taking possession rather than that for completion may be specified.

A.7.1.64   Usually the purchaser's lawyer will:—

(a) arrange for a survey, termite inspection and electrical engineer's inspection; and

(b) request a title insurance company for a title report.

A.7.1.65   If the title is less than marketable this may not satisfy the conditions in the lender's commitment. However, many theoretical title imperfections are overcome by the insurance company's willingness to insure the mortgagee (perhaps not the buyer) against loss arising from such defects.

A.7.1.66   Present at completion are:—

(a) the two parties;

(b) their lawyers;

(c) a representative from the buyer's mortgagee; and

(d) a title insurance company "closer" who makes final telephone searches to cover matters insured by his company and issues a cover note. He arranges for the recording of deeds and the payment of taxes on behalf of both the vendor and purchaser.

Texas

A.7.1.67   The majority of Texans do not employ lawyers when purchasing a house. This summary is based on information about transactions in which an attorney is instructed by the purchaser.

A.7.1.68   The contract is usually drafted by an estate agent using a one-page standard form published by estate agents' associations and title insurance companies. These contracts, and sometimes the language in which they are completed, are sometimes not adequate, and the purchaser's attorney may rewrite the contract, or append an addendum to it, in order to afford his client proper protection. The contract is submitted via the purchaser's estate agent to the vendor as an offer to purchase which must be accepted within a specified time. This may be followed by a counter offer from the vendor. These negotiations are usually handled by the parties' estate agents.

A.7.1.69   When agreement is reached as to terms and price the purchaser's attorney engrosses the contract, which when signed by both parties is submitted to a title insurance company together with the deposit and an order for a title report. Most contracts are conditional on the availability of a mortgage loan. Contracts usually do not have a specific date for completion, the "on or before" formula is commonly used. The purchaser applies for a mortgage.

A.7.1.70   An attorney acting for the title insurance company reports on the title to the insurer who then issues a commitment to insure, the purchaser's attorney advises his client and settles matters relating to the title report and mortgage offer, and the lender's attorney drafts the transfer, mortgage deed and settlement statement.

A.7.1.71   Completion usually takes place at the title insurance company's office. This company sends all executed deeds and commitments to insure to the mortgagee for final approval. When this is received the title insurance company will disburse the sale money to the vendor and his mortgagee, pay the surveyor's fees, deduct its own fees and record all executed deeds. The purchaser's attorney checks the buyer's title insurance policy.

170

ANNEX 7.2

List of consultees

(paragraph 7.4)

Northern Ireland
W. B. Cumming, Esq (solicitor and past President of the Incorporated Law Society of Northern Ireland).

Sweden
Legal Department of Svenska sparbanksföreningen (Swedish Savings Banks Association).

Australia
New South Wales
    Law Society of New South Wales
South Australia
    Law Society of South Australia Incorporated
    The Honourable P Duncan (formerly Attorney General of South Australia)
    L K Gordon, Esq (formerly Director-General of Legal Services)
Victoria
    Law Institute of Victoria

New Zealand
    New Zealand Law Society

Canada
Maritime States
    Land Registration and Information Service

Ontario
    H Allan Leal, Esq, QC

United States of America
California
    Carlisle B Lane, Esq (attorney)
    William B Christy, Esq (attorney)

Illinois
    E W Saunders, Esq (attorney)
    T M Schroeder, Esq (attorney)

Missouri
    Hugh B Kuder Jnr, Esq (attorney)

New York
    Carrol J Cavanagh, Esq (attorney)

Texas
    Kraft W Eidman, Esq (attorney and Past President of the American College of Trial Lawyers).

SECTION 8

Survey of Users and Non-users of Legal Services in England and Wales

This survey was undertaken on behalf of the Commission by its consultants, Social & Community Planning Research who also prepared the report which follows

Contents

Introduction

8.1   This report covers a survey of the use of lawyers' services by the general public in England and Wales carried out by Social and Community Planning Research at the request of the Royal Commission on Legal Services.

Sampling
8.2   The survey was spread over 125 Parliamentary constituencies in England and Wales. These were selected randomly with probability proportional to size of electorate after stratification by region and population density and by car ownership (as an indicator of social composition).

8.3　Within each constituency, two polling districts were selected randomly with probability proportional to size of electorate and within each polling district, forty private addresses were selected randomly with equal probability from the electoral registers. Special measures were taken in addition to this to cover private addresses which do not appear in the electoral registers.

8.4　The survey was intended to cover all private households at these addresses, seeking information on the use of lawyers' services by all persons aged 18 or over living in these households.

Fieldwork
8.5　Fieldwork was carried out by 186 interviewers between 6 January and 2 April 1978.

8.6　After deletions of addresses found to be empty, demolished or institutions and inclusion of addresses which do not appear in the electoral registers, the number of addresses traced which were found to be occupied by private households was 9,753. The number of households living there was 9,902. The total number of households successfully interviewed was 7,941, a response rate of 80 per cent.

8.7　A fuller account of the sampling and fieldwork methods and of the achieved sample is given in annex 8.1.

Questionnaire
8.8　The questionnaire used in this survey was in three parts:—

(a) *Household questionnaire*

This covered background information on the household and its members and information on the use of lawyers' services by each member of the household aged 18 or over.

(b) *Use sheet*

If a member of the household had been the sole or main contact between the household and a lawyer over some personal matter during 1977, a use sheet was completed with that person on that matter. The use sheet sought information on the nature of the matter, contact and dealings with the lawyer and the respondent's attitudes to the services provided by the lawyer. The number of use sheets to be completed with any one individual respondent was limited to two. If the respondent had been sole or main contact from his household on three or more matters during 1977, use sheets were completed only for the first two matters on which consultation took place.

(c) *Individual questionnaire*

This covered a number of other topics of interest to the Commission. It was completed with each person who completed one or more use sheets

178

and with a randomly selected one in ten of all other persons aged 18 or over in the households covered. Information from these two groups was weighted together at the data processing stage to produce data representative of the population aged 18 and over as a whole.

Copies of these three parts of the survey questionnaire are included at annex 8.2.

Source of further information

8.9   Arrangements have been made for the main body of survey material to be deposited in the survey archive of the Social Science Research Council at the University of Essex, in a form which does not allow individuals to be identified. It includes the magnetic tapes on which the data are recorded and related documentation. Any application for the use of this material should be made to:—

Social Science Research Council,

Survey Archive,

University of Essex,

Wivenhoe Park,

Colchester,

Essex, CO4 3SQ.

Notes on the tables in this report

8.10   For convenience of layout, some tables in this report are set out with percentage breakdowns running vertically and some with percentage breakdowns running horizontally. The placing of percentage signs in the tables indicates the direction in which percentages should be read.

8.11   Where percentages are shown in this report, they are shown to the nearest whole percentage unit. The cumulative effect of this rounding means that percentage figures do not always total exactly to 100 per cent or whatever other overall total is appropriate. Where tables are not intended to total to 100 per cent (for instance, because of multiple answers) this is indicated in the text.

8.12   Figures for sample size shown in this report for individual questionnaire data are based on the sample before weighting. They show the actual number of interviews carried out which form the base for the data. All percentage figures shown, however, are calculated from the data after weighting.

8.13   The symbol * is used in tables in this report to stand for quantities less than 0·5 per cent. The letters "n.a." are used in tables to stand for "not applicable". The symbol — is used to indicate zero.

179

The numbers using lawyers' services

Summary
8.14   The majority of people aged 18 or over in England and Wales (57 per cent) have had professional help or advice from a lawyer over personal business at some time in their lives. Use of lawyers' services tends, however, to be infrequent. About one in three adults made use of lawyers' services in personal business during the past five years. Fifteen per cent did so during 1977.

8.15   It quite often happens that two or more members of a household get help or advice from a lawyer jointly. One in five of those using lawyers' services in 1977 was not the main contact between his or her household and the lawyer on any matter. Limiting the definition of use to those who were main contacts between their households and a lawyer over some personal matter, the number of users during 1977 reduces to 12 per cent.

8.16   Very few people (2 per cent of all adults) used lawyers' services in more than one matter of personal business in 1977. The numbers of matters of personal business about which lawyers were consulted during 1977 can be estimated at about 14 per 100 adults or about 27 per 100 households. On a quarter of these matters, the consultation with the lawyer started before 1977. The number of new matters on which consultation with lawyers started during 1977 can be estimated at about 10 per 100 adults or about 20 per 100 households.

Defining the use of lawyers' services
8.17   An important objective of the survey was to find out how many of the people aged 18 or over in England and Wales use the services of lawyers for advice or help in their personal affairs over a year. 'Using lawyers' services' is, however, a rather imprecise concept. It needs closer definition before the findings of the survey can be discussed.

(a) *Who are lawyers?* The intention was to cover professional legal services of all sorts, not only those provided by solicitors in private practice. It was intended to include, for example, professional advice or services provided through a law centre or legal advice centre, a citizens advice bureau or a trade union. But in ordinary language the term 'solicitor' is sometimes reserved for solicitors in private practice. Hence respondents were asked about the help or advice they had from 'solicitors or other lawyers'.

(b) *What counts as personal affairs?* Many people use lawyers' services in the course of their jobs. In most cases, it is easy to distinguish such dealings from dealings with lawyers on personal matters. But there is a difficulty with the self-employed. The distinction between their work and their personal affairs is often blurred. Hence it was decided that all help or advice given to self-employed people by solicitors or other lawyers should be included as relevant use of lawyers' services. For employees, however, any matters in which they were acting on behalf of their employers were excluded.

(c) *What counts as use of lawyers' services?* People can get professional legal help or advice without being in direct personal contact with a lawyer. For example, a trade union member with a claim for compensation for an

180

industrial injury may get professional legal advice through his union without being in personal contact with the advising lawyer. Contact might be through a union official only. Such cases were included within the definition of use of lawyers' services.

On the other hand, it sometimes happens that someone will seek a lawyer's help or advice on behalf of a third person rather than on his own account. Providing this was not done in the course of work as an employee, both the person directly seeking the help and the person on whose behalf it was sought were counted as users.

Often, of course, two or more people seek a lawyer's help jointly. The commonest example is the buying or selling of a house in the joint names of a married couple. In the survey, each person on whose behalf solicitors' help or advice was given was counted as a user.

In the instances given above, two or more people could count as users of the same lawyer's services in the same matter. Usually this arises through two or more members of a household being involved in the same matter. To give a closer estimate of the numbers of matters involved, respondents were asked, for each of the first two matters in which they were counted as users, whether any other member of their household was involved in any way. If any other member of the household was involved, the respondent was asked to say which member of the household was most closely in contact with the lawyer over the matter. This gives a count of people who were sole or main contacts between their household and a lawyer over some matter.

Within the household, it was possible for the interviewer to sort out occasional disputes between household members over who was the main contact with the lawyer. This would not have been practicable had the scope of the question been extended to include persons outside the household who were involved. The degree of over-counting of matters because of this was, however, small.

(d) *What is a matter?* It sometimes happens that people use the services of lawyers over a complex of problems or that one problem can give rise to another. It may sometimes be unclear whether a series of complications with a lawyer is over one matter or several matters. As an example, a divorce may lead to problems over division of property and custody of children. Depending on circumstances, people may see this as one single matter or as a series of separate though related matters. It seemed impracticable to produce simple general rules about what should count as one matter and what should count as more than one. Respondents were asked to decide this for themselves.

(e) *What counts as use over a year?* The interviewing for the survey took place during the early months of 1978 and the whole of 1977 was chosen as a convenient reference period for measuring use of lawyers' services over a year. The intention was to measure the numbers who had any help or advice from lawyers during 1977. There was no requirement that the

181

lawyers should have started or concluded giving this help or advice during the year. Any matter on which a respondent had help or advice from a lawyer during 1977 was counted as an instance of use, even though the lawyer had started giving help or advice earlier or was still in the process of giving help or advice at the end of the year.

Use of lawyers' services during 1977

8.18 Using the definitions discussed above, 15 per cent of all the people aged 18 or over for whom data were obtained from the survey had made some use of the services of lawyers for help or advice in their personal affairs during 1977. Twenty two per cent of all the households covered in the survey included one or more such person.

8.19 Generally, those who had used the services of lawyers during 1977 had used them in one matter only. The number using lawyers' services in more than one matter was very small.

TABLE 8.1

Number of personal matters in which lawyers were consulted during 1977

	All adults	All using lawyers' services in 1977
Sample	15,441	2,363
	%	%
Number of matters of use during 1977:		
none	85	n.a.
1	13	85
2	2	12
3	* →	2
4 or more	*	1
not stated	*	1

8.20 Fifteen per cent of adults used a lawyer's services in some matter during 1977. Of those who used a lawyer's services in that year, 15 per cent used them in two or more matters. It is sometimes said that some people use lawyers' services very frequently. There is a stereotype of a person constantly consulting his solicitor, perhaps about very trivial matters. The survey results suggest that, if such people do exist, their number is extremely small.

8.21 To limit the maximum length of the interview, those who had used lawyers' services in three or more matters during 1977 were questioned in detail only on the first two matters on which they had help or advice during the year. Given the small numbers making frequent use of legal services, this did not seriously limit the coverage of the survey. With coverage limited to the first two matters, detailed questions were asked about 96 per cent of all instances of use shown in Table 8.1.

8.22 The first of the detailed questions was about the involvement of other members of the household in the matter. The answers are summarised in Table 8.2.

TABLE 8.2
Degree of contact with lawyer in 1977

	All adults	All using lawyers' services in 1977
Sample	15,441	2,363
	%	%
Made no use of legal services in 1977	85	n.a.
Was sole contact from household with lawyer over one or more personal matters	8	49
Was main but not sole contact from household with lawyer over one or more personal matters	5	30
Was subsidiary contact only with lawyer	3	21

8.23 One in five of those using lawyers' services during 1977 had only subsidiary contact with the lawyer. Another member of the household was the person most closely in contact with him. Excluding those with subsidiary contact only, 12 per cent of all persons aged 18 or over were main or sole contacts from their households with lawyers over one personal matter or more during 1977.

8.24 Of those who were main or sole contacts with lawyers, 14 per cent were main or sole contacts in two matters. The rest were sole or main contacts in one matter only. These figures imply a total of 14 personal matters on which lawyers give help or advice per hundred adults per year or 27 matters per hundred households per year.

8.25 These figures should be treated with caution. They contain an element of underestimate, because of the exclusion of third and subsequent instances of use. They also contain an element of overestimate because, in some matters, members of more than one household were involved.

8.26 When respondents were questioned in detail about matters in which they had been the sole or main contact from their households with a lawyer, they were asked whether the lawyer's help or advice was given solely on their own behalf, solely on someone else's behalf or jointly for them and other people. In 14 per cent of cases they mentioned that someone outside their household was involved. If we assume that members of no more than two households were involved in any particular consultation (the number of cases involving more must be very small), this means that the survey counts 100 matters involving individual households for every 93 actual consultations on personal matters given by solicitors or other lawyers. Thus, the survey method leads to an overestimate of the total number of personal cases dealt with by lawyers of about $7\frac{1}{2}$ per cent. The limitation of detailed questioning to two matters per person meant that only 96 per cent of the matters people mentioned were covered by these questions. Putting together the overestimate of $7\frac{1}{2}$ per cent because of matters involving more than one household and the underestimate of 4 per cent because of the limitation to two matters per person gives a net overestimate of about 3 per cent. This is too small a net bias to suggest any revision of the figures given in paragraph 8.24.

8.27 The figures in paragraph 8.24 are for matters on which people had help or advice from lawyers at any time during 1977. They include matters in which the lawyer started helping or advising in 1976 or earlier. One in four of all the matters mentioned were of this sort. Allowing for this, the number of new matters on which people started getting help or advice from lawyers during 1977 can be estimated at about 10 per hundred adults or 20 per hundred households.

Use of lawyers' services prior to 1977
8.28 Information on earlier use of lawyers' services was sought from those who had been the sole or the main contact from their households with a lawyer over some personal matter during 1977. The same information was sought from one in ten of all other adults in the households covered. The answers of these two groups, weighted together, show how many of the adult population have ever used the services of lawyers and when they last did so. Details are given in Table 8.3.

8.29 It will be noted that the figure shown for use during 1977 in this table is 14 per cent as compared to the 15 per cent shown earlier. This results from random variation in the figures when reducing to a sub-sample of all those covered by this survey. The earlier figure, based on the total sample, is more reliable.

8.30 Over half of all people aged 18 or over (57 per cent) have made some use of lawyers' services at some time in their lives. Use of lawyers' services tends, however, to be rather infrequent. Of those who had ever used lawyers' services, only one in four did so during 1977 and only three in five said they had done

184

so in the past five years. Overall, the proportion of all people aged 18 or over saying they had used lawyers' services during the past five years was one in three (34 per cent).

TABLE 8.3

Past use of legal services

	All adults	All ever using lawyers' services
Sample (unweighted)	3,016	2,409
	%	%
Have never used lawyers' services	41	n.a.
Have used lawyers' services	57 →	100
Not stated	2	n.a.
Last used lawyers' services in:		
1977	14 ⎫	25 ⎫
1976	8 ⎪	14 ⎪
1975	4 ⎬ 34	7 ⎬ 59
1974	4 ⎪	6 ⎪
1973	3 ⎭	6 ⎭
earlier	23	40
not stated when	1	1

8.31 Beyond the past year, people's memories for dates can become very hazy. The five-year figures should, therefore, be treated with some caution. It should be taken as more liable to error through poor recall than the figure for numbers using lawyers' services in 1977.

8.32 In considering the figures in table 8.3, it should be borne in mind that the figures for 1977 are not comparable to those for earlier years. Somewhat over one in four of the matters in which people had help or advice from lawyers in 1977 carried over into 1978. The figures for 1976 and earlier years include only matters which ended in these years.

The sorts of people who use lawyers' services

Summary
8.33 The age group using lawyers' services most is those aged 25–34. More than one in five people in this age group had help or advice from a lawyer in some personal matter during 1977. After the age of 35, incidence of use drops gradually to less than one in ten among those aged 65 or over. In part, this probably reflects the life cycle of the household. It probably also reflects a difference between generations. Beyond the age of 45, the numbers saying they have ever

185

used lawyers' services drops off markedly. Older people make less use of lawyers' services than those now 25–34. They also appear to have made less use of lawyers when they themselves were younger.

8.34   Men are somewhat more likely than women to be main or sole users of lawyers' services. This applies in all age groups.

8.35   Incidence of use varies with household tenure. One in five of those living in owner-occupying households used a lawyer's services in some personal matter in 1977 as compared to less than one in ten of those living in rented accommodation. This may partly explain the variation in level of use by age, since older people are less likely than average to live in owner-occupying households.

8.36   Incidence of use also varies with socio-economic group. Socio-economic group and tenure are, of course, themselves linked, but each is independently related to incidence of use. The relationship between tenure and use is stronger than that between socio-economic group and use.

8.37   The part of the country in which people live and whether they live in urban or rural areas does not appear to have a great deal to do with whether they use the services of lawyers or not.

Introduction
8.38   This chapter is about the variation in incidence of use of lawyers' services between different groups within the adult population. This is discussed under three heads:—

demographic characteristics—sex, age and household size.

socio-economic characteristics—home tenure & socio-economic group.

region and area type—where in the country people live & whether they live in urban or rural areas.

Demographic characteristics
8.39   (a) *Sex and age.*
The incidence of use of lawyers' services during 1977 varied between men and women and varied markedly with age. The differences are shown in Table 8.4.

8.40   During 1977 rather more men than women used lawyers' services. In particular, men were more likely than women to have been the main contact between the household and the lawyer.

8.41   Incidence of use of lawyers' services is somewhat below the general average among those aged under 25. It is highest among those aged between 25 and 34. More than one in five people in that age group claimed to have had help or advice from a lawyer in some personal matter during 1977. After the age of 35 incidence of use gradually falls. Among those aged 65 or over, fewer than one in ten used lawyers' services during 1977. The variation in incidence of use by sex is independent of age. In all age groups, men were more likely than women to have used lawyers' services during 1977 and, both among men and women, those over 55 were less likely to have done so than younger people.

186

TABLE 8.4

Use of lawyers' services in 1977: by sex and age

	Sample	Used lawyers' services on some personal matter in 1977		Was main or sole contact with lawyer on some personal matter during 1977
All adults	15,441	%	15	12
Sex men	7,341	%	17	15
women	8,051	%	14	10
Age 18–24	1,691	%	14	10
25–29	1,473	%	23	17
30–34	1,540	%	22	17
35–44	2,502	%	19	15
45–54	2,604	%	15	12
55–64	2,316	%	12	10
65+	3,035	%	9	7
Age within sex				
men: under 30	1,539	%	19	16
30–54	3,304	%	21	17
55+	2,377	%	11	10
women: under 30	1,612	%	17	11
30–54	3,335	%	16	12
55+	2,947	%	10	8

8.42   The variation in level of use by age may relate to the life cycle of the household. It may be, for example, that people between 25 and 34 are more likely than older people to buy houses or get divorced. This is not the whole explanation, however. Were it so, the numbers who had ever used lawyers' services would rise sharply through the 25–34 age group and then continue to rise, but more slowly, through the higher age groups. The number who had ever used lawyers' services would be highest among old people. The survey results show a quite different pattern. The numbers saying they have ever used lawyers' services vary with age as shown in Table 8.5.

8.43   Above the age of 45, the number saying they have ever used a lawyer's services drops off sharply. It may be that some people who last had a lawyer's help or advice a very long time ago forgot to mention it. This could account, perhaps, for an understatement of a few percentage points in the figures for older people. It seems very unlikely, however, that this could account for a difference of the order shown in Table 8.5. It is much more likely that people now under 35 make more use of lawyers' services than older people did when they themselves were under 35. Thus the incidence of use of lawyers' services has almost certainly risen over the past 20 to 25 years.

TABLE 8.5

Past use of lawyers' services: by age

	Sample (unweighted)	Ever used lawyers' services	
All adults	3,016	%	57
Age: 18–24	340	%	31
25–29	343	%	60
30–34	361	%	72
35–44	543	%	71
45–54	512	%	59
55–64	420	%	55
65+	449	%	55

8.44   (b) *Household size.*

We noted earlier that 15 per cent of people aged 18 or over made some use of lawyers' services during 1977 and that 22 per cent of households contained someone in this category. Incidence of use varied with the number of persons aged 18 or over in the household. Details are given in Table 8.6.

8.45   There is hardly any difference in incidence of use between households with one, two and three adults. This means that incidence of use is not randomly distributed among adults irrespective of the size of the households they live in. If this were so, incidence of use among one-adult households would be the same as incidence of use among adults in general, about 15 per cent. Incidence of use among two-adult households would be approximately 28 per cent, (15 per cent + 15 per cent of 85 per cent) and, by a similar calculation, incidence of use among three-adult households would be approximately 39 per cent. The explanation is, almost certainly, that many of the matters about which lawyers are consulted refer to the household as a unit rather than to the individuals within it.

8.46   It will also be noted that the incidence of two users in households where someone has made use of legal services is much higher than one would expect if use were randomly distributed among adults. The reason for this is probably that in matters concerning the household as a whole, the consultation with a lawyer may be made jointly by two members of the household.

Socio-economic characteristics

8.47   (a) *Tenure.* Buying a house involves a conveyance and as one would expect, the level of use of lawyers' services, as shown in Table 8.7, was higher among owner-occupiers than among those who rent their houses.

188

TABLE 8.6

Use of lawyers' services in 1977: by number of adults in household

	Sample	Households containing:			
		one or more users	one user only	two users	three or more users
All households	7,941	% 22	15	7	*
Number aged 18+ in household:					
one person	1,695	% 20	20	—	—
two people	4,941	% 22	12	10	—
three people	972	% 22	15	6	1
four or more people	333	% 31	22	7	2

8.48 Incidence of use of lawyers' services was twice as high among those in owner-occupying households as it was among those who live in rented accommodation. It was particularly high among those who own their houses with a mortgage. By tenure, incidence of use of lawyers' services in 1977 was lowest among council tenants.

TABLE 8.7

Use of lawyers' services in 1977: by household tenure[1]

	Sample	Used lawyers' services on some personal matter in 1977	Was main or sole contact with lawyer on some personal matter in 1977
All adults	15,441	% 15	12
Household tenure: Own	8,907	% 20	15
own outright	3,702	% 16	13
own with a mortgage	5,205	% 22	16
Rent	5,995	% 9	8
rent from council	4,370	% 8	7
rent from private landlord	1,625	% 11	10

[1]Table 8.7 excludes just over 500 people who had housing provided by their employer or whose tenure was not established.

8.49 A similar pattern was evident in the numbers who have ever had help or advice from a lawyer. Seventy three per cent of those living in owner-occupying households said they had used lawyers' services at some time as compared to only 36 per cent of those in rented accommodation.

8.50   (b) *Socio-economic group*. At each household covered in the survey, the interviewer sought details of the present or last occupation of the head of the household and this was subsequently coded into the Registrar General's socio-economic groups. Excluding widows who have never had a career job and those giving insufficient detail for coding, Table 8.8 shows the variation in incidence of use of lawyers' services by a condensed version of the socio-economic groups.

TABLE 8.8

Use of lawyers' services in 1977: by socio-economic group of household head

	Sample	Used lawyers' services on some personal matter in 1977		Was main or sole contact with lawyer on some personal matter in 1977
All adults	15,441	%	15	12
Socio-economic group of household head:				
professional	779	%	25	18
employers and managers	2,199	%	21	16
intermediate and junior non-manual	2,703	%	19	15
skilled manual and own-account workers	5,510	%	13	9
semi-skilled manual	2,171	%	11	9
unskilled manual	801	%	10	8

8.51   Incidence of use was highest among those who live in households where the head was in a professional job and lowest among those living in households whose head was in semi-skilled or unskilled manual work. The biggest drop was that between the intermediate and junior non-manual group and the skilled manual group. The distinction between manual and non-manual work does seem to be relevant to incidence of use of lawyers' services. Among all the non-manual groups taken together, incidence of use of lawyers' services during 1977 was 21 per cent. Among all the manual groups taken together it was 12 per cent.

8.52   Given this difference in level of use over a year, the difference by socio-economic group in the numbers who have ever had help or advice from a lawyer, although large, is, perhaps, less than one would expect. Sixty seven per cent of those in households where the head was in a non-manual job said they had used lawyers' services at some time as compared to 51 per cent of those where the household head was a manual worker. The numbers who had ever used lawyers' services varied little between the three non-manual groupings. They varied more among the three manual categories. Fifty five per cent of those in households with skilled manual heads said that they had had help or advice from a lawyer at some time as compared to 46 per cent of those with semi-skilled and 39 per cent of those with unskilled household heads.

TABLE 8.9

Use of lawyers' services in 1977: by socio-economic group within tenure group

| | Tenure | | | |
| | own | | rent | |
	sample	used lawyers' services on some personal matter in 1977	sample	used lawyers' services on some personal matter in 1977
All adults	8,907	% 20	5,995	% 9
Socio-economic group of household head: professional/employer/manager	2,390	% 24	482	% 13
intermediate and junior non-manual	1,789	% 22	795	% 12
skilled manual and own-account workers	3,078	% 16	2,304	% 8
semi-skilled or unskilled manual	1,058	% 16	1,822	% 8

8.53 (c) *Tenure and socio-economic group.* There is, of course, a relationship between the socio-economic group of the household's head and the household's domestic tenure. The variation in incidence of use of lawyers' services in 1977 by socio-economic group within tenure is shown in Table 8.9.

8.54 Incidence of use of lawyers' services is affected both by tenure and by the socio-economic group of the household head. Of the two factors, however, tenure is the more important.

8.55 (d) *Tenure and age.* As was noted earlier, the number saying they have ever used a lawyer's services drops off sharply after the age of 45. Domestic tenure, which is clearly linked to incidence of use of lawyers' services, also varies with age. People aged 45 and over are less likely than those between 30 and 44 to live in owner-occupying households.

8.56 Details of the comparison by age group between the numbers who said they had ever used lawyers' services and the numbers living in owner-occupying households are given in Table 8.10.

TABLE 8.10
Past use of lawyers' services and tenure: by age

	Sample[1] (un-weighted)	Ever used lawyers' services		Sample[1]	Living in owner-occupying households	
All adults	3,016	%	57	15,441	%	58
Age: 18–24	340	%	31	1,691	%	50
25–29	343	%	60	1,473	%	56
30–34	361	%	72	1,540	%	66
35–44	543	%	71	2,502	%	66
45–54	512	%	59	2,604	%	59
55–64	420	%	55	2,316	%	53
65+	449	%	55	3,035	%	54

[1]Samples differ since figures for those ever using lawyers' services are based on the individual questionnaire sample while figures for tenure are based on the total sample.

8.57 Except for those under 25, the pattern by age in the two sets of figures is very similar. The variation by age in the numbers living in owner-occupying households may partly explain the variation by age in the numbers who said they had ever used lawyers' services.

Region
8.58 Table 8.11 shows the incidence of use, by region, of lawyers' services among adults during 1977.

8.59 Incidence of use did not vary greatly by region. It was slightly below average in the Inner London Education Authority (ILEA) area and in the North. It was slightly above average in the South West and, perhaps, the East Midlands and East Anglia. Beyond this the variation is no more than one would expect from random sampling error.

8.60 Regions, of course, vary in character. An analysis which takes into account the characteristics of particular areas within regions might be more useful. It is, for example, sometimes said that people in rural areas have less recourse to lawyers than those who live in the main towns.

8.61 As an approximation to a measure of urban or rural character, the areas covered in the survey were divided into seven groups as follows:—

(a) the Inner London Education Authority Area;

(b) the rest of the area covered by the Greater London Council (GLC);

(c) other metropolitan counties;

(d) other high density areas (other constituencies with a mean density of four electors per acre or more);

(e) other medium density areas (other constituencies with a mean density of 0·9 to 3·9 electors per acre);

(f) other low density areas (other constituencies with a mean density of 0·8 electors per acre or less except for polling districts defined below as very rural);

(g) very rural areas (polling districts whose character is such that their electoral registers are arranged alphabetically by surname of elector. All such polling districts covered in the survey were in constituencies with a mean density of 0·8 electors per acre or less).

TABLE 8.11

Use of lawyers' services in 1977: by region

	Sample	Used lawyers' services on personal matters in 1977		Was main or sole contact with lawyer on personal matter in 1977
All adults	15,441	%	15	12
Region:				
GLC—ILEA area	562	%	11	10
North	1,104	%	12	10
Wales	881	%	13	11
West Midlands	1,794	%	14	11
GL—Outer area	1,371	%	14	12
South East other than GLC	2,896	%	15	12
Yorkshire and Humberside	1,511	%	16	12
North West	2,060	%	17	13
East Anglia	565	%	18	13
East Midlands	1,382	%	18	14
South West	1,315	%	18	15

8.62 By this division, the incidence of use of lawyers' services during 1977 varied as shown in Table 8.12.

8.63 Again, the variation in incidence of use was small. As noted already, use was slightly below average in the ILEA area. It was slightly above average in low density areas which are not very rural in character. Apart from this, the variation is negligible.

TABLE 8.12
Use of lawyers' services in 1977: by area type

	Sample	Used lawyers' services on personal matters in 1977	Was main or sole contact with lawyer on personal matter in 1977
All adults	15,441	15	12
Area type:			
GLC—ILEA area	562	% 11	10
GLC—outer area	1,371	% 14	12
Other metropolitan counties	3,580	% 15	12
Other high density	2,744	% 15	12
Other medium density	3,667	% 15	12
Other low density	2,471	% 18	14
Very rural	1,046	% 16	12

8.64 It would appear that the parts of the country in which people live and the urban or rural character of the places where they live do not have a great deal to do with whether they use lawyers' services or not.

TABLE 8.13
Profile of those using legal services in 1977

		All adults	Used lawyers' services on personal matters in 1977	Was main or sole contact with lawyer on personal matter in 1977
Sample		15,441	2,370	1,869
		%	%	%
Sex:	Men	48	53	57
	Women	52	47	43
Age:	18–24	11	10	9
	25–29	10 ⎫	14 ⎫	13 ⎫
	30–34	10 ⎬ 36	15 ⎬ 49	14 ⎬ 47
	35–44	16 ⎭	20 ⎭	20 ⎭
	45–54	17	12	17
	55–64	15	17	12
	65+	20	11	12
	Not stated	2	2	2
Household tenure:	Own	58	74	72
	Rent	39	22	25
	Other	3	3	3

Profile of users

8.65 So far, the discussion has been entirely in terms of incidence of use. It may be helpful to show the figures discussed another way, comparing the distribution of users and non-users by what have been found to be some of the more important variables. Details are given in Table 8.13.

8.66 Half of those who used lawyers' services in 1977 were aged between 25 and 44 as compared to just over one in three of the general adult population. Just over one in ten users was aged 65 or over as compared to one in five of all adults.

8.67 Three-quarters of those who used lawyers' services in 1977 lived in owner-occupying households as compared to less than three in five of all adults.

The matters on which people consult lawyers

Summary
8.68 Three in ten of all the matters on which members of the public were given help or advice by lawyers during 1977 related to the buying or selling of houses. No other type of matter accounted for anything like this proportion of all consultations. Other matters of common consultation were dealing with the estates of people who have died, making or altering wills, divorce and problems stemming from it, motoring or other offences, compensation for personal injuries and matters relating to rights or title to domestic property which did not involve conveyancing. Beyond this, the matters about which lawyers are consulted are very various, no one particular type of matter being very common.

8.69 The peak years for using lawyers' services on domestic conveyancing are 25–34. This age group, which accounts for one in five of the adult population, accounts for more than a third of those mainly concerned in consultations with lawyers about buying or selling houses over a year. The particular prominence of conveyancing among all users of lawyers' services accounts for there being more users of lawyers' services in the 25–34 age group than in any other. Most consultations about domestic conveyancing are made on behalf of a married couple.

8.70 Consultation with lawyers about offences and about compensation for injuries in road traffic accidents is particularly common among men aged under 25.

8.71 The peak years for consultations about divorce are 30–34 and most consultations about divorce are made by women.

8.72 The majority of consultations with lawyers about making or altering wills are made by people aged 55 or over. Consultations on this sort of matter are equally divided between men and women.

8.73 The peak years for consultation about the winding up of estates are 45–64 and most consultations of this sort are made by women. It is very common for members of more than one household to be involved in matters of this sort.

195

8.74　The high proportions of all consultations with lawyers made by people in households with heads in non-manual occupations and by people in owner-occupier households arise largely because such people are more likely than others to consult lawyers on matters concerning property.

Sample sizes

8.75　In this and subsequent chapters, the discussion will move between people consulting lawyers, the matters about which they consult lawyers and their consultations with lawyers. It may help to make the discussion clearer if we start by setting out the distinction between the different groupings used and the numbers of interviews involved in each.

8.76　Respondents were questioned in detail about personal matters in which they had help or advice from lawyers during 1977 and in which they were the sole or main contact between their households and the lawyer. In cases in which respondents had been the main or sole contact in three or more matters, they were asked only about the first two on which they had help or advice during the year. The screening questions indicate that the detailed questions should have been asked of 1,869 people and that they should have been questioned about 2,131 matters. In practice, a few respondents were never available to answer the questions and a few were unwilling to answer them. The loss because of this was 5 per cent. 1,784 people in fact answered detailed questions about 2,040 matters.

8.77　In 14 matters, the respondent had dealt with a lawyer practising outside England and Wales and, therefore, outside the Commission's area of interest. These matters are excluded from the analyses shown below. The number of matters on which respondents were questioned and in which lawyers in England and Wales were consulted is, therefore, 2,026.

8.78　In 38 of these matters (2 per cent of the total), respondents were helped or advised during 1977 by two different lawyers working quite independently (that is, excluding cases in which people dealt with two or more members of the same firm and cases in which one lawyer consulted another). In such cases respondents were questioned separately about their dealings with each of the lawyers. The total number of consultations with lawyers in England and Wales about which people were questioned is, therefore, 2,064.

8.79　We have already mentioned the question of overlap between 1977 and other years. People were questioned about all the matters on which they consulted lawyers during 1977, including both those matters in which the process of consultation started before 1977 and those in which consultation was still going on at the end of the year. To give a picture of the matters people take to lawyers over a year, we show separate figures below for the 1,569 matters on which the first consultation with the lawyer took place during 1977.

The matters about which lawyers were consulted

8.80 The matters about which people consulted lawyers were grouped into 27 categories. These are based on the nature of the matter rather than any action the lawyer took. Thus the "divorce" category, for example, includes cases in which someone merely sought advice about the position of the law on divorce. An entry in this category does not imply that the person concerned has obtained a divorce or necessarily intends to do so.

8.81 In a few complex cases (37 in all, 2 per cent of the total) the matter was assigned to two or more categories. The most common multiple allocation was to "divorce" and "custody or property problems following divorce". With that overlap allowed for, the categories can be taken as, for all practical purposes, mutually exclusive and, therefore, additive.

8.82 The matters about which people consulted lawyers in 1977 are shown in Table 8.14.

8.83 By far the most important category is domestic conveyancing, accounting for 30 per cent of all the personal matters on which lawyers gave help or advice during 1977.

8.84 There are six other important categories—dealing with the estates of people who have died (11 per cent), making or altering wills (10 per cent), divorce (7 per cent), motoring and other offences (7 per cent), compensation for personal injuries (7 per cent), and matters other than conveyance which deal with rights or titles to domestic property (5 per cent).

8.85 Between them these seven main categories cover more than three out of every four personal matters on which lawyers gave help or advice during 1977. The range of the other personal matters on which they were consulted is very wide. No other particular type of matter stands out as very important.

8.86 At this level of analysis, it makes little difference whether we look at all the matters about which lawyers were consulted during 1977 or only at those consultations which started during 1977. The two approaches produce almost identical results. A more detailed analysis of types of matter by when they started is given in paragraphs 8.277–289.

The people involved in the consultation

8.87 As we have noted earlier, those questioned in detail about matters in which they had been sole or main contacts between their households and a lawyer during 1977 were asked on whose behalf the lawyer was giving his help or advice.

197

TABLE 8.14
Nature of matters about which lawyers were consulted in 1977

	All matters about which lawyers were consulted in 1977	All consultations starting in 1977
Sample	2,026	1,569
	%	%
Buying or selling a house or flat	30	31
Other matters concerning title or rights to domestic property	5	5
Dealing with estate of deceased person	11	11
Making or altering a will	10	12
Divorce	7 ⎫	5 ⎫
Custody or property problems following divorce	3 ⎬ 12	2 ⎬ 9
Other matrimonial or family problems	3 ⎭	3 ⎭
Motoring offences	4	4
Other offences	3	3
Compensation for industrial injury	3 ⎫	2 ⎫
Compensation for road traffic injury	3 ⎬ 7	2 ⎬ 5
Compensation for other injury	1 ⎭	1 ⎭
Problems about purchase of goods or services/faulty goods	2	2
Money owed to client	2	1
Money owed by client	1	1
Buying or selling a shop or business	2	2
Insurance, taking out insurance	1	1
Advice or help on investment	1	1
Problems of self-employment not specified elsewhere	2	2
Problems as a landlord	1	1
Problems as a tenant	1	1
Problems with neighbours	1	1
Problems about employment/dismissal	1	1
Problems about social security/welfare rights	*	*
Setting up/administering trusts	*	*
Tax or capital transfer matters	1	1
Other matters	4	5
Nature of matter not clearly stated	*	*

8.88 In 51 per cent of consultations, the help or advice was given wholly on behalf of the respondent. In 49 per cent of cases it was given wholly or partly for other people. The other person or persons involved were members of the respondent's household in 35 per cent of cases and people outside the respondent's household in 14 per cent of cases (the incidence of others from inside and outside the household being involved was negligible). Where the advice or help obtained was not solely on behalf of the person interviewed, it was almost always partly on his or her behalf. It was only in 4 per cent of all consultations that it was obtained solely on someone else's behalf.

8.89 Where someone else was involved, it was, in most cases, the respondent's husband or wife. The only other sort of person commonly involved was a relative outside the household.

TABLE 8.15
Persons on whose behalf lawyer's help or advice was given:
by type of matter[1]

	All consultations in 1977	buying/selling house	winding up estates	offences other than motoring	making wills	divorce/other family problems	motoring offences	personal injury compensation
				Nature of matter				
Sample	2,064	602	228	60	199	249	78	133
Advice/help given to main/sole household contact was:	%	%	%	%	%	%	%	%
wholly on own behalf	51	29	42	58	70	74	82	82
for self and other jointly	45	69	50	27	26	22	14	9
wholly on other's behalf	4	2	8	15	5	3	4	9
Other person involved was:								
spouse	30	60	7	10	25	5	55	3
other adult in household	3	2	4	5	3	4	3	6
child in household	2	*	3	12	1	10	1	4
Relative outside household:	9	5	43	10	4	5	3	2
partner/customer in own-account business	1	*	*	—	—	—	—	1
employee/workmate	1	—	—	—	—	—	1	—
neighbour	*	*	—	—	—	—	1	—
others outside household	3	3	4	8	—	1	4	2

[1]In some cases more than one category of other person was involved.

199

8.90   There were very large differences by type of matter in the numbers and sorts of people whom the lawyer was helping or advising. For the main types of matter in which there were enough cases for separate analysis, these differences are shown in Table 8.15.

8.91   Three in five consultations about domestic conveyancing were made on behalf of a husband and wife jointly. Less than three in ten were made by one person acting solely on his or her own behalf. For other matters concerning rights or titles to domestic property (not shown in the table) the figures are virtually identical.

8.92   Almost three in five of those questioned about consultations with lawyers on winding up estates said that the lawyer's help was given on behalf of others as well as themselves. Most of the others involved were people, usually relatives, outside the respondent's own household. People outside the household were much more commonly involved in the winding up of estates than in any other of the main types of matter.

8.93   The figures shown earlier for the types of matter on which lawyers were consulted are based on counting people from different households consulting lawyers on the same matter separately. If one were to move to counting each matter of consultation separately, however many households were involved, the proportion of all matters of consultation accounted for by the winding up of estates would fall from 11 per cent to 9 per cent.

8.94   In about three out of five consultations about offences other than motoring offences, the person questioned was getting help or advice on his or her behalf only. In most instances where another person was involved, it was the spouse of the respondent or a juvenile member of the same household.

8.95   People made their wills either by themselves or, in a quarter of the cases, jointly with their husbands or wives.

8.96   Three-quarters of consultations about divorce, the problems following divorce, judicial separation and other family problems were made on behalf of one person only. Where the lawyer was giving help or advice on someone else's behalf as well, this was usually a child living with the main person involved in the consultation.

8.97   Four out of five consultations about compensation for personal injuries and about motoring offences were made by someone acting solely on his or her own behalf.

Type of matter and age
8.98   Different groups within the population consult lawyers about different sorts of matter. The most striking differences are by age. The age profiles of

those who were sole or main contacts between their households and lawyers during 1977 on one or more matters for some of the main types shown in Table 8.14 are given in Table 8.16.

TABLE 8.16
Age profile of people consulting lawyers about main types
of matter during 1977

	Sample	Age							
		18–24	25–29	30–34	35–44	45–54	55–64	65+	age not stated
All adults	15,441	% 11	10	10	16	17	15	20	2
All who were main or sole contact during 1977 on: any matter	1,784	% 10	13	14	20	17	12	12	2
motoring offences	75	% 31	11	12	24	13	5	1	3
other offences	52	% 27	12	10	23	12	10	4	2
road traffic injury compensation	54	% 26	17	7	20	16	7	6	—
domestic conveyance	579	% 13	20	17	20	12	9	8	1
divorce	148	% 7	18	24	29	18	2	1	1
industrial injury compensation	51	% 6	16	14	22	18	16	8	2
winding up estates	215	% *	3	7	18	24	22	23	3
making and altering wills	195	% *	3	7	11	17	23	35	3

8.99 It will be noted that some of the sample bases are extremely small. A very large margin for sampling error must be allowed with percentages on these bases. The differences in the age profiles for different types of matter are so large, however, that conclusions can be drawn even when a very large allowance for sampling error has been made.

8.100 People aged 18–24 account for one in ten of the adult population. In 1977, they accounted for more than a quarter of all those who, over the year, consulted lawyers about motoring or other offences or about compensation for injuries in road traffic accidents.

8.101 People aged between 25 and 34 account for one in five of the adult population. They accounted for more than a third of all those consulting lawyers during 1977 about buying or selling houses.

201

8.102 The peak years for consultation with lawyers about divorce are 30–34. Just under one in four of those consulting lawyers about divorce during 1977 was aged between 30 and 34, as compared to one in ten of the adult population in general. Seven out of ten consultations about divorce were by people aged between 25 and 44, an age range which includes only just over a third of all adults.

8.103 Only one in ten of those consulting lawyers during 1977 about the winding up of an estate was aged under 30. Almost seven out of ten were aged 45 or over. People consulting lawyers about making or altering wills tended to be still older. Almost three in five of those consulting lawyers on such matters during 1977 were aged 55 or over.

Type of matter and sex

8.104 There are also striking differences by sex in the sorts of matters about which people consult lawyers. In two sorts of matter, motoring offences and compensation for industrial injury, four out of five main household contacts with lawyers during 1977 were men. In three other sorts of matter, offences other than motoring offences, compensation for injuries in road traffic accidents

TABLE 8.17
Types of matter about which lawyers were consulted in 1977:
by sex and age of main contact

		All matters about which lawyers were consulted in 1977:					
		main/sole contact with lawyer was:					
		men aged:			women aged:		
	total	under 30	30–54	55+	under 30	30–54	55+
Sample	2,026	268	636	241	185	417	241
Type of matter:	%	%	%	%	%	%	%
domestic conveyance	30	41	29	27	46	25	16
other matters concerning domestic property	5	4	7	5	3	5	2
motoring offences	4	9	5	2	4	2	—
other offences	3	7	2	2	3	3	2
road traffic injury compensation	3	6	2	1	4	2	2
industrial injury compensation	3	4	3	3	1	1	2
divorce	7	3	5	2	14	17	*
winding up estates	11	2	7	12	2	15	28
making/altering wills	10	1	7	20	2	6	27
other/not stated	24	23	33	27	21	25	22

and domestic conveyancing, about three in five main contacts with lawyers were men. In consultations on making or altering wills, the sexes were evenly balanced and in two sorts of matter, divorce and winding up the estates of people who have died, over three in five of those who were main contacts between their households and lawyers during 1977 were women.

Type of matter, age and sex
8.105   Taking age and sex together, the incidence of different types of matter among all those about which people consulted lawyers during 1977 varied between men and women of different ages as shown in Table 8.17.

8.106   Despite what has been said about the varying sex and age profiles of people consulting lawyers about different sorts of matter, domestic conveyancing remains the one main single subject of consultation among all groups except older women. Varying incidence of involvement in buying or selling houses explains much of the difference between sex and age groups in overall incidence of use of lawyers' services.

8.107   This comes out most clearly if one compares the profile by sex and age of those who were main contacts with lawyers during 1977 over matters of domestic conveyancing to the profile of those using lawyers in other matters. Details are given in Table 8.18.

TABLE 8.18
Sex and age profile of those consulting lawyers about conveyancing and other matters in 1977

| | All who were main or sole contacts with lawyers in any matter in 1977 | All who were main or sole contacts in: | | All adults |
		domestic convey- ancing	other matters only	
Sample	1,784	579	1,205	15,441
	%	%	%	%
Sex: men	56	61	54	48
women	44	39	46	52
Age: 18–24	10	13	8	11
25–34	27	37	22	20
35–44	20	20	20	16
45–64	29	21	34	32
65 or over	12	8	15	20
age not ascertained	2	1	2	2

8.108   If those who had dealings with lawyers over the buying and selling of houses are set aside, the profile by age and sex of people using lawyers' services during 1977 is much closer to that of the adult population in general. Those using lawyers' services in other matters are, however, still somewhat more likely than average to be men and under 65.

Type of matter and socio-economic group

8.109 There are also differences by socio-economic group between the people who consult lawyers about different sorts of matter, although these are not as marked as the differences by age. In terms of the distribution by socio-economic group of the heads of household of those who consulted lawyers during 1977, the main sorts of matter can be grouped into three categories.

8.110 The first category consists of matters in which the majority of main contacts with lawyers during 1977 came from households where the head's present or last main occupation was non-manual. These matters largely concern property. There are three main types of matter in this category—the buying and selling of houses, dealing with the estates of deceased persons and making or altering wills. In all three of these types of matter, slightly over half of all main or sole users of lawyers' services were people from households whose heads were in non-manual occupations, a group which accounts for only a little over a third of the adult population in general.

8.111 The second category consists of matters in which the distribution of users of lawyers' services by socio-economic group is quite close to that of the adult population in general. The more important matters in this category are divorce, motoring offences and seeking compensation for injuries in road traffic accidents.

8.112 The third category consists of matters in which people in non-manual households are represented among users in less than their population proportions. This is, marginally, the case of offences other than motoring offences. It is clearly the case (as one would expect) with matters of compensation for industrial injury.

8.113 We have shown earlier that the incidence of use of lawyers' services is much higher among those in non-manual households than it is among others. We now see that lawyers are consulted much more frequently by the public about matters concerning property than they are about matters concerning, say, offences or industrial injuries. Consultations about property are made mainly by those living in non-manual households and matters of this sort account for most of the higher incidence of use among people living in such households.

8.114 Out of the 27 categories into which the matters which people take to lawyers were grouped in this survey, 10 clearly concern property. These are domestic conveyancing, other matters concerning rights or title to domestic property, conveying businesses and other problems concerning self-employment, matters concerning wills, estates, trusts, tax or capital transfer, insurance or investment. A comparison of these matters with the others in terms of the socio-economic group of the household heads of those who were main or sole contacts with lawyers on them is given in Table 8.19.

TABLE 8.19
Socio-economic group profile of consultations with lawyers
in 1977: by type of matter

	All matters on which lawyers were consulted in 1977			All adults
	total	matters specifically concerning property	others matters	
Sample	2,026	1,247	779	15,441
Socio-economic group of household head of main/sole contact:	%	%	%	%
professional	8 ⎫	9 ⎫	7 ⎫	5 ⎫
employer or manager	19 ⎬ 49	22 ⎬ 54	16 ⎬ 42	14 ⎬
intermediate and junior non-manual	22 ⎭	23 ⎭	19 ⎭	18 ⎭ 37
skilled manual and own-account workers	28	26	31	36
semi-skilled manual	11	9	13	14
unskilled manual	4	2	5	5
uncodeable/never worked	9	8	9	8

8.115 In matters which do not specifically concern property, the profile of users of lawyers' services by socio-economic group is not greatly different from that of the adult population in general.

Type of matter and tenure
8.116 A similar pattern is evident when we look at the types of matter about which people in owner-occupying households and renting households consult lawyers. We saw earlier that the incidence of consultation is much higher among those in owner-occupied households than it is among those who rent. But, in fact, 70 per cent of the matters about which those in owner-occupied houses consulted lawyers were matters in the group defined above as specifically concerned with property. Only 34 per cent of the matters about which people in rented accommodation consult lawyers fell in this group.

8.117 More than four out of five consultations with lawyers about property were made by people living in owner-occupied households. On other matters, the split of consultations by tenure reflected the split by household tenure among the population in general.

Domestic conveyancing

8.118 The one type of matter accounting for the largest proportion of private consultations with lawyers is the buying and selling of domestic property. It may be useful to look at such consultations in more detail.

8.119 Conveying domestic property accounted for 30 per cent of all the matters on which people had help or advice from lawyers during 1977. In 7 per cent of all the households covered in the survey, there was one or more persons who had help or advice from a lawyer over this during 1977.

8.120 In one case in four, the consultation had not, at the time of interview, led to a completed conveyance. Mainly this was because the solicitor still had the matter in hand (17 per cent of all cases). In 5 per cent of all cases, however, the solicitor had been asked for advice only and in 3 per cent of cases he had taken some action, but the matter had been dropped with the conveyance not completed.

8.121 The proportion of households containing one or more persons who had help from a lawyer during 1977 which had led to a completed conveyance by the time of interview was 5 per cent. This is higher than the proportion of households living in owner-occupied accommodation who had occupied their property for less than a year (4 per cent of all households). The reasons for this difference were very varied. Some were buying property as sitting tenants or buying the freehold on leasehold property. Some were buying second homes, retirement homes or had some other reason for postponing occupation. Some had sold a house and moved to rented accommodation or accommodation which went with a job. Some were buying or selling domestic property as a financial transaction. No one reason was particularly prominent.

Finding a lawyer

Summary

8.122 In three out of four matters on which people consulted lawyers during 1977, those making the consultation had no advice or help from people outside their households before a lawyer was contacted. Where it was given, such previous advice or help came most commonly from friends or workmates, relatives, the citizens advice bureau or, in cases of conveyancing, from an estate agent. Most of those who had previous advice had been advised to see a lawyer.

8.123 Less than half the consultations in 1977 were with lawyers used previously in any personal matter by the client or other members of his household. In a third of cases where there had been previous consultations over other matters, the first consultation with that lawyer had taken place during the past five years. Consultations with lawyers who had a longstanding connection with the household were very much the minority.

8.124   Most people going to a particular lawyer for the first time were led to him through their personal or informal contacts—through the recommendation or experience of their relatives, friends, neighbours or workmates. It was in only a quarter of cases of first consultation in 1977 that the client found a lawyer through recommendation or mention by an official body or by someone else with whom he already had business or professional dealings. The formal contacts most commonly mentioned were the citizens advice bureau and, in conveyancing matters, estate agents or building societies.

8.125   When those who had not used a lawyer during 1977 were asked how they would go about choosing a lawyer if they wanted one, almost all were able to give some answer and the pattern of their answers closely followed the pattern of answers among those who had actually used one.

8.126   Ninety four per cent of all consultations with lawyers in 1977 were with solicitors in private practice.

Advice from others before consulting a lawyer

8.127   Those questioned in detail about matters in which they had been main or sole contacts with lawyers during 1977 were asked whether they had any help or advice of any sort about the matter from anyone outside their own household, before the lawyer was consulted. In the considerable majority of cases (73 per cent of all consultations), respondents said they had not.

8.128   There was no notable difference between the sexes on this point, nor between people of different socio-economic group. There was some difference by age. Older people (perhaps because of wider experience) were more likely than young people to have gone straight to a lawyer without any prior help or advice from anyone outside their household. Thirty eight per cent of those aged 18 to 24 said they had prior help or advice as compared to 30 per cent of those between 25 and 44 and only 20 per cent of those aged 45 or over.

8.129   There were also some differences in the incidence of prior help or advice by type of matter. Those seeking compensation for personal injuries were more likely than others to have had prior advice, very often from a trade union. Those seeking to make wills or wind up the estates of deceased people (who tend, as we have seen earlier, to be older people), were less likely than average to have had prior help or advice.

8.130   In three-quarters of the cases where people had prior help or advice, someone had suggested that they should go on to get help or advice from a lawyer. In considering this finding, it must be borne in mind that at this point we are discussing the situation of those who actually did go on to consult a lawyer. The situation of people who had problems but did not consult a lawyer about them is discussed in paragraphs 8.371–8.400.

8.131   People got help or advice before consulting a lawyer from a considerable variety of sources. The main sources are shown in Table 8.20.

TABLE 8.20
Source of help or advice before consulting a lawyer[1]

	All giving prior help or advice
Sample: All consultations in which help or advice was given previously by someone other than a lawyer	548
Prior helpers and advisors:	%
friends or workmates	15
relatives outside the household	10
citizens advice bureau	13
estate agent	10
bank manager	6
insurance broker	5
building society	5
accountant	5
employer	4
trade union	6
local authority department	6
DHSS/benefit office	3
non-governmental advice centre/pressure group	3
police	5
other	12

[1]Some respondents had several advisors.

8.132   Estate agents, of course, had given help or advice mainly on the buying and selling of houses.

8.133   There were 71 matters in which people had help or advice from a citizens advice bureau before consulting a lawyer. The largest single group of these (21 matters) related to divorce, to the problems following it or to other family matters. Two other types of matter on which a citizens advice bureau had commonly been consulted were problems relating to the purchase of goods and compensation for personal injuries. Between them, these three types of matter accounted for half of all the matters on which a citizens advice bureau was consulted prior to consultation with a lawyer.

8.134   Overall, however, the most common sources of advice were friends, workmates and relatives outside the household. These helped and advised on a very wide variety of matters.

Type of lawyer consulted
8.135   The types of lawyer people consulted about personal matters in 1977 are shown in Table 8.21.

TABLE 8.21
Type of lawyer consulted

	All consultations with lawyers in England and Wales
Sample	2,064
Type of lawyer:	%
a solicitor in private practice	94
a solicitor or other lawyer in a citizens advice bureau	1
a solicitor or other lawyer in a law centre or legal advice centre	1
a solicitor or other lawyer working in a trade union	1
a solicitor or other lawyer working for the AA or RAC	1
a personal friend or relative consulted informally	*
other	1
not stated	*

8.136   Note that Table 8.21 refers to the type of lawyer initially consulted by the client. The number of matters which subsequently led to a barrister being consulted is discussed in paragraphs 8.206–8.209.

8.137   So far in this report we have talked about lawyers. Since 94 per cent of all consultations are with solicitors in private practice and many of the rest are with other solicitors, it seems reasonable to switch to talking about solicitors from this point on.

8.138   There was negligible variation between the sexes, between different age groups and between socio-economic groups in the types of solicitor used. There were some small differences, however, by area and tenure. In the GLC area and among those living in rented accommodation the proportion of consultations which were made with solicitors in law centres, legal advice centres and CABx was above the general average.

8.139   The numbers involved are too small for any detailed conclusions to be drawn about the types of matter about which the different types of solicitor outside private practice are consulted. Few of them, however, involved conveyancing, the making of wills or the winding up of estates. Most consultations with trade union solicitors (16 out of 25) were about compensation for industrial injuries.

Previous consultations with the solicitor
8.140   Those questioned in detail about consultations with solicitors during 1977 were asked whether the solicitor they consulted had ever been consulted before about other matters concerning them or other members of their present household. Those who said he had were asked when he was first consulted about a matter concerning a member of the household.

8.141   Somewhat over half the consultations in 1977 (54 per cent) were with solicitors who had never been consulted about the household's affairs before. In a third of all cases in which the solicitor had been consulted before, the first consultation was within the past five years. It would appear that consultations with "family solicitors", used in various matters over a long period to time, account for very much a minority of all consultations.

8.142   Where the consultation was with a solicitor outside private practice, it was almost always a first consultation. In more than nine out of 10 such consultations, the client and his household had never had help or advice from that particular solicitor before.

8.143   The pattern of answers did not vary with sex, but, as one might expect, the older the person consulting the solicitor, the more likely it was that the solicitor had been consulted about other matters affecting the household before. Even among those aged 65 and over, however, 44 per cent of all consultations were first consultations with that particular lawyer.

TABLE 8.22
Previous consultations with solicitor: by tenure,
socio-economic group and area type

	Sample	Never consulted that solicitor before	Solicitor first consulted in:			Not stated
			1973–77	1960–72	before 1960	
All consultations in 1977	2,064	% 54	16	18	10	1
Tenure:						
own	1,508	% 48	18	21	12	2
rent	496	% 73	13	9	4	1
SEG of household head:						
professional/employer/ manager	576	% 40	18	24	17	1
intermediate/junior non- manual	444	% 57	16	16	10	2
skilled manual	571	% 59	18	16	5	2
semi-skilled/unskilled manual	289	% 67	15	15	3	—
Area type:[1]						
GLC/metropolitan county	704	% 62	15	15	7	1
other high or medium density	812	% 53	17	17	12	1
other low density and very rural	548	% 46	17	23	12	2

[1]See paragraph 8.61 for the definition of an area type.

8.144 There were also substantial differences in the pattern of answers by tenure, socio-economic group and area type, shown in Table 8.22.

8.145 The higher incidence of previous use among those living in owner-occupied accommodation may largely reflect a higher incidence of use in conveyancing and this explanation may carry through to the differences in incidence of previous use by socio-economic group.

8.146 The difference by area type is more difficult to explain. We have seen earlier that the incidence of use of lawyers' services during 1977 varies hardly at all between different types of area, but it does appear that people in rural areas who go to solicitors are less likely than those in the big cities to be consulting that particular solicitor for the first time. One possibility is that in more rural areas the choice of solicitors within easy reach is narrower.

How solicitors are chosen
8.147 People making their first use of the services of a solicitor or firm of solicitors were asked how they came to choose that particular solicitor or firm. Also, those who had used particular solicitors before in other matters but had done so for the first time during the past five years were asked how they came to be chosen in the first place. The question was not asked if the first consultation was more than five years ago, since it was thought that people's memories of their original reasons for choosing a solicitor so long ago would often have become rather hazy.

8.148 Table 8.23 lists the reasons people gave for their choice of solicitors.

8.149 The figures for first consultations in 1977 and those for first consultations in the past five years are very similar. Respondents' answers fall into three main groups.

8.150 The largest group of answers refers to informal, personal recommendation or connection. Main answers in this group are that the solicitor had worked for or was recommended by relatives, friends or neighbours, or that the respondent had some previous acquaintance or connection with the solicitor or his firm. Taken together, these accounted for just under half of all the answers given. In some cases where previous acquaintance or connection with the solicitor was mentioned, the connection seemed fairly remote or quite irrelevant to the solicitor's professional competence. It appears that some people prefer to go to a solicitor of whom they have some previous knowledge, however slight, rather than go to a complete stranger.

8.151 In about a quarter of cases of first consultation, the solicitor had been recommended by or was on a list held by some official body or by someone with whom the respondent had business dealings. The most common references were

211

to estate agents and building societies (almost always in connection with conveyancing), to the citizens advice bureau (most commonly in cases of divorce and other family problems) and to trade unions (in the majority of cases over matters of compensation for personal injury).

TABLE 8.23
How solicitor used in 1977 came to be chosen

	All first consultations in 1977	All first consultations in past five years
Sample:	1,120	1,460
	%	%
Solicitor had worked previously for relatives or friends	16	16
Recommended by friends or neighbours	15	14
Recommended by relatives	5	5
Household member dealt with solicitor in course of work	3 }48	4 }50
Solicitor/member of solicitor's firm was an acquaintance/ friend	9	11
Recommended/mentioned by/on list held by:		
—estate agent	5	5
—building society	4	3
—vendor of house	1	1
—citizens advice bureau	5	4
—trade union	3	3
—social services dept/welfare dept/ other official body	2	2
—bank manager	2	2
—employer	1	*
—other professional/non-governmental organisation	5	4
Recommended by other solicitor as specialist/by other solicitor who could not handle matter	3	3
Office is convenient/near home or work	10	9
Chosen from telephone directory/yellow pages	3	3
Other answer	8	7
Not stated/cannot recall	2	6

8.152 In one case in ten, the respondent mentioned explicitly that the solicitor's office was conveniently situated as a main reason for choosing to go to him.

8.153 Between them, these three groups account for more than four in five of the answers given. It appears to be very unusual for solicitors to be chosen from the telephone directory and very unusual for one solicitor to send a possible client to another specialist solicitor.

How non-users would find a lawyer

8.154 The discussion so far has concerned those who were sole or main contacts between their households and a solicitor during 1977. One tenth of all the adults in the households covered who did not come into this category were asked how they would choose a solicitor if they wanted help or advice from one.

8.155 The non-users fall into two groups, those who had not been sole or main contacts with a solicitor in 1977 but had, at some time in their lives, made use of lawyers' services and those who had never made use of lawyers' services

TABLE 8.24

How those who were not main or sole users of lawyers'
services in 1977 would find a solicitor

	All who were not main or sole contacts with lawyers in 1977	Previous personal experience of using lawyers' services:	
		some	none
Sample (unweighted):	1,234	627	607
	%	%	%
Go back to solicitor used personally/by household for domestic conveyance	9	15	3
Go back to solicitor used personally/by household in other matters	18	34	2
Go to solicitor used previously by relatives	8	5	11
Get relatives' recommendation	14	8	21
Get friends'/neighbours'/workmates' recommendation	21	16	5
Go to solicitor who is an acquaintance/personally known	5	6	5
Go to solicitor used by employer of household member	2	2	2
Get recommendation of:			
—citizens advice bureau	9	5	13
—trade union	1	1	1
—social services dept/marriage guidance council/other official body	3	3	3
—other advice centre/pressure group	*	*	1
Go to local one/one whose offices are convenient	9	7	11
Choose from telephone directory/yellow pages	5	4	6
Other answer	5	3	6
Don't know/not stated	6	5	6

at all. Split between these two groups, the ways in which people said they would set about choosing a solicitor are analysed in Table 8.24.

8.156 It will be noted that almost everyone gave some answer. Hardly any had no ideas on how they would set about looking for a solicitor.

8.157 Quite a number mentioned several approaches they might take and their answers are coded into several different categories in Table 8.24. The totals of the percentage figures thus come to considerably over 100 per cent.

8.158 Among those who had used solicitors' services at some time in the past, almost half said they would go back to a solicitor they had used previously. Apart from this, the largest group of answers referred to informal, personal recommendation of friends, neighbours, workmates or relatives, going to a solicitor who had been used before by a relative or to a solicitor with whom they happened to be acquainted.

8.159 Next most frequently mentioned was seeking the recommendation of some official body or formal advisory service, most commonly the citizens advice bureau.

8.160 Finally, 7 per cent said they would go to a local solicitor or one whose offices were convenient.

8.161 Among those who had never at any time had the help or advice of a solicitor, by far the most common answers were that they would seek the recommendations of friends, neighbours or relatives or that they would go to one used in the past by a relative or another member of the household. Other common answers were that they would ask the citizens advice bureau to recommend one (13 per cent) and that they would go to a local one or one whose offices were convenient (11 per cent).

8.162 Thus the ways in which those who had not been main users of legal services in 1977 said they would seek a solicitor if they needed one are very similar to the ways in which those who had been main users had actually chosen their solicitors.

The initial approach to the solicitor
8.163 Those questioned in detail about matters in which they had been the sole or main contact between their household and a solicitor during 1977 were asked whether they themselves had approached the solicitor directly or whether someone else had approached him on their behalf. In 80 per cent of cases the main contact had made the initial approach. In 4 per cent of cases, it had been made by another member of the household (usually the main contact's husband or wife) and in a further 4 per cent of cases the initial approach had been made

214

by a relative outside the household. In 12 per cent of cases, however, the initial approach was made by someone wholly outside the family.

8.164 The main sorts of people from outside the family who had made initial approaches to solicitors on people's behalf were workmates or friends (2 per cent of all cases), trade unions (2 per cent of all cases), estate agents (2 per cent of all cases), building societies, insurance brokers, bank managers, employers and the citizens advice bureau (1 per cent each of all cases).

8.165 Cases in which the initial approach to the solicitor had been made by trade unions almost all concerned compensation for personal injuries. A trade union had made the first approach to the solicitor in 21 per cent of all cases about compensation for personal injury.

8.166 Where the initial approach to the solicitor was made by an estate agent or a building society, it was almost always over a matter of domestic conveyancing. The first approach to the solicitor was made by an estate agent or a building society in 7 per cent of such matters, in most cases on behalf of people from households with heads in manual work.

The nature of the solicitor's services

Summary
8.167 In one consultation in six, the client did not visit the solicitor's office. Occasionally, this was because the solicitor came to see his client, but it was mainly because all contact was handled by letter or telephone.

8.168 Where clients visited solicitors, more than one visit was usually involved. In one case in six, there were five visits or more. Numbers of visits varied considerably with type of matter. Making or altering wills usually involved no more than two visits. In more than one in three cases of divorce, its consequences or other family matters, five visits or more were involved.

8.169 In one case out of 10, the solicitor gave the client advice only and took no action of any sort on his behalf. Most commonly, the client was advised how to deal with the matter himself or advised on the state of the law. Only one in ten of those given advice said it was not clear. One in five, however, did not follow it, usually because they had their own ideas or because they decided not to proceed with the matter.

8.170 Where the solicitor had taken some action, 87 per cent of clients said the final outcome of the solicitor's action was as they had expected. Three per cent said it was better and 7 per cent said it was worse. Matters involving offences and matters involving divorce, its consequences or other family matters, were more likely than average to turn out worse than the client expected.

8.171 Fourteen per cent of all completed matters in which a solicitor had taken action came before a court or tribunal at some stage. The main types of matter involved were offences, divorce, its consequences and other family problems. Young people were more likely than

215

older people to be involved in court or tribunal cases. More than seven out of 10 of those whose cases came before courts or tribunals were aged under 45.

8.172 In two-thirds of the matters which came before a court or tribunal, the client was represented there by his solicitor. In a quarter of cases, he was represented by a barrister. Taking into account also matters in which barristers were only consulted and matters in which they were briefed, but did not actually appear in court, they were said to be involved in 4 per cent of all the completed matters handled by solicitors.

Contact with the solicitor

8.173 One in six consultations with solicitors in 1977 which had been completed by the time of interview did not involve the client visiting the solicitor. Most commonly this was because all contact was by letter or telephone (12 per cent of completed consultations). In some cases, however, it was because the solicitor came to visit the client (3 per cent) or because there was no direct contact between solicitor and client, the whole matter being handled through a third party (2 per cent).

8.174 Where the solicitor came to see the client, the client was quite often an old person. In two cases out of five where this happened, the client was aged 65 or over.

8.175 Dealing with a solicitor exclusively by letter or telephone, on the other hand, was related in some degree to socio-economic group. Eighteen per cent of consultations by people in households with professional, employer or manager heads were made this way as compared to 14 per cent in households where the head's job was intermediate or junior non-manual, 10 per cent where it was skilled manual and 6 per cent where it was semi-skilled or unskilled manual.

8.176 Where the client went to see the solicitor, one visit was seldom enough to deal with the matter. Two in five completed matters had involved three or more visits. One in six involved five visits or more.

8.177 Nature and number of contacts varied, of course, with type of matter. Table 8.25 gives details for the types of matter for which the sub-samples of completed consultations are large enough for separate analysis.

8.178 Of the main types of matter solicitors deal with, the making and altering of wills involved fewest visits to the solicitor. Less than one in seven clients in this sort of matter had visited the solicitor more than twice. Offences also involve fewer visits on average than most other matters. The type of matter most likely to involve a large number of visits was divorce, separation and other family problems.

Whether the solicitor took action or gave advice

8.179 Respondents were asked whether the solicitor they consulted gave them advice only or took some sort of action on their behalf. The definition of action used was minimal. The solicitor was counted as having taken action even if he had only made a telephone call or consulted someone else on behalf of the client.

TABLE 8.25
Contacts with solicitor: by type of matter

	All cases where action/ advice was completed	Type of matter					
		wills	offences	estates	dom- estic convey- ancing	personal injury compen- sation	divorce & other family problems
Sample	1,444	187	119	120	493	52	130
	%	%	%	%	%	%	%
Nature of contact:							
no direct contact	2	3	2	7	*	4	2
letter/telephone only	12	5	8	12	13	21	2
solicitor visited client	3	7	5	5	2	6	—
Client visited solicitor:							
once	21	20	30	20	11	21	22
twice	21	49	29	9	17	12	13
three times	17	12	13	21	24	12	13
four times	7	1	4	8	12	4	10
five + times	16	1	9	17	21	21	37
not stated	*	1	—	—	*	—	—

8.180 In nine cases out of ten, the solicitor was said to have taken some action. Only one case in ten involved giving advice only.

8.181 It was particularly unusual for solicitors to be consulted for advice only on buying or selling houses. Ninety six per cent of such cases involved taking some action. Solicitors were more likely than average to give advice only in cases of motoring offences. Their services were limited to advice in 20 per cent of consultations over these. Also, they were more likely than average to give advice only on a range of types of matter which, individually, account for only a small proportion of the matters on which they are consulted—problems over goods, problems over employment, problems as a tenant or with neighbours and matters of tax or capital transfer.

The advice solicitors gave
8.182 The matters on which solicitors gave advice only were very varied. In total, the numbers of cases in which their services were limited to advice are quite small and the nature of the advice given cannot be reliably broken down in detail by type of matter. Table 8.26 shows, grouped into broad categories, the advice respondents said they were given.

217

TABLE 8.26
Advice given by solicitor[1]

	All cases in which solicitor gave advice only
Sample	215
	%
Advice given:	
told client how to deal with matter himself	47
advised client on state of the law	23
civil matters—client had no case	6
civil matters—not financially worthwhile proceeding	6
civil matters—other advice against proceeding	4
offences—advice on plea	3
suggested taking case to another/specialist lawyer	2
suggested taking case to tribunal	1
suggested taking case to other advice agency etc	1
advised on choice of professional other than lawyer	1
other answer	7
not stated	1

[1]Table totals over 100 per cent as some answers are classified in more than one category.

8.183   In most cases where the solicitor gave advice only, he advised the client how to set about handling the matter himself or advised the client on the position in law with regard to the matter.

8.184   Eighty six per cent of all clients who were given advice only said the advice they were given was clear. Nine per cent said it was not. The remaining 5 per cent did not give a definite answer on this point.

8.185   Four out of five (80 per cent) said they followed the advice they were given, 19 per cent said they did not and one per cent did not say definitely whether they did or not.

8.186   Where the solicitor's advice was not followed, it was mainly because the client either disagreed with the advice and had his own ideas (6 per cent) or because the client decided not to proceed with the matter (4 per cent).

The action solicitors took
8.187   The action solicitors took in clients' affairs was, of course, even more various than the sorts of advice they gave. No attempt was made to classify it in detail. An attempt was made, however, to classify the action the solicitor took in terms of whether the client thought he had done everything they agreed or not. This classification was somewhat difficult and in some cases, possibly, the decision on allocation was somewhat arbitrary. The results should, therefore, be treated with caution.

8.188   In 92 per cent of cases, the solicitor appeared to have done what the client expected of him. In 3 per cent of cases he did not. In 5 per cent of cases, it was unclear how his action matched his client's wishes. There were only small differences by type of matter.

8.189   In three in ten cases in which solicitors had taken action, the action was still in progress at the time of interview. In those cases where action had been completed, respondents were asked whether the final outcome was as they expected, better than they expected or worse than they expected. Eighty seven per cent said the outcome was what they had expected, 3 per cent said it was better and 7 per cent said it was worse. The rest were unable to answer on this point.

8.190   There were substantial differences by type of matter. Details of the main types of matter are given in Table 8.27.

TABLE 8.27
Outcome: by type of matter

	All cases where action was completed	Type of matter					
		wills	estates	domestic convey-ancing	divorce & other family problems	offences	personal injury compen-sation
Sample	1,267	177	105	469	104	94	44
	%	%	%	%	%	%	%
Final outcome was:							
as expected	87	96	96	93	82	65	64
better than expected	3	—	1	*	4	13	5
worse than expected	7	2	—	3	8	20	25
not stated	3	2	3	3	7	2	5

8.191   Some of the sample sizes are small, particularly that for cases of compensation for personal injury. It does appear, however, that the outcome of cases of compensation for personal injury and offences are more likely than average to be worse than the client had expected.

Use of courts
8.192   In 14 per cent of all the matters in which solicitors had acted on behalf of private clients in 1977 and completed their action by the time of interview, the matter had come before a court or tribunal. Taking into account consultations in which the solicitor gave advice only, this represents 12 per cent of all completed consultations.

8.193   Two types of matter accounted for almost four-fifths of completed consultations which had involved court or tribunal cases. These were offences

(44 per cent) and divorce, separation and their consequences (34 per cent). Of the offences which led to a court case, half were motoring offences.

8.194 It is important here to be quite clear that what is being referred to are matters on which clients consulted solicitors in which court or tribunal cases ensued. Thus, in a case of, say, dispute between divorced people over custody of a child, there may have been two separate clients from separate households consulting separate solicitors. If the matter came to court, however, there would be only one court case. The survey estimates the number of people whose dealings with solicitors led to court or tribunal cases. It cannot give an estimate of the number of court or tribunal cases.

8.195 The figures given above for the number of consultations with a solicitor which involved a court or tribunal case are based on consultations complete at the time of interview. In fact, some of the matters which solicitors were still handling had also gone before a court or tribunal. These matters were rather different from those in which the consultation was complete by the time of interview. It was unusual for a solicitor to be involved in action over an offence which had already been before a court. It was not at all unusual for a solicitor to be still dealing with the consequences of a divorce after the court case had been completed. The uncompleted matters which had already been before a court or tribunal are included in the figures given below except where it is specifically stated that they are not.

TABLE 8.28
Type of court or tribunal: by type of matter

	All matters coming before a court or tribunal	Type of matter		
		divorce & other family problems	offences	all other matters
Sample	274	126	83	65
	%	%	%	%
Magistrates' court	51	41	81	32
County court	28	40	5	32
Crown Court	8	6	13	6
High Court	6	8	1	9
Other court/type not stated	7	6	5	11
Industrial tribunal	1	—	—	5
Other tribunal/type not stated	2	—	—	8
Not stated whether court or tribunal	3	1	1	3

Type of court or tribunal

8.196   Those whose cases had been before a court or tribunal were asked at which sort of court or tribunal they had been heard. Their answers should be treated with caution. Some gave answers which were almost certainly wrong. Others could not give the correct technical name of the type of court or tribunal.

8.197   Table 8.28 shows, by main type of matter, the types of courts or tribunals at which respondents stated the matter had been heard.

8.198   In Table 8.28 columns total over 100 per cent, since some cases came before more than one sort of court or tribunal.

8.199   It will be noted that the main types of matter which come before courts or tribunals are matters which were shown in Table 8.16 to be more common among younger than among older people.

8.200   In fact, those whose cases are heard at courts and tribunals are predominantly people from the younger half of the population. Details are given in Table 8.29.

TABLE 8.29
Age profile of persons whose cases came before courts or tribunals

	All Adults	All main or sole contacts with lawyers on personal matters in 1977	Case came before		
			any court or tribunal	magis- trates' court	county court
Sample	15,441	1,869	274	140	76
	%	%	%	%	%
Age:					
18–24	11	9	14	18	5
25–29	10	13	16	15	18
30–34	10	14	19	19	21
35–44	16	20	23	19	28
45–54	17	17	16	16	17
55+	35	24	12	12	9
not stated	2	2	1	1	1

8.201   The 47 per cent of the adult population aged under 45 account for 56 per cent of all those who were main or sole contacts with solicitors over personal matters during 1977. They account, however, for 72 per cent of those whose cases came before courts or tribunals.

8.202   Those whose cases went before magistrates were particularly likely to be young. More than half were aged between 18 and 34. Those whose cases were heard at county courts tended to be a little older. Few were under 25. Two in three were aged between 25 and 44.

8.203   There was little difference by sex between those whose cases were heard at courts or tribunals and the rest of those who had the help or advice of solicitors in 1977. Those whose cases went before magistrates were, however, predominantly men (61 per cent men to 39 per cent women) while those whose cases were heard at county courts were almost equally divided by sex (49 per cent men to 51 per cent women).

8.204   We have noted earlier that people using solicitors' services are more likely than average to come from households with heads in non-manual occupations. This does not apply to those whose cases were heard at courts or tribunals. By socio-economic group, they were quite close to the general adult population, with the exception that they were less likely than average to come from skilled manual households.

Representation
8.205   Most people whose cases had come before a court or tribunal said they had representation there. Sixty five per cent said they were represented by their solicitor. Twenty four per cent said they were represented by a barrister. The numbers saying they were represented by any other sorts of person were negligible.

Use of barristers
8.206   Of all the matters about which solicitors were consulted during 1977 which were complete by the time of interview, 2 per cent involved a barrister representing the client in court at some stage. This represents 3 per cent of all the completed consultations in which the solicitor took any action on the client's behalf.

8.207   In a further 2 per cent of all completed consultations, the respondent said a barrister was consulted or briefed, although he did not actually represent the client in a court or tribunal hearing.

8.208   Barristers were involved at some stage, therefore, in 4 per cent of all the completed matters handled by solicitors or 5 per cent of all the matters in which they took action on the client's behalf.

8.209   Table 8.30 shows main types of completed matter in which barristers were said to have been involved.

222

TABLE 8.30
Types of completed matter in which barrister was used

	All completed matters in which barrister was consulted or represented client in court or tribunal
Sample	62
	%
Nature of matter:	
offences	29
divorce/problems following divorce/other family matters	27
personal injury compensation	13
all other matters	32

Overall satisfaction with solicitors' services

Summary

8.210 More than nine out of ten of those who consulted solicitors during 1977 said they found them easy to deal with. The numbers who said they were completely satisfied with the way the solicitor had handled their affairs were, however, rather smaller—two in three. One in eight clients expressed some dissatisfaction. One in sixteen expressed strong dissatisfaction.

8.211 The most common reasons given for dissatisfaction were that the solicitor appeared not to show enough interest in the client's problem or appeared not to do enough about it, that the matter took too long to complete or that the client was not kept informed of progress. It was much less common for people to suggest that the solicitor made any actual mistake in the advice he gave or the action he took or to say that it cost too much.

8.212 There was very little difference in the levels of satisfaction expressed by clients of different sex or of different age groups or social groups. Nor were there great differences in level of satisfaction by the type of matter about which the solicitor was consulted or the nature of the consultation.

The level of satisfaction with solicitors' services

8.213 Respondents questioned in detail on matters about which they consulted solicitors during 1977 were asked how satisfied they were, overall, with the way the solicitor handled the matter. Their answers reflect how they feel about the services given them. But we have seen already that most people use solicitors infrequently. In most cases, their judgment of the quality of the services given them is probably not professional or expert. That they are dissatisfied does not mean that they necessarily have good reason for dissatisfaction. Nor, conversely, does the fact that they are satisfied mean that the services given them are necessarily of a high professional standard.

223

8.214 The levels of satisfaction stated are given in Table 8.31.

TABLE 8.31
Satisfaction with solicitors' services

	All consultations with solicitors in England and Wales
Sample:	2,064
Completely satisfied	67 ⎱ 84
Fairly satisfied	17 ⎰
Neither satisfied nor dissatisfied	3
Somewhat dissatisfied	7 ⎱ 12
Very dissatisfied	6 ⎰
Not stated	*

8.215 Two-thirds of clients said they were completely satisfied and more than four out of five said they were either completely or fairly satisfied. One in eight expressed dissatisfaction and one in sixteen expressed strong dissatisfaction.

8.216 It might be expected that the level of client satisfaction would vary with the background of the client, the nature of the matter concerned and the nature of the consultation. In fact, variations in level of satisfaction by these factors were very minor. This is a very important finding and the evidence for it needs, therefore, to be set out in detail.

Type of client
8.217 The variation in level of satisfaction with solicitors' services by the main demographic and social factors discussed earlier in this report is shown in Table 8.32.

8.218 Women were marginally more likely than men to say they were completely satisfied with the services of their solicitor. Also, older people, particularly those aged 65 or over, were somewhat more likely than average to say they were completely satisfied. Among those over 65, the number saying they were somewhat or very dissatisfied (the combined figure is shown in the right hand column of Table 8.32) was 7 per cent, compared to an overall average of 12 per cent.

8.219 These differences are, however, quite small. The sex and age of clients appears to have little to do with whether they are satisfied with solicitors' services or not.

8.220 Home tenure and socio-economic group appear to have nothing whatsoever to do with client satisfaction. There is no significant variation of any sort in client satisfaction by either of these variables.

TABLE 8.32

Satisfaction with solicitors' services: by sex, age, tenure and socio-economic group

	Sample	Completely satisfied	Fairly satis-fied	Neither /not stated	Some-what dissatis-fied	Very dissatis-fied	Some-what or very dissatis-fied
All consultations	2,064	% 67	17	4	7	6	12
Sex:							
men	1,186	% 65	18	5	7	6	13
women	877	% 71	15	3	7	5	12
Age:							
18–24	195	% 63	20	5	7	6	13
25–29	264	% 60	24	3	7	5	12
30–34	296	% 64	18	4	8	6	14
35–44	428	% 65	17	4	7	7	14
45–54	355	% 66	18	5	6	5	11
55–64	249	% 74	10	3	6	7	13
65 or over	240	% 81	9	3	4	3	7
Household tenure:							
own	1,508	% 67	17	4	7	5	12
rent	496	% 67	16	5	6	6	12
Socio-economic group of household head:							
professional/em-ployer/manager	576	% 66	18	3	6	7	13
intermediate or junior non-manual	444	% 68	17	2	7	6	13
skilled manual and own account workers	571	% 65	16	6	7	5	12
semi/unskilled manual	289	% 66	16	6	6	7	12

8.221 By region, there is a slight difference between the GLC area and the rest of the country. In the GLC area, only 60 per cent of clients said they were completely satisfied with the way the solicitor handled the matter they took to him as compared to 68 per cent of clients elsewhere. Nineteen per cent of clients in the GLC area said they were somewhat or very dissatisfied as compared to 11 per cent of clients elsewhere. Outside the GLC area, differences in level of satisfaction by area and area type were trivial.

225

Type of matter and type of consultation

8.222 Table 8.33 shows stated levels of satisfaction among clients by type of lawyer, previous experience with the lawyer, nature of the service given and nature of the matter in question.

TABLE 8.33
Satisfaction with solicitors' services: by type of lawyer,
nature of services and type of matter

	Sample	Completely satisfied	Fairly satis-fied	Neither /not stated	Some-what dissatis-fied	Very dissatis-fied	Some-what or very dissatis-fied
All consultations	2,064	% 67	17	4	7	6	12
Type of lawyer:							
solicitor in private practice	1,947	% 68	16	3	7	6	12
other lawyer	111	% 59	19	12	7	3	10
Previous consultation with that lawyer:							
never before	1,120	% 63	19	4	7	6	14
first consultation in past five years	340	% 70	14	3	6	6	12
first consultation longer ago	575	% 74	13	3	5	4	9
Service given:							
advice only	215	% 66	12	4	10	8	18
took some action	1,849	% 67	17	3	6	5	12
Nature of matter:							
making/altering wills	199	% 89	5	1	4	2	6
domestic conveyancing	602	% 70	17	2	7	3	10
personal injury compensation	133	% 57	20	10	5	8	13
offences	138	% 60	19	7	7	7	14
winding up estates	228	% 67	15	4	7	7	14
divorce and other family problems	249	% 60	21	4	8	7	15
other matters concerning domestic property	105	% 62	14	4	10	10	20
all other matters	410	% 64	18	7	7	4	11

8.223 Those who were going to a particular solicitor for the first time were a little more likely to be dissatisfied with the service they got than those going back to one they had first used more than five years ago. Fourteen per cent of clients going to a particular solicitor for the first time said they were dissatisfied with the way he handled the matter as compared to 9 per cent of those who were going back to a solicitor they had first used more than five years ago. It is not surprising that this difference should exist. It seems quite surprising that it is so small.

8.224 People making or altering their wills were somewhat less likely than average to say they were dissatisfied and people who went to a solicitor about a matter concerning domestic property other than conveyancing were somewhat more likely than average to say that they were dissatisfied. Beyond this, the level of dissatisfaction did not vary greatly by type of matter.

8.225 Clients were slightly more likely than average to say they were dissatisfied if the solicitor was giving advice only. Again, however, the difference was not a large one.

Reasons for dissatisfaction
8.226 We have seen that clients said they were somewhat or very dissatisfied with the way the solicitor handled the matter in one in eight consultations. Dissatisfaction is not, however, closely linked to any particular type of client, to any particular type of matter or to any particular type of consultation. How, then, does it arise?

8.227 Those who said they were dissatisfied were asked what they were dissatisfied with. Details of their answers, analysed by degree of dissatisfaction, are given in Table 8.34.

8.228 Two sorts of reasons were very commonly given—that the solicitor took too little interest in the matter or did not appear to do enough about it and that the matter took too long. That the matter took too long was the most common reason for clients saying they were somewhat dissatisfied. That the solicitor took too little interest in the matter was the most common reason for clients saying they were very dissatisfied.

8.229 These two main types of reason for dissatisfaction do not imply that the client felt that any action the solicitor actually took or any advice he gave was not soundly based. Nor do they imply that he made any particular mistakes in handling the matter. They refer to the client's perception of the solicitor's interest and diligence in pursuing the matter.

8.230 The next most common reason given for dissatisfaction was that there was a lack of communication between solicitor and client (15 per cent), a reason which can, perhaps, be grouped in the same general category as the first two. A further fairly common reason for dissatisfaction which may also be taken as falling in the same general category is that the client did not like the solicitor's manner (8 per cent).

227

TABLE 8.34

Reasons for dissatisfaction[1]

	All who were dissatisfied	Degree of dissatisfaction	
		somewhat dissatisfied	very dissatisfied
Sample	255	138	117
	%	%	%
Reasons for dissatisfaction:			
solicitor did not take an interest in it/did not do enough	30	25	36
matter took too long/solicitor was too slow	29	38	19
lack of communication/not kept informed of progress	15	14	16
solicitor made mistakes/was forgetful	9	11	8
solicitor gave bad advice/disagreed with the action he took	9	6	12
complaints about solicitor's manner	8	6	11
charged too much	8	7	9
incurred unnecessary costs/outside costs too high	3	2	3
solicitor lacked specialist knowledge for case	3	1	5
solicitor was guilty of malpractice/unprofessional behaviour	1	—	3
other answer	6	5	7
reason not stated	3	2	3

[1]Answers total over 100 per cent as some gave more than one reason for dissatisfaction.

8.231 The second general category of reasons for dissatisfaction was that the client saw the solicitor as having given poor advice or as having taken the wrong sort of action, that the client thought the solicitor had made mistakes in handling the matter or that the client thought the solicitor lacked specialist experience in this particular sort of case. Nine per cent of those who said they were dissatisfied with their solicitor's handling of the matter said they thought he had actually made mistakes or been forgetful in the way he handled it. Three per cent thought he lacked specialist experience.

8.232 The third general category of reasons for dissatisfaction was the cost of the solicitor's services. The wording of the actual question put to respondents must be borne in mind. It referred specifically to the way the solicitor handled the matter. It could be that some respondents took this to exclude the amount they had to pay for the solicitor's services. Nevertheless, 8 per cent of those who said they were dissatisfied with the way the solicitor handled the matter mentioned as a reason that he charged too much and 3 per cent said that he incurred unnecessary or excessive outside costs.

8.233   It was decided to include in the frame for coding answers to the question on reasons for dissatisfaction a specific code to cover any case where the client's answer could be taken to imply that the solicitor was guilty of malpractice or unprofessional behaviour. In fact, only 1 per cent of those who said they were dissatisfied gave answers which implied this.

8.234   In summary, therefore, the most important causes of client dissatisfaction appear to be related to clients' perceptions of solicitors' interest in their problems and diligence in dealing with them. Complaints about errors or misjudgment on the solicitors' part or about cost are less common.

8.235   As we have stressed earlier, this is the client's judgment and the client is probably no expert in the law or in the time legal procedures take to complete. In many cases, complaints about solicitors' lack of interest or about matters taking a long time to complete may be justified. In some cases, also, clients may have quite unreasonable expectations. It is possible, however, that dissatisfaction of this sort may arise through a failure on the part of the solicitor to communicate to the client just what he is doing and how long it is likely to take. This is discussed in more detail in paragraphs 8.252–8.272.

Likes and dislikes about solicitors

8.236   Respondents answering about matters on which they consulted solicitors during 1977 were asked if there was anything they particularly liked or particularly disliked about the way the solicitor handled the matter. These questions were put to all users of solicitors' services whether they were satisfied with the services they received or not.

8.237   The majority (58 per cent) said there was something they particularly liked. The points they mentioned are listed in Table 8.35.

8.238   Half the people saying there was something they particularly liked about the way the solicitor handled the matter, or just over a quarter of all those who dealt with solicitors in 1977, commented favourably on the solicitor's personal manner towards them during their dealings. In considering this, it must be borne in mind that the question was an open-ended one. The respondents were not prompted to say anything about the solicitor's manner.

8.239   The only other favourable comments made by substantial numbers of respondents were that the solicitor was efficient or businesslike (17 per cent of all respondents) and that he explained things clearly (14 per cent of all respondents).

8.240   There were no notable differences by sex, age, socio-economic group or area in the numbers making favourable comments about their solicitors. Women were, however, rather more likely than men to comment favourably on the solicitor's personal manner. Those dealing with solicitors over divorce, the consequent problems or other family matters (who as we have seen earlier were mainly women) were particularly likely to comment favourably on the solicitor's personal manner. So also were those engaged in making or altering wills. Apart from this, differences by type of matter were trivial.

TABLE 8.35

Points particularly liked about solicitor's handling of matter[1]

	All consultations with solicitors in England and Wales in 1977	All mentioning points particularly liked
Sample	2,064	1,188
	%	%
Particularly liked:		
nothing mentioned	42	n.a.
solicitor was nice/friendly/easy to talk to	28	49
solicitor was efficient/businesslike	17	30
solicitor explained things clearly	14	25
solicitor handled things promptly/quickly	6	10
solicitor was professionally expert	5	9
solicitor was personal friend/acquaintance	2	3
favourable comment on costs	2	3
solicitor's manner was confident	1	2
did what I asked/no problems/did a good job/ other general favourable comments	4	7
other answers	*	*

[1]Answers total over 100 per cent as some mentioned more than one point they particularly liked.

8.241 Far fewer people (17 per cent) said there was anything they particularly disliked about the way their solicitors handled the matters they took to them.

8.242 Table 8.36 shows their answers, analysed by their degree of overall satisfaction with the way their solicitors handled the matter.

8.243 These answers follow very closely the pattern of answers on reasons for dissatisfaction.

8.244 Once again, variations by type of client and type of matter were fairly minor. Clients aged 65 or over and those who were making or altering their wills were less likely than average to say there was anything they disliked about the way the solicitor handled the matter. People in the GLC area were somewhat more likely than average to say that there was something that they disliked. Twenty-four per cent of clients in the GLC area said there was something they disliked as compared to the overall average of 17 per cent. Londoners were particularly likely to say that the solicitor had not shown enough interest or had not done enough.

TABLE 8.36
Points particularly disliked about solicitor's handling of matter[1]

	All con-sultations with solici-tors in Eng-land & Wales in 1977	All mention-ing points disliked	Overall satisfaction		
			satisfied/ neither satisfied nor dis-satisfied	somewhat dis-satisfied	very dis-satisfied
Sample	2,064	361	1,799	138	117
	%	%	%	%	%
Particularly disliked: nothing mentioned	82	n.a.	92	22	11
matter took too long/solici-tor too slow	5	30	3	21	26
solicitor did not take an interest in it/did not do enough	5	26	1	23	37
lack of communication/not kept informed of progress	4	20	1	15	24
solicitor made mistakes/was forgetful	2	9	1	9	6
complaints about solicitor's manner	2	8	1	7	9
charged too much	1	7	1	4	7
solicitor gave bad advice/ disagreed with action taken	1	6	1	4	6
solicitor lacked specialist knowledge for case	1	3	*	2	4
incurred unnecessary costs/ outside costs too high	*	2	*	1	2
solicitor was guilty of mal-practice/unprofessional be-haviour	*	1	—	1	1
other answers	1	6	1	4	4

[1]Answers total over 100 per cent as some mentioned more than one point they particularly disliked.

How easy the solicitor was to deal with

8.245 Respondents who had used solicitors in 1977 were also asked whether they found the solicitor easy to deal with. Ninety-two per cent said they did. Six per cent said they did not. Once again, there was little variation in the pattern of answers by type of client or type of matter.

8.246   The ways in which people said they found solicitors not easy to deal with are listed in Table 8.37.

TABLE 8.37
Ways in which solicitor was not easy to deal with[1]

	All saying solicitor was not easy to deal with
Sample	127
	%
Difficult to contact/did not keep me informed	30
Not interested/negative approach	28
Did not explain things clearly/at all	21
Too slow	13
Inefficient/forgetful	12
Incompetent	3
Old/infirm/ill	2
Other answers	20

[1]Answers total over 100 per cent as some found solicitors difficult to deal with in several ways.

8.247   The main difficulties mentioned were over contact on progress, the client's perception of the solicitor's attitude to the matter and lack of clear explanation of the matter by the solicitor. Once again, actual mistakes on the solicitor's part were mentioned by a small minority. As one might expect, there was quite a strong relationship between the client's view on whether the solicitor was easy to deal with and his overall level of satisfaction with the way the solicitor handled the matter. Three-quarters of those who said the solicitor was not easy to deal with (76 per cent) said they were not satisfied with the way he handled the matter as compared to only 8 per cent of those who said he was easy to deal with.

Attitude to repeat consultation
8.248   As a final check on level of overall satisfaction, respondents who had been main or sole contacts with solicitors during 1977 were asked whether, if a similar matter arose in the future and they wanted the help or advice of a solicitor, they would go back again to the same one.

8.249   Seventy per cent said they would and 17 per cent said they would not. An unusually large number, 12 per cent, did not give a definite answer to this question one way or the other. In some cases, this was because of changes in circumstances (they or the solicitor had moved, the solicitor had retired etc). In most cases, however, the failure to give a definite answer appeared to indicate that respondents were actually unsure about what they would do.

8.250 Once again, the pattern of answers did not vary greatly with type of client or type of matter.

8.251 As one might expect, clients' attitudes to consulting the same solicitor again were closely linked to their satisfaction with the way he handled the matter in question. Four out of five of those who were completely or fairly satisfied with his handling of the matter said they would use the same solicitor again in similar circumstances. Four out of five who were somewhat or very dissatisfied with their solicitor's handling of the matter said they would not.

Communication, outcome and satisfaction

Summary
8.252 Three in four of those on whose behalf solicitors took action said that the solicitor had explained at the outset what he was going to do. Young people and people in manual households were more likely than average to have had an explanation of the intended action. In most cases where no explanation had been given the client had not asked for one. Five per cent said they asked for an explanation and were not given one.

8.253 There was some relationship between overall satisfaction with the solicitor and whether an explanation of the intended action was given.

8.254 Four in five of those on whose behalf solicitors took action said they had been kept sufficiently informed of progress by the solicitor during the course of the matter. Eight per cent, however, had had difficulty in finding out how matters stood and 4 per cent had had a lot of difficulty. There was a very strong relationship between how well the client thought he had been kept informed of progress and his overall satisfaction with the solicitor. This was the closest correlate of overall satisfaction of all topics covered in the survey.

8.255 There was some relationship between the client's view of how the matter finally turned out and his satisfaction with the solicitor's services. This was not so strong, however, as the relationship between satisfaction and information on progress.

Communication
8.256 We have shown that a main cause of client dissatisfaction is a feeling on the part of the client that the solicitor is not doing enough on his behalf or lacks interest in his problem and have suggested that this may sometimes arise through a failure of communication between solicitor and client.

8.257 In the following paragraphs we deal with two aspects of communication between solicitor and client in cases where the solicitor took action on the client's behalf—whether he told the client what action he proposed to take on his behalf and whether he kept him informed of progress. Whether he gave the client a clear idea of probable time and a clear idea of probable cost are covered in paragraphs 8.290–8.296 and 8.338–8.344 respectively.

Explanation of intended action
8.258 Three in four of those on whose behalf lawyers took action during 1977 (75 per cent) said that when the solicitor started dealing with the matter

233

he explained to them what he was going to do. One in four (25 per cent) said he did not. Of these, however, almost all said that they did not ask him to. Three per cent said that they asked for an explanation but did not get one. Twenty per cent had not asked for an explanation of the intended action.

8.259   Answers to this question did not vary greatly by type of matter, with the exception that few who were consulting the solicitor about matters of divorce, separation, their consequences or other family problems had failed to ask the lawyer for an explanation of his intended course of action. Possibly as a consequence, they were more likely than average to have got one.

8.260   As Table 8.38 shows, there were differences in the answers given to this question by the youngest and oldest respondents. Those under 25 were more likely than average and much more likely than old people to have been given an explanation. Old people were more likely than average and much more likely than young people not to have asked for one.

TABLE 8.38
Explanation of intended action: by age

	All cases in which solicitor took action	Age		
		18–24	25–64	65+
Sample	1,849	175	1,420	222
	%	%	%	%
Explanation of intended action:				
given	75	84	75	68
not given	24	15	24	31
not stated	1	1	1	2
asked for	3	2	3	1
not asked for	20	13	20	28
not stated	1	—	1	3

8.261   There was also a difference by socio-economic group. Those in households with semi-skilled or unskilled manual heads were more likely than average to have been given an explanation of what the solicitor intended to do. They were more likely than average to have asked for one.

8.262   Overall client satisfaction varied with the information they said they had been given or asked for. Among those who said the solicitor had explained to them what he was going to do, 8 per cent said they were somewhat or very dissatisfied with the way he handled the matter. Among those who said they had not been given an explanation but had not asked for one, the level of dissatisfaction rose to 17 per cent. Of the 49 people who said they had asked the solicitor for an explanation but had not been given one, the majority (26) expressed dissatisfaction with his handling of the matter. More than one in three (17) expressed strong dissatisfaction.

Information on progress

8.263 Four out of five of those on whose behalf solicitors took some action (79 per cent) said that, while the solicitor was dealing with the matter, he kept them sufficiently informed of progress. One in five (20 per cent) said he did not.

8.264 Of those who said the solicitor had not kept them sufficiently informed of progress, 11 per cent said that they had not at any time had difficulty finding out from him how matters stood. Eight per cent said they had in fact had such difficulties. Half of these said this had happened once or twice. Half said it had happened a lot.

8.265 Table 8.39 shows respondents' views on how well they were kept informed, analysed by overall level of satisfaction with the solicitor's handling of the matter.

TABLE 8.39

Information on progress: by satisfaction with solicitors' handling of the matter

	All cases in which solicitor took action	Overall level of satisfaction		
		very dis-satisfied	somewhat dis-satisfied	all others
Sample	1,849	99	117	1,633
	%	%	%	%
Kept sufficiently informed	79	24	39	85
Not kept sufficiently informed	20	73	59	14
Not stated	2	3	2	2
No difficulty in finding out how matters stood	11	13	21	10
Difficulty in finding out how matters stood	8	59	36	3
Not stated	1	1	2	1
Happened once or twice	4	17	18	2
Happened a lot	4	40	18	1
Not stated	*	2	—	*

8.266 Almost three in four of those who said they were very dissatisfied with the way the solicitor handled the matter said he did not keep them sufficiently informed as compared to one in seven of those who did not express dissatisfaction. Two in five of those who said they were very dissatisfied said they had a lot of trouble in finding out how matters stood as compared to one in a hundred of those who expressed no dissatisfaction.

8.267 Of all the topics covered in the survey, the client's view on how well he was kept informed of progress correlates most closely with overall satisfaction and dissatisfaction. It is worthwhile, therefore, to present the same figures again in a different way. Details of the level of satisfaction with the way the solicitor handled the matter among those with different views on how well or badly they were kept informed of progress are shown in Table 8.40.

TABLE 8.40

Satisfaction with solicitor's handling of matter:

by information given on progress

	All cases in which solicitor took action	Kept informed of progress	Not kept informed		
			no difficulty finding out	difficulty once or twice	a lot of difficulty
Sample	1,849	1,455	199	74	71
	%	%	%	%	%
Satisfaction with solicitor's handling of matter:					
completely satisfied	67	76	47	14	—
fairly satisfied	17	16	25	27	11
neither satisfied nor dissatisfied	3	2	8	7	3
somewhat dissatisfied	6	3	13	28	29
very dissatisfied	5	2	7	23	56
not stated	1	*	2	1	—

8.268 Three-quarters of those who said they had been kept sufficiently informed of progress by their solicitor said they were completely satisfied with the way he handled the matter. Among those who had to ask to find out how matters stood, even though they had no difficulty in finding out, the numbers who were completely satisfied fell to less than half. If they did have difficulty finding out, the level of general satisfaction fell further. Among those who said they had a lot of difficulty over this, more than half said they were very dissatisfied with the way the solicitor had handled the matter.

Outcome and satisfaction

8.269 We have already discussed (paragraphs 8.187–8.191) the outcome of matters in which solicitors' action had been completed in relation to the client's expectations. It seems reasonable to expect that there should be a relationship between this and the client's satisfaction and dissatisfaction with the way the solicitor handled the matter, particularly since in quite a number of cases the solicitor's views may have influenced the client's expectations.

8.270 There is in fact such a relationship, but it is not as strong as the relationship between information on progress and satisfaction.

8.271 In cases where the solicitor had taken action which had been completed by the time of interview, the client's view of the solicitor's handling of the matter was not affected by whether the matter turned out as he had expected or better than he had expected. If the outcome had been worse than the client expected, however, the client was more likely than average to say he was dissatisfied with the way the solicitor had handled it.

8.272 Of the 88 clients with completed matters which had turned out worse than they expected, 40 per cent expressed themselves somewhat or very dissatisfied with the way the solicitor handled the matter as compared to an average for all completed cases of action of 10 per cent. Thirty-one per cent said they were very dissatisfied as compared to an average for all completed cases of 4 per cent.

Time

Summary

8.273 Different types of matter took different lengths of time to complete. The making or altering of a will was over within two months in five cases out of six. In most cases, action on behalf of a client over an offence was over within two months. Most domestic conveyancing took between one and four months. In winding up estates, seeking compensation for personal injuries and divorce, separation and other family problems, however, the time the solicitor took to complete the matter was very much more variable. The matter might be dealt with quite quickly or might take a very considerable time to complete.

8.274 Less than half of those on whose behalf solicitors had taken action said they had been given a clear idea how long the matter would take to complete. Most of those who had not did not ask for one, but one in ten said they had asked for an estimate of time and had not been given one. In cases of estates and personal injury compensation, two of the sorts of matter in which actual time taken varied a lot, more people than average said they had not asked the solicitor for an estimate. In cases of divorce and family problems, where time taken was also variable, more people than average said they had asked for an estimate but had not been given one.

8.275 Just under one in five said the matter had taken less time to complete than they expected. One in four said it took longer. There was little variation on this point by type of

237

matter. Where the matter had taken longer to complete than expected, people were often vague about the reasons. The responsibility for the delay was put wholly or partly on the client's solicitor in less than one case in five.

8.276 Satisfaction with the solicitor's services did not vary greatly with the length of time the matter took to complete. Those who said it took longer than they expected, however, and those who said they had asked for an estimate of time but had not been given one were much more likely than average to say they were dissatisfied with the way the solicitor had handled the matter.

When matters started

8.277 The matters covered in the survey were those in which respondents had help or advice from lawyers during 1977, whether the consultations with the lawyer over the matter started in 1977 or started earlier. In just under one in four cases (23 per cent) consultations started before 1977. Sixteen per cent of cases started in 1976. Seven per cent had been going on since 1975 or earlier.

8.278 Different sorts of matter take different lengths of time to complete. Table 8.41 gives a broad comparison between different sorts of matter by analysing matters handled during 1977 in terms of when they started.

TABLE 8.41

Consultations with solicitors in 1977: by when consultations started

	All consultations with solicitors in England and Wales in 1977	Consultation with solicitor started in:		
		1977	1976	1975 or earlier
Sample	2,064	1,569	333	148
	%	%	%	%
Type of matter:				
domestic conveyancing	29	31	33	7
other matters concerning title or rights on domestic property	5	5	6	5
winding up estates	11	11	12	16
making or altering a will	10	12	2	1
divorce/consequent problems/other family problems	12	9	19	29
offences	7	7	5	—
compensation for personal injury	6	5	10	14
money owed to client	2	1	1	7
setting up/administering trusts	*	*	*	3
matters of tax or capital transfer	1	1	*	3
all other matters	17	17	14	17

8.279 The sorts of matter which had been going on since 1975 or earlier were different in character from those which had started more recently. Divorce, its consequences and other family problems (separation, maintenance, etc) accounted for 29 per cent of all the consultations which had been going on since 1975 as compared to only 9 per cent of those which started in 1977. Personal injury compensation cases accounted for 14 per cent of the matters going on since 1975 as compared to 5 per cent of those which started in 1977. The winding up of estates also figured more prominently among long-term cases than among cases in general.

8.280 Some types of matter, which formed only a very small proportion of all the matters solicitors dealt with, figured more prominently among long-term cases. The main types of matter in this category were the recovery of debts, trust matters and matters of tax or capital transfer.

8.281 Offences and wills, on the other hand, figured hardly at all among the matters on which the consultation with the solicitor had been going on since 1975 or earlier. Few cases of domestic conveyancing, the largest single category of business for solicitors, had been going on for so long.

Duration of matter

8.282 In cases where the solicitor had taken some action and the matter had been completed by the time of the interview, the time the matter took to complete was analysed by the nature of the matter.

8.283 In fact, in three out of ten of all the matters in which the solicitor had taken action, action was still incomplete at the time of interview. This applied particularly in cases of compensation for personal injuries and in cases of divorce and its consequences or other family problems, as one might expect from the findings on when matters started.

8.284 Also, analysis of the time the matter took depended on respondents being able to give the month the consultation with the solicitor started and the month the solicitor finished dealing with it. In 7 per cent of cases where the solicitor took some action and the matter had been completed by the time of interview, the respondent was unable to give one or other of these dates, usually the date the consultation started.

8.285 Because of these two factors, the sample sizes in Table 8.42 below are small for all types of matter except domestic conveyancing. They are particularly small for cases of compensation for personal injuries. There is also a possibility of bias in the figures. Starting months which respondents could not recall may have tended to be further back in the past than those they could recall. Thus the figures shown below should be treated with extreme caution.

8.286 Five out of six consultations about making or altering wills were over in no more than two months. Almost half took less than a month.

TABLE 8.42

Duration of completed matters: by type of matter

Sample: all cases where action completed and duration given	Type of matter					
	wills	offences	domestic conveyancing	estates	personal injury compensation	divorce/ other family problems
	160	90	432	96	41	93
	%	%	%	%	%	%
Duration of consultation:						
less than 1 month	47	20	3	10	7	8
1–2 months	37	36	29	16	12	16
3–4 months	6	18	38	25	10	8
5–6 months	6	11	14	16	17	15
7–12 months	2	12	10	23	32	27
over 1–2 years	1	3	4	6	17	15
over 2–3 years	1	—	*	1	2	6
3 years or more	—	—	*	3	2	5

8.287 Consultations over offences where the solicitor took some action on the client's behalf also tended to be completed quite quickly. Half took no more than two months. Three in four were over within four months.

8.288 Two in three conveyances took between one and four months.

8.289 The time it takes for action to be completed on the winding up of estates, on compensation for personal injury and on divorce, its consequent problems and other family problems was very much more variable. In some cases, such matters were dealt with quite quickly. In others, they took a very long time indeed to complete.

Advice on how long action would take

8.290 All those on whose behalf solicitors took action were asked whether, when the solicitor started dealing with the matter, he gave them a clear idea of how long he thought it would take. If they said he did not, they were asked whether in fact they had asked him how long he thought it would take.

8.291 Less than half of those on whose behalf solicitors had acted (46 per cent) said they had been given a clear idea of how long the solicitor thought the matter would take.

8.292 Most of those who said the solicitor had not given them a clear idea of how long he thought the matter would take, however, said they had not in fact asked him for one. Only one in ten said they had asked the solicitor how long he thought the matter would take but had not been given a clear answer.

8.293 There were substantial differences by type of matter. In matters concerning the winding up of estates and compensation for personal injuries, people were less likely than average to say they had been given a clear idea of how long the matter would take and were less likely than average to have asked for one. As we have seen earlier, these are among the sorts of matter whose duration is very variable and it is possible some clients are aware of this.

8.294 In matters concerning divorce and its consequences and other family problems, people were more likely than average to say that they had asked the solicitor for his opinion on how long the matter would take but had not been given a clear answer. They were also more likely than average, however, to have asked about how long the matter would take and, overall, were as likely as average to have been given a clear idea of probable timing.

8.295 Table 8.43 shows the advice given about duration, split by type of matter.

TABLE 8.43

Advice on duration: by type of matter

	All cases where solicitor took action	Type of matter					
		wills	domestic convey- ancing	divorce/ other family problems	offences	estates	personal injury compen- sation
Sample	1,849	185	571	218	113	209	121
	%	%	%	%	%	%	%
How long matter would take:							
clear idea given	46	58	57	50	39	33	31
not given	53	39	42	49	59	66	69
not stated	2	2	1	1	1	1	1
asked for	10	2	9	18	9	7	13
not asked for	41	37	31	29	47	55	54
not stated	2	1	1	1	4	3	2

241

8.296 There were only negligible differences in answers to this question by sex. socio-economic group or tenure. There was, however, a difference by age, Young people were considerably more likely than old people to say they had been given a clear idea of how long the matter would take. They were also more likely than old people to say they had asked for an opinion but had not been given a clear answer, and were much less likely than old people not to have asked about timing.

TABLE 8.44

Advice on duration: by age of client

	All cases where solicitor took action	Age		
		under 30	30–64	65 or over
Sample	1,849	415	1,180	222
	%	%	%	%
How long matter would take:				
clear idea given	46	55	45	33
not given	53	42	54	65
not stated	2	2	1	2
asked for	10	14	9	4
not asked for	41	27	43	60
not stated	2	1	2	*

Opinion of time taken

8.297 Among those for whom solicitors took action which had been completed by the time of interview, just over half (53 per cent) said the matter had taken about as long as they expected. Eighteen per cent said that it was completed more quickly than they expected and 25 per cent said it took longer than they expected. Five per cent could not answer this question.

8.298 People concerned in making or altering wills were extremely unlikely to say the matter took longer than they expected. Apart from this, there were no very notable differences by type of matter.

8.299 We have seen earlier that it is mainly older people who make wills. Probably because of this, older people were less likely than younger people to find that matters took longer than they expected. Only 16 per cent of clients aged 65 or over said this as compared to 31 per cent of those aged under 30.

8.300 Asked why the matter took longer than expected, just under one in five of those who thought this put the responsibility wholly or partly on their solicitor. Ten per cent said it was wholly due to him and 8 per cent said it was partly due to him and partly due to other factors.

8.301 Half said the delay was not due to their solicitors in any way. The remainder were vague about the responsibility for the delay.

Time and satisfaction with solicitors

8.302 For completed matters, there was some variation in level of satisfaction with the way the solicitor handled the matter by the amount of time it took to complete. Six per cent of those where the solicitor's action was completed within two months said they were somewhat or very dissatisfied with the way he handled it, compared to 16 per cent of those whose affairs took over a year to complete. The difference is not a large one. Given the differences in the length of time it takes to complete different sorts of matter, a simple analysis of satisfaction by duration of matter is not, perhaps, very helpful. Sample sizes are too small, however, for an analysis of time by satisfaction within type of matter.

8.303 There were larger differences in levels of satisfaction by whether the matter had taken a longer or shorter time than the client expected. Few of those whose affairs had taken less time to handle than they expected or about as long a time to handle as they expected expressed any dissatisfaction. Four per cent of the clients in this situation said they were fairly or very dissatisfied with their solicitors' handling of the matter. Where the matter had taken longer than the client expected, 25 per cent said they were dissatisfied with the solicitor's handling of it. Ten per cent said they were very dissatisfied.

8.304 There was an equally great difference in level of satisfaction by the advice the client had been given on the time the matter would take. Table 8.45 shows that clients who had asked for a clear idea of how long it would take and had not been given one were much more likely than average to be dissatisfied.

TABLE 8.45
Satisfaction with solicitor: by information given on probable duration of matter

	All cases in which solicitor took action	Idea of how long matter would take		
		given	not asked for	asked for but not given
Sample	1,849	848	762	176
	%	%	%	%
Satisfaction with solicitor:				
completely satisfied	67	78	62	39
fairly satisfied	17	14	19	27
neither satisfied nor dissatisfied	3	2	5	4
somewhat dissatisfied	6 ⎫	4 ⎫	7 ⎫	16 ⎫
	⎬ 12	⎬ 7	⎬ 13	⎬ 30
very dissatisfied	5 ⎭	3 ⎭	6 ⎭	14 ⎭
not stated	1	*	1	1

243

8.305 Three in ten of those who said they had asked for a clear idea of timing but had not been given one said they were not satisfied with the way their solicitor had handled the matter.

Costs

Summary

8.306 In many cases, respondents were unable to say how much solicitors' services had cost. This very often applied when the costs had been borne by someone else and also when the solicitor had been handling money on the client's behalf and had deducted his fees before passing the money to the client. Even where the solicitor had billed the client directly, one in eight was unable to remember the amount at the time of the interview. The information given on the costs of solicitors' services is, therefore, unreliable.

8.307 Amounts stated as paid varied considerably with type of matter. Mean amount stated as paid for domestic conveyancing was £300, for making or altering wills £14. Clients were so frequently uncertain about the breakdown of the bill between fees and disbursements that it is not worthwhile reporting answers on this.

8.308 Where all or part of the bill had been paid by the client or his household, one in five thought they had had poor value for money. There was some relationship between amount paid and opinion on value for money. Among those who had paid £20 or less few thought they had had poor value for money. This was not as strong, however, as the relationship between opinion on value for money and satisfaction with the way the solicitor handled the matter.

8.309 Only one in four of those on whose behalf solicitors took action said that at the outset the solicitor had given them a clear idea of how much it would cost. Most of the rest said they had not asked, but 9 per cent said they had asked and had not been given a clear answer. As with information on how long matters would take, those who said they had asked for an indication of how much the solicitor's services would cost but had not been given a clear answer were more likely than average to say they were dissatisfied with the way he handled the matter.

The reliability of the information on cost

8.310 If respondents were main contacts between their households and solicitors for advice or action over some matter during 1977 and the consultation was complete by the time of interview, they were asked whether the solicitor had issued a bill and, if so, whether it was paid by members of their households or by others. They were also asked for the actual amount paid by themselves or other members of their households, the amount out of this total which was for disbursements (money paid out by the solicitor on the client's behalf) and the amount paid by people outside the household who paid all or part of the bill.

8.311 The questionnaire for this survey was piloted twice and the questions on cost were substantially altered after each pilot because of difficulties interviewers met in administering them and difficulties respondents had in answering them. Despite these changes, the final version of the cost questions did not work well in the field and most of the questions on cost cannot be regarded as having produced very reliable information.

8.312   The main reason for this was that, in many cases, we were seeking information from respondents which they did not have. If the solicitor had not issued a bill directly to them, which they had paid, they were quite often uncertain about how he had been paid for his services and in very many cases had no idea of the amount of this payment. This applied in cases in which the solicitor had issued a bill to someone else. It also appeared frequently to apply in cases in which the solicitor had handled money due to his client and had deducted his fees before passing on the balance.

8.313   A further factor was that a number of respondents who had actually paid solicitors for their services had forgotten the amount of the bill and did not have the receipt readily to hand to check it at the time of the interview. How this failure to remember the amount paid relates to the actual amount paid and to the time since it was paid is not clear. It is certainly possible, however, that the sums forgotten may, on average, have been different from the sums remembered.

8.314   This applies to the total amount of the solicitor's bill. It applies even more strongly to the proportion of this bill which was for expenses or disbursements paid by the solicitor on the client's behalf.

8.315   The replies respondents gave on cost are summarised below. They should be treated with extreme caution.

Who paid the solicitor

8.316   Thirty per cent of those whose dealings with solicitors in 1977 had been completed by the time of interview said the solicitor had issued no bill. Of the rest, 47 per cent said he had issued a bill which had been paid wholly by themselves or others in their households, 3 per cent said it had been paid partly by their households and partly by others and 7 per cent said it had been paid wholly by others. The remaining 2 per cent were unable to give a clear answer on who paid for the solicitor's services.

8.317   Where others were said to have paid all or part of the bill, those most commonly mentioned as paying were relatives outside the household (3 per cent), the legal aid fund, employers and insurance companies (1 per cent each).

8.318   If the solicitor concerned was not one specifically said to be in private practice, it was hardly ever the case that the respondent said that he issued a bill.

8.319   Table 8.46 shows, by main type of matter, the situation stated with regard to the solicitor's fees.

TABLE 8.46

Who paid the bill: by type of matter

	All com-pleted matters	Type of matter					
		domestic convey-ancing	wills	estates	divorce/ other family problems	offences	personal injury com-pensation
Sample	1,444	493	184	118	128	118	52
No bill issued	% 30	% 10	% 21	% 24	% 54	% 57	% 56
Bill paid:							
all by household	57	82	76	46	34	22	15
some by household	3	2	—	10	3	4	6
none by household	7	5	3	16	7	15	23
not stated	2	1	—	4	1	2	—
Others paying:							
relatives outside household	3	3	3	13	5	1	—
legal aid fund	1	—	—	—	5	5	10
employer	1	2	—	—	—	1	8
insurance company	1	—	—	1	—	8	8
trade union	*	—	—	—	—	—	6
other/not stated	3	2	—	11	—	3	4

8.320 In most cases people said they paid the bills for solicitors' services in domestic conveyancing and the making of wills themselves. This was usually not so, however, in cases of offences or personal injury compensation.

8.321 Those in non-manual households were slightly more likely than those in manual households to say they paid the bill themselves. This can be related to the greater likelihood of their being involved in matters of domestic conveyancing and the making of wills. The difference is not, however, a large one. Three out of five of those in professional, employer or managerial households said their households paid the whole of the bill as compared to half of those in semi-skilled and unskilled manual households.

Amounts paid

8.322 The numbers saying directly that others had paid all or part of the solicitor's bill were small. It seems certain that quite a number of the cases where the solicitor was said not to have issued a bill should, in fact, have fallen into this category. Also a number who said that something was paid by others were unable to state the amount. Given this, the figures quoted for amounts paid by others seem so unlikely to be reliable as a guide to the general situation with regard to costs that it would be misleading to report them.

8.323 The amounts people reported as paid by themselves or other members of their household are shown in Table 8.47.

TABLE 8.47

Amount paid by household: by type of matter

	All completed consultations in which solicitor's bill paid wholly or partly by household	Type of matter	
		domestic conveyancing	making/ altering wills
Sample	877	417	143
	%	%	%
Amount paid by household:			
£1–10	12	1	41
£10–20	9	*	27
£20–40	9	2	12
£40–80	8	5	3
£80–120	7	8	1
£120–160	9	14	—
£160–200	8	14	1
£200–300	10	18	—
£300–400	7	12	—
£400–500	3	4	—
over £500	6	10	—
amount not stated	13	11	17
Mean	£190	£300	£14

8.324 Three in five of those whose cases had been completed by the time of interview said that any of the solicitor's bill had been paid by themselves or other members of their households. Also, 13 per cent of those who said their households had paid something could not state the amount. The numbers stating an amount paid are, therefore, small relative to the total sample and the amounts they give should not be taken as necessarily giving a very accurate picture of the actual situation. By type of matter, only the sub-samples of those whose consultations with solicitors had been about domestic conveyancing or the making or altering of wills are large enough to be presented separately.

8.325 The mean amount paid to solicitors by those giving a figure was £190. It will be noted, however, that the actual amounts quoted varied greatly. Three in ten said they paid no more than £40. Only one in four said they paid over £200, a figure little higher than the overall mean. The mean is high because a few of those quoting amounts over £200 quoted very large sums indeed. Median amount paid was between £80 and £120.

8.326 Mean amount stated as paid for matters of domestic conveyancing was £300. Again the amounts actually quoted were very widely dispersed.

8.327   Mean amount stated as paid for consultations on the making or altering of wills was £14. Four in five of those quoting an amount paid for this sort of work stated payments of no more than £20.

8.328   Respondents who said the bill had been paid by their household wholly or in part were also asked if it included any items the solicitor had to pay out on the client's behalf. Of the 877 who said their household had paid all or part of the bill, 52 per cent said it included no disbursements and a further 21 per cent either did not know whether there were or did not know the amount. Given the very large number who were unclear on this point, it would be misleading to quote the figures given by those who did state amounts.

Value for money

8.329   All those who said that they or other members of their household had paid all or part of the solicitor's bill were asked whether, taking into account what he did, they thought the amount they paid the solicitor in fees was good, reasonable or poor value for money. It was intended that this question should refer specifically to the solicitor's own fees, excluding the disbursements he made on the client's behalf. Given the high degree of uncertainty among clients about disbursements, however, it would probably be more reasonable to regard the answers as a general reaction to the whole bill.

8.330   More than a third (38 per cent), thought the amount they had to pay good value for money and more than a third (36 per cent) thought it reasonable value for money. More than one in five, however, (22 per cent) thought they had poor value for the money they paid.

8.331   By type of matter, the sub-samples were large enough for reliable separate analysis only for domestic conveyancing, the making or altering of wills and the winding up of estates.

8.332   Those who had paid solicitors to make or alter wills were much more likely than average to think they had good value for money. Sixty five per cent of them said this. Nine per cent said they had poor value for money.

8.333   People who had paid for the winding up of estates were slightly more likely than average to think they had had good value for money and people who had paid for domestic conveyancing were slightly less likely than average to think this. In domestic conveyancing cases, 33 per cent thought what they had to pay was good value for money and 26 per cent thought it poor value.

8.334   Domestic conveyancing, of course, tends to cost more than making a will and there was some relationship between the amounts people paid and their opinions of the value for money they got. Details are given in Table 8.48.

TABLE 8.48

Opinion of value for money: by amount paid

	All completed consultations where solicitor's bill was paid wholly or partly by household	Amount paid				
		up to £20	£20– £100	£100– £250	over £250	amount not stated
Sample	877	181	173	234	173	116
	%	%	%	%	%	%
Opinion of value for money:						
good	38	57	39	28	24	51
reasonable	36	31	34	41	39	34
poor	22	10	27	24	34	4
not stated	3	1	—	7	2	11

8.335 If the bill was no more than £20, most people felt they were getting good value for money. The number thinking this dropped to one in four if the bill was over £100 and the number thinking it poor value for money became as large as the number thinking it good value.

8.336 There was little difference in opinions on value for money by socio-economic group.

8.337 Where people did think the solicitor's bill was poor value for money, it was almost always because they thought the solicitor's charges were too high. Hardly any thought the solicitor had done unnecessary work for which they had been charged.

Advice on cost

8.338 One in four of those on whose behalf solicitors took any action said that, when he started dealing with the matter, the solicitor had given them a clear idea of what his bill to them would be. Seventy four per cent said he had not, but out of these 64 per cent said they had not in fact asked him. Nine per cent said that they had asked the solicitor what his bill to them would be but had not been given a clear answer.

8.339 The numbers who said they were not given a clear idea of cost at the outset are considerably greater than the numbers who said they were not given a clear idea of probable timing. This was usually because they did not ask and can be related in part to the fact that many did not, in fact, pay the solicitor's bill themselves.

249

8.340 As with the questions on information about the amount of time the matter would take, there were differences by type of matter. Details about advice on cost for the main types of matter are given in Table 8.49.

TABLE 8.49

Advice on cost: by type of matter

	All cases where solicitor took action	Type of matter					
		domestic convey- ancing	divorce and other family problems	offences	wills	personal injury compen- sation	estates
Sample	1,849	571	218	113	185	121	209
	%	%	%	%	%	%	%
How much bill would be:							
clear idea given	25	37	28	27	26	12	8
not given	74	61	70	73	72	83	91
not stated	2	1	2	1	2	5	1
asked for	9	12	8	7	3	10	6
not asked for	64	49	60	64	70	71	84
not stated	1	1	2	2	—	2	*

8.341 People involved in domestic conveyancing were more likely than average to say they had been given a clear idea of probable cost at the outset. Even among these, however, less than two in five said this happened.

8.342 People seeking compensation for personal injury were less likely than average to say they had been given a clear idea of cost. This was also the case with people involved in the winding up of estates, but few of these said they had asked about cost.

8.343 As with advice on how long the matter would take, young people were more likely than old people to say they had been given a clear idea at the outset of how much the solicitor's bill would be. Thirty four per cent of those aged under 30 said this as compared to 18 per cent of those aged 65 or over. Young people were also more likely than old people to say they had asked for an indication of cost but had not been given one. They were considerably less likely than old people to say they had not asked the solicitor for an indication of likely cost.

8.344 On this point there were no notable differences in the pattern of answers by sex or socio-economic group.

Cost and satisfaction

8.345 There was no relationship between the client's satisfaction or dissatisfaction with the way the solicitor handled the matter and who was said to have paid the bill. Nor, in cases where the client's household paid all or part of the bill, was there any relationship between the actual sum paid and satisfaction or dissatisfaction with the way the solicitor handled the matter.

8.346 There was, however, a relationship between whether the client thought he got value for money and satisfaction with how the solicitor handled the matter. Clients who said they were somewhat or very dissatisfied with the solicitor's handling of the matter and who had paid for his services were much more likely than average to think they had had poor value for money. Of the 96 respondents who had paid for the solicitor's services and who said they were very dissatisfied with the way he handled the matter, 83 per cent thought that they had been given poor value for money. This compared with an overall figure of 22 per cent saying they thought the service they got was poor value for money.

8.347 We noted earlier the relationship between client satisfaction and the information the client said the solicitor gave at the outset about how long the matter would take. There was a similar relationship between client satisfaction and the information the client said the solicitor gave at the outset about how much his bill would be. Details are given in Table 8.50.

TABLE 8.50

Satisfaction with solicitor: by information given on probable cost

	All cases where solicitor took action	Idea of how much bill would be		
		given	not asked for	asked for but not given
Sample	1,849	459	1,176	162
	%	%	%	%
Satisfaction with solicitor:				
completely satisfied	67	80	66	44
fairly satisfied	17	14	17	27
neither satisfied nor dissatisfied	3	1	4	3
somewhat dissatisfied	6 ⎫	3 ⎫	7 ⎫	11 ⎫
	⎬ 11	⎬ 4	⎬ 12	⎬ 26
very dissatisfied	5 ⎭	1 ⎭	5 ⎭	15 ⎭
not stated	1	*	1	1

8.348 Clients who said they had been given a clear idea of probable cost at the outset were, on average, somewhat more satisfied with their solicitor's handling of their affairs than those who said they had not been given a clear idea of cost but had not asked for one. People who had asked for an indication of cost but had not been given one were much more likely than average to be dissatisfied.

Complaints against solicitors

Summary

8.349 Eleven per cent of those who had ever used solicitors' services said that at some time they had felt they had cause for complaint against a solicitor for unsatisfactory work. In many cases, however, this had happened a considerable time ago. Six per cent of those who had made use of solicitors' services during 1977 said they had cause for complaint during 1977 or 1978. The grounds on which people said they had cause for complaint the last time this happened were very similar to the reasons given for dissatisfaction with solicitors' handling of matters, which have been discussed earlier.

8.350 One in three of those who said they had had cause for complaint had actually made a complaint the last time this happened. Compared with those who thought they had cause, the people who actually made complaints were more likely to come from professional, employer and managerial households and were more likely to be older people.

8.351 Two in three of all the complaints said to have been made were made to the solicitor or his firm. Six per cent were made to the Law Society.

8.352 One in three of those who made a complaint on the last occasion they thought they had cause was satisfied with the outcome of the complaint.

The incidence of complaints against solicitors

8.353 We have already discussed client satisfaction and dissatisfaction with solicitors' handling of matters on which they worked during 1977. Those who had been main or sole contacts between their households and a solicitor during 1977 and those others selected for individual interview who had used solicotors' services at some time in their lives were also asked whether they had ever felt they had cause for complaint against a solicitor for unsatisfactory work.

8.354 Eleven per cent of all those who had ever used solicitors' services said that at some time they had felt they had cause for such complant. Many of the occasions on which people felt they had cause for complaint were, however, well in the past. Six per cent of those who had made any use of solicitors' services during 1977 said they felt they had cause for such complaint during 1977 or 1978. Nine per cent of those who had made any use of lawyers' services in the past five years said that they felt they had cause for complaint during that time. Almost half of those who said they had had cause for complaint (47 per cent) said that it had last happened more than five years ago.

8.355 There were no great differences by region, area, type or sex in the numbers of those who had used solicitors who said that at some time they had had cause for complaint over unsatisfactory work. There was some difference, however, by the socio-economic group of the head of the household and by age, as shown in Table 8.51.

TABLE 8.51

Cause for complaint against solicitors: by socio-economic group

	All ever using solicitors' services	Socio-economic group of household head			
		profes-sional/ employer/ manager	inter-mediate/ junior non-manual	skilled manual	semi-skilled/ unskilled manual
Sample (unweighted)	2,409	602	519	727	357
	%	%	%	%	%
Had cause for complaint:					
at any time	11	16	10	10	10
never	86	81	87	89	87
not stated	3	3	3	1	3
Last occasion:					
1977-78	2	2	2	1	2
1976	2	2	1	2	2
1975	1	1	1	1	*
1974	1	1	*	1	—
1973	1	1	*	*	1
1972 or earlier	5	8	5	4	6
not stated when	*	*	*	*	*

8.356 Users of solicitors' services in professional, employer or managerial households were somewhat more likely than average to say they had cause for complaint at some time, but they were no more likely than others to have had cause for complaint over the last two years.

8.357 Naturally enough, users under 25 were less likely than average ever to have had cause for complaint. They were as likely as others, however, to say they had had cause for complaint recently. Also, people aged 65 and over were slightly less likely than average to say they had ever had cause for complaint.

Reasons given for complaints against solicitors

8.358 The main reasons people gave for saying they had cause for complaint on the last occasion this had happened were broadly similar to those given earlier by people saying they were dissatisfied with the way a solicitor had handled matters in 1977. Table 8.52 compares the reasons given.

TABLE 8.52

Reasons client last had cause for complaint and reasons for dissatisfaction[1]

	Reasons had cause for complaint on last occasion	Reasons for dissatisfaction with solicitor used in 1977
Sample (unweighted):	371	255
	%	%
Solicitor did not take an interest in it/did not do enough	33	30
Matter took too long/solicitor was too slow	25	29
Lack of communication/not kept informed of progress	6	15
Solicitor made mistakes/was forgetful	19	9
Solicitor gave bad advice/disagreed with the action he took	14	9
Complaints about solicitor's manner	6	8
Charged too much	15	8
Incurred unnecessary costs/outside costs too high	2	3
Solicitor lacked specialist knowledge for case	2	3
Solicitor was guilty of malpractice/unprofessional behaviour	4	1
Other answer	7	6
Reason not stated	3	3

[1]Answers total over 100 per cent as some had several reasons for complaint or dissatisfaction.

8.359   In both cases, the most common reasons given were that the solicitor took too little interest in the matter or did not appear to have done enough about it and that the solicitor took too long to complete the matter. The numbers giving these as reasons for saying they had cause for complaint were similar to the numbers giving them as reasons for dissatisfaction with solicitors' handling of matters in 1977.

8.360   Other causes for complaint commonly mentioned were that the solicitor was forgetful or made mistakes, that the solicitor gave bad advice or the client disagreed with the action he took and that the solicitor charged too much. People mentioned these somewhat more commonly as causes for complaint than as reasons for saying they were dissatisfied with the solicitor's handling of the matter.

8.361   As when giving their reasons for dissatisfaction, few clients when giving their causes for complaint gave answers which implied that the solicitor had been guilty of any actual malpractice or unprofessional conduct. Only 4 per cent of the answers given about most recent causes for complaint could be interpreted in this way.

Making complaints

8.362 We have talked so far about people who thought they had cause for complaint. In fact, only one in three of those who said they had cause for complaint had actually made a complaint to anyone on the last occasion this happened. Those who said they had cause for complaint at some time and had actually made a complaint the last time this happened thus formed only 4 per cent of those who had ever used solicitors' services.

8.363 The sample of those who said they had actually made a complaint the last time they had cause was small—only 138 people before weighting. Results based on it should be treated with some caution. There are, however, some marked differences between the people who said they had cause for complaint and the people who said they had actually made a complaint the last time this happened. Table 8.53 compares the profiles of all those who had ever used solicitors' services, those who said they had cause for complaint and those who had actually made a complaint the last time this happened.

TABLE 8.53

People with cause for complaint and people who complained:
by age and socio-economic group

	Ever used solicitor's services	Ever had cause for complaint	Complained last time they had cause
Sample (unweighted)	2,409	371	138
	%	%	%
Age:			
18–24	7	5	1
25–29	10	15	8
30–44	32	34	34
45–64	32	36	37
65+	17	9	17
not stated	1	1	2
Socio-economic group of household head:			
professional/employer/manager	22	31	43
intermediate/junior non-manual	21	20	19
skilled manual	34	30	22
semi-skilled/unskilled manual	16	14	8
uncodeable/never worked	7	5	7

8.364 We have noted earlier that people in professional, employer and managerial households were more likely than average to say they had had cause for complaint. They were very much more likely than users of solicitors' services

255

in general to have actually made a complaint to someone the last time this happened. Users in manual households, on the other hand, were less likely than average to have actually made a complaint.

8.365   There was also a difference by age. People under 30 accounted for one in five of those who said they had had cause for complaint but less than one in ten of those who actually complained the last time this happened. People aged 65 and over, on the other hand, who were less likely than average to feel they had cause for complaint, were particularly likely to have complained if they thought they had cause.

8.366   There were no notable differences by sex on this point.

8.367   Where complaints had been made, they had in the considerable majority of cases been made to the solicitor concerned or to his firm. Sixty nine per cent of the complaints respondents said they had made were directed to their solicitors.

8.368   Six per cent of all complaints had been made to the Law Society. The number of complaints said to have been made to the Law Society was too small for anything to be said about them as a separate group.

8.369   Beyond the solicitor himself and the Law Society, 3 per cent of complaints were made to Members of Parliament and the rest were made to a wide variety of other persons and organisations.

8.370   Of those who said they had made a complaint only one in three was satisfied with what was done about it.

Matters which are not taken to solicitors

Summary

8.371   Respondents were asked whether, during 1977, there were any occasions when they felt the sort of help or advice solicitors can give might possibly be useful to them, but they did not in fact contact one. Nine per cent said there were. The sorts of problems they mentioned were very different from the problems actually taken to solicitors. The commonest type mentioned was problems with neighbours. Other problems more commonly mentioned in this context than they were among matters actually taken to solicitors were problems over goods and services, landlord and tenant problems, social security and welfare problems and problems about employment.

8.372   People with problems they did not take to solicitors were more likely than those who consulted solicitors about their problems to have had help or advice from other sources— particularly friends and workmates, the citizens advice bureau or a local authority department. It was only in one case in four where they had such other help or advice that it was suggested they consult a solicitor.

8.373   More than a third said they had not taken the matter to a solicitor because they decided to drop it and a quarter said they did not take it to a solicitor because they managed to resolve the matter without one. A third, however, specifically mentioned cost as a reason for not seeking a solicitor's help or advice.

Matters in which solicitors are not consulted

8.374 Some problems in which solicitors could help are not taken to them. When this study was being designed, there was discussion on whether an attempt should be made to assess how often this happens. It was decided that it should not. The reason for the decision not to attempt to cover this area was that it was considered impossible to make any reliable assessment of this in the context of a large-scale survey with a highly structured questionnaire administered by lay interviewers. Any attempt to do so might produce very misleading data.

8.375 Problems are of many sorts. In some a solicitor can be of no help whatsoever. Deciding whether a problem is one in which a solicitor's services might be helpful or one in which they would not is a technical judgment which lay interviewers are not competent to make. Problems vary in their nature so much that it is impracticable to specify what data should be collected so that this judgment could be made by a qualified person at a later stage.

8.376 It did seem reasonable, however, to ask respondents about problems they had which they did not take to a solicitor but in which they felt at some stage that a solicitor's help or advice might have been useful. It must be stressed, however, that this is quite different from trying to make an objective estimate of the incidence of problems in which solicitors might have been helpful but were not consulted. There are three main differences. First, a person faced with a problem may simply not realise that it is the sort of matter with which a solicitor might deal. Secondly, a person faced with a problem may consider going to a solicitor, but defer this until he has tried to resolve the matter himself or until he has made a final decision whether to take the matter further or not. If his own efforts to resolve the matter are successful or if he decides not to proceed, he has, ultimately, no need for recourse to a solicitor, although this is something that at some stage he has thought might be useful. The third difference concerns people's attitudes to solicitors' services in general. Those whose attitude is wholly negative may be unlikely to think solicitors' services potentially useful, even in situations where others would have immediate recourse to them.

8.377 All those answering the individual questionnaire (those who were main contacts between their households and a solicitor during 1977 and one in ten of all others) were asked whether, during 1977, there were any occasions when they felt that the sort of help or advice solicitors can give might possibly have been useful to them but they did not in fact contact a solicitor. Their answers, weighted together, show that 9 per cent of all adults had some problem of this sort during 1977 which they did not take to a solicitor. This compares with 15 per cent who actually used solicitors' services during the year. In most cases, there was only one matter over the year in which a solicitor might have been used but was not. Only one in eight of those mentioning any matter mentioned more than one.

8.378   Incidence of mention of problems not taken to solicitors in which it was thought they might have been useful varied with socio-economic group. Ten per cent of adults in non-manual households and 8 per cent of those in skilled manual households mentioned such a problem as compared to 5 per cent in semi-skilled manual households and 3 per cent in unskilled manual households.

8.379   Incidence of mention was slightly higher among men than women (11 per cent to 7 per cent). By age it was highest in the 25–34 age group (14 per cent), lowest among those aged 65 and over (4 per cent).

8.380   In these respects, incidence of mention of problems not taken to solicitors follows the pattern of actual use of solicitors, which might suggest that recognition of problems in which a solicitor's advice might be useful goes with a general propensity to use a solicitor. In other respects, however, incidence of mention of problems not taken to solicitors does not follow the pattern of actual use of their services. By tenure, incidence of problems in which it was thought a solicitor might have helped, but in which no solicitor was consulted, was highest among those living in privately rented accommodation (16 per cent). Use of solicitors' services in 1977 was below average among this group. Also, by region, mention of problems not taken to a solicitor was highest in the GLC area (12 per cent). This was the part of the country with the lowest actual incidence of use of solicitors' services.

8.381   There was no close relationship between use of solicitors' services and mention of problems not taken to them in which people thought they might have been of help. Incidence of mention of such problems did not vary between those who were in fact main contacts with solicitors in 1977 and those who were not. A comparison between those who had never at any time made use of solicitors' services and those who had at some time done so shows only a small difference. Ten per cent of those who had used a solicitor's services at some time mentioned a problem not taken to a solicitor in 1977 as compared to 6 per cent of those who had never used a solicitor.

Type of matter

8.382   The types of matter in which people said they had thought, at some time during 1977, that a solicitor's help or advice might be useful but which had not led to consultation with a solicitor were, like the matters actually taken to solicitors, very varied.

8.383   When asked about matters on which solicitors actually were consulted, respondents were asked for a description of the matter which was coded to categories at a later stage. For matters they did not take to solicitors, respondents were asked to pick a category to describe the matter from a show card. The two methods are not strictly comparable. With every allowance made for this, however, it is clear that the matter in which people consider a solicitor's help might be useful, but which they do not take to a solicitor, are very different from the matters on which solicitors are actually consulted. Table 8.54 shows, by type of matter, the matters on which a solicitor's help was not sought.

TABLE 8.54

Matters in which solicitor not consulted in which he might had been useful

	Matters in which a solicitor's help might have been useful but solicitor was not consulted
Sample: all matters (unweighted)	322
	%
Type of matter:	
problems with neighbours	13
buying or selling a house or flat	10
problems about faulty goods or services	10
landlord and tenant problems	9
making or altering a will	7
matrimonial or family problems	6
social security or welfare problems	5
problems about employment, dismissal, etc.	5
debt or hire purchase problems	5
motoring offences	4
other offences	1
compensation for personal injuries	1
dealing with the estate of someone who had died	2
tax or capital transfer problems	4
other financial problems	7
all other problems	9

8.384 Matters of domestic conveyancing, the main type of matter about which solicitors are actually consulted, figure far less prominently in this list than they do among the problems solicitors actually deal with. This is also the case with matters concerning the winding up of estates.

8.385 Types of matter appearing much more frequently in this list than among matters about which solicitors actually are consulted are problems with neighbours, problems over goods and services, landlord and tenant problems, social security and welfare problems and problems about employment.

8.386 In some respects, the matters on which a solicitor's help was considered possibly useful but not sought are closer to the matters on which solicitors, when consulted, gave advice only than to matters in which they took any action. Problems with neighbours, the commonest problem on which a solicitor's help might have been useful but was not sought, accounted for 4 per cent of all consultations with solicitors in which the solicitor gave advice only but for only 1 per cent of the matters in which they took action. Similarly, problems over goods accounted for 7 per cent of consultations in which solicitors gave advice only but for only 2 per cent of cases in which they took any action.

8.387 It will be recalled that the commonest form of advice given by solicitors in cases in which they took no action was on how the client could deal with the matter himself. It may be that some of the problems not taken to solicitors are ones in which all solicitors could have done was to advise clients how to handle the problem themselves. It may be that they can get this advice from other sources.

8.388 Mention of landlord and tenant problems as matters on which a solicitor's advice was thought possibly useful but not sought was, naturally enough, highest among those living in privately rented accommodation. One in twenty of those living in this sort of accommodation mentioned a landlord-tenant problem which they had not taken to a solicitor during 1977. Mention of landlord-tenant problems was also particularly high in the GLC area, where it was the type of problem most commonly mentioned.

8.389 The number of those who had never at any time used a solicitor's services who mentioned problems they had in 1977 in which a solicitor might have been of help was too small for a detailed analysis of the problems they mentioned to yield very reliable results. The sorts of problems they mentioned did not, however, differ substantially from the problems mentioned by people who had experience of using a solicitor.

Advice from people other than solicitors

8.390 We have noted earlier that, in cases where solicitors were consulted, only 27 per cent of people had help or advice in the matter from anyone outside their household before the solicitor was contacted. In matters in which a solicitor's help was thought possibly useful but not sought, the number receiving help or advice from people outside their household was higher – 42 per cent.

8.391 The main sources of outside help or advice are shown in Table 8.55, with the incidence of prior help and service from other sources in cases which actually did lead to consultation with a solicitor shown beside for comparison.

8.392 Three sources of help or advice are commonly mentioned in connection with matters not taken to solicitors—friends or workmates, the citizens advice bureau and local authority departments. All three are a good deal more commonly mentioned in connection with matters not taken to solicitors than in connection with matters which are. It seems plausible to see them as, to some extent, alternatives to the solicitor as sources of help or advice.

TABLE 8.55

Sources of help or advice other than solicitors[1]

	All matters in which solicitors help or advice might have been useful, but solicitor was not consulted	All consultations with solicitors in England and Wales in 1977
Sample (unweighted)	322	2,064
	%	%
Other helpers or advisors:		
friends or workmates	10	4
relatives outside the household	5	3
citizens advice bureau	9	3
estate agent	1	3
bank manager	*	2
insurance broker	*	1
building society	—	1
accountant	1	1
employer	*	1
trade union	*	2
local authority department	8	2
DHSS/benefit office	1	1
non-governmental advice centre/pressure group	4	1
police	3	1
other	3	3
no-one	55	73
not stated	3	—

[1]Table totals to over 100 per cent as some respondents mentioned more than one helper.

8.393 There was no difference between people in manual and non-manual households in the numbers saying they had had help or advice from others in matters which they did not take to solicitors. Their helpers or advisors were, however, somewhat different. Those in non-manual households were particularly likely to get help or advice from friends or workmates. None of them mentioned help or advice from advice centres or pressure groups or help or advice from the police. These were mentioned exclusively by people in manual households.

8.394 The citizens advice bureau was mentioned equally frequently by people in manual and in non-manual households.

261

8.395   We have noted earlier that, in three-quarters of cases where a solicitor was consulted but help or advice was obtained from someone else first, someone had suggested that the matter be taken to a solicitor. With matters in which respondents had thought a solicitor's help or advice might be useful but a solicitor was not consulted, the situation was quite different. A quarter of those who had help or advice from others in such matters said that someone had suggested they should take the matter to a solicitor.

Reasons for not using solicitors

8.396   Those mentioning matters in which they had considered a solicitor's advice might be useful, but who had not consulted one were asked whether there was any particular reason why they had not done so. Their answers are shown in Table 8.56.

TABLE 8.56

Reason matter not taken to solicitor[1]

	All matters in which solicitor's help or advice might have been useful but solicitor was not consulted
Sample (unweighted):	322
	%
Deterred by cost of solicitor's services	33
Matter resolved without outside help	16
Matter resolved with help of friend/other non-lawyer	8
Matter dropped on advice of friend/other non-lawyer	3
Matter dropped for other reasons	33
Do not trust solicitors	3
Did not know a solicitor	*
Other reasons	7
Not answered	8

[1]Table totals over 100 per cent as some respondents gave more than one reason.

8.397   In 36 per cent of cases, the reason the matter was not taken to a solicitor was that it was dropped. In 24 per cent of cases the reason was that it was resolved without need for recourse to a solicitor.

8.398   In one case in three, however, the cost of the solicitor's services was given as a reason for not going to one.

8.399   Very few people (3 per cent) gave distrust of solicitors as a reason for not using them. Hardly anyone gave the fact he did not know a solicitor as a reason for not using one (as we saw earlier, most people have fairly clear ideas on how they would find a solicitor if they wanted one).

8.400   People in manual households were somewhat more likely than those in non-manual households to give cost as a reason for not using solicitors (38 per cent to 27 per cent) and people in rented accommodation were somewhat more likely to mention cost than those in owner-occupied accommodation (39 per cent to 29 per cent).

Other topics of enquiry

Summary

8.401   Almost two in three adults claimed to have heard of the Law Society, but only one in three could give some account of what it is and what it does. One in six specifically mentioned that it investigates complaints by the public against solicitors. Among those who had been sole or main contacts with solicitors during 1977, half could give some account of the nature and functions of the Law Society. Just over one in four mentioned that it investigates complaints.

8.402   More than four in five had heard of the legal aid scheme and more than three in five were aware that people on lower incomes can qualify for help under it.

8.403   Five per cent said there was someone in their household with professional legal training and 16 per cent said there was some such person among their other relatives or close friends. The professional legal training referred to, however, was usually study of some aspects of law as part of the training for some other job.

Awareness of the Law Society

8.404   This chapter covers some topics covered in the survey which were not directly related to the use of solicitors' services. The first of these is awareness of the Law Society. Respondents to the Individual Questionnaire were asked whether they had ever heard of the Law Society. If they said they had, they were asked to say what it is and what it does. Their answers were then checked against the main actual functions of the Law Society. The answers given, analysed by past use of legal services, are shown in Table 8.57.

8.405   Almost two in three respondents claimed to have heard of the Law Society. Half of these, however, were unable to give even a partially correct account of what it is and what it does. The proportion of all adults who were able to give some account of its functions was 32 per cent.

8.406   The point most commonly made about the Law Society was that it investigates complaints against solicitors by members of the public. This point was mentioned spontaneously by one adult in six. Other points commonly mentioned were that it is the solicitors' professonal organisation and sets rules for the professional behaviour of solicitors.

263

TABLE 8.57

Awareness of the Law Society: by past use of solicitors

		Past use of legal services		
	All adults	main/sole contact with a solicitor in 1977	other past users of solicitors' services	never used solicitors' services
Sample (unweighted)	3,016	1,782	627	607
	%	%	%	%
Heard of Law Society	64	78	72	53
Law Society:				
investigates complaints against solicitors by the public	17	28	23	6
sets rules for the professional behaviour of solicitors	11	12	15	5
the professional organisation for solicitors	11	22	12	8
helps run the legal aid scheme	3	5	3	3
advises on charges for legal work	1	2	1	*
licenses solicitors to practice	1	1	1	*
advertises solicitors' services on press or TV	*	1	*	1
all mentioning any of these points	32	51	42	19
claimed to have heard of Law Society but mentioned none of these points	32	27	30	34
have not heard of Law Society	35	18	28	47
not stated	1	4	*	—

8.407 As one might expect, awareness of the Law Society and its functions was higher among those who had used the services of solicitors than among those who had not. Among those who had been main or sole contacts between their households and a solicitor during 1977, half (51 per cent) said they had heard of the Law Society and were able to give at least a partially correct account of what it does. This compares with one person in five among those who had never used a solicitor.

8.408 Of those who had been main or sole contacts with solicitors in 1977, just over one in four (28 per cent) said spontaneously that one of the functions of the Law Society is to investigate complaints made against solicitors by members of the public.

8.409 Awareness of the Law Society and what it does varied with use of solicitors' services. Among different groups within the population it varied in the same way as use of solicitors' services. More men than women could give a wholly or partly correct account of the nature or functions of the Law Society (40 per cent to 26 per cent). People under 25 were slightly less likely than average to be able to do so, as were people between 55 and 64. Those aged 65 and over were particularly unlikely to be able to do so. Only 18 per cent in that age group could give a wholly or partly correct account of the Law Society and its functions.

8.410 Table 8.58 shows the level of awareness of the Law Society by socio-economic group of household head.

TABLE 8.58

Awareness of the Law Society: by socio-economic group of household head

	Sample (un-weighted)	Claimed to have heard of Law Society	Gave partly/ wholly correct account of Law Society	Mentioned Law Society investigates complaints
All Adults	3,016	% 64	32	17
Socio-economic group of household head:				
professional	191	% 87	64	33
employer/manager	502	% 75	48	23
intermediate and junior non-manual	601	% 76	41	19
skilled manual and own-account workers	947	% 62	28	16
semi-skilled manual	382	% 52	21	12
unskilled manual	133	% 45	14	6

Awareness of the legal aid scheme

8.411 Individual questionnaire respondents were also asked whether they had ever heard of the legal aid scheme and, if they had, under what circumstances people could qualify for legal aid. More than four in five respondents (84 per cent) said they had heard of the scheme. More than three in five (62 per cent) said it was for people of low income or gave examples of low-income people who might qualify.

8.412 Awareness of the legal aid scheme varied less with experience of using solicitors' services than awareness of the Law Society. Eighty nine per cent of those who had been sole or main contacts with a solicitor during 1977 and 89 per cent of those who had used a solicitor's services previously to that said they had heard of the scheme. Among those who had never used a solicitor's services, claimed awareness was 79 per cent. The level of spontaneous connection of the scheme with people on low incomes was 72 per cent among 1977 main or sole contacts, 67 per cent among others who had used solicitors' services and 52 per cent among those who had never used them.

Legal Training

8.413   Individual questionnaire respondents were asked whether they themselves had any professional legal training, whether any other member of their household had any professional legal training and whether any of their other relatives or close friends had any professional legal training.

8.414   Three per cent claimed to have some professional legal training themselves. Five per cent claimed that either they or some other member of their household had professional legal training. Sixteen per cent said they had other relatives or close friends with professional legal training.

8.415   In almost all cases, however, the professional legal training referred to was not professional legal training as a solicitor or barrister. In most cases, the people mentioned as having professional legal training had done some courses in aspects of law as part of training for some other profession (most commonly banking, accountancy, etc.).

8.416   Incidence of professional legal training in the household and among other relatives or close friends varied sharply, as one might expect, with the socio-economic group of the household head.

TABLE 8.59

Contact with people with professional legal training: by socio-economic group

	Sample (un-weighted)	Member of household has professional legal training	Other relative or close friend has profes-sional legal training
All adults	3,016	% 5	16
Socio-economic group of household head:			
professional	191	% 28	44
employer/manager	502	% 9	25
intermediate and junior non-manual	601	% 8	22
skilled manual and own-account workers	947	% 2	11
semi-skilled manual	382	% 1	7
unskilled manual	133	% *	10

ANNEX 8.1

Sampling, field work and sample structure

The sample covered

A8.1.1   The survey was intended to cover persons aged 18 or over living in private households in England and Wales. Those living in institutions (hospitals, hotels, army barracks, etc.) were excluded. They form a very small proportion of the total population and the special measures which would have been required to deal with them were not felt to be justified.

A8.1.2   The sample issued to interviewers consisted of 10,000 addresses selected from the electoral registers, split into 250 batches of 40 addresses each. The 250 batches of addresses were spread over 125 constituencies randomly selected with probability proportional to size of electorate after stratification by region and population density and by level of car ownership (as an indicator of social composition). Within each selected constituency, two polling districts were randomly selected with probability proportional to size of electorate and within each polling district, 40 addresses were randomly selected from the district register with equal probability.

Selection of constituencies

A8.1.3   The 552 parliamentary constituencies in England and Wales were divided into 20 groups as follows.

(a)   Constituencies were split between the Registrar General's nine standard regions.

(b)   Constituencies in the South East region were further split between those in the GLC area and others. Constituencies in the other four regions which contain metropolitan counties were further split between metropolitan county constituencies and others.

(c)   Constituencies in the East Midlands, the South West, Wales and the GLC area were further divided into two groups on the basis of the numbers of electors per acre in each constituency. Constituencies in the South East outside the GLC area were divided in this way into three groups.

Within each of the 20 groups of constituencies so created, constituencies were listed in order of the percentage of their households who owned or had the use of cars at the time of the 1971 census.

A8.1.4   The electorate of each constituency was recorded and electorates were cumulated throughout the list. One hundred and twenty five constituencies were then selected from the list by the random starting point and fixed interval method, working on the cumulated electorate figures. This gives a sample of constituencies selected randomly with probability proportional to electorate after stratification by region, an indicator of population density and an indicator of social composition.

A8.1.5   The spread of the selected constituencies between the 20 groups is shown in Table A8.1.1.

Selection of polling districts

A8.1.6   The polling districts within each selected constituency were listed from the electoral registers and their electorates recorded. Some rural polling districts are very small and their selection would have entailed an undesirably close clustering of addresses. To avoid this, before proceeding with selection polling districts with electorates below 400 were combined with adjacent districts on the list to produce units with electorates of 400 or more.

A8.1.7   After this operation, district electorates were cumulated within constituencies and two districts (or district groups) selected for each constituency by the random starting point and fixed interval method.

267

TABLE A8.1.1
Distribution of constituencies

		Number of constituencies	Number of constituencies selected
North	—metropolitan counties	14	3
	—other	23	5
North West	—metropolitan counties	46	10
	—other	30	7
Yorkshire & Humberside	—metropolitan counties	40	9
	—other	15	3
West Midlands	—metropolitan counties	32	7
	—other	24	6
East Midlands	—1+ electors per acre	22	5
	—less than 1 elector per acre	17	5
East Anglia		17	4
South West	—1+ electors per acre	19	4
	—less than 1 elector per acre	27	7
GLC	—10+ electors per acre	72	15
	—less than 10 electors per acre	20	4
Rest of South East	—3+ electors per acre	32	7
	—1+ but under 3 electors per acre	34	9
	—less than 1 elector per acre	32	8
Wales	—1+ electors per acre	21	4
	—less than 1 elector per acre	15	3
	Total	552	125

Selection of Addresses

A8.1.8 The final aim was to include in the sample all adults living at each address selected. This meant that, if each adult living at addresses on the register was to have an equal chance of selection, addresses should be selected from the register with equal probability. But an address appears in the register once for each elector living there. On average across England and Wales, there are 215 register entries for every 100 addresses.

A8.1.9 Addresses were selected from the register by the random starting point and fixed interval method. The problem of multiple mention of addresses was dealt with by adjusting the fixed interval. To select a sample of 40 electors from a register with equal probability, one would set the fixed interval by dividing the electorate by 40. To select a sample of addresses with equal probability, we set the fixed interval by dividing the electorate by 92 (40 x 2.3). A sample of electors was then selected but their addresses were included in the sample only if the selected elector was the first elector listed for that address in the register. Thus each address had one and only one chance for inclusion.

A8.1.10   A factor of 2·3, higher than the average elector-address ratio, was used to allow for variation in the elector-address ratio between polling districts and to allow for institutional addresses. Any address which was clearly institutional in character was deleted from the sample. After deletion of institutional addresses, the sample in each polling district was reduced to 40 by random deletion.

Addresses which do not appear in the registers

A8.1.11   The electoral registers do not list all the addresses in England and Wales where private households currently live. The main reasons for omission are that the address was empty or in other use at the time the register was compiled but has since been occupied by a private household, that the people occupying the premises are aliens, that the occupants have failed to complete the statutory return to the Registration Officer or that the premises have been newly built since the time the register was compiled.

A8.1.12   It is to be expected that, as time passes, the accuracy of the registers as a list of private household addresses will decrease. The registers used to select the sample were those published in February 1977, for which data were collected in October 1976. At the time fieldwork started, they were 15 months old.

A8.1.13   The deficiencies of the registers were partly dealt with by a special sampling technique. Most registers are arranged by street and, within a street, by physical order of addresses, first down one side of the street, then down the other. The only cases where this does not happen are very rural polling districts where a substantial proportion of addresses are not in streets. In these cases, the register is arranged by alphabetic order of surname of elector. There were 17 sampling points of this sort out of the 250 covered in the survey.

A8.1.14   At all other points, the sample issue sheets given to interviewers showed not only the addresses selected from the registers, but also, for each address, the next address listed in that street in the register. In the field, interviewers checked whether, between the sampled address and the next listed address, there were any other residential premises occupied by a private household. (If the sampled address was the last shown in the street in the register, interviewers were told this and checked to see whether there were, in fact, any more.) Any intervening address so identified which was currently occupied by a private household was added to the sample.

A8.1.15   This method covers many of the private household addresses which do not appear in the registers. It does not, however, cover all. We have already noted that it cannot be used in polling districts with alphabetic registers. It also, clearly does not cover cases of wholly new developments, where a new street was occupied for the first time since October 1976.

Fieldwork—the interviewer's task

A8.1.16   Interviewers were instructed to seek to interview at each private household living at the addresses selected from the registers and at each private household living at any intervening addresses they identified. If more than one household lived at an address, they sought separate interviews with each.

A8.1.17   In the interview, the interviewer had to seek information on any use of legal services during 1977 by any adult member of the household. This information was sought personally from each adult, with the sole exception that a husband might be taken as a proxy respondent on his wife's use of legal services in 1977 and a wife might be taken as a proxy respondent on her husband's. Beyond this, no proxy response was permitted. Interviewers were instructed to make a minimum of four suitably spaced calls at an address before abandoning any adult living there as impossible to contact.

A8.1.18   If someone in the household was identified as a main contact between the household and a lawyer over some matter during 1977, the interviewer was instructed to seek to complete a use sheet with that person about that matter. In this case, no proxy response of any sort was permitted.

A8.1.19   In some cases, some members of a household were willing to co-operate while others were unwilling or were impossible to contact. In such cases, a household was classed as successfully covered if the screening information on use of legal services was obtained for the head of the household and, where this was another person, for the housewife. If information on these people was not obtained, the partial interview was discarded.

Fieldwork organisation

A8.1.20   Fieldwork on the survey was carried out by a total of 186 interviewers, between 6 January and 2 April, 1978. All interviewers taking part in the survey were personally briefed by a researcher or field supervisor before starting interviewing.

A8.1.21   As a routine field control measure, 20 addresses at each of 50 sampling points were issued to supervisors for personal recall. Also, six addresses at each of 200 points were selected for postal checking, which was carried out at such of these addresses as produced completed questionnaires.

Result of fieldwork

A8.1.22   The results of fieldwork are given in Table A8.1.2. Overall response rate was 80 per cent. The special measures taken to cover addresses which do not appear in the electoral registers increased the number of occupied residential addresses covered and the total number of interviews carried out by 2 per cent.

Response rate in screening

A8.1.23   We have noted earlier that, in screening for use of legal services in 1977, husbands and wives could be accepted as proxy respondents on each other's behalf. We have also noted that, in some cases, interviews were accepted which did not include screening data for all household members.

A8.1.24   In the 7,941 households where acceptable interviews were carried out, there were in total 15,907 people aged 18 or over. The success rate in screening is shown in Table A8.1.3. The total number of people from whom data were collected was 11,707. They reported on the behaviour of 15,441 people.

A8.1.25   Screening information was obtained for 97 per cent of the people aged 18 or over in the households at which acceptable interviews were carried out. The comparison between those for whom screening information was obtained and those for whom it was not is shown in Table A8.1.6.

Response to the use sheet

A8.1.26   If, from the screening data, it appeared that a person had been the sole or main contact between his or her household and a lawyer over any personal matter during 1977, interviewers were instructed to complete a use sheet with that person about that matter. A limit of two was set on the number of use sheets to be completed with any one respondent. If a respondent had been the main or sole contact with a lawyer over three or more matters, use sheets were completed only on the first two in which he or she had dealings with a lawyer during 1977.

270

TABLE A8.1.2

Fieldwork results

	Main sample		Intervening addresses		Total sample	
	No.	%	No.	%	No.	%
Issued addresses	10,000					
Less:						
empty/derelict/demolished	314					
business/industrial premises only	19					
institution only	11					
untraceable	113					
Traced, residential and occupied	9,543		210		9,753	
Plus:						
additional households found at addresses	144		5		149	
Total possible household interviews	9,687	100	215	100	9,902	100
Less:						
refused	928	10	15	7	943	10
no contact with anyone after 4+ calls	641	7	11	5	652	7
no contact with qualified respondent after 4+ calls	81	1	1	*	82	1
qualified respondent broke appointment and could not be recontacted	44	*	1	*	45	*
qualified respondent away/in hospital	94	1	4	2	98	1
qualified respondent ill/senile/ incapacitated	75	1	—	—	75	1
inadequate English spoken	35	*	13	6	48	*
other reasons for no interview	18	*	—	—	18	*
Total households not interviewed	1,916	20	45	21	1,961	20
Total households interviewed	7,771	80	170	79	7,941	80

A.8.1.27 The screening data obtained indicated that use sheets should have been completed with 1,869 people about 2,131 matters. In fact, use sheets were completed with 1,784 people (96 per cent of the indicated total) about 2,040 matters (96 per cent of the indicated total).

A8.1.28 It has been noted earlier that, if a married person in the household was unavailable, his or her spouse could be used as a proxy respondent on use of legal services, but that no proxy response was accepted for the completion of use sheets. The main reason for use sheets not being completed where they were indicated was that use information was obtained by proxy on a spouse who was temporarily away, sick or otherwise unable to give an interview or who could not be contacted by the interviewer after repeated calls.

TABLE A8.1.3

Response rate in screening

	All persons aged 18+ in households interviewed	
Sample	15,907	
	No.	%
Screening data obtained—personally	11,707	74
—by proxy from spouse	3,734	23
Screening data not obtained	466	3

Response to the individual questionnaire

A8.1.29   The individual questionnaire was to be asked of all those completing use sheets and in fact was successfully completed with all but two such persons. In addition, it was to be asked of a randomly selected one in ten of all people in the household who had not been sole or main contacts with a lawyer over any matter during 1977.

A8.1.30   Of the 15,907 people aged 18 or over identified in the households where successful interviews were carried out, 14,038 either had not been main or sole contacts with lawyers during 1977 or no screening information was obtained for them.

A8.1.31   The method used in random selection of one in ten adults was itself subject to sampling error and indicated that 1,399 individual interviews with non-users should have been sought as compared with the theoretical figure of 1,404. In fact, the number of individual questionnaires completed with such people was 1,234, 92 per cent of the indicated total.

A8.1.32   It was noted earlier that screening data were not obtained for 4 per cent of the adults in the households covered. Where this occurred, completion of an individual questionnaire could not be expected either. Beyond this, the main reasons for failure to complete individual questionnaires were that persons for whom screening data were obtained from a spouse by proxy were temporarily away, ill or otherwise unable to be interviewed or that they could not be contacted by the interviewer after repeated calls.

Sample structure: households

A8.1.33   By household size and tenure, the comparison between the households covered in this survey and those covered in England and Wales by the 1976 OPCS General Household Survey, is shown in Table A8.1.4.

Sample structure: region

A8.1.34   Table A8.1.5 shows the comparison between the spread by region of the individuals aged 18 or over identified in households successfully interviewed in this survey and the spread of the total England and Wales population shown by the 1971 census.

Demographic characteristics of sample

A8.1.35   The characteristics of the survey sample by sex, age and marital status are compared in Table A8.1.6 with 1971 census figures. Four breakdowns of the survey figures are shown below.

(a) All persons aged 18 plus reported in households at which acceptable interviews were carried out.

TABLE A8.1.4

Household size and tenure

	This survey	General Household Survey 1976
Sample: all households	7,941	
	%	%
Number of persons in household (all ages)		
1 person	19	21
2 people	34	32
3 people	17	17
4 people	18	17
5 or more people	12	13
not ascertained	*	—
Tenure		
owned: outright	25	23
on a mortgage	31	30
rented: from council/new town	29	31
privately furnished	3	3
privately unfurnished	9	} 13
other	2	
not ascertained	1	—

TABLE A8.1.5

Region

	This survey (all persons 18+)	1971 census (all persons)
Sample	15,907	
	%	%
Region: North	7	7
North West	13	14
Yorkshire & Humberside	10	10
West Midlands	12	10
East Midlands	9	7
East Anglia	4	3
South West	9	8
Wales	6	6
GLC Area	13	15
Rest of South East	19	20

(b) All persons aged 18 plus reported in such households for whom screening information on use of legal services in 1977 was obtained.

(c) All persons aged 18 plus reported in such households for whom screening information was not obtained.

(d) All persons asked the individual questionnaire. Interviewers sought to complete this questionnaire with all those who were sole or main contacts with a solicitor over some personal matter during 1977 and one in ten of all others aged 18 or over in the household covered. The figures below are based on the sample after weighting to correct this imbalance.

A8.1.36 Those for whom screening data were not obtained were predominantly young, single people and the sample for whom screening data were obtained was slightly short on people of this sort. The difference was, however, extremely small.

A8.1.37 Despite the random exclusion of nine in ten adults who were not sole or main contacts with a lawyer in 1977, the sample asked the individual questionnaire after weighting also closely matches population data from the census.

TABLE A8.1.6
Sex, age and marital status

	All persons 18+ in households interviewed	Persons 18+ for whom screening data were not obtained	Persons 18+ for whom screening data were obtained	Individual question- naire sample	All persons 18+ (1971 census)
Sample (unweighted)	15,907	466	15,441	3,016	
	%	%	%	%	%
Sex: men	48	53	48	46	48
women	52	46	52	54	52
not ascertained	*	1	*	*	—
Age: 18–24	12	43	11	13	14
25–29	10	10	10	9	9
30–34	10	6	10	10	8
35–44	16	10	16	16	16
45–54	17	8	17	17	17
55–64	15	8	15	16	17
65+	19	12	20	18	18
not ascertained	2	4	2	1	—
Marital status:					
married	72	24	73	71	71
single	15	60	14	16	18
widowed	9	9	9	⎫	10
divorced	2	3	2	⎬ 12	1
separated	1	1	1	⎭	included as married
not ascertained	1	3	1	1	—

ANNEX 8.2

Survey questionnaire

(paragraph 8.8)

SOCIAL & COMMUNITY PLANNING RESEARCH
Main Office: 16 Duncan Terrace, London N1 8BZ   Tel: 01-278 2061

P.491

P.491 (1–3)
Record No. (4–7)
Card 100 (8–10)

LEGAL SERVICES SURVEY
Household Questionnaire

Area Code [ ][ ][ ][ ] (11–14)

No. of electors listed at
address (from S.I.S.)   [ ][ ] (19–20)

Address Serial No. [ ][ ] (15–16)

No. of households at address
(from Address Contact Sheet)   [ ] (21)

Household No. [ ] (17)   last digit ↑

Day	Month
[ ][ ]	[ ][ ]

Date of interview   (22–25)

Intervening Address: (18)

Hours	Mins
[ ][ ]	[ ][ ]

Identified	1
Not identified	2
This is intervening address	3

Time interview started   (26–29)

24 hour clock

1.

THE INFORMATION AT Q.1 MAY BE OBTAINED FROM ANY HOUSE-HOLD MEMBER AGED 18 OR OVER.

(a)   First I'd like to check what people aged [18 or over] live with you in this household

Person number	Relationship to Head of Household	Sex M F	Age last birth-day	Marital status					Employment status Working Full time (31+ hrs a week)	Part time (10–30 hrs a week)	Not work-ing	
				M	S	Wid	Div	Sep				
1	Head of Household	1 2							1	2	3	(30–34)
2		1 2							1	2	3	(35–39)
3		1 2							1	2	3	(40–44)
4		1 2							1	2	3	(45–49)
5		1 2							1	2	3	(50–54)
6		1 2							1	2	3	(55–59)
7		1 2							1	2	3	(60–64)
8		1 2							1	2	3	(65–69)

No. of persons aged under 18 in household   [ ]   (70)

Total no. of persons in household   [ ][ ]   (71–72)

Card 100

Col./ Code	Skip to

PUT QUESTION 2 INDIVIDUALLY TO EACH PERSON
18+ IN HOUSEHOLD.
THE ONLY EXCEPTION IS THAT YOU MAY ASK
HUSBANDS AND WIVES FOR INFORMATION ABOUT
THEIR SPOUSES IF AND ONLY IF YOU FIRST ASK:

"Are you able to answer these questions about your husband/
wife with certainty?"

AND THE ANSWER IS A CLEAR YES.

	Person number (from H/H Grid)							
	1	2	3	4	5	6	7	8
	(73)	(74)	(75)	(76)	(77)	(78)	(79)	(80)
Information obtained —personally	1	1	1	1	1	1	1	1
—from spouse	2	2	2	2	2	2	2	2
Information not obtained	3	3	3	3	3	3	3	3
Reason not obtained (WRITE IN)								
O.U.O.								

	Col./Code	Skip to
ASK SEPARATELY OF EACH PERSON AGED 18+	P.491 (1–3) Record No. (4–7) Card 200 (8–10)	

2. I am going to ask some questions about any dealings of any sort you may have had with solicitors or other lawyers *last year*, during 1977. SHOW CARD A. These are the sorts of people and the sorts of matters I mean.

(a) During 1977, did any solicitor or other lawyer do any work for you, start doing any work for you or give you help or advice of any sort? (PLEASE INCLUDE ANYTHING THAT STARTED EARLIER AND CARRIED ON INTO 1977) RECORD IN GRID BELOW.

(b) During 1977, did anyone else *outside this household* get any help or advice from a solicitor or other lawyer on your behalf, *or* have anything done by one on your behalf?

IF YES TO (a) OR (b) ASK (c) OR (d) OF THAT PERSON

(c) In any of these matters, were you acting as an employee *on behalf of your employer*?

(d) (Excluding matters where you were acting on behalf of your employer) on how many separate matters did you have advice or help from a solicitor or other lawyer during 1977?

NOW REPEAT Q.2 FOR NEXT PERSON.
IF NO OTHER PERSON SKIP TO Q.6.

		Person number (from H/H Grid)							
		1	2	3	4	5	6	7	8
(a)	Yes	(11) 1	(15) 1	(19) 1	(23) 1	(27) 1	(31) 1	(35) 1	(39) 1
	No	2	2	2	2	2	2	2	2
(b)	Yes	(12) 1	(16) 1	(20) 1	(24) 1	(28) 1	(32) 1	(36) 1	(40) 1
	No	2	2	2	2	2	2	2	2
(c)	Yes—acted for employer	(13) 1	(17) 1	(21) 1	(25) 1	(29) 1	(33) 1	(37) 1	(41) 1
	No—did not	2	2	2	2	2	2	2	2
(d)	Number of personal matters (WRITE IN) ...	(14)	(18)	(22)	(26)	(30)	(34)	(38)	(42)

277

Card 200

	Col./ Code	Skip to

3. ASK SEPARATELY OF EACH PERSON MENTIONING
ANY MATTER AT Q.2(d)

(a) On the matter on which you had help or advice from a solicitor
(lawyer) most recently, was any other member of your household who lives with you now involved in any way? RECORD
BELOW.

(b) IF YES TO (a) Which of the people in this household now
was the person most closely in contact with the solicitor
(lawyer) about this matter? Was it you or was it someone else?

Person number (from H/H Grid)									
	1	2	3	4	5	6	7	8	
	(43)	(44)	(45)	(46)	(47)	(48)	(49)	(50)	
(a) Other H/H member was involved	A	A	A	A	A	A	A	A	
No other H/H member was involved	1	1	1	1	1	1	1	1	COMPLETE USE SHEET FOR THIS MATTER
(b) This person was main contact	2	2	2	2	2	2	2	2	
Other H/H member was main contact	3	3	3	3	3	3	3	3	NO USE SHEET REQUIRED

IF 1 MATTER ONLY FOR THAT PERSON AT Q.2(d)
SKIP TO NEXT PERSON OR Q.6
IF 2+ MATTERS ASK Q.4

4. ASK SEPARATELY OF EACH PERSON MENTIONING
2+ MATTERS AT Q.2(d)

(a) On the matter on which you had help or advice from a solicitor
(lawyer) next most recently, was any other member of your
household who lives with you now involved in any way?
RECORD BELOW.

(b) IF YES TO (a) Which of the people in this household now
was the person most closely in contact with the solicitor
(lawyer) about this matter? Was it you or was it someone else?

Person number (from H/H Grid)									
	1	2	3	4	5	6	7	8	
	(51)	(52)	(53)	(54)	(55)	(56)	(57)	(58)	
(a) Other H/H member was involved	A	A	A	A	A	A	A	A	
No other H/H member was involved	1	1	1	1	1	1	1	1	COMPLETE USE SHEET FOR THIS MATTER
(b) This person was main contact	2	2	2	2	2	2	2	2	
Other H/H member was main contact	3	3	3	3	3	3	3	3	NO USE SHEET REQUIRED

IF 2 MATTERS ONLY FOR THAT PERSON AT Q.2(d)
SKIP TO NEXT PERSON OR Q.6.
IF 3+ MATTERS ASK Q.5.

Card 200

	Col./ Code	Skip to

5.

ASK SEPARATELY OF EACH PERSON MENTIONING 3+ MATTERS AT Q.2(d).

SHOW CARD B. So far I have asked about two matters. You mentioned earlier that there were ....(NUMBER) more. What were these other matters about? Anything else? PROBE TO "No".

CODE AS MANY AS APPLY

	Person number (from H/H Grid)							
	1	2	3	4	5	6	7	8
	(59)	(61)	(63)	(65)	(67)	(69)	(71)	(73)
Buying or selling a house or flat ...	1	1	1	1	1	1	1	1
Making a will	2	2	2	2	2	2	2	2
Dealing with the estate of someone who has died	3	3	3	3	3	3	3	3
Matrimonial or family problems (divorce etc.)	4	4	4	4	4	4	4	4
Social security or welfare rights problems	5	5	5	5	5	5	5	5
Problems about employment, dismissal etc.	6	6	6	6	6	6	6	6
Problems about faulty goods or services	7	7	7	7	7	7	7	7
Debt or hire purchase problems ...	8	8	8	8	8	8	8	8
Landlord and tenant problems ...	9	9	9	9	9	9	9	9
Problems with neighbours ...	0	0	0	0	0	0	0	0
Compensation for personal injuries	X	X	X	X	X	X	X	X
Motoring offences	Y	Y	Y	Y	Y	Y	Y	Y
	(60)	(62)	(64)	(66)	(68)	(70)	(72)	(74)
Other offences or criminal charges	1	1	1	1	1	1	1	1
Tax or capital transfer problems...	2	2	2	2	2	2	2	2
Other financial problems ...	3	3	3	3	3	3	3	3
Other (SPECIFY)								

(75–80) Blank

279

		Col./ Code	Skip to

FOR ALL HOUSEHOLDS

6. (a) AT QUESTIONS 3 & 4 YOU HAVE
IDENTIFIED THE PEOPLE FOR WHOM
USE SHEETS MUST BE ASKED.
SUMMARISE THIS BELOW.

P. 491   (1–3)
Record No.   (4–7)
Card 300   (8–10)

Use sheet required					No use sheet required	
Person No. (H/H Grid)	No. of Sheets required	Completed Yes	No		Person No. in H/H Grid (write in)	Non-user Code
	1 2	1	2	(11–13)		A
	1 2	1	2	(14–16)		B
	1 2	1	2	(17–19)		C
	1 2	1	2	(20–22)		D
	1 2	1	2	(23–25)		E
	1 2	1	2	(26–28)		F
	1 2	1	2	(29–31)		G
	1 2	1	2	(32–34)		H

TOTAL No. FOR WHOM NO USE SHEET   ☐   (35)
REQUIRED

IF EVERYONE AGED 18+ IN THE HOUSEHOLD HAS
TO COMPLETE ONE OR MORE USE SHEETS, SKIP TO
Q.7. OTHERWISE CHECK ON GRID AT (b) WHETHER
INDIVIDUAL INTERVIEW WITH NON-USER (PERSON
NOT SOLE OR MAIN USER) IS REQUIRED.

280

Card 300

		Col./ Code	Skip to

(b) REFER TO TOTAL No. OF NON-USERS AND LAST DIGIT OF ADDRESS SERIAL NUMBER. THIS WILL LEAD YOU TO ONE BOX ON THE GRID BELOW. IF THE BOX IS BLANK, NO INDIVIDUAL INTERVIEW WITH A NON-USER IS REQUIRED. IF THERE IS A CODE LETTER IN THE BOX, SEEK AN INDIVIDUAL INTERVIEW WITH THE PERSON WITH THAT NON-USER CODE IN THE LIST ABOVE.

Total non-users 18+	Last digit of Address Serial Number									
	1	2	3	4	5	6	7	8	9	0
1	A			NO INDIVIDUAL						
2	B	A		INTERVIEW WITH NON-USER						
3	C	B	A	REQUIRED						
4	D	C	B	A						
5	E	D	C	B	A					
6	F	E	D	C	B	A				
7	G	F	E	D	C	B	A			
8	H	G	F	E	D	C	B	A		

INDIVIDUAL INTERVIEW REQUIRED WITH NON-USER OF CODE INDICATED

(36)

WRITE IN:
No individual interview required with non-user   1   Q.7
Individual interview required with non-user   2

Person No. of selected non-user (from H/H Grid) ... [ ]   (37)

(38)
Interview achieved with selected non-user   1   Q.7
Interview not achieved with selected non-user   2

Reason for no interview...

Card 300

	Col./ Code	Skip to

INFORMATION AT Q.7 AND Q.8 MAY BE OBTAINED FROM HEAD OF HOUSEHOLD OR HOUSEWIFE ONLY.

FOR ALL HOUSEHOLDS

7. (a) Do you own this accommodation or do you rent it?.

IF OWNED Do you own it outright or on a mortgage?

IF RENTED Do you rent it from the council or from a private landlord?

IF PRIVATE LANDLORD Do you rent it furnished or unfurnished?

(39)

OWNED
outright 1
on a mortgage 2
RENTED
from Council or New Town Corporation 3
from private landlord furnished 4
from private landlord unfurnished 5

Other (SPECIFY)..........

(40)

(b) For how many years have you lived at this address?
Under 1 year 1
1 but under 2 years 2
2 but under 3 years 3
3 but under 4 years 4
4 but under 5 years 5
5 but under 10 years 6
10 years or more 7

FOR ALL HOUSEHOLDS

8. Occupation of Head of Household (Present or last main job)

Name/title of job ....

Description of activity..........

Skill/qualifications/experience required..........

O.U.O.

Supervision/management responsibilities (including number supervised)..........

(41)   (42)

Industry/business/profession of employer..........

No. of people employed at place of work: 1 only   A
2–24   B
25+   C

Employment status: Employee   A
Self-employed   B

	Hrs.	Mins.	
Time interview completed			(43–46)
Interviewer No.			(47–50)

Signature of Interviewer

....

(51–80)   Blank

282

P.491   LEGAL SERVICES SURVEY

USE SHEET   January 1978

		Col./ Code	Skip to

| | P.491 Record No. Card 5 | (1–3) (4–7) (8) | |

Person Number (from H/H Grid) ☐ (9)   Area Code ☐☐☐☐   (11–14)

(10)
Serial Number of Use Sheet for this person   1   Address Serial No. ☐☐   (15–16)
2
8 (2nd SOLICITOR/ LAWYER ONLY (SEE Q.2))   Household Number ☐   (17)

COMPLETE ONE OF THESE SHEETS FOR EACH CASE OF SOLE OR MAIN USE IDENTIFIED ON HOUSEHOLD QUESTIONNAIRE Q.3 OR Q.4.
THIS SHEET *MUST* BE COMPLETED WITH THE SOLE OR MAIN USER ONLY.
SPOUSES MAY *NOT* BE USED AS PROXIES.

1. Now I would like to ask you for some more details about the .... (1st/2nd) matter you mentioned on which you had help or advice from a solicitor (lawyer) last year. What was this matter about? PROBE FULLY.

O.U.O.

(18)   (19)

2. (a) SHOW CARD C. There are various places where solicitors and other lawyers work and can be consulted. When you first had advice or help from a solicitor (lawyer) about this matter in 1977, where was he working?   (20)
On his own or in a partnership or firm of solicitors   1
In a law centre or a legal advice centre...   2
In a Citizens' Advice Bureau   3
In a Trade Union   4
In the AA or RAC   5

Somewhere else (SPECIFY) ....

....

(b) Apart from this solicitor (lawyer), did you get any help or advice from any other solicitor (lawyer) about this matter during 1977?   (21)
Yes   A
No   1   Q.3

(c) IF YES TO (b) Was this other solicitor (lawyer) someone working in the same firm as the first one, someone the first solicitor (lawyer) consulted *or* quite a separate solicitor (lawyer)?
Worked in same firm   ...   .   3 ⎫
Consulted by first one   ...   .   4 ⎬
Separate solicitor ...   .   5 ⎭

SEE Instruc-tion below (d)

Card 5

		Col./ Code	Skip to

(d) IF SEPARATE SOLICITOR AT (c) In which of these was the second solicitor (lawyer) working when he was first consulted about the matter?   (22)

On his own or in a partnership or firm of solicitors   1
In a law centre or a legal advice centre   2
In a Citizens' Advice Bureau   3
In a Trade Union   4
In the AA or RAC   5

Somewhere else (SPECIFY) ....

....

IF *ANY OTHER* SOLICITOR WAS USED (YES TO Q.2(b)) PREFACE Q.3 BY SAYING:
"I would like you to answer the next questions just about the *first* solicitor (lawyer)."

IF A *SEPARATE* SOLICITOR WAS USED (CODE 6 AT Q.2(c)), ON COMPLETING THIS USE SHEET DO A FURTHER USE SHEET FOR THIS MATTER (SERIAL No. 8) COVERING 2nd SOLICITOR AND STARTING RECORDING AT Q.2(d).

3. Can I check, at the time he helped you or gave you advice, was the solicitor (lawyer) working in England or Wales or was he working elsewhere?   (23)
England and Wales   1   END THIS SHEET HERE
Elsewhere—Scotland   2
Elsewhere—other   3

ASK ALL WITH SOLICITORS IN ENGLAND OR WALES   (24)

4. (a) Was the advice or help you got from the solicitor (lawyer) *wholly* for yourself *or* wholly for someone else *or* for you and someone else jointly?
Wholly on own behalf   1   Q.5
Wholly on other's behalf   2
Self and other jointly   3

(b) IF OTHER INVOLVED (CODES 2 OR 3 AT (a))
Who else was involved apart from yourself?   (25)
CODE AS MANY AS APPLY
Member of same household—spouse   1
Member of same household—other adult 18+   2
Member of same household—child (0–17)   3
Relative outside household   4

Other (SPECIFY)...

ASK ALL   (26)
5. (a) Before the solicitor (lawyer) was consulted, did you get any help or advice of any sort about the matter from anyone outside your household?   Yes   1
No   2   Q.6

IF YES TO (a) ASK (b) AND (c)   O.U.O.

(b) Who helped you or gave you advice? Anyone else?   (27)   (28)
PROBE TO NO.

284

Card 5

		Col./ Code	Skip to
(c)	Did .... (HELPERS/ADVISERS) ever suggest you might get help or advice from a solicitor (lawyer) about this matter?	(29)	
	Yes	1	
	No	2	Q.6
		O.U.O.	
(d)	IF YES TO (c) and 2+ ADVISERS MENTIONED at (b) Who was it who suggested this?	(30)	(31)

6. When was the solicitor (lawyer) *first* consulted about this matter?

WRITE IN MONTH .... & CODE

Month			Year		
		1	9			(32–35)

		Col./ Code	Skip to
7. (a)	Had that solicitor (lawyer) ever been consulted before about other matters concerning you or other members of your present household?	(36)	
	Yes	1	
	No	2	(c)
(b)	IF YES TO (a) When was he *first* consulted about *any* matter concerning you or other members of your present household?	(37)	
	Before 1960	1	
	1960–1964	2	Q.8
	1965–1969	3	
	1970–1972	4	
	1973	5	
	1974	6	
	1975	7	
	1976	8	
	1977	9	
	IF NO TO Q.7(a) OR 1973–1977 (CODES 5–9) AT Q.7(b) ASK (c)	O.U.O.	
(c)	How did that particular solicitor (lawyer) come to be chosen (originally)? PROBE FULLY AND RECORD ANSWER FULLY.	(38)	(39)
8. (a)	Coming back now to .... (MATTER OF THIS USE SHEET) again, who first approached the solicitor (lawyer) about this matter? Did you yourself approach him directly *or* did someone else approach him on your behalf?	(40)	
	Approached self	1	Q.9
	Other approached	2	
		O.U.O.	
(b)	IF SOMEONE ELSE AT (a) Who was that?	(41)	(42)

285

Card 5

		Col./ Code	Skip to
9. (a)	Did you ever go to see the solicitor (lawyer)?	(43)	
	Yes—went to see him	1	(c)
	No—did not go to see him	A	
(b)	IF DID NOT GO TO SEE HIM Did he come to see you *or* was your contact with him by letter or telephone only *or* did you have no direct contact with him at all?		
	Solicitor came to see client	3 }	
	Contact by telephone/letter only	4 }	Q.10
	No direct contact	5 }	
	IF WENT TO SEE HIM (YES TO (a)) ASK (c) & (d)	(44)	
(c)	How often in all did you see him about the matter?		
	Once	1	
	Twice	2	
	Three times	3	
	Four times	4	
	Five or more times	5	
(d)	The first time you went to see him, did you go by yourself or did anyone else go with you?	(45)	
	Went self	1	Q.10
	Other accompanied	2	
(e)	IF ACCOMPANIED AT (d) Who went with you?	O.U.O.	
		(46)	(47)
	ASK ALL		
10.	Did the solicitor (lawyer) do anything at all on your behalf (even if it was only witnessing a document, making a telephone call or writing a letter) *or* did he just give you advice?	(48)	
	Took some action	1	Q.12
	Gave advice only	2	
	ASK ALL GETTING ADVICE ONLY (CODE 2 AT Q.10)	O.U.O.	
11. (a)	What advice did he give you? PROBE FULLY AND RECORD ANSWER FULLY.	(49)	(50)
(b)	Have you followed this advice?	(51)	
	Yes	1	(d)
	No	2	
(c)	IF NO TO (b) Why is that? PROBE FULLY AND RECORD ANSWER FULLY.	O.U.O.	
		(52)	(53)
(d)	When he was giving you advice, did he explain things clearly to you?	(54)	
	Yes	1	
	No	2	

286

Card 5

		Col./ Code	Skip to
(e)	Is the solicitor (lawyer) still giving you advice about this matter?	(55)	
	Yes	1	Q.16
	No	2	

(f) IF NO TO (e) When was the *last* time he gave you advice about it?

Month	
WRITE IN MONTH................AND CODE	1977
(56–57)	

NOW SKIP TO Q.16

ASK ALL WHERE ACTION TAKEN (CODE 1 AT Q.10)

12. (a) What did the solicitor (lawyer) do for you? PROBE FULLY AND RECORD ANSWER FULLY. O.U.O.

		(58)	(59)
(b)	When the solicitor (lawyer) started dealing with the matter, did he explain to you what he was going to do?	(60)	
	Yes	1	(d)
	No	A	
(c)	IF NO TO (b) Did you in fact ask him to explain what he was going to do?		
	Yes	3	
	No	4	
(d)	When the solicitor (lawyer) started dealing with the matter, did he give you a clear idea of how long he thought it would take?	(61)	
	Yes	1	(f)
	No	A	
(e)	IF NO TO (d) Did you in fact ask him how long he thought it would take?		
	Yes	3	
	No	4	
(f)	When the solicitor (lawyer) started dealing with the matter, did he give you a clear idea of how much his bill to you would be?	(62)	
	Yes	1	(h)
	No	A	
(g)	IF NO TO (f) Did you in fact ask him how much his bill to you would be?		
	Yes	3	
	No	4	
(h)	While he was dealing with the matter, did the solicitor (lawyer) keep you sufficiently informed of progress?	(63)	
	Yes	1	Q.13
	No	A	
(i)	IF NO TO (h) Did you ever have difficulty finding out from him how matters stood?		
	Yes	3	
	No	4	Q.13

Card 5

		Col./ Code	Skip to
(j)	IF YES TO (i) Did this happen a lot or just once or twice?	(64)	
	Happened a lot	1	
	Happened once or twice	2	
	ASK ALL WHERE ACTION TAKEN	(65)	
13. (a)	Was the matter one which might possibly at some stage have come before a court or tribunal?		
	Yes	1	
	No	2	Q.14
(b)	IF YES TO (a) Did it in fact come before a court or tribunal?	(66)	
	Yes	1	
	No	2	Q.14
	Not yet, but might	3	Q.14
	IF YES TO (b) ASK (c) & (d)	(67)	
(c)	Which kind of court/tribunal did it come before?		
	COURTS: Magistrates' Court	1	
	County Court	2	
	CODE AS MANY AS APPLY Crown Court	3	
	High Court	4	
	Other Court (SPECIFY)...		
	....		
	TRIBUNALS: Industrial	6	
	Supplementary Benefits	7	
	National Insurance	8	
	Rents	9	
	Other Tribunal (SPECIFY)...		
	....		
(d)	Did anyone represent you in the court/tribunal?	(68)	
	Yes	1	
	No	2	Q.14
(e)	IF YES TO (d) Who represented you?	(69)	
	Anyone else? Solicitor	1	
	CODE AS MANY AS APPLY Barrister	2	Q.15
	Other (SPECIFY)..		
	....		
	ASK ALL WHERE ACTION TAKEN UNLESS BARRIS-TER MENTIONED AT Q.13(e)	(70)	
14.	Did your solicitor (lawyer) ever consult or brief a barrister about the matter?		
	Yes	1	
	No	2	Q.15
	ASK ALL WHERE ACTION TAKEN	(71)	
15. (a)	Is the solicitor (lawyer) still dealing with the matter *or* has he stopped dealing with it?		
	Still dealing	1	Q.16
	Stopped dealing	2	

288

Card 5

	Col./Code	Skip to

IF STOPPED AT (a) ASK (b)–(f)

(b) When did he stop dealing with it?

WRITE IN MONTH...............AND CODE [Month] 1977

(72–73)

	Col./Code	Skip to
(c) Considering what was done, what do you think of the time it took? Was it: READ OUT:	(74)	
A shorter time than you had expected	1	(e)
or about as long as you expected	2	(e)
or a longer time than you expected?	3	
(d) IF LONGER THAN EXPECTED AT (c) Is there any particular reason why it took longer than you expected?	O.U.O.	
PROBE FULLY AND RECORD ANSWER FULLY	(75)	
	O.U.O.	
(e) IF STOPPED DEALING WITH IT AT (a) How did the matter stand when the solicitor (lawyer) stopped dealing with it? PROBE FULLY AND RECORD ANSWER FULLY.	(76)	(77)
	(78–80)	Blank
P.491	(1–3)	
Record No.	(4–7)	
Card 6	(8)	
Person No. [ ]	(9)	
Use Sheet No. [ ]	(10)	
(f) IF STOPPED DEALING WITH IT AT (a) Was this the outcome you had expected?	(11)	
Yes	1	Q.16
No	2	
IF NO TO (f) ASK (g) and (h)	O.U.O.	
(g) In what way was the outcome different from what you had expected? PROBE FULLY AND RECORD ANSWER FULLY.	(12)	
	(13)	
(h) Was the actual outcome better or worse than you had expected?	(14)	
Better	1	
Worse	2	
ASK ALL	(15)	
16. (a) Was the solicitor (lawyer) easy to deal with?		
Yes	1	(c)
No	2	
	O.U.O.	

Card 6

		Col./ Code	Skip to
(b)	IF NO TO (a) In what way was he not easy to deal with? PROBE FULLY AND RECORD ANSWER FULLY.	(16)	
		(17)	
(c)	Was there anything you particularly liked about the way the solicitor (lawyer) handled the matter? PROBE FULLY AND RECORD ANSWER FULLY.	(18)	
	No, nothing	0	
		(19)	
(d)	Was there anything you particularly disliked about the way the solicitor (lawyer) handled the matter? PROBE FULLY AND RECORD ANSWER FULLY.	(20)	
	No, nothing	0	
		(21)	
(e)	Overall, taking everything into account, were you satisfied or dissatisfied with the way the solicitor (lawyer) handled the matter? IF SATISFIED: Completely satisfied or just fairly satisfied? IF DISSATISFIED: Were you very dissatisfied or just somewhat dissatisfied?	(22)	
	Completely satisfied	1	(g)
	Fairly satisfied	2	(g)
	Somewhat dissatisfied	4	
	Very dissatisfied	5	
	Neither satisfied nor dissatisfied	3	(g)
(f)	IF SOMEWHAT OR VERY DISSATISFIED AT (e) Can you tell me what you were dissatisfied with?	O.U.O.	
	PROBE FULLY AND RECORD ANSWER FULLY.	(23)	(24)
(g)	ASK ALL If a similar matter arose in the future and you wanted the help or advice of a solicitor (lawyer), would you go to the same one again?	(25)	
	Yes	1	
	No	2	
	Other answer (WRITE IN)		
	....		
	IF SOLICITOR GAVE ADVICE ONLY, CHECK Q. 11(e). IF STILL GIVING ADVICE END HERE. IF SOLICITOR TOOK ANY ACTION, CHECK Q. 15(a). IF STILL DEALING WITH MATTER END HERE.		

290

Card 6

	Col./Code	Skip to

ASK ALL WHERE SOLICITOR HAS STOPPED ADVISING OR DEALING WITH MATTER.

17. (a) Did the solicitor (lawyer) issue a bill in connection with this matter?

	Col./Code	Skip to
	(26)	
Yes	1	
No	2	END HERE

(b) IF BILL ISSUED   How much of the bill did you or other people in your household pay?   Was it: READ OUT:

		Col./Code	Skip to
		(27)	
	all of it	1	Q.18
(NOTE: IF BILL OUTSTANDING,	or some of it	2	
CODE ON BASIS OF WHO *WILL* PAY)	or none of it?	3	

IF PAID PARTLY OR WHOLLY BY OTHERS (CODE 2 OR 3 AT (b)) ASK (c) AND (d)

	Col./Code	Skip to
	O.U.O.	

(c) Who else paid the bill/paid part of the bill?

	Col./Code	Skip to
	(28)	(29)

(d) Do you know how much they paid?

	Col./Code	Skip to
	(30)	
Yes	1	
No	2	CHECK Q.18

(e) IF YES TO (d)   How much was that?   £ ☐☐☐☐ (31–34)

Record to nearest £

IF BILL PAID ENTIRELY BY OTHER PEOPLE (CODE 3 AT (b)), END HERE.

ASK ALL PAYING ALL OR PART OF THE BILL (CODE 1 OR 2 AT Q.17(b))

18. (a) What was the total amount you paid to the solicitor (lawyer)?

£ ☐☐☐☐ (35–38)

Record to nearest £

(NOTE: SUGGEST REFERENCE TO BILL IF NECESSARY)

(b) Did this include any items the solicitor had to pay out on your behalf?

	Col./Code	Skip to
	(39)	
Yes	1	
No	2	(d)

(c) IF YES TO (b)   How much of the bill was for items like that?

£ ☐☐☐☐ (40–43)

Record to nearest £

(d) Taking into account what he did, do you think the amount you paid to the solicitor (lawyer) for his own fees was:

	Col./Code	Skip to
	(44)	
READ OUT: Good value for money	1	
or Reasonable value for money	2	
or Poor value for money	3	

(e) IF POOR VALUE AT (d)   Why do you say that? PROBE FULLY.

	Col./Code	Skip to
	O.U.O.	
	(45)	(46)
	(47–80)	Blank

291

P.491   LEGAL SERVICES SURVEY
               Individual Questionnaire

		Col./ Code	Skip to
	P.491 Record No. Card 4	(1–3) (4–7) (8)	

OUO

Person Number ☐ (9) | 0 | (10) Household No. ☐ | (17)
(from H/H grid)

Area Code ☐☐☐ (11–14)	This individual: —has completed use sheet(s) —is a selected non-user	(18) 1 2	
Address ☐☐ (15–16) Serial No.			

THIS SCHEDULE IS FOR:
—ALL COMPLETING USE QUESTIONNAIRES
—SELECTED NON-USERS (H/H SCHEDULE Q.6)

1. (a) SHOW CARD B AGAIN. I have asked already about occasions when you got help or advice from a solicitor (lawyer) last year. During 1977, were there any (other) occasions when you felt that the sort of help or advice that solicitors (lawyers) can give might possibly have been useful to you but you did not in fact contact one?

		(19)	
	Yes No	1 2	 Q.4

IF YES TO (a) ASK (b) AND (c).

(b) Was this about just one matter, *or* over last year were there several different matters on which you felt a solicitor's (lawyer's) help or advice might possibly be useful to you?
IF SEVERAL: How many?
No. of different matters ☐ (20)

292

	Card 4	Col./ Code	Skip to

(c)   SHOW CARD B. What was the (most recent) matter about?
IF 2+ MATTERS REPEAT FOR 2nd MATTER.

IF 3+ MATTERS, THEN ASK: What were the other
matters about? Anything else? (CODE AS MANY AS
APPLY).

	Most recent	2nd most recent	Other matters
	(21)	(23)	(25)
Buying or selling a house or flat	1	1	1
Making a will	2	2	2
Dealing with the estate of someone who has died	3	3	3
Matrimonial or family problems (divorce, etc.)	4	4	4
Social security or welfare rights problems ...	5	5	5
Problems about employment, dismissal etc.	6	6	6
Problems about faulty goods or services ...	7	7	7
Debt or hire purchase problems	8	8	8
Landlord and tenant problems	9	9	9
Problems with neighbours	0	0	0
Compensation for personal injuries ...	X	X	X
Motoring offences	Y	Y	Y
	(22)	(24)	(26)
Other offences or criminal charges... ...	1	1	1
Tax or capital transfer problems	2	2	2
Other financial problems	3	3	3
Other (SPECIFY)			

2. (a)   ASK ALL SAYING YES TO Q.1(a)   (27)
Now about .... (matter mentioned as most recent at
Q.1(c)). Did you in fact get any help or advice of any sort
about this matter from anyone outside your household?

                                    Yes   1
                                    No   2   (d)

IF YES TO (a) ASK (b) and (c)

(b)   Who helped you or gave you advice? Anyone else?

                                          O.U.O.

                                      (28–29)

(c)   Did .... (HELPERS/ADVISERS) ever suggest that you   (30)
might get help or advice from a solicitor (lawyer) about this
matter?

                                      Yes   1
                                    No   2

(d)   ALL SAYING YES TO 1(a) Did you ever consider getting   (31)
help or advice from a solicitor (lawyer) about the matter?

                                      Yes   1
                                    No   2

	Card 4	Col./ Code	Skip to
(e)	Is there any particular reason why you did not get help or advice/consider getting help or advice from a solicitor (lawyer) about it? PROBE FULLY. RECORD ANSWER FULLY.		
		O.U.O.	
		(32–33)	

IF ONE MATTER ONLY AT Q.1(b) NOW SKIP TO Q.4

		Col./Code	Skip to
	ASK ALL MENTIONING 2 OR MORE MATTERS AT Q.1(b)	(34)	
3. (a)	Now about .... matter mentioned as 2nd most recent. Did you in fact get any help or advice of any sort about this matter from anyone outside your household? Yes No	1 2	(d)
	IF YES TO (a) ASK (b) and (c)		
(b)	Who helped you or gave you advice? Anyone else?		
		O.U.O	
		(35–36)	
(c)	Did .... (HELPERS/ADVISERS) ever suggest that you might get help or advice from a solicitor (lawyer) about this matter?	(37)	
	Yes No	1 2	
		(38)	
(d)	ALL MENTIONING 2 + MATTERS AT Q.1(b) Did you ever consider getting help or advice from a solicitor (lawyer) about the matter?		
	Yes No	1 2	
(e)	Is there any particular reason why you did not get help or advice/consider getting help or advice from a solicitor (lawyer) about it? PROBE FULLY. RECORD ANSWER FULLY		
		O.U.O.	
		(39–40)	
	ASK ALL	(41)	
4. (a)	Apart from anything you have mentioned already, *before* last year (1977), have you yourself ever had help or advice from a solicitor (lawyer) about any matter?		
	Yes No	1 A	(c)

	Card 4	Col./ Code	Skip to

(b) IF NO TO (a) Before 1977, has anyone ever got help or advice from a lawyer (solicitor) for you, on your behalf?

		Col./Code	Skip to
	Yes	3	
	No	4 →	Selected Non-User → Q.8
			User → Q.5

(c) IF YES TO (a) OR (b) When was the last time this happened? IF MORE THAN ONE YEAR GIVEN, TAKE MOST RECENT

(42–43)

1	9		

IF 1972 OR EARLIER AT (c) SKIP TO Q.5. IF 1973 OR LATER ASK (d)

(d) SHOW CARD B What was the matter about? (44)

	Col./Code
Buying or selling a house or flat	1
Making a will	2
Dealing with the estate of someone who has died	3
Matrimonial or family problems (divorce, etc.)	4
Social security or welfare rights problems	5
Problems about employment, dismissal etc.	6
Problems about faulty goods or services	7
Debt or hire purchase problems	8
Landlord and tenant problems	9
Problems with neighbours	0
Compensation for personal injuries	X
Motoring offences	Y

(45)

	Col./Code
Other offences or criminal charges	1
Tax or capital transfer problems	2
Other financial problems	3

Other (SPECIFY)...

5. ASK ALL USERS AND ALL SAYING YES TO 4(a) or 4(b) (46)

(a) Have you personally ever felt you had cause for complaint against a solicitor (lawyer) for unsatisfactory work?

		Col./Code	Skip to
	Yes	1	
	No	2	Q.8

(b) IF YES TO (a) When did this happen (last)?

(47–48)

1	9		

IF USER AND IF DATE AT (b) IS 1977 ASK (c). OTHERS SKIP TO Q.6

(c) Was this in connection with something we have talked about in detail already? (49)

	Col./Code
Yes—matter of use sheet 1	1
matter of use sheet 2	2
No—no use sheet completed for that matter	3

295

	Card 4	Col./ Code	Skip to

ASK ALL WHO HAVE HAD CAUSE FOR COMPLAINT (YES TO 5(a))

6. (a) On the last occasion you felt you had cause for complaint, what was this complaint about? PROBE FULLY. RECORD ANSWER FULLY

		O.U.O.	
		(50)	
		(51)	

(b) Did you actually make a complaint to anyone on that occasion?

		(52)	
	Yes	1	
	No	2	Q.8

IF YES TO (b) ASK (c)–(e)

(c) To whom did you complain?

CODE AS MANY AS APPLY

		(53)	
—to the solicitor or his partnership		1	
—to the Law Society		2	
—to an MP		3	

—to someone else (SPECIFY)...

....

(d) What happened as a result of your complaint? PROBE FULLY. RECORD ANSWER FULLY

		O.U.O.	
		(54)	
		(55)	

(e) Were you satisfied with what was done about your complaint?

		(56)	
	Yes	1	Q.7
	No	2	

		O.U.O.	

(f) IF NO TO (e) Why were you not satisfied? PROBE FULLY. RECORD ANSWER FULLY

		(57)	

296

		Card 4	Col./ Code	Skip to
7.		ASK ALL WHO HAVE HAD CAUSE FOR COMPLAINT (YES TO 6(a))	(58)	
	(a)	Have you ever tried to sue a solicitor for professional negligence?		
		Yes	A	
		No	0	Q.8
		IF YES TO (a) ASK (b) AND (c)		
	(b)	Was a writ actually issued against him? Yes	2	
		No	3	
	(c)	Did you have any difficulties of any sort in trying to sue him?	(59)	
		Yes	1	
		No	2	Q.8
	(d)	IF YES TO (c) What difficulties? PROBE FULLY. RECORD ANSWER FULLY	O.U.O.	
			(60)	
			(61)	
8.		ASK ALL	(62)	
	(a)	Have you ever heard of the Law Society?		
		Yes	1	
		No	2	Q.9
	(b)	IF YES TO (a) What is it and what does it do? PROBE FULLY. RECORD ANSWER FULLY	(63)	
9.		ASK ALL	(64)	
	(a)	Have you ever heard of the Legal Aid Scheme?		
		Yes	1	
		No	2	Q.10
	(b)	IF YES TO (a) Can you tell me under what circumstances people qualify for legal aid? PROBE FULLY. RECORD ANSWER FULLY	O.U.O. (65)	
		ASK ALL	(66)	
10.	(a)	Do you yourself have any professional legal training?		
		Yes	1	
		No	2	(c)
	(b)	IF YES TO (a) What sort of legal training? RECORD IN GRID BELOW		
			(67)	
	(c)	Does any other member of your household have any professional legal training?		
		Yes	1	
		No	2	(e)

297

| | Card 4 | Col./ Code | Skip to |

(d)   IF YES TO (a)   What sort of legal training?
RECORD IN GRID BELOW

	(b) Respon- dent	(d) Other H/H member
	(68)	(69)
Qualified solicitor	1	1
Qualified barrister	2	2
Qualified legal executive	3	3
Law degree	4	4
Law student/articled clerk	5	5
Police training	6	6
Other (banking, accounting exams etc.) (SPECIFY):		

(e)   Do any of your other relatives or close friends have any professional legal training?

		(70)	
	Yes	1	
	No	2	

USERS END HERE.   NON-USERS ASK Q.11

ASK ALL SELECTED NON-USERS — O.U.O.

11.   If you wanted to get help or advice from a solicitor now, how would you choose one? PROBE FULLY. RECORD ANSWER FULLY

(71)

(72)

(73–80) Blank

298

SECTION 9

Analysis of Complaints concerning Legal Services

Contents

Introduction

9.1 This section is based on information the Commission received concerning complaints about legal services. The information was obtained from the following three sources:—

(a) the survey of households conducted for the Commission by Social and Community Planning Research (SCPR); the full SCPR report is given in Section 8 of this Volume;

(b) letters received by the Commission;

(c) a survey by the National Association of Citizens Advice Bureaux (NACAB).

9.2 The first source of information is the SCPR survey. This survey was conducted among a random sample of 10,000 households in England and Wales during 1977 and covered many matters other than complaints about legal services, as can be seen from the consultants' report at Section 8 of this Volume. There were 15,441 adults in the survey of whom 1,770 had consulted a solicitor in 1977, some more than once, so that a total of 2,026 matters were concerned. In answer to a question in the survey 224 respondents expressed some dissatisfaction with the legal service obtained covering 255 matters. An analysis of the information obtained is given later in this section.

9.3 The 224 respondents who expressed dissatisfaction with the legal services they obtained were approached by the consultants, SCPR, with a view to the Commission enquiring further into the nature and cause of their dissatisfaction. However, only 28 agreed that their names could be released to the Commission and only eight of these answered letters from the Commission.

9.4 The second source of information on complaints about legal services was in response to the advertising campaign carried out by the Commission in 1976, designed to reach 97 per cent of the adult population, inviting the public to submit evidence to the Commission. The advertisements invited evidence on all matters relevant to the Commission's inquiry and a large volume of correspondence was received. Of the letters received from the public, 1,473 contained complaints of one sort or another about legal services. No enquiry was made by the Commission into the circumstances of these complaints and the Commission did not attempt to ascertain if the complaints were justified. An analysis from the information contained in the 1,473 letters is given later in this section.

9.5 Thirdly, in 1977, NACAB conducted a survey of legal services throughout its 654 bureaux. Records were kept over a four-week period of all enquiries containing complaints about solicitors. In this period 901 matters giving rise to complaint were recorded. This represents approximately one complaint for every 100 enquiries of a legal nature. An analysis of the 901 matters is given later in this section.

Analysis of complaints by class of work

9.6 Table 9.1 gives an analysis of the recorded complaints by class of work. In the last column the table shows, for comparison, the distribution by class of work of all matters about which lawyers were consulted in 1977, as shown by the SCPR survey.

9.7 Table 9.1 shows that the main areas of complaint in the three sources we have analysed were civil litigation, matrimonial matters and conveyancing. If the distribution of complaints is compared with the distribution of all legal business, as shown by the last column of Table 9.1, it can be seen that the proportion of complaints arising in conveyancing matters was relatively low whilst the proportion of complaints concerning matrimonial matters was relatively high.

TABLE 9.1

Analysis of recorded complaints by class of work

| Class of work | Source of information and percentage of complaints analysed by class of work | | | All work taken to lawyers according to SCPR survey |
	SCPR survey %	letters to Commission %	NACAB survey %	
Civil litigation[1]	16	29	11	13
Matrimonial	15	18	33	13
Conveyancing	25	17	21	32
Probate	13	12	8	11
Property	9	10	4	7
Crime	8	5	3	7
Miscellaneous	15	9	20	18
Total	100[2]	100	100	100[2]
Number of matters	255	1,473	901	2,026

[1] Including matters which may lead to civil litigation.
[2] Totals add to more than 100 due to rounding.

Analysis of complaints by reason for complaint

9.8 Table 9.2 gives an analysis of the reasons for dissatisfaction with legal services as expressed in the complaints analysed from the three sources of information referred to in paragraph 9.1.

9.9 Table 9.2 shows that, in the complaints analysed, the most common reasons given for complaint can broadly be classed as assertions of inefficiency or negligence. However, it is not possible from the information available to enquire further into these allegations. No conclusions can therefore be drawn from the data available. The other main reasons given for complaint were delay and cost of providing legal services.

9.10 At annexes 9.1 to 9.3 to this section further analyses are given of the recorded complaints from the three sources of information referred to in paragraph 9.1. Details are given in these annexes of the proportion of complaints analysed by class of work and by the reason given for complaint. In two of the three sources of information a high proportion of the recorded complaints about conveyancing and probate matters were related to delay or cost, while for criminal matters the majority of the recorded complaints referred to matters which fell into the broad categories of inefficiency or negligence. But in general there was no particular pattern shown between the reason given for complaint and the type of work involved.

TABLE 9.2

Analysis of recorded complaints by the reasons expressed for dissatisfaction

Reasons expressed for dissatisfaction	SCPR survey %	Letters to Commission %	NACAB survey %
Inefficiency or negligence on part of solicitor	42	20	44
Delay	24	19	17
Cost	9	18	23
	75	57	84
Other reasons:			
restrictions on legal aid	—	9	—
difficulty in pursuing complaint	—	7	—
complaint against third party solicitor	—	6	—
complaint involving conflict of interest	—	4	—
complaint against counsel	—	3	—
lack of communication/not kept informed of progress	12	—	—
complaints about solicitor's manner	7	—	—
miscellaneous	7	13	16
	26	42	16
Total	100[1]	100[1]	100

[1] Totals do not add to 100 due to rounding.

Conclusion

9.11   In this section various analyses have been set out of the complaints about legal services recorded in three sources of information available to the Commission. Information was not available to compare the number of complaints with the number of cases which were not the subject of complaint in the case of the NACAB survey and the letters to the Commission. The analyses in this section do not therefore indicate the extent of dissatisfaction with legal services, which is discussed in paragraphs 8.210 to 8.251.

9.12   The main areas of complaint concerned civil litigation, matrimonial matters and conveyancing. In comparison with the distribution of all legal work, the proportion of complaints arising in conveyancing matters appeared relatively low while that for matrimonial matters appeared relatively high.

9.13 The reasons given for complaint were varied and generally vague. Many of the complaints can broadly be classified by an assertion that the lawyer was in some way inefficient or negligent. The other main causes for complaint were delay and cost, which arose most often in conveyancing and probate work. It is important to bear in mind that it was not possible to obtain information from the solicitor concerned to ascertain his view of the complaint and its validity, or to verify the complaint from other sources. To this extent, therefore, the complaints set out in this paper impart a one-sided view.

**Complaints about legal services recorded in SCPR survey:
analysis of complaints by class of work and reason for complaint[1]**

(paragraph 9.10)

| Class of work | Reason for complaint | | | | Total |
	inefficiency or negligence %	delay %	cost %	other %	%
Civil litigation	50	13	9	29	100[2]
Matrimonial	57	27	9	7	100
Conveyancing	34	22	12	32	100
Probate	33	40	5	23	100[2]
Property	38	22	6	34	100
Crime	63	8	4	25	100
Miscellaneous	35	32	6	27	100
All matters	42	24	9	26	100[2]

[1] The figures are based on all the reasons given for dissatisfaction, and not the number of matters. Sometimes several reasons for dissatisfaction were given in a single matter.
[2] Totals do not add to 100 due to rounding.

**Complaints about legal services recorded in letters to the Commission:
analysis of complaints by class of work and reason for complaint**

(paragraph 9.10)

| Class of work | Reason for complaint | | | | Total |
	inefficiency or negligence %	delay %	cost %	other %	%
Civil litigation	19	20	16	45	100
Matrimonial	18	20	17	45	100
Conveyancing	26	13	28	32	100[1]
Probate	17	33	22	28	100
Property	28	17	11	42	100[1]
Crime	20	8	12	60	100
Miscellaneous	10	10	14	66	100
All matters	20	19	18	42	100[1]

[1] Totals do not add to 100 due to rounding.

Complaints about legal services recorded in NACAB survey:

analysis of complaints by class of work and reason for complaint
(paragraph 9.10)

| Class of work | Reason for complaint | | | | Total |
	inefficiency or negligence %	delay %	cost %	other %	%
Civil litigation	51	24	11	15	100[1]
Matrimonial	49	17	19	15	100
Conveyancing	32	13	40	15	100
Probate	31	27	25	16	100[1]
Property	55	14	15	14	100[1]
Crime	66	11	8	15	100
Miscellaneous	41	16	25	16	100[1]
All matters	44	17	23	16	100

[1] Totals do not add to 100 due to rounding.

Complaints about legal services recorded in RACAD survey:

analysis of complaints by class of work and reason for complaint

(paragraph 9.10)

Class of work	Reason for complaint				Total
	misconduct or negligence %	delay %	cost %	other %	%
Civil litigation	51	24	11	13	100
Matrimonial	62	17	10	11	100
Conveyancing	32	15	40	13	100
Probate	31		23	36	100
Property	57	14	15	14	100
Co or	65	11	8	15	100
Miscellaneous	41	16	25	18	100
All matters	44	17	22	16	100

Totals do not add to 100 due to rounding.

306

SECTION 10

Time taken to Dispose of Actions in the Queen's Bench Division

Contents

Introduction

10.1 Information on time taken for actions to be disposed of in the Queen's Bench Division of the High Court has already been given in Volume I, paragraph 22.25 and Table 22.14. This section gives more detailed information on waiting times and draws on material from sources other than "Judicial Statistics", which is the sole source of published information on this subject; the main additional sources are unpublished data collected and held by the Lord Chancellor's Department and the results of a survey conducted in 1977 by Sir Jack Jacob, Senior Master in the Queen's Bench Division, in conjunction with the Lord Chancellor's Department.

Stages before an action is disposed of by the court

10.2 For those actions which, having been set down, were tried or otherwise disposed of in 1977, on average nearly four years elapsed between the date on which the cause of action arose and the date when the trial started or the case was otherwise disposed of. This interval may be divided into three periods: first, the time between the cause of action and the issue of the writ, secondly, the time between the issue of the writ and the action being set down for hearing, and thirdly, the time between the action being set down for hearing and the start of the trial or disposal of the case. It should be noted that about 95 per cent of actions in which writs are issued are settled or otherwise disposed of without ever being set down for hearing. The figures dealt with in the remainder of this Section exclude actions withdrawn or settled before being set down for hearing.

Nature of actions

10.3 Table 10.1 sets out the nature of the actions disposed of in 1977, from which it can be seen that personal injuries were the subject matter of 74 per cent of all actions.

308

TABLE 10.1
Actions for trial disposed of in the Queen's Bench Division in 1977

Nature of claim	In London		Outside London		All regions	
	number	%	number	%	number	%
Breaches of contract other than those included below	336	10	243	6	579	8
Goods sold and delivered	268	8	297	7	565	7
Libel and slander	96	3	8	—	104	1
Personal injuries including Fatal Accidents Act	2,061	63	3,640	82	5,701	74
Other claims	505	16	238	5	743	10
All claims	3,266	100	4,426	100	7,692	100

Source: Lord Chancellor's Department.

Time lapse from cause of action to disposal of case

10.4   For those set down actions which were tried or otherwise disposed of in 1977, Table 10.2 gives an indication of the average time taken between various stages. It should be noted that the time lapse between setting down and start of the trial or disposal represents less than a quarter of the total time between the cause of action and the hearing, and that the time taken between cause of action and issue of writ is equal to the period between issue of writ and setting down.

TABLE 10.2
Actions for trial in the Queen's Bench Division: average time intervals in months
for cases disposed of in 1977

Stage of action	Months		
	In London	Outside London	All regions
Cause of action to issue of writ	17	17	17
Issue of writ to setting down	18	17	17
Setting down to start of trial or disposal	14	9	11
Cause of action to start of trial or disposal	49	43	45
Number of actions disposed of	3,266	4,426	7,692

Source: Lord Chancellor's Department.

309

The time lapse varies to some extent according to the nature of the claim, as can be seen from annexes 10.1 and 10.2 which show the actions disposed of in 1977 (Table 10.1) analysed in more detail according to the average time taken to dispose of them (Table 10.2).

10.5   Figure 10.1 shows the profile of total time from cause of action to start of trial or disposal of action in relation to the types of claims set out in Table 10.1. Actions generally have a similar time profile with the exception of libel and slander actions which are dealt with more promptly.

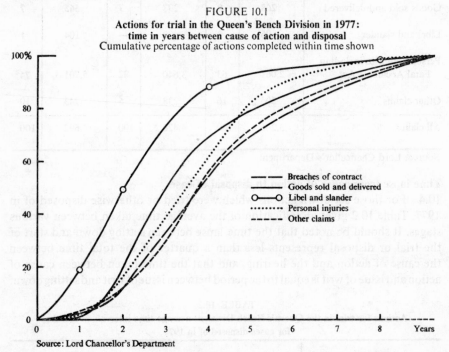

FIGURE 10.1
**Actions for trial in the Queen's Bench Division in 1977:
time in years between cause of action and disposal**
Cumulative percentage of actions completed within time shown

Source: Lord Chancellor's Department

The results of Figure 10.1 for all actions as as follows:—

Time lapse in years	Percentage of actions disposed of
	%
Less than 1	2
1–2	14
2–4	46
4–8	35
More than 8	3
	100

The summary indicates that the majority of cases take from two to five years from cause of action to start of trial or disposal.

310

Time lapse from cause of action to issue of writ

10.6   Figure 10.2 shows the time profile between cause of action and issue of writ. In some types of case there is a long period between the cause of action and the issue of a writ. In the case of personal injury actions 40 per cent of writs were issued in the year following the cause of action, and a further 34 per cent in the second year. In 26 per cent of personal injury actions, writs were issued more than two years after the cause of action. By contrast, in libel and slander actions 80 per cent of writs were issued within six months of the cause of action.

FIGURE 10.2

Actions for trial in the Queen's Bench Division in 1977:
time in months between cause of action and issue of writ
Cumulative percentage of writs issued within time shown

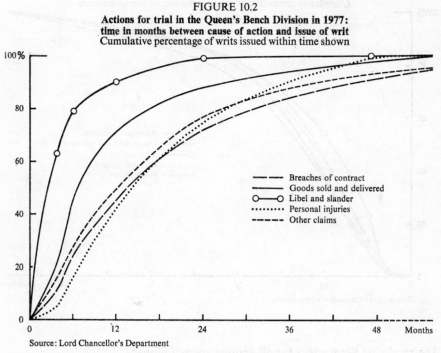

Source: Lord Chancellor's Department

The results of Figure 10.2 for all actions are as follows:—

Time lapse in months from cause of action	Percentage of actions disposed of
	%
Less than 6	21
6–12	25
12–24	31
24–48	22
More than 48	1
	100

311

Issue of writ to setting down

10.7   Figure 10.3 shows the time profile between issue of writ and setting down. In over 55 per cent of all types of action, except libel and slander, a period of more than one year elapsed at this stage.

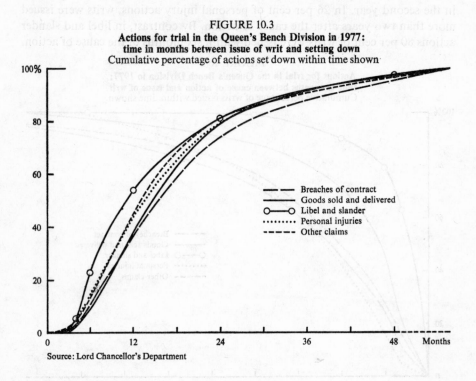

FIGURE 10.3
Actions for trial in the Queen's Bench Division in 1977:
time in months between issue of writ and setting down
Cumulative percentage of actions set down within time shown

Breaches of contract
Goods sold and delivered
Libel and slander
Personal injuries
Other claims

Source: Lord Chancellor's Department

The results of Figure 10.3 for all actions are as follows:—

Time lapse in months from issue of writ	Percentage of actions disposed of
	%
Less than 6	14
6–12	28
12–24	36
24–48	19
More than 48	3
	100

Requests for further and better particulars

10.8 The period between the issue of a writ and setting down an action is occupied by the exchange of pleadings and other steps in the proceedings. The plaintiff delivers a statement of claim (which may be endorsed on the writ) to the defendant. The defendant delivers a defence and, in some cases, a counter-claim to which the plaintiff delivers a reply. In complex actions, further exchanges of pleadings may take place. Further and better particulars of the statement of claim may be requested by the defence, and of the defence by the plaintiff. If the request is refused an application may be made to the court for an order that particulars be given which, if contested, is dealt with at an oral hearing before the master or registrar. After pleadings have been exchanged, directions are given by the court for the preparation of the case for trial and for setting it down. This may be followed by discovery of documents relevant to the issues, agreement of maps and drawings and of experts' reports and other work preparatory for trial. The time occupied by exchanges of pleadings and parti-culars was examined in the 69 cases which were listed for hearing at London and Birmingham between December 1976 and January 1977. Information from this study is given in Tables 10.3, 10.4 and 10.5.

TABLE 10.3

Actions listed for hearing in the Queen's Bench Division in December 1976 and January 1977: incidence of requests for further and better particulars

Nature of claim	Number of actions in which further and better particulars were requested		Number of actions in sample
	in respect of statement of claim	in respect of defence	
Breaches of contract other than those included below	6	4	8
Goods sold and delivered	2	0	3
Libel and slander	0	2	5
Personal injuries including Fatal Accidents Act	23	10	45
Other claims	3	4	8
Total	34	20	69

Source: Unpublished study of time taken in the Queen's Bench Division.

Time intervals between pre-trial stages

10.9 Table 10.4 shows the intervals of time between the issue of the writ and the statement of claim, between statement of claim and defence and counterclaim and between counterclaim and reply. Statements of claim were served within one month of the issue of the writ in over half (38) of the cases; in four cases they were not served until more than one year after the issue of the writ. A defence was pleaded in nearly all cases (66) and in 55 cases the defence was served within three months of service of the statement of claim. Replies to the defence were made in a minority of cases (13).

TABLE 10.4

Actions disposed of in the Queen's Bench Division in December 1976 and January 1977: time intervals in exchange of pleadings

Time interval in months.	Stage		
	from issue of writ to statement of claim	from statement of claim to defence	from defence to reply
Less than 1	38	23	1
1– 3	13	32	6
3– 6	9	8	2
6–12	5	2	3
12–24	3	1	1
More than 24	1	0	0
All actions	69	66	13

Source: Unpublished study of time taken in the Queen's Bench Division.

Time intervals relating to further and better particulars

10.10   Table 10.5 shows the incidence of requests for further and better particulars in the cases examined in 1976–77. Out of the 69 cases, further and better particulars were requested of the statement of claim in 34 cases and of the defence in 20 cases. In 11 cases (not shown in the table) further and better particulars were requested of both the statement of claim and the defence.

10.11   In the majority of cases, requests for further and better particulars were made within three months of receiving the statement of claim or defence. Longer periods of time elapsed before the further and better particulars were served: in the 34 cases in which further and better particulars of the statement of claim were requested, further and better particulars were given in 13 cases within three months, in 16 cases in more than three months and in five cases the particulars requested were not given.

Setting down to trial or disposal

10.12   Figure 10.4 sets out the time profile from setting down to trial or disposal. Libel and slander actions were again dealt with more promptly: 42 per cent within three months and 80 per cent within one year.

TABLE 10.5

Actions disposed of in the Queen's Bench Division in December 1976 and January 1977: time intervals relating to further and better particulars

Time interval in months	Stage			
	from statement of claim to request for further and better particulars of statement of claim	from request to receipt of further and better particulars of claim	from service of defence to request for further and better particulars of defence	from request to receipt of further and better particulars of defence
Less than 1	11	2	1	0
1 — 3	14	11	10	6
3 — 6	4	12	2	4
6 — 12	2	3	4	3
12 — 24	3	1	2	2
More than 24	0	0	1	1
All actions	34	29	20	16

Source: Unpublished study of time taken in Queen's Bench Division.

FIGURE 10.4

Actions for trial in the Queen's Bench Division in 1977:
time in months between setting down and disposal

Cumulative percentage of actions disposed of within time shown

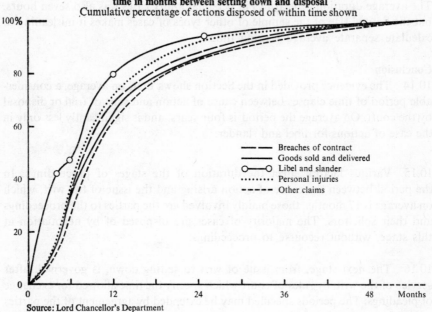

Source: Lord Chancellor's Department

315

The results of Figure 10.4 for all actions are as follows:—

Time lapse in months after setting down	Numbers of cases disposed of
	%
Less than 3	15
3–6	21
6–12	35
12–24	20
24–48	8
More than 48	1
	—
	100

Fifteen per cent of all actions were disposed of within three months of being set down, and 71 per cent within one year. A small proportion of actions (9 per cent) were not disposed of more than two years after setting down.

Hearing time

10.13 Of the 69 cases examined in 1976–77, 36 were settled shortly before the hearing without prior notice. The remainder went to trial, and of the 31 cases where the hearing time was given, the average time was seven hours. This figure, however, is distorted by a few cases which lasted for several days. The average duration of hearings in personal injury cases was also seven hours, but the limited size of the sample of other types of cases makes it misleading to calculate separate average hearing times.

Conclusion

10.14 The evidence provided in the Section shows that, on average, a considerable period of time elapses between cause of action and start of trial or disposal by the court. On average the period is four years, and is significantly less only in the case of actions for libel and slander.

10.15 Various factors affect the duration of the stages of proceedings. In the period between the cause of action arising and the issue of the writ, which on average is 17 months, those mainly involved are the parties to the proceedings and their solicitors. The majority of cases are disposed of by negotiation at this stage, without recourse to proceedings.

10.16 The next stage, from issue of writ to setting down, is governed, after service of the writ, by rules of court which specify the time allowed for exchange of pleadings. The periods specified may be extended by agreement of the parties or by the court. The time allowed after service of the writ for service of the statement of claim is 14 days, for service of the detence, 14 days thereafter and for the reply, if any, 14 days. It is clear that these periods are extended in all but a few cases. Those involved at this stage are barristers, who settle the pleadings and advise, solicitors, who conduct the case, clients and witnesses who provide instructions and statements, and experts who make reports. Until pleadings have been exchanged, the court has no opportunity to intervene unless one of the parties makes an application, for example for a contested extension of time. It is not apparent why the average period of 17 months is far longer than that provided in the rules of court nor why, for example, it takes an average of three months to request, and six months to provide, particulars of pleadings.

10.17 When an action is set down it must be ready for trial. The period which elapses between setting down and trial is governed by the availability of courts and judges. The present average period of 11 months is not affected in general by the conduct of the parties.

10.18 Since compiling this information on time taken in the Queen's Bench Division, the report of the personal injuries litigation procedure working party, the "Cantley Committee", has been published (Cmnd. 7478, HMSO, March 1979). The effect of the working party's recommendations is that the High Court should be given greater control over the conduct of proceedings in personal injury cases. The recommendations provide, *inter alia*, for the replacement of summons for directions by automatic directions without summons and without order. A further recommendation is that if an action has not been set down within 18 months of the issue of the writ, the plaintiff's solicitor should be required to report to the court the stage which the proceedings have reached. After such a period the court should have discretion, upon consideration of the plaintiff's report or otherwise, to issue a court summons for the purpose of giving directions in the action. The working party considered that these recommendations would prevent the more serious examples of delay in cases being heard.

ANNEX 10.1

Actions for trial in the Queen's Bench Division in London: average time intervals in months for cases disposed of in 1977

(paragraph 10.4)

Nature of action	Average interval from cause of action to issue of writ	Average interval from issue of writ to setting down	Average interval from setting down to start of trial or disposal	Average interval from cause of action to start of trial or disposal	Number of actions disposed of
Breaches of contract other than those listed below	18	19	16	53	336
Goods sold and delivered	12	18	15	45	268
Libel and slander	5	14	9	28	96
Personal injuries including Fatal Accidents Act	18	18	14	50	2,061
Other claims:					
hire purchase and conditional sale agreements	10	16	12	38	11
return of goods other than under hire purchase agreements	13	22	12	47	13
money lent, paid or received	19	13	16	48	9
bank loans	14	13	18	45	23
nuisance and/or breach of statutory duty	16	23	16	55	17
possession of land (other than landlord and tenant)	13	18	15	46	24
other claims for debt	14	18	15	47	85
other torts	19	20	18	57	73
wrongful dismissal	14	21	14	49	18
miscellaneous	18	16	14	48	232
Total	17	18	14	49	3,266

Source: Lord Chancellor's Department.

ANNEX 10.2

Actions for trial in the Queen's Bench Division outside London: average time intervals in months for cases disposed of in 1977
(paragraph 10.4)

Nature of action	Average interval from cause of action to issue of writ	Average interval from issue of writ to setting down	Average interval from setting down to start of trial or disposal	Average interval from cause of action to start of trial or disposal	Number of actions disposed of
Breaches of contract other than those listed below	22	20	9	51	243
Goods sold and delivered	11	18	9	38	297
Libel and slander	4	19	11	34	8
Personal injuries including Fatal Accidents Act	17	16	9	42	3,640
Other claims:					
hire purchase and conditional sale agreements	13	18	6	37	15
return of goods other than under hire purchase agreements	13	18	11	42	8
money lent, paid or received	8	15	9	32	13
bank loans	18	18	12	48	9
nuisance and/or breach of statutory duty	25	23	11	59	11
possession of land (other than landlord and tenant)	8	13	4	25	6
other claims for debt	21	22	11	54	46
other torts	16	16	8	40	22
wrongful dismissal	18	22	12	52	15
miscellaneous	21	20	11	52	1,033
Total	17	17	9	43	4,426

Source: Lord Chancellor's Department.

SECTION 11

International Comparisons of the Duration of Litigation

Contents

Introduction

11.1 Enquiries were made at the request of the Commission in a number of jurisdictions about the duration and cost of litigation. The purpose of the exercise was to compare experience in the various jurisdictions.

11.2 Court procedures were not included in our terms of reference and we draw attention in Part VI of Volume I to a number of proposals in this category, many of which are intended to reduce the complexity of litigation and hence its cost. We propose in Part VI the creation of an expert body to review procedures in detail. We hope that this process will be assisted by the results of our enquiries concerning litigation in other jurisdictions, which are summarised in this Section.

322

Comparisons—the difficulties

11.3   It was not the purpose of our enquiries to obtain information on which to base conclusions as to the relative efficiency or economy of different legal professions or systems. Such a comparison would only be possible following detailed research designed to quantify, in respect of a carefully selected range of jurisdictions, the factors which determine the duration and cost of legal proceedings. For example, the interval between initial consultation between lawyer and client and the eventual determination of a dispute depends upon the procedural stages required under rules of court, the volume of other business to be dealt with by the courts and the degree of proof required. Because a particular class of litigation may be dealt with quickly in a particular country does not mean that that country's legal system should necessarily be copied. What is right for one country may not be right for another.

11.4   A problem may under some systems be susceptible to a legal solution, while in others it may be dealt with administratively and not come before the courts at all. For example, in a number of jurisdictions adoption applications are dealt with by social welfare authorities and are not the subject of legal proceedings; similarly, a personal injury case may not lead to litigation where there is a no-fault system of compensation. Where there are proceedings in some form, procedures vary greatly under different legal systems. For example, claims for wrongful dismissal from employment are dealt with in some juris-dictions by courts, in others by tribunals, and in others by arbitration. Some jurisdictions have developed small claims courts where small consumer claims may be dealt with quickly and cheaply. The extent of intervention by the courts also varies: in some jurisdictions with "adversary" systems, the courts' sole function is to resolve the issues on the evidence presented by the parties; in others the court staff, or the judicial officers themselves, are actively involved in the proceedings and may, on their own initiative, make enquiries about the case or encourage a settlement between the parties. The availability of state assistance for litigation varies from one jurisdiction to another. The rules of law also vary, so that a particular set of facts will result in different decisions in different jurisdictions. In all these circumstances, one cannot reach conclusions with the same certainty as where like is compared with like.

The nature of our enquiries

11.5   The availability of statistics about the duration and cost of proceedings in different countries is uneven. Where comprehensive statistics exist, they tend to concentrate on volume of court business, the number of cases heard or settled out of court and similar information. Some statistics give the duration of certain stages of the litigation process, but direct comparison of stages between jurisdictions is not usually possible.

11.6   We concluded that the best means of obtaining general information was to ask the views of people working in the various jurisdictions as to the duration and the amount of professional time likely to be expended in certain cases. In order to make these enquiries as specific as possible, we devised a set of hypothetical cases, the facts of which we thought were likely to arise in any part of the world, and we asked selected consultees (mainly practitioners and professional bodies) in eighteen jurisdictions for their views on the probable duration of each case and the amount of lawyers' time involved.—

11.7   We received replies from the following jurisdictions:

Northern Ireland

Sweden

USA   —New York
      —Illinois
      —California
      —Texas
      —Missouri

Canada —Ontario

Australia—New South Wales
         —Victoria

New Zealand

Zambia

The names of the organisations which assisted us, to which we here record our gratitude, are set out in annex 11.1.

11.8   We asked the Law Society and the Senate for their views on the duration and cost of our hypothetical cases in England and Wales. In addition, the Law Society asked legal practitioners in thirteen countries (including some consulted by us) how long our cases would take in these countries.

11.9   We specifically asked our consultees to base their assessments of the duration of our cases not on theoretical time limits laid down, for example, by rules of court, but on normal experience in such cases, taking account of human fallibility, congestion in court lists, missing witnesses and other difficulties. It must be emphasised that the figures we received were estimates and were not arrived at by means of taking statistical samples or any similar procedures. This is borne out by the fact that the estimates we received as to the duration of cases frequently varied from those received by the Law Society, and indeed the Law Society found that in some instances they were given widely varying estimates in the same country, while some of their correspondents, like ours, felt that it was not possible to give useful estimates at all.

11.10   It must be recognised that it is impossible to estimate how long any case will take simply from knowing its basic facts and its eventual outcome. This was put to us succinctly by our Canadian consultee in this way.

324

Factors affecting solicitors' fees may be the firm involved, the experience of the solicitor involved, the complexity, seriousness and monetary value of the matter in question, the amount of preparation the solicitor does, the financial situation of the parties involved and the results achieved. The time involved will vary with the solicitors involved, with the court's backlog of cases, the court's locality, the availability of witnesses, the bitterness of the dispute and many other factors.

11.11   Our consultees calculated the duration of cases in various ways, some from the events giving rise to them, some from the first consultation with a lawyer, others from arrest or from the issue of proceedings. As far as possible we have compensated for these discrepancies. It should also be mentioned that the replies we received did not cover all our cases or deal with every aspect in all instances.

11.12   Our enquiries did not bring to light detailed statistical information on the levels of lawyers' charges for different classes of work. Such information as was available concerning laywers' earnings did not indicate the levels of charges in specific classes of case. Our consultees provided us with some estimates of cost, but it was difficult in some instances to distinguish between lawyers' fees and charges made by others involved, such as expert witnesses and the courts themselves. This section is therefore confined to comparisons between estimates given to us of the amount of time likely to be spent on the specimen cases by the lawyers involved.

The results of our enquiries

11.13   In the paragraphs that follow we describe the hypothetical cases used in the exercise. Each description is followed by a commentary on the estimates we received of the duration of the case and the professional time likely to be expended.

11.14   Our hypothetical cases concerned the following matters:—
(a) Consumer transaction:
     (i) small claim
     (ii) large claim
(b) Landlord and tenant
(c) Undefended divorce
(d) Defended divorce
(e) Adoption
(f) Personal injury
(g) Wrongful dismissal from employment
(h) Shoplifting—prosecution
(j) Armed robbery—prosecution:
     (i) not guilty plea
     (ii) guilty plea

325

(k) Dangerous driving:
     (i) prosecution
     (ii) civil proceedings
(l) Probate action.

Consumer transaction—small claim

Facts

11.15 The central heating system in A's house ceased to function properly, and A asked B Ltd, a firm specialising in the maintenance and repair of such equipment, to overhaul it. In due course he was told by B Ltd that they system was in working order (no demonstration of that fact was given by B Ltd or asked for by A). A paid B Ltd's charge of £150. A few days later A found that the system was again not operating properly. B Ltd examined it at A's request and claimed to have discovered a defect that was not present when they had previously worked on it. They contended that the new defect had been caused either by some unknown supervening cause for which they were in no way responsible or by A's incompetent usage. A denied this and alleged that B Ltd had not repaired the system competently in the first place. After an exchange of letters between A and B Ltd, A consulted solicitors, telling them he wished to enforce the terms of the contract against B Ltd. He was advised that he could not obtain an order in a county court requiring B Ltd to do the work, but that he should have his heating system repaired by another contractor and instruct the solicitors to claim as damages from B Ltd the cost of those repairs. This he did. B Ltd refused to pay the sum claimed, £250, and A's solicitors, as instructed, commenced proceedings.

11.16 At the hearing A gave evidence on his own behalf, and called one witness, the heating engineer who repaired the system. A director of B Ltd and the senior member of the team who carried out the original repairs gave evidence for B Ltd.

11.17 At the end of the hearing judgment was given in favour of A.

Comparison

11.18 The claim described in our hypothetical case concerns a sum of money above the limit of the small claims arbitration service offered by the county courts in England, Wales and Northern Ireland. It would therefore be heard in the county court itself and, in England and Wales, may take about a year. In Northern Ireland it would take an estimated four months. In Ontario the case would probably be heard in the small claims court, which provides a quick and economical service. If it were to be heard in a county court it would take up to two years. In some jurisdictions (New South Wales, New Zealand, and Zambia) small claims are heard by magistrates with civil jurisdiction and take about five months on average, though this time may vary considerably. In all these countries the amount of professional time involved is much the same: about 9–12 hours for the plaintiff and generally slightly less for the defendant. In those continental countries (Denmark, Holland, Sweden, Belgium, Luxembourg, France, Germany, Italy and the Republic of Ireland) consulted by the Law Society, the length of time estimated for the case varied between one month and eighteen months.

11.19 Several jurisdictions (New York, Missouri, Victoria and Ontario (up to $400)) have introduced small claims courts or (in Victoria) tribunals to hear these claims. In these the case takes only a matter of months. In some courts legal representation is excluded and legal fees are low. In Victoria and Missouri no legal fees are payable.

Consumer transaction—large claim

Facts

11.20 The central heating system in the head office of A Ltd ceased to function properly and A Ltd instructed B Ltd, a specialist firm whom A Ltd had employed on previous occasions, to overhaul it. Two days later B Ltd reported to A Ltd that various parts of the central heating system were defective and had had to be replaced, but that it was now in full working order again. On putting it into operation, A Ltd found that it was still not functioning correctly and they so informed B Ltd. After a further three days, B Ltd reported that their engineers had carried out further adjustments to the system and were satisfied that it was in working order. B Ltd then submitted a statement of their charge for the work they had carried out, amounting to £1,800. A Ltd contended that neither in terms of quality nor extent did the work done by B Ltd justify a charge of such an amount and they refused to pay B Ltd.

11.21 After protracted negotiations, A Ltd offered to pay £700, but B Ltd insisted that they were entitled to the full amount of their charge. A Ltd refused to increase their offer and B Ltd then instructed solicitors, who commenced proceedings in the High Court (at the time this example was prepared the limit of the jurisdiction of the county court in actions based on contract was £1,000; it has since been increased to £2,000).

11.22 At the hearing, A Ltd called two witnesses, the director who had authorised the work and given instructions to B Ltd, and the office manager responsible for operating the heating system. B Ltd called the foreman in charge of the work of overhaul and an independent expert witness, a heating engineer. At the end of the hearing, B Ltd were held to be entitled to be paid £1,000 in respect of the work they had carried out for A Ltd.

Comparison

11.23 In all jurisdictions consulted, large consumer claims are the subject of ordinary civil court proceedings. In most countries such cases would be heard in the High Court or its equivalent, although in some a claim of this size would in fact be within the jurisdiction of the lower courts. In some jurisdictions (including Sweden, Belgium, Germany, Western Australia and Missouri) such a case would take a matter of months. In most countries, however, it would take about a year or so, and in some cases up to three years. In England and Wales the case would take about two years. The amount of professional time involved seems to be greatest (45 hours each for plaintiff and defendant) in England and Wales. In other countries it varies but the average is around 30 hours for each.

11.24 In New York (where the case takes about 8–18 months and legal fees, charged on a lump sum basis, are among the highest) the judge may actively mediate in the dispute, and may summon the parties and their lawyers several times to try to reach a settlement.

Landlord and tenant

Facts

11.25 Mr and Mrs F with their two children aged three and six had for a period of three years occupied a flat comprising the upper floor of a house owned by Mr G. Mr G with his family occupied the remainder of the house as their residence. Mr G gave Mr F three months' notice of the termination of his tenancy on the ground that he himself required the premises occupied by Mr F and his family for his elderly parents to live in. Mr F refused to quit the premises and Mr G instructed solicitors who applied to the county court for an order giving him possession.

11.26 At the hearing Mr G was represented by his solicitor; Mr G and his mother gave evidence, and medical evidence was given concerning the state of health of Mr G's father. Mr and Mrs F were granted legal aid and were represented by a solicitor working in a law centre, and both gave evidence.

11.27 The court refused an order for possession on the general basis of Mr F's greater need.

Comparison

11.28 The substantive law relating to landlord and tenant varies greatly among the jurisdictions consulted. The proceedings would in most cases be heard by the equivalent of county courts or magistrates' courts with civil jurisdiction, and the parties would usually be legally represented. In Ontario, where tenants often either represent themselves or are assisted by law students from a legal aid clinic, landlords represent themselves or are represented by their agents. In Sweden the proceedings are before a rent tribunal and the parties are usually represented by ombudsmen. This case would in the jurisdictions consulted normally be heard quickly and cheaply, generally with less than 10 hours' professional time taken on behalf of each party. In several jurisdictions (including Denmark, California, Illinois, Ontario and Victoria) it would take only a month or so. In most countries it would take less than six months. In some jurisdictions, however (including England, Wales, France, Italy, Holland and New York), it may take longer, on average between six months and a year.

Undefended divorce

Facts
11.29 Mrs A petitioned for divorce in the county court on the ground of irretrievable breakdown of the marriage resulting from Mr A's adultery. Mr A entered no defence. There were two children of the marriage aged 9 and 11, whose legal custody Mr A agreed should be given to Mrs A; Mr A's proposals with regard to access to the children were agreed to by Mrs A. Maintenance for Mrs A and the children was agreed. Mrs A then consulted her solicitor who with her agreement proposed that Mr A should be responsible after the termination of their marriage for payment of the rent and rates on the flat he and Mrs A had occupied as their matrimonial home and that Mrs A should continue to live in it. After negotiations between Mr and Mrs A's respective solicitors this was agreed. At the hearing of her petition, Mrs A was granted a divorce and the agreed arrangements in relation to custody and maintenance were confirmed by the court.

Comparison
11.30 Divorce proceedings in most of the jurisdictions consulted are heard in the High Court or its equivalent. Although the hearing in undefended proceedings is very short the time taken to negotiate a financial settlement varies between different jurisdictions. In most of the jurisdictions consulted (including England and Wales) undefended divorce proceedings are completed in less than six months. In a number of jurisdictions this period includes a compulsory period (of six weeks or three months) between decree nisi and decree absolute. In Sweden there is a compulsory consideration period of six months to one year before the divorce is granted in all cases where there are children under 16. The amount of professional time taken in England and Wales (ten hours for the petitioner, six for the respondent) is about average.

Defended divorce

Facts
11.31 Mrs A petitioned for divorce on the grounds that her marriage had irretrievably broken down by reason of the fact that Mr A had left the matrimonial home against her wishes and that he had been continually in desertion for a period which would enable a divorce to be granted. Mr A opposed the grant of a decree to Mrs A on the ground that the marriage had not irretrievably

broken down, that his withdrawal from the matrimonial home was solely due to Mrs A's conduct towards him and that he would willingly return to live with her if she would behave properly towards him. Both parties were represented by solicitors and counsel. At the hearing evidence was given by Mrs A and a neighbour, and by Mr A on his own behalf.

11.32 The court, after hearing evidence and argument by counsel, awarded a decree to Mrs A and made an order in regard to maintenance for Mrs A (there were no children of the marriage).

Comparison
11.33 Substantive divorce law varies greatly between the jurisdictions consulted. In some jurisdictions (among them New York and Illinois) divorce is still based on fault, while in others (such as Sweden and Australia) there could be no obstacle to a divorce in the circumstances described in our hypothetical case. Defended divorce proceedings generally take longer than undefended ones; in England and Wales our case would take about two and a half years. This is in fact longer than any of the periods quoted by those consulted by ourselves or the Law Society; the range was from three months in California to two years in Italy. It is, however, particularly difficult to guage a "normal" duration for such a case, as so much will depend on the parties, and indeed two of our consultees (in Illinois and New York) felt unable to give any estimate at all. The amount of professional time taken will also vary greatly. Assuming a contested application for permanent maintenance, 70 hours for petitioner and respondent was estimated in England and Wales. The amount of time involved (quoted for the petitioner only) was thought to be similar in New York, but in most other jurisdictions the estimates were appreciably less, ranging from about four hours in Sweden (where the divorce could not be contested) to about 40 in Ontario (where the substantive law is similar to that in England and Wales), with a rough average of about 10 hours. In most jurisdictions somewhat more professional time would be involved on the petitioner's behalf than on the respondent's.

Adoption

Facts
11.34 A (unmarried) gave her three month old child (whereabouts of putative father unknown) to Mr and Mrs D with the express intention (admitted by A) that they should at the appropriate time adopt the child. When the child was one year and eight months old, A withdrew her consent to its adoption on the ground that her material circumstances having improved and she having a settled home with her parents she was in a position to bring up the child herself. Mr and Mrs D consulted a solicitor and subsequently instituted adoption proceedings in the county court. At the hearing of their application both they and A were legally represented. The court held that Mr and Mrs D were entirely

suitable adoptive parents for the child, that it would be harmful to the child to break its established relationship with them, and that A was withholding her consent to the adoption unreasonably. Adoption application granted.

Comparison

11.35 The law and practice relating to adoption vary considerably among the jurisdictions consulted. In several jurisdictions the case described could not arise: in Sweden adoption is not permitted if the natural parents oppose it; in Victoria consent could not be withdrawn after so long a time; in New Zealand consent would have been obtained at an early stage and could not thereafter be withdrawn; and in New York (under relatively new statutory provisions) there is a statutory period within which consent may be withdrawn. In New Zealand adoption is dealt with by the Social Welfare Department, apart from the formal application for legal adoption which is heard by a magistrate. In the other jurisdictions consulted, in which court proceedings are involved, their duration is fairly uniform, generally about six months, although it may be less in some jurisdictions (Northern Ireland, Belgium, Luxembourg, Texas and Zambia) and more in others (nine months in England and Wales, 18 in Holland). In England and Wales about 12 hours of professional time would be involved on behalf of both applicant and respondent. This is a little less than in most other jurisdictions, where roughly 17 hours is generally involved for the applicant and somewhat less for the respondent—although in Illinois over 100 hours was estimated to be needed for both applicant and respondent, including 50 hours' preparation for the hearing and 30 hours at the hearing itself.

Personal injury

Facts

11.36 A, employed as a builder by Y Ltd, was injured at his place of work when the chain supporting an iron girder while it was being lifted by a crane broke and the girder struck A as it fell to the ground. As a result of his injuries A was permanently incapacitated from earning his living in the building trade. A claimed damages through his trade union. Y Ltd, through their insurers, disclaimed liability maintaining that A should not have been standing as close as he had been to the crane while it was hoisting the girder and that a written instruction to that effect had been circulated by Y Ltd to all their employees. A then instructed solicitors to commence proceedings on his behalf.

11.37 At the hearing of the action evidence was given on behalf of A by A himself and two workmates. Evidence for Y Ltd was given by the crane driver, their safety officer (who had drafted the written instruction) and by A's foreman. An agreed medical report was put before the court, and no doctor was called to give oral evidence.

11.38   Y Ltd were held to have been to blame for the accident on the ground that they ought to have, and as a matter of fact had not, laid down and enforced a rule that no crane driver employed by them should start lifting any load until everyone in the vicinity had moved to a safe distance. A was found to have contributed to the accident by his negligence in standing too close to the crane, contrary to the written instruction of which (though he did not admit it) he was found to be aware. A was awarded £30,000 damages, less 20 per cent.

Comparison

11.39   In an increasing number of jurisdictions forms of compensation, rules as to legal liability and the method of obtaining compensation for personal injuries incurred at work are regulated by legislation. Many systems of compensation were to be found in the jurisdictions where we made enquiries. In New Zealand, for example, no legal proceedings would arise, since there is a state no-fault compensation scheme. In Sweden proceedings are rare since compensation is normally paid by the state work injury insurance scheme. Any compensation additional to that provided by the state scheme is generally settled by negotiation with the employer's insurers. When proceedings do occur in Sweden, they are preceded by extensive investigation and negotiations between the parties' ombudsmen. In a number of states of the USA and in Ontario workmen's compensation legislation has been introduced under which claims for work injuries are heard before statutory boards (before the Industrial Commission of Illinois, the Workmen's Compensation Appeals Board of California, Referees in Missouri and Workmen's Compensation Boards in Ontario) and liability is often on a no-fault basis, so that negligence does not have to be proved. In the United States the parties are normally legally represented, while in Ontario claimants normally represent themselves or have lay (for example union) representatives, and are assisted without charge by Board workers and advisers. In the other jurisdictions consulted there would be court proceedings (usually with a jury), at the equivalent of High Court level in Northern Ireland, New York, Victoria and New South Wales. Personal injury proceedings are often protracted, even in those jurisdictions where they are heard by tribunals. One reason is that it may be in the plaintiff's interest to delay matters until the final outcome of his injuries can be assessed medically, although the defendants may also wish to delay. In England and Wales the specimen case would take about three years. In New York it was thought likely to take longer. In many of the continental jurisdictions consulted by the Law Society, and also in Victoria and New South Wales, such a case would take up to about two years. In Zambia, however, it would take less than a year, in Sweden (despite lengthy negotiations) about 15 months, in Illinois (before the Industrial Commission) about six months to a year and in Missouri (before Referees) about six weeks. The amount of professional time taken on the plaintiff's behalf would be about 75 hours in England and Wales, roughly 30 hours in Sweden, California, New South Wales and Zambia, and about 114 hours in New York. The estimate for England and Wales was based on the assumption that it would be necessary in a case of this character, to obtain a number of experts' reports, although at the hearing only one agreed medical report would be put before the court. Slightly less time would be needed on the defendant's behalf in each of these jurisdictions. In the U.S.A., the fees of the plaintiff's lawyer may be payable on a contingency basis.

Wrongful dismissal from employment

Facts

11.40 W was employed as a wood turner by X Ltd. A large consignment of wooden bowls made by W was found to be defective and W was summarily dismissed by X Ltd from their employment (with full pay in lieu of the appropriate notice of termination). W maintained that the materials with which he had been supplied by X Ltd were not suitable for turning on a lathe and that he had done the best any skilled operator could do with the materials provided.

11.41 W brought an action against X Ltd claiming that he was wrongfully dismissed by them and that he was entitled to reinstatement in the job he had held until his dismissal.

11.42 At the hearing, at which both parties were represented by solicitors and counsel, W gave evidence on his own behalf and evidence was given on behalf of X Ltd by W's foreman and by a quality control inspector. It was held that W had been wrongfully dismissed and that he was entitled to damages, but not to reinstatement.

Comparison

11.43 In only a few of the jurisdictions consulted (Australia and Zambia) would these proceedings be heard before an ordinary court. In England and Wales, Northern Ireland and New Zealand they would be heard by an industrial tribunal and in Sweden (assuming the employee was a trade union member) by a labour court. In the United States and Ontario the employee would be unlikely to have a cause of action in the civil courts under his contract of employment, as such contracts are normally terminable at will. In those jurisdictions, under collective bargaining agreements with the employee's union, the matter would be dealt with by arbitration, following agreed grievance procedures. In England and Wales, Northern Ireland and New Zealand such proceedings were estimated to last about six months. Estimates of their duration in the USA suggest that they may take longer there than in England and Wales. In Zambia they would take about 10 months (which is the standard duration quoted for High Court proceedings there) and in Victoria and New South Wales, about a year to 18 months. Of those continental countries consulted by the Law Society, the proceedings would take six months or less in Denmark, Luxembourg, Germany and Italy, and six months to a year in Holland, Belgium, France and the Republic of Ireland. In most of the jurisdictions which produced estimates, the amount of professional time taken would be much the same, that is between 20 and 30 hours for both plaintiff and defendant. In Illinois the estimate was 48 hours each whereas in New Zealand only a few hours would be taken.

Shoplifting—prosecution

Facts

11.44　Mrs E was charged with shoplifting from a departmental store owned by XYZ Ltd involving the theft of goods valued at £10.90. A shop assistant was the only witness of the alleged theft. Mrs E claimed that the allegedly stolen goods found in her shopping basket when she was interviewed by a security officer employed by XYZ Ltd were purchased by her at another shop and were in her basket when she entered XYZ's store. She named the shop at which the goods were, she alleged, purchased by her, but no-one in that shop could recall serving her. In the magistrates' court she pleaded not guilty. She was granted legal aid for the purpose of her defence and retained a solicitor.

11.45　At the hearing the shop assistant, the security officer and a police officer gave evidence for the prosecution. Mrs E gave evidence on her own behalf and a former employer gave evidence of her good character. She was acquitted.

Comparison

11.46　This case would normally be tried by a subordinate court without a jury, although in California and, usually, Missouri there would be a jury trial. In most of the jurisdictions consulted, Mrs E would be tried within one to three months of being charged, in England and Wales, within about six weeks. In some of the continental countries consulted by the Law Society, however, the case would take up to six months or longer (in Italy, about three years). The amount of time spent on the case by Mrs E's lawyer would, in England and Wales, be about eight hours. In Victoria and New Zealand it would be about an hour and a half, in Sweden about four hours and in Ontario six to seven hours. In Missouri Mrs E's lawyer would spend about four to 14 hours on a summary trial, and about two hours more if (which would be normal) there was a jury trial. In California the trial, by jury, was thought likely to last about three days, increasing the professional time spent on the case to 35 to 36 hours.

Armed robbery—prosecution, not guilty plea

Facts

11.47　A was charged with shooting a night watchman who interrupted three men while they were in the process of preparing to blow the safe at a factory. All three men escaped immediately after the shooting, but one of them was seen by Mr and Mrs R, passing pedestrians, running from the factory gates towards a parked car in which two men were already waiting. The other men were never apprehended. A was identified by Mr and Mrs R at a police identification parade. A, when being questioned, said he was elsewhere at the time.

11.48　A was charged, denied his guilt and after preliminary proceedings was committed for trial in the Crown Court where he pleaded not guilty.

334

11.49   Evidence for the prosecution was given by the night watchman, a surgeon (concerning the night watchman's wounds), a forensic scientist (concerning the materials found on and near the safe and the bullet recovered from the night watchman's wound), Mr and Mrs R and four police officers. Evidence for the defence was given by A and two alibi witnesses, one of whom changed his story under cross-examination.

11.50   After a trial lasting four days, A was convicted.

Comparison

11.51   In most jurisdictions this case would be tried by a jury. In England and Wales A would be tried about nine months after being charged. In Sweden, Denmark, Western Australia, New Zealand, California, Missouri and, if A was in custody, Ontario, the trial would take place between one and a half and five months after charge. In New York the case would take anything between four and 11 months. In Victoria, Quebec, Ontario (if A was not in custody), Holland, Belgium, Luxembourg, Italy and Zambia it might take between six months and a year, while in the Republic of Ireland, although on average it would take about four months, it might take anything from two to 28 months. The amount of time spent on the case by A's lawyers would, in England and Wales, be about 80 hours. This is similar to the times quoted for California and Ontario. In Sweden, New Zealand and Missouri, only about half that time would be taken.

Armed robbery—prosecution, guilty plea

Facts

11.52   As described in paragraph 11.47 above; but on being charged, A admitted the offence and pleaded guilty in subsequent proceedings.

Comparison

11.53   The effect of admitting the offence is that, in all the jurisdictions consulted, the case would come to trial more quickly and in most jurisdictions no jury would be needed. In England and Wales the case would take about six months. It would take about the same length of time in several of the continental countries consulted by the Law Society and (if A was not in custody) in Ontario. In the other continental countries consulted, and in New Zealand, Ontario (if A was in custody), Missouri, California, Western Australia and Zambia, it would take only between one and three months. The amount of professional time spent on A's behalf would vary greatly from country to country. In England and Wales it would be about 18 hours; in Missouri between three and $8\frac{1}{2}$; in New Zealand $5\frac{1}{2}$; in Sweden $8\frac{1}{2}$; and in Ontario 30.

Dangerous driving—prosecution

Facts

11.54 A car being driven by D, on approaching a bend in the road, mounted the footpath and struck and seriously injured a passing pedestrian. D was charged with dangerous driving.

11.55 At his trial in the magistrates' court D pleaded not guilty. The prosecution called four witnesses: the injured pedestrian, a driver who had been following D and who had stopped at the scene of the accident, the arresting officer and a police officer who had taken measurements and photographs at the scene of the accident. The prosecution's case was that, although the road along which D was travelling was not subject to a speed limit of 30 or 40 mph, the speed at which D had been travelling was excessive in the prevailing conditions (narrow carriageway, approaching bend in road, bad weather) and that the manner of his driving had been the overriding cause of the accident.

11.56 D gave evidence on his own behalf and said that immediately before the accident he had felt his car veering towards the edge of the road and that he had been unable to rectify this movement or to stop the car before it mounted the kerb. He contended that the accident had been entirely due to a mechanical failure in the car (steering mechanism defect or burst tyre) for which he was in no way responsible and that his speed had had no bearing on the occurrence of the accident or its consequences. The damage done to D's car in the collision was such that no reliable evidence could afterwards be obtained, either in support of or in contradiction of his contention that the accident had been due to mechanical defect.

11.57 D was convicted as charged.

Comparison

11.58 This case would in most jurisdictions be tried by a subordinate court. In California the trial would be by jury and in New York and Illinois it could be although this would be unusual in the latter jurisdiction. In Canada the trial could (on the election of the Crown) be summary or on indictment; if the latter, D could elect whether to be tried by judge alone or by jury. In the other jurisdictions we consulted the trial would be by judge alone. In England and Wales D would be tried about six months after committing the offence. In some jurisdictions he would be tried very quickly: in New York, Missouri, California, New Zealand, Western Australia, Victoria and Denmark, about a month or two after receiving his summons or seeking legal advice. In New Zealand, a date of hearing in the magistrates' court a minimum of ten days and usually about two weeks ahead, is specified in the summons. In Sweden, Luxembourg and (if D were in custody) Ontario, D would be tried after three or four months. In Ontario, however, the case would take about seven to nine months if D were on bail, and it would (according to figures supplied to the Law Society) probably take a similar length of time (in some instances somewhat less, in others up to a year) in Quebec, Holland, Belgium, Germany and the Republic of Ireland. In Italy it is estimated to take about six years. The amount of time spent on the case by D's lawyers varies from jurisdiction to jurisdiction. In England and Wales it would be about eight hours. In Missouri it would only be about two and a half hours, in Victoria and New Zealand about four, in Sweden about seven and a half, in Ontario about 20 or 30 (if D was tried summarily, and about four more if he was tried on indictment), and in California 36 to 37 hours including a three-day jury trial. In Illinois D's lawyers would do a considerable amount of preparation for the trial, because of its being a possible prelude to a civil suit for damages.

Dangerous driving—civil proceedings

Facts
11.59   As in paragraphs 11.54–57 above; in subsequent civil proceedings which were contested by D on the issues of liability and quantum, the pedestrian with whom D's car had collided claimed damages in respect of his injury. D was held liable in full on the ground that on the evidence adduced in those proceedings (which was essentially the same as that adduced in the previous criminal proceedings) the plaintiff's injuries had been caused by D's negligent driving. The plaintiff was awarded £12,000 in damages.

Comparison
11.60   In certain jurisdictions no proceedings would arise. In New Zealand the claim would be met out of the state no-fault compensation scheme, while in Sweden a traffic insurance company would normally pay the pedestrian's damages, and any dispute (and trial) would be merely concerned with the amount of damages and would be between the pedestrian and D's insurance company. In England and Wales the case would be heard in the High Court and would take about 2½ years, with about 40 hours' preparation by lawyers for both plaintiff and defendant. The duration of the proceedings in the other jurisdictions consulted varied considerably. In Denmark, Belgium and Germany it was thought likely to be about six months. In Holland it would be about a year to 18 months and in the Republic of Ireland one to three years (about 18 months on average). In Zambia it would (like all High Court proceedings) be about 10 months, with about 25 hours spent on the case by the plaintiff's lawyers and about 22½ hours by the defendant's. In Missouri it would be about 1½ to two years, with about 90 hours' preparation by the plaintiff's lawyers and about 83 for the defendant's (who would be lawyers instructed by D's insurance company for the previous criminal proceedings as well). In Ontario (where personal injury cases are often tried by jury) it would be about two years but could be more than three years. The plaintiff's lawyers would spend about 40 hours on the case, and the defendant's about 35. Information obtained by the Law Society suggests that in New York (where D's insurance company would provide the defence lawyers) it would be about five years, and in Italy about six years.

337

Probate action

Facts

11.61 On 16th February 1976 Miss A, aged 85, who had been seriously ill and bedridden for some years, executed a will prepared for her by her nurse. The will gave legacies of £50 to each of her two sisters and the residue of a considerable estate to the nurse. Miss A died on 18th February 1976. Miss A's sisters, who knew that they were the only beneficiaries under a will of Miss A made in 1968, instructed their solicitor to contest the later will. The solicitor took preliminary steps to ensure that the 1976 will could not be admitted to probate uncontested: he entered a caveat in the Principal Probate Registry. The caveat was warned and an appearance entered to the warning and the nurse accordingly issued a writ seeking to establish the 1976 will.

11.62 In the ensuing High Court proceedings at which both parties were represented by solicitors and counsel evidence was given by the nurse on her own behalf and by one of the witnesses to the will. Evidence for the sisters was given by one of the sisters, a friend of the family and Miss A's doctor. Miss A's sisters sought to establish that Miss A did not know or approve the contents of the 1976 will, that the execution of the 1976 will was obtained by undue influence, and that the testatrix was not of sound mind, memory or understanding by virtue of her illness and old age when she executed the will. The Court held that the nurse was unable to show that Miss A knew and approved of the contents of the 1976 will, and that the deceased did not have the necessary testamentary capacity when executing the 1976 will, but made no finding on the issue of undue influence. The Court pronounced against the 1976 will and in favour of the 1968 will.

Comparison

11.63 The length of time taken by this case would be greatly affected by the length of negotiations or even (in some instances) by deliberate delaying tactics by one side or the other. In some jurisdictions it would very rarely come to trial, so that the figures quoted are only rough estimates. In England and Wales the proceedings would probably last about three years from the date of entry of the caveat. In most jurisdictions they would be quicker. They would take about two months in Denmark, and under six months in Sweden, Quebec, Missouri (where the trial would be by jury), and New South Wales. Estimates given for New Zealand indicated a possible range of six months to three years. In Ontario (for surrogate court proceedings—proceedings involving a large estate would be heard in the Supreme Court), Victoria, Zambia (where actions of this kind are extremely rare), Germany and the Republic of Ireland the proceedings would generally take six months to a year. Most such cases in Illinois are settled, but, if contested, could be expected to take between one and two years, possibly two to three years for a large estate. Between one and two years is said to be the normal period in Texas, Italy, Luxembourg, France and Belgium. In California there was thought to be a possibility that one side or the other would delay the proceedings to gain advantage in a settlement. In New York no probate contest on such simple facts would come to trial without settlement and in any case the parties could be expected to try to settle in the course of taking depositions outside the court before the trial, which would probably be by jury. The amount of professional time spent on the action would, in England and Wales, be about 75 hours for both plaintiff and defendant. In Sweden it would be about 15 hours for each. In Ontario, New South Wales and Zambia it would be roughly 20 hours for the plaintiff and slightly less for the defendant. In Missouri and New York State about 50 hours would be needed for the defendant and, in Missouri, slightly more for the plaintiff. In Texas (where the trial would last a week) over 160 hours would be needed for the plaintiff's case and over 180 for the defendant's, while in Illinois (where there would probably be two separate hearings, one for the initial proof of the will and one for its subsequent contest) 180 hours would be needed for the plaintiff and over 200 hours for the defendant. It should be noted that due to procedural variations, proceedings in Sweden, Zambia, Missouri and Illinois would be started by Miss A's sisters, rather than her nurse.

ANNEX 11.1

Organisations consulted
(paragraph 11.7)

England and Wales	The Law Society
	The Senate of the Inns of Court and the Bar
Northern Ireland:	The Incorporated Law Society of Northern Ireland
United States of America:	American College of Trial Lawyers
Canada:	Ontario Law Reform Commission
Sweden:	Ministry of Justice
Australia:	The Law Council of Australia
New Zealand:	New Zealand Law Society
Zambia:	Ministry of Legal Affairs

SECTION 12

The Accounts and Finances of the Four Inns of Court

This memorandum was prepared for the Commission by its consultants Coopers & Lybrand, and submitted by them in November 1977.

Contents

Tables (continued) *number*

Introduction

12.1   This memorandum has been prepared from our review of the audited financial accounts of the four Inns of Court:—

The Honourable Society of The Inner Temple (Inner Temple)

The Honourable Society of The Middle Temple (Middle Temple)

The Honourable Society of Lincoln's Inn (Lincoln's Inn)

The Honourable Society of Gray's Inn (Gray's Inn)

and from information supplied by the Under Treasurer of each Inn. We have not carried out any work in the nature of an audit.

12.2   The Under Treasurer of each Inn has seen a draft copy of this memorandum and has agreed that the facts in respect of the Inn concerned are fairly stated. We acknowledge the willing assistance we have received from each of the Inns.

Background

History and activities

12.3   For many centuries barristers were answerable for their conduct to the governing body of the Inn to which they belonged. In 1965 the Senate of the Four Inns of Court was created to which the Inns surrendered many of their functions in relation to the governance of the profession. The Senate of the Inns of Court and the Bar was established in 1974. In submission No. 2 to the Royal Commission, the Senate says that the main functions of the Inns are at present:—

(a) Providing chambers for their members in the vicinity of the courts and financing the provision of such accommodation in London and elsewhere.

(b) Providing law libraries for students and for barristers.

(c) Providing communal accommodation (halls, common rooms, etc) and catering, so that barristers as well as students can associate regularly for "talking shop".

(d) Providing the collegiate element in the training of Bar students by communal dining, moots, talks and exercises after dining in which judges and senior barristers participate and at weekends at Cumberland Lodge.

(e) Providing scholarships for students and young barristers.

Membership

12.4 There are three grades of members of the individual Inns—benchers, barristers and students.

12.5 The Inns admit as students all applicants "of good character" and who possess the necessary educational qualifications. In Table 12.1 the number of admissions of students of UK origin are set out for each year since 1971.

TABLE 12.1

UK students admitted to the Inns of Court, 1971–1976

	Student admissions				
	Lincoln's Inn	Inner Temple	Middle Temple	Gray's Inn	Total
1971	94	171	195	199	659
1972	101	164	254	226	745
1973	122	193	305	218	838
1974	111	186	304	239	840
1975	162	188	339	334	1,023
1976	119	144	263	272	798

Source: Senate Submission No. 7 to the Royal Commission.

12.6 A fee of £85 is payable on admission (comprising admission fee, composition fee and payment to the Council of Legal Education). A deposit of from £75 to £150 is also payable by an applicant who is not a graduate or undergraduate of a United Kingdom university, which is returnable on call to the Bar. The student can use the hall, library and common rooms of the Inn.

344

12.7 Having passed the Bar examinations and attended the prescribed number of dinners in his Inn the student is qualified for call to the Bar. Upon call he becomes a barrister member of the Inn. A call fee, normally of £75, is payable to the Inn.

12.8 There are some 70–130 benchers (or Masters of the Bench) of each Inn, elected from senior members of the Inn by the existing benchers. We were informed that, ignoring temporary vacancies, some 40–65 of these are practising barristers and the remainder are judges or honorary benchers. Most of the practising barristers who are benchers are senior QCs and few of them are juniors. A fee is payable on call to the Bench, £350 for Middle Temple and £400 for the other three Inns.

12.9 The government of each Inn is vested in the benchers assembled in general meeting. Administration of each Inn is controlled by various committees made up of both benchers and non-benchers.

Staff

12.10 Each Inn has a permanent staff under an Under Treasurer (Sub-Treasurer at Inner Temple). We set out in Table 12.2 the approximate numbers of full-time staff at present.

TABLE 12.2

Numbers of full-time staff employed by the Inns of Court

	Lincoln's Inn	Inner Temple	Middle Temple	Gray's Inn	Total
Treasurer's office	12	13	8	9	42
Library	5	8	10	5	28
Kitchen and catering	26	40	25	15	106
Works department/Surveyor's office	11	14	13	5	43
Miscellaneous, including porters and gardeners	19	13	8	12	52
Total	73	88	64	46	271

In addition to the above there are part-time cleaners, clerks and others. Middle Temple does not employ any gardeners. Inner Temple is responsible for the Temple gardens and recovers one-third of the cost from Middle Temple.

Pensions

12.11 Lincoln's Inn, Middle Temple and Gray's Inn operate non-contributory pension schemes for their staff. Inner Temple provides pensions for its staff having more than ten years' service, out of current income, on an ex-gratia basis. We comment below on the schemes operated by the other Inns.

345

12.12   The Lincoln's Inn scheme started in 1973 and is open to all full-time staff over the age of 25 years provided they have at least two years' service and are not within 5 years of retiring age (65 men, 60 women). The pension is based on 1/60th of final salary for each year's service (though those who would have benefited under the previous ex-gratia scheme receive a pension based on 1/50th of final salary rising to 1/40th for service in excess of 15 years). In addition there are benefits for widows and upon death. The fund, which is uninsured, is managed by three trustees appointed by the Masters of the Bench. Levels of contribution from the Inn are assessed on actuarial advice. We have been informed that Lincoln's Inn does not intend to contract out of the new state pension scheme when it comes into operation and as a result the pension scheme will be revised next year.

12.13   The Middle Temple scheme, which started in 1968, is open to all full-time employees. The pension is based on 1/60th of the final salary per year of service. In addition there are death benefits and provisions for widows. The fund is managed by the Inn's own trustees through the Legal and General Assurance Company and, on the basis of actuarial valuation, the Inn currently contributes 19·6 per cent of the annual salary bill.

12.14   The Gray's Inn scheme, which started in 1974, is open to all male members of the staff under 60 with at least one year's service and all female members under 55 with five years' service. The principal benefit is a pension of 1/45th of the average of the employee's last three years' salaries for each year of service. In addition there are death benefits and provisions for widows. The fund is with Commercial Union and the Inn receives financial advice from Pension and Capital Planning Limited on the level of its contribution.

Charitable status of the Inns

12.15   Lincoln's Inn and Gray's Inn have no written constitutions; the properties of Inner Temple and Middle Temple are held under Royal Charter of James I, although we are told that the terms of the Charter are unclear. Certain of the activities of the Inns were regarded by the Inland Revenue as charitable and therefore exempt from corporation tax, broadly being those relating to the churches, to legal education and to the library. To segregate these activities the Inns some years ago set up the following trusts:—

Inn	Trust
Lincoln's Inn	Special trustees account.
	Students trustees account.
Inner Temple	The Charitable Trust Fund of the Inner Temple.
Middle Temple	Special Trust account.
Gray's Inn	The Honourable Society of Gray's Inn Charitable Trust.

12.16   Until 31 December 1973 the Inns were assessed to corporation tax on their income, other than that relating to the trusts referred to in the previous paragraph. From 1 January 1974 the Inns were not assessed to tax except on income deemed to be used for non-charitable purposes—this income has been taken as an amount equal to the deficit, if any, of the collegiate, or members, account. Gray's Inn has, therefore, in its accounts to 31 December 1976, provided for corporation tax on the deficit on its collegiate account at the rate of 42 per cent. Lincoln's Inn and Middle Temple made a surplus on collegiate account in the year and have, therefore, made no provision for tax. Inner Temple showed a deficit for the year of £54,850 but has an accumulated surplus on its collegiate account and has, therefore, also not provided for tax.

12.17   Although therefore treated to some extent by the Inland Revenue as charities since 1 January 1974, the Inns are not registered as charities with the Charity Commissioners. With regard to other professional bodies, the Royal College of Surgeons is a registered charity, but so far as we are aware, none of the other main professional bodies has obtained full charity status. For example, the Institute of Chartered Accountants in England and Wales is not a registered charities since 1 January 1974, the Inns are not registered as charities with the a wholly owned trust company.

12.18   Following consideration of our draft report the Inns jointly gave us the following comments:—

> Although they conduct some activities of a non-charitable nature, the Inns of Court are *sui generis* and are not comparable to the professional bodies referred to in paragraph 12.17. No Inn has made an application to be registered as a charity with the Charity Commissioners and, indeed, no Inn would assert that all its activities are charitable. Informal discussions did take place with the Charity Commissioners a few years ago; and following the decision of the Court of Appeal in upholding the charitable status of the Incorporated Council of Law Reporting, the Inland Revenue have agreed to treat the Inns of Court as charities from January 1 1974, except to the extent that their income/gains are applied to non-charitable purposes, viz. subscriptions to the Senate and deficit upon catering for members other than the students.

Special trust funds

12.19   In addition to the charitable trusts set up by the Inns to segregate their own expenditure of a charitable nature the Inns manage a number of scholarship and other funds which are the result of endowments from former members and others. These trust funds are shown in Table 12.3.

Accounts

12.20   In 1975 the Inns agreed that the presentation of their accounts should be on a uniform basis. In accordance with this policy, Inner Temple changed its accounting year-end to 31 December and prepared accounts for the period from 26 March 1975 to 31 December 1975. Accounts for each of the Inns were prepared as at 31 December 1975 and 1976 and in these accounts an attempt was made to present items on a consistent basis from Inn to Inn. However, as we mention below, there are still instances where the Inns allocate expenditure or describe items differently in their accounts.

TABLE 12.3

Trust funds managed by the Inns of Court

	Net assets per accounts £'000	as at
Gray's Inn:		
Gray's Inn Charitable Trust	48	
Gray's Inn Scholarships Trust	182	
	230	31 December
		1976
Inner Temple:		
The Charitable Trust Fund of the Inner Temple	(6)	
Inner Temple General, Prize and Scholarships Trust Fund	34	
	28	31 December
		1976
Middle Temple:		
The Astbury Scholarship Fund	200	
Harmsworth Memorial Fund	229	
Eight other trust funds	53	
	482	30 September
		1976
Lincoln's Inn:		
Twenty one separate trust funds	154	31 December
		1975

12.21   The accounts are approved in detail by each Inn's finance committee and formally adopted by the Masters of the Bench. Although they are not published, the Inns exchange copies and copies are sent to the Senate and, we were told, are available for inspection by the members. Lincoln's Inn, Inner Temple and Gray's Inn provide an abbreviated version of their accounts at their annual meetings.

12.22   The accounts of Lincoln's Inn and Middle Temple are audited by Clark Pixley, chartered accountants, and those of Inner Temple and Gray's Inn by Hill Vellacott, chartered accountants. In the accounts to 31 December 1976 Hill Vellacott qualified their audit reports on the grounds that certain assets are not recorded in the books and, in the case of Gray's Inn, buildings are recorded at a 1950 valuation; subject to this their audit reports state that the accounts of Inner Temple and Gray's Inn give a true and fair view of the state of affairs and income and expenditure. The audit reports of Clark Pixley on the other two Inns' accounts to 31 December 1976 are unqualified and state that the accounts give a true and fair view of the state of affairs and of the results.

348

Form of the accounts

12.23 Although the form of the accounts differs slightly from Inn to Inn, they all include:—

(a) A balance sheet (or "statement of balances" for Lincoln's Inn) and supporting detailed notes. The principal omissions from the balance sheets are the great majority of the fixed assets, although Gray's Inn includes buildings at a 1950 valuation and subsequent additions at cost.

(b) A general income and expenditure account and supporting schedules. This account reflects all income and expenditure, including most expenditure of a capital nature, other than that deemed to relate to the members (see (c) below). The principal income is from renting the buildings (estate income) and the main expenditure is on the administration of the Inn and the cost of the charitable activities.

(c) A collegiate income and expenditure account and supporting schedules. This is an income and expenditure account of the activities of the members. The principal sources of income are admission fees and call fees and the principal expenditures are catering and a subscription to the Senate.

12.24 In the following two sections of this memorandum we set out and comment on the income and expenditure and assets and liabilities shown in the audited accounts at 31 December 1976. For this purpose we have combined the general and collegiate income and expenditure accounts. We have also included expenditure reimbursed by each Inn to its related charitable trusts—that is the amount of the trusts' expenditure less income from the trusts' own sources, normally a very small income from dividends.

Income and expenditure

Introduction

12.25 We set out in Table 12.4 a summary of the income and expenditure of the four Inns of Court for the year ended 31 December 1976 as shown by the audited accounts. In showing comparative figures for 1975, we have apportioned the figures for Inner Temple on a time basis.

12.26 There are a number of differences between the Inns in the allocation of expenses between the heads shown above. For example, Middle Temple includes under "administration" the wages of the surveyor and car park attendants, whereas the other Inns include these under "estate expenses". Information is not readily available to adjust for these differences and we have made no adjustment for them. However, we note below where we have been told that these differences could materially distort comparisons between the Inns.

TABLE 12.4

Summary of income and expenditure of the Inns of Court: year ended 31 December 1976

	Paragraph	Lincoln's Inn	Inner Temple	Middle Temple	Gray's Inn	1976 total	1975 total
		£'000	£'000	£'000	£'000	£'000	£'000
Income: estate, net of expenses	12.27–12.33	267	406	309	460	1,442	1,256
members	12.34–12.36	26	29	43	43	141	213
investment	12.37	24	12	39	1	76	90
miscellaneous	12.38	8	4	9	2	23	61
		325	451	400	506	1,682	1,620
Expenditure: administration	12.39–12.41	185	118	207	175	685	563
education	12.42–12.44	59	66	26	70	221	221
catering net loss	12.45–12.46	32	66	34	67	199	182
library	12.47	44	57	55	46	202	180
subscription to Senate	12.48–12.51	20	20	20	25	85	67
church	12.52	2	11	17	3	33	39
donations		3	3	3	5	14	12
miscellaneous		1	1	5	—	7	4
		346	342	367	391	1,446	1,268
Surplus/ (deficit) before tax and exceptional items		(21)	109	33	115	236	352
Tax	12.53	—	—	—	(19)	(19)	(10)
		(21)	109	33	96	217	342
Exceptional and prior year items	12.54–12.55	23	(33)	21	(8)	3	(78)
Surplus		2	76	54	88	220	264

The Middle Temple surplus of £54,000 is reduced to £4,000 in its accounts by a transfer to the New Building Fund (see paragraph 12.71). Income and expenditure accounts of the four Inns for the years ended 31 December 1974, 1975 and 1976 are set out at annex 12.1.

Estate income, net of expenses

12.27 The bulk of the income of the Inns comes from rents from letting the Inns' premises. We set out in Table 12.5 an analysis of the income from lettings for the year ended 31 December 1976.

TABLE 12.5

Estate income of the Inns of Court: year ended 31 December 1976

	Lincoln's Inn	Inner Temple	Middle Temple	Gray's Inn	1976 total	1975 total
	£'000	£'000	£'000	£'000	£'000	£'000
Rents:						
chambers	180	451	290	82	1,003	823
offices	327	81	59	531	998	848
residential	43	29	42	28	142	131
	550	561	391	641	2,143	1,802
Sundry income	44	20	11	33	108	96
Total estate income	594	581	402	674	2,251	1,898
Estate expenses	(327)	(175)	(93)	(214)	(809)	(642)
Net estate income	267	406	309	460	1,442	1,256

Rents

12.28 Chambers are leased to barristers. There is no requirement on the head tenant of a set of chambers to be a member of the Inn in which his chambers are situated except in Inner Temple. The office accommodation is leased mostly to firms of solicitors though some is occupied by other professional people such as architects and surveyors. Residential accommodation is nearly all occupied by members of the Inn in which the accommodation is situated. The proportion of accommodation let to barristers is lowest in Gray's Inn, where there are only 17 chambers within the Inn, and greatest in Inner and Middle Temples. It should be noted that the different Inns use different terminology to describe accommodation occupied by barristers and non-barristers; for the purposes of this memorandum we have confined ourselves to the terms "chambers", "offices" and "residential" defined as in this paragraph.

12.29 The Under Treasurers at the Inns informed us that the rent payable by chambers was, in the case of Inner and Middle Temples and Gray's Inn, two-thirds of a full rack rent and in the case of Lincoln's Inn at present one-half of a full rack rent, although it is proposed to increase this to two-thirds at the March 1978 rent review. Chambers' leases are reviewable quarterly in the cases of Inner and Middle Temples, annually in Lincoln's Inn and every three years for Gray's Inn. Further details are given at annex 12.2.

351

Sundry income

12.30 Sundry income principally consists of service charges and income from parking permits enabling the holder to park within the boundaries of the Inn. Each Inn has a different scale of charges for such permits which range from £20–£125 per annum.

Estate expenses

12.31 Expenditure in the year ended 31 December 1976 may be analysed as shown in Table 12.6.

TABLE 12.6

Estate expenditure of the Inns of Court: year ended 31 December 1976

	Lincoln's Inn	Inner Temple	Middle Temple	Gray's Inn	1976 total	1975 total
	£'000	£'000	£'000	£'000	£'000	£'000
Repairs and maintenance	185	94	46	120	445	336
Services	97	60	11	72	240	221
Mortgage interest	36	—	—	—	36	41
Other expenses	9	21	36	22	88	44
	327	175	93	214	809	642

12.32 Included in the above expenses are the wages of the works departments. As we have noted, Middle Temple include some expenses under administration (see paragraph 12.26) which is classified as estate expenses in the other Inns. Also included in estate expenses is the cost of professional advice on property matters; the Inns take advice from several firms of professional property advisers.

12.33 Lincoln's Inn's mortgage interest is in respect of a mortgage loan secured on Hale Court and 24, Old Buildings. We are informed that the mortgage, which was taken out in 1969 in an amount of £600,000, is for 40 years with interest at $7\frac{1}{4}$ per cent for the first 20 years and then subject to revision. Lincoln's Inn has had to incur very heavy repairs expenditure for a number of years.

Members

12.34 Income recorded in the members' accounts for the year ended 31 December 1976 may be analysed as shown in Table 12.7.

Admission fees

12.35 Admission fees are charged to each person who wishes to become a member of an Inn. The great majority of these are students but there are a number of *ad eundem* admissions—members of one Inn becoming members of another, normally because they are tenants of a chamber of that Inn. Current

TABLE 12.7

Membership income of the Inns of Court: year ended 31 December 1976

	Lincoln's Inn	Inner Temple	Middle Temple	Gray's Inn	1976 total	1975 total
	£'000	£'000	£'000	£'000	£'000	£'000
Admission fees	14	14	19	24	71	127
Calls to the Bar	11	12	17	16	56	68
Calls to the Bench	—	3	1	3	7	7
Life commutation of duties and fees and other income	1	—	6	—	7	11
	26	29	43	43	141	213

admission fees for students are £85 for each Inn and *ad eundem* admission fees range from £50 to £200 depending on the Inn and seniority of the barristers. Lincoln's Inn reduce charges for benchers' sons and certain students are admitted free on scholarships provided by the Inn.

Call fees

12.36 Call fees are levied when a member is called to the Bar or becomes a bencher. Call to the Bar fees are £75 for each Inn; call to the Bench fees are £350 for Middle Temple and £400 for each of the other Inns. Benchers of the Middle Temple have to pay an additional fee of £5 per term.

Investment income

12.37 Investment income comprises dividends and interest on quoted and unquoted securities and loans (see paragraph 12.61).

Miscellaneous income

12.38 This is virtually all students' deposits written off after being unclaimed for fifteen years (see paragraph 12.67).

Administration expenses

12.39 We set out in Table 12.8 an analysis of administration costs for the year ended 31 December 1976.

12.40 Salaries and wages are mainly in respect of the Under Treasurers' office, although Middle Temple informed us that they include wages which the other Inns show under different heads, for example under estate expenses.

12.41 Accommodation costs include rates, repairs, heating, lighting and insurance, mainly applicable to the administrative buildings although there again appear to be differences between the Inns in the allocation of costs.

TABLE 12.8

Administrative costs of the Inns of Court: year ended 31 December 1976

	Lincoln's Inn	Inner Temple	Middle Temple	Gray's Inn	1976 total	1975 total
	£'000	£'000	£'000	£'000	£'000	£'000
Salaries and wages	79	39	76	41	235	197
Pension fund	30	—	27	35	92	76
Pensions and donations	19	21	19	21	80	41
Accommodation	21	42	59	51	173	155
Printing, stationery and telephone	8	4	8	12	32	24
Legal and professional	9	8	7	1	25	25
Bank interest	—	—	—	6	6	16
Miscellaneous	19	4	11	8	42	29
	185	118	207	175	685	563

Education

12.42 We set out in Table 12.9 an analysis of expenditure on education for the year ended 31 December 1976.

TABLE 12.9

Expenditure on education by the Inns of Court: year ended 31 December 1976

	Lincoln's Inn	Inner Temple	Middle Temple	Gray's Inn	1976 total	1975 total
	£'000	£'000	£'000	£'000	£'000	£'000
Scholarships and prizes	17	20	35	24	96	116
Less amount met out of trust funds	(8)	(4)	(30)	(11)	(53)	(57)
	9	16	5	13	43	59
Contribution to catering costs	28	39	17	35	119	98
Other expenses	22	11	4	22	59	64
	59	66	26	70	221	221

12.43 The number of students who received scholarships, prizes and grants from the Inns in 1975 is given in Table 12.10.

TABLE 12.10

Number and value of scholarships, prizes and grants awarded by the Inns of Court in 1975

	Lincoln's Inn	Inner Temple	Middle Temple	Gray's Inn
Value	£18,000	£28,000	£42,000	£47,000
Number	45	88	96	179
Average value	£400	£318	£438	£263

Catering

12.44   The contribution to catering costs represents approximately one-third to one-half of the deficit on the catering account (see paragraph 12.45). We understand that each Inn has agreed with the Inland Revenue an appropriate allocation to arrive at the cost of subsidised meals to students.

12.45   We set out in Table 12.11 an analysis of the catering income and expenditure for the year ended 31 December 1976.

TABLE 12.11

Catering income of and expenditure by the Inns of Court: year ended 31 December 1976

	Lincoln's Inn	Inner Temple	Middle Temple	Gray's Inn	1976 total	1975 total
	£'000	£'000	£'000	£'000	£'000	£'000
Income	36	62	82	34	214	179
Expenditure:						
salaries	64	86	70	65	285	244
cost of food	32	55	34	37	158	144
cost of drink	7	13	16	11	47	36
other	2	25	17	34	78	69
staff meals	(9)	(12)	(4)	(11)	(36)	(34)
	96	167	133	136	532	459
Deficit	(60)	(105)	(51)	(102)	(318)	(280)
Less attributable to students and included in education costs	28	39	17	35	119	98
Net deficit	(32)	(66)	(34)	(67)	(199)	(182)

12.46 The net deficit is attributable to members and will include costs of entertaining. The costs shown in Table 12.11 do not include an allocation of general administration expenses and include no rental for use of the premises. The costs are therefore mainly direct costs of providing meals.

Library

12.47 Each Inn has its own library and the expenditure in the year to 31 December 1976 is in Table 12.12.

TABLE 12.12

Expenditure on library facilities by the Inns of Court: year ended 31 December 1976

	Lincoln's Inn	Inner Temple	Middle Temple	Gray's Inn	1976 total	1975 total
	£'000	£'000	£'000	£'000	£'000	£'000
Salary costs	19	27	36	19	101	88
Books and binding	10	18	18	13	59	50
Accommodation and other costs	15	12	1	14	42	42
	44	57	55	46	202	180

Accommodation costs include heating, lighting and related costs allocated to the library, except Middle Temple which has not allocated any accommodation costs to its library account.

Subscription to Senate

12.48 The subscriptions of the Inns to the Senate of the Inns of Court and the Bar in the years ended 31 December 1975 and 1976 are shown in Table 12.13.

TABLE 12.13

The Inns subscriptions to the Senate: years ended 31 December 1975 and 1976

	1975 £'000	1976 £'000
Lincoln's Inn	19	20
Inner Temple	15	20
Middle Temple	19	20
Gray's Inn	14	25
	67	85

12.49   On formation of the new Senate in July 1974 regulations were made which included "Understandings" as to the contributions to be made by the Inns to the finances of the Senate. These are reproduced at annex 12.3. In summary, these provided that:—

(a) The annual running costs of the Senate up to the 1974 level should be paid from its subscription income and from contributions from the Inns, in the same proportions as previously.

(b) Further costs, including the costs of special projects should be borne between subscription income and contributions from the Inns in equal proportions, or such other proportion determined by the Senate.

In effect the contribution is decided by each Inn following discussion with the Senate.

12.50   We summarise in Table 12.14 the income and expenditure of the new Senate since its incorporation in July 1974.

TABLE 12.14

Income and expenditure of the Senate: 1974/75–1976/77

	28 July 1974 to 5 April 1975		Year to 5 April 1976		Year to 5 April 1977	
	£'000	%	£'000	%	£'000	%
Income:						
subscriptions from members of the Bar	50	62	142	62	158	62
contributions from Inns of Court	24	30	80	35	80	32
other income	6	8	6	3	15	6
Total income	80	100	228	100	253	100
Expenditure:						
salaries and payroll overheads	67		130		117	
rent, rates and other establishment expenses	6		25		29	
other expenses	12		28		23	
Total expenses	85		183		169	
Surplus/(deficit)	(5)		45		84	

12.51   It can be seen from Table 12.14 that subscriptions from members of the Bar provided 62 per cent of the Senate's income in the period since it was formed until 5 April 1977.

357

Church expenses

12.52   The expenses relate to the Lincoln's Inn and Gray's Inn chapels and to the Temple church.

Tax

12.53   Gray's Inn has provided for corporation tax at 42 per cent on the deficit in its collegiate accounts for the years ended 31 December 1975 and 1976 (see paragraph 12.16 above).

Exceptional and prior year items

12.54   Exceptional and prior year items for the year ended 31 December 1976 aer set out in Table 12.15.

TABLE 12.15

Exceptional and prior year items in the accounts of the Inns of Court: year ended 31 December 1976

	Lincoln's Inn	Inner Temple	Middle Temple	Gray's Inn	1976 total	1975 total
	£'000	£'000	£'000	£'000	£'000	£'000
Capital expenditure	(33)	(24)	(7)	—	(64)	(78)
Depreciation	—	—	—	(3)	(3)	(3)
Profit/(loss) on sale of investments	19	(11)	26	—	34	(4)
Other items	37	2	2	(5)	36	7
	23	(33)	21	(8)	3	(78)

In addition to the above, students' deposits written off of £51,000 were shown under exceptional items in the 1975 accounts; in this memorandum we have shown this item against the comparative figure in the 1976 accounts under "miscellaneous income".

12.55   Apart from certain specific exceptions, mentioned in paragraph 12.58 below, expenditure of a capital nature is charged in the general income and expenditure account.

Students

12.56   In Table 12.16 we show the income from admission and call fees and a broad estimate of the expenditure of the Inns on students. We have included the expenditure on education shown in paragraph 12.42 above. Lincoln's Inn prepares a statement of the amount of expenditure for the benefit of students: this statement incorporates an allocation of two-thirds of the expenditure on the library and approximately ten per cent of the administration expenditure.

We were told that these proportions were derived from calculations of the amount of staff time spent, and that the basis has been agreed with the Inland Revenue. We do not know whether similar proportions would be appropriate for the other Inns, but in the absence of actual figures we have applied these proportions to the library and administration expenditure of the other Inns in preparing the table below. It should be noted that the expenditure does not include amounts met out of privately established trusts administered by the Inns.

TABLE 12.16

Income from, and estimated expenditure on, students by the Inns of Court: year ended 31 December 1976

	Lincoln's Inn	Inner Temple	Middle Temple	Gray's Inn	1976 total	1975 total
	£'000	£'000	£'000	£'000	£'000	£'000
Income:						
admission fees	14	14	19	24	71	127
call fees	11	12	17	16	56	68
	25	26	36	40	127	195
Expenditure:						
scholarships and prizes	9	16	5	13	43	59
catering	28	39	17	35	119	98
other expenses	22	11	4	22	59	64
library (two-thirds)	29	38	37	30	134	120
administration (10%)	19	12[1]	21	17	69	55
	107	116	84	117	424	396
Excess of expenditure over income	(82)	(90)	(48)	(77)	(297)	(201)

[1] Inner Temple has assessed the amount of administration expenses relating to students in the year ended 31 December at £15,487. However, for purposes of comparison we have included only 10 per cent of total expenses.

Assets and liabilities

Introduction

12.57 We summarise in Table 12.17 the assets and liabilities shown by the audited balance sheets of the Inns as at 31 December 1976.

TABLE 12.17

Assets and liabilities of the Inns of Court: at 31 December 1976

	Paragraphs	Lincoln's Inn	Inner Temple	Middle Temple	Gray's Inn
		£'000	£'000	£'000	£'000
Fixed assets	12.58–12.60	40	—	148	2,612
Investments	12.61	349	208	350	88
Current assets:					
stocks	12.62	47	11	47	39
tax recoverable		—	—	36	—
debtors	12.63–12.64	270	286	171	235
bank		—	31	1	—
		317	328	255	274
Current liabilities:					
overdraft	12.65	—	88	46	78
tax	12.66	—	—	—	37
creditors		146	136	135	140
		146	224	181	255
Net current assets		171	104	74	19
Repayable student deposits	12.67–12.68	(153)	(80)	(86)	(64)
Net assets		407	232	486	2,655
Accumulated funds:					
general funds		(82)	96	71	374
collegiate fund		173	109	177	2,281
special reserves	12.69–12.71	316	27	238	—
		407	232	486	2,655

The balance sheets of the Inns at 31 December 1974, 1975 and 1976 are set out at annex 12.4.

Fixed Assets

12.58   The fixed assets listed in Table 12.18 were recorded in the books of the Inns at 31 December 1976. The freehold property at Southampton is owned jointly by the three Inns below. The heating installation is being amortised over 20 years. The cost of the leasehold property, Devereux Chambers, is being amortised over the life of the lease of $19\frac{1}{2}$ years. No depreciation is provided on the other properties.

TABLE 12.18

Fixed assets of the Inns of Court: as recorded in the Inns' books of account at 31 December 1976

	Lincoln's Inn	Middle Temple	Gray's Inn	Total
	£'000	£'000	£'000	£'000
Buildings at 1950 valuation or subsequent cost	—	—	2,533	2,533
Heating installation	—	—	48	48
Freehold chambers in Southampton	30	31	31	92
13 Cotsford Avenue, New Malden	10	—	—	10
2 New Street, Leicester	—	20	—	20
Devereux Chambers—leasehold	—	97	—	97
	40	148	2,612	2,800

12.59   Most of the properties are of nineteenth century or earlier origin. The buildings of the Inner and Middle Temples, with the exception of a few recent additions, are held on trust under a Royal Charter of James I and we were informed that they cannot be sold or mortgaged. There is probably no such legal restriction on the buildings of Gray's Inn or Lincoln's Inn. With the exception of the buildings and heating installation shown above, all the fixed assets of the Inns are unrecorded in the books of account. No depreciation charge is made in respect of such assets and, in general, no renewals funds are maintained. However, Lincoln's Inn was advised by its surveyor in 1974 that expenditure on reconstruction and non-routine maintenance on all its buildings would amount, over the next 15 years, to approximately £1 million. Lincoln's Inn intends making transfers to its reconstruction and maintenance reserve to ensure that costs are charged evenly over this period.

12.60   The only available valuations are those for insurance purposes and these we summarise in Table 12.19.

TABLE 12.19

Fixed assets of the Inns of Court: valuations for insurance purposes

	Lincoln's Inn	Inner Temple	Middle Temple	Gray's Inn	Total
	£'000	£'000	£'000	£'000	£'000
Buildings	29,843	32,396	26,764	14,145	103,148
Silver, pictures and other chattels	1,116	678	1,125	149	3,068
	30,959	33,074	27,889	14,294	106,216

Investments

12.61   The investments of the Inns are summarised in Table 12.20.

TABLE 12.20
Investments held by the Inns of Court: at 31 December 1976

	Lincoln's Inn	Inner Temple	Middle Temple	Gray's Inn
	£'000	£'000	£'000	£'000
Mortgages	17	—	—	10
Loans:				
staff	—	11	—	1
chambers	—	14	—	13
loan scheme	—	—	—	64
Securities:				
government and convertible stocks	55	16	167	—
quoted investments	277	167	183	—
Total book value	349	208	350	88
Market value, per accounts	421	225	361	88

The Gray's Inn loan scheme was started three years ago to make interest-free loans to newly-qualified barristers. Individual loans vary from £500 to £750 and are repayable half after three years and half after four years.

Stocks

12.62   Stocks principally consist of wine. The notes to the accounts state that the valuation of stocks is as follows:—

(a)   Lincoln's Inn—lower of cost and net realisable value,

(b)   Inner Temple—professional stocktakers' valuation at cost,

(c)   Middle Temple—lower of cost and net realisable value,

(d)   Gray's Inn—cost.

Debtors

12.63   Debtors are analysed in the accounts as shown in Table 12.21.

TABLE 12.21
Debtors of the Inns of Court: at 31 December 1976

	Lincoln's Inn	Inner Temple	Middle Temple	Gray's Inn
	£'000	£'000	£'000	£'000
Tenants	173	179	130	156
Members	2	7	3	8
Sundry, including prepayments	95	100	39	71
	270	286	172	235

12.64   Many rents are payable in arrears on quarter days. The amounts shown in Table 12.21 as due from tenants therefore include substantial amounts due on 25 December 1976 and not received by the year-end.

Overdrafts

12.65   It will be noted that three Inns showed substantial overdrafts in their accounts at 31st December 1976: Inner Temple (£88,000), Middle Temple (£46,000) and Gray's Inn (£78,000). The Under Treasurer at Middle Temple informed us that, by agreement, the overdraft on the Inn's general accounts is offset by balances on Middle Temple trust accounts and the EEC library account, with the result that the Inn bears no interest charge. The EEC library account is administered without charge by the Middle Temple on behalf of the four Inns.

Tax

12.66   Only Gray's Inn has provided for corporation tax (see paragraph 12.16).

Repayable students' deposits

12.67   Deposits made on admission by students against future call fees are credited to profit and loss account by the Inns if they are unclaimed after 15 years. The balances therefore represent deposits received since 1960 and not repaid. The amounts received from students as deposits are not separately banked or invested from the Inn's other monies. Deposits are only required from students who are not graduates or undergraduates of a United Kingdom university and in recent years the amounts received have diminished considerably—the amounts received in 1976 were:—

	£'000
Lincoln's Inn	3
Inner Temple	3
Middle Temple	–
Gray's Inn	6
	12

12.68   Deposits are reclaimable upon death or withdrawal and on call to the Bar, whether or not the amounts have been written off in the accounts of the Inn. The Inns told us that they would favourably consider requests for repayment from continuing students who are in financial difficulties.

Special reserves

12.69   We set out in Table 12.22 a summary of the special reserves of the Inns at 31st December 1976.

363

TABLE 12.22

Special reserves held by the Inns of Court: at 31 December 1976

	Lincoln's Inn	Inner Temple	Middle Temple	Gray's Inn
	£'000	£'000	£'000	£'000
North Garden Compensation Fund	291	—	—	—
Reconstruction and maintenance reserve	25	—	—	—
New Building Fund	—	20	209	—
Others	—	7	29	—
	316	27	238	—

12.70   The North Garden Compensation Fund is the unexpended balance of an amount received by Lincoln's Inn from the Department of the Environment as compensation after planning permission for the North Garden was refused. We understand that if the proposed development is eventually allowed, some or all of the compensation received may have to be refunded and consequently the amount of the compensation is invested separately from Lincoln's Inn's other funds.

12.71   In the year to 31 December 1976 Middle Temple charged improvements at Fountain Court against the New Building Fund, as follows:—

	New Building Fund £'000
as at 1st January 1976	259
transfer from general reserves	50
	309
less improvements at Fountain Court	100
as at 31st December 1976	209

Summary

Background

12.72   The government of each Inn is vested in the benchers in general meeting. Benchers are elected by existing benchers of the Inns. According to the Inns, about half of the benchers are practising barristers and the remainder are judges or honorary benchers (paragraphs 12.4–12.11).

12.73   Each of the Inns has a permanent staff, varying from 46 full-time staff at Gray's Inn to 88 full-time staff at Inner Temple. A substantial proportion of these are kitchen and catering staff and other staff are engaged in the maintenance of the buildings and gardens. Each Inn has about 20 staff employed in the Treasurer's office or library (paragraph 12.10).

12.74 Inner Temple does not have a pension scheme. The other three Inns have recently started their own non-contributory pension schemes which in general are open to all full-time staff and provide for pensions based on final salaries. The Middle Temple and Gray's Inn schemes are invested with insurance companies (paragraphs 12.11–12.14).

12.75 The Inns are not registered charities with the Charity Commissioners but since 1st January 1974 they have been treated to some extent by the Inland Revenue as charities (paragraphs 12.15–12.17). Gray's Inn made a small provision for tax in its 1976 accounts. The other Inns made no such provision (paragraph 12.53). The Inns jointly gave us comments concerning their charitable status which we set out at paragraph 12.18.

12.76 Each Inn prepares annual accounts which are audited by firms of chartered accountants. The auditors' reports on the 1976 accounts state that the accounts give a "true and fair view" of the state of affairs and results, but the accounts of Inner Temple and Gray's Inn were qualified on the grounds that certain assets are not recorded in the books and that the accounts of Gray's Inn include buildings at a 1950 valuation. Although the first matter also applies to the accounts of Lincoln's Inn and Middle Temple, their accounts, which are audited by a separate firm, were not qualified (paragraphs 12.20–12.22).

12.77 In the 1975 accounts an attempt was made by the Inns for the first time to present their accounts on a uniform basis. There are, however, still certain differences between the Inns in the allocation of costs and presentation of the 1976 accounts (paragraphs 12.20 and 12.26).

12.78 The accounts of the Inns are approved and adopted by the benchers. The accounts are not published although we were told that they are available for inspection by members of the Inn concerned. Lincoln's Inn, Inner Temple and Gray's Inn provide an abbreviated form of accounts at their annual meetings (paragraph 12.21).

12.79 The accounts of each Inn include a balance sheet and statement of income and expenditure of the Inns which are intended to reflect all of their activities. In addition, the Inns manage a number of scholarship and other trust funds for which separate accounts are prepared (paragraph 12.23).

Income and expenditure
12.80 In 1976 Lincoln's Inn made a very small surplus of £2,000. The other Inns had surpluses of £76,000 (Inner Temple), £54,000 (Middle Temple) and £88,000 (Gray's Inn). However, the Middle Temple surplus of £54,000 is before

making any provision towards improvements at Fountain Court of £100,000; in its accounts the Inn charged this expenditure against its New Building Fund (paragraphs 12.25 and 12.71).

12.81   Most of the income of the Inns comes from letting their premises. The combined net rental income of the four Inns amounted in 1976 to about 86 per cent of total income; the proportion varied from 77 per cent in Middle Temple to 91 per cent in Gray's Inn. There are two other main sources of income: admission and call fees to members, and investment income (paragraph 12.25).

12.82   While Inner Temple and Middle Temple obtained in 1976 well over 70 per cent of their rental income from letting chambers, Lincoln's Inn obtained 33 per cent of its rents from chambers and Gray's Inn only 13 per cent, the remainder of their income mainly coming from letting offices to commercial tenants (paragraph 12.27).

12.83   The Inns informed us that rents for chambers were less than full rack rents, one-half of a full rack rent in the case of Lincoln's Inn and two-thirds in the cases of the other Inns. Chambers' leases are reviewable quarterly in the case of Inner and Middle Temples, annually in Lincoln's Inn and every three years in Gray's Inn, where there are only 17 sets of chambers within the Inn (paragraphs 12.28–12.29).

12.84   Income from members mainly comprises admission fees (£85 for each Inn) and call to the Bar fees (£75 for each Inn) (paragraphs 12.34–12.36).

12.85   Apart from repairs and maintenance of their buildings almost all of the expenditure of the Inns in 1976 was incurred in general administration (£685,000); education (£221,000); catering for members (£199,000); the library (£202,000); and in paying a subscription to the Senate (£85,000) (paragraph 12.25).

12.86   Administration costs mainly comprised salaries and related costs (including pensions) and rates, maintenance, heating and lighting of the administrative buildings (paragraphs 12.39–12.41).

12.87   Education costs in 1976 comprised the costs of scholarships and prizes (£43,000), catering costs attributable to students (£119,000) and other costs (£59,000). In 1976 the Inns attributed in all just over one-third of their catering losses to the provision of meals to students in arriving at the costs included under "education" (paragraphs 12.42–12.44).

12.88   Catering losses attributable to members came in total for the four Inns in 1975 to £182,000 and in 1976 to £199,000. These losses are before making any charge for general administration expenses or rental of the premises, and represented 102 per cent of catering income in 1975 and 93 per cent of catering income in 1976 (paragraphs 12.45–12.46).

366

12.89   Library costs for the four Inns combined amounted to £202,000 in 1976, which includes £101,000 for salary costs and £59,000 for the purchase or binding of books (paragraph 12.47).

12.90   Subscriptions to the Senate in 1976 totalled £85,000, Gray's Inn paying £25,000 and all the other Inns each paying £20,000. There are "Understandings" of the new Senate. Since the new Senate was formed in July 1974 the Inns have contributed about one-third of its income, the rest almost all coming from subscriptions of barristers (paragraphs 12.48–12.51).

12.91   Apart from a few specific exceptions, capital expenditure is charged to income and expenditure account in the year it is incurred. In 1975 the amount charged by the four Inns combined was £78,000 and in 1976 it was £64,000, excluding the £100,000 referred to in paragraph 12.80 above (paragraphs 12.54–12.55).

12.92   Lincoln's Inn estimated that two-thirds of its library costs and 10 per cent of its general administration costs were attributable to students. Using these proportions for each of the Inns, the total expenditure on students in 1976 was £424,000 and income from admission and call fees was £127,000, an excess of expenditure over income of £297,000 (1975: £201,000) (paragraph 12.56).

Assets and liabilities

12.93   Gray's Inn includes certain buildings in its 1976 balance sheet at a 1950 valuation (excluding site value) or subsequent cost totalling some £2·5 million. The four Inns include in their 1976 balance sheets the cost of certain freehold and leasehold provincial chambers amounting in total to a cost of £219,000, and Gray's Inn has capitalised the cost of a heating installation of £48,000. There are no other fixed assets recorded in the books of the Inns. Current insurance valuations of the Inns' buildings total some £103 million and silver, pictures and chattels are insured for some £3 million (paragraphs 12.58–12.60).

12.94   Depreciation is provided in the accounts of the Inns on one provincial property and on the heating installation. No depreciation charge is made in respect of other assets nor are any other provisions made against income for reconstruction or replacement. We understand that Lincoln's Inn intends to provide in future for reconstruction and non-routine maintenance, which its surveyor estimated in 1974 would cost £1 million over the next 15 years (paragraph 12.59).

12.95   Lincoln's Inn, Inner Temple and Middle Temple had substantial investments at 31 December 1976, mostly in quoted securities and government stocks. Gray's Inn owned no securities at that date, but had made loans totalling £88,000 mainly to chambers and newly-qualified barristers (paragraph 12.61).

12.96   At 31 December 1976 Inner Temple, Middle Temple and Gray's Inn had bank overdrafts of £88,000, £46,000 and £78,000 respectively (paragraphs 12.57 and 12.65).

12.97   Each of the Inns shows in its accounts a substantial liability for students' deposits received since 1960 and not reclaimed or written-off (paragraphs 12.57 and 12.67–12.68).

ANNEX 12.1

**Combined income and expenditure accounts of the four Inns of Court
for the years ended 31 December 1974, 1975 and 1976**
(paragraph 12.25)

	1974	1975	1976
	£'000	£'000	£'000
Income:			
estate, net of expenses	895	1,256	1,442
members	162	213	141
investment	59	90	76
miscellaneous	5	61	23
	1,121	1,620	1,682
Expenditure:			
administration	409	563	685
education	203	221	221
catering net loss	156	182	199
library	131	180	202
subscription to Senate	20	67	85
church	37	39	33
miscellaneous	21	16	21
	977	1,268	1,446
Surplus before tax and exceptional items	144	352	236
Tax	(11)	(10)	(19)
	133	342	217
Exceptional and prior year items	(86)	(78)	3
Surplus	47	264	220

369

ANNEX 12.2
Rental policies of the Inns
(paragraph 12.29)

	Gray's Inn	Inner Temple	Middle Temple	Lincoln's Inn
Chambers:				
rent	2/3 FRR[1]	63% FRR	2/3 FRR	50% FRR (⅔ proposed March 1978)
length of lease	6 years (review after 3 years)	quarterly	quarterly	annual
type of lease	tenants repairing	tenants repairing	tenants repairing	tenants repairing
must head tenant be a member of the Inn?	no	yes	no	no
number of sets of chambers[2]	17[3]	——— 131 ———		44
Offices:				
rent	FRR	FRR	FRR	FRR
length of lease	6 years (review after 3 years)	quarterly	quarterly	20 years (with reviews after 5, 10 and 15 years) or 21 years (with breaks after 7 or 14 years)
type of lease	tenants repairing	tenants repairing	tenants repairing	tenants repairing
number of offices	70[4]	27	16	37
Residential:				
rent	"fair rent" (2/3 fair rent to members)	63% FRR	approx. 70% of estimated registered rent[5]	registered rent (less 10% for members)
length of lease	3 years	quarterly	for 1 year certain	3 years
type of lease	tenants repairing	tenants repairing	tenants repairing	tenants repairing
number of units of accommodation	62	63	81	70

[1] FRR=Full Rack Rent (or Precinct Rent). All proportions quoted are approximate and vary from time to time.

[2] Per 1976 Law List—the number of separate lettings will be greater.

[3] In addition, the Council of Legal Education and the Senate occupy accommodation in Gray's Inn.

[4] In addition, the Clergy Benevolent Association and the Barristers' Benevolent Association have offices in Gray's Inn. Neither association has paid rent in the past though we have been informed that the Clergy Benevolent Association will be charged rent in the future.

[5] We are informed that it is the current policy of the Middle Temple to move towards charging tenants of residential accommodation the registered rent.

ANNEX 12.3

Regulations of the Senate of the Inns of Court and the Bar

Annexure A—The Understandings

(paragraph 12.49)

The purpose for which the Inns hold and must conserve their property are the education and training of new entrants to the profession, the provision of accommodation and facilities for those who wish to practise, and the well-being of the Bar as a whole, and accordingly:—

(a) The undertakings by the Inns give rise to a moral obligation but not to any legally enforceable liabilities.

(b) In setting the contributions of the Inns to the Senate regard will be had to the general principle:

that no Inn will be required, except with its consent, to make annual contributions to amounts which, taking one year with another

    (i) would result in its being compelled to reduce its capital assets or the provision of proper reserves for their maintenance; or

    (ii) would disable it from continuing to provide:

        (1) scholarships or other financial assistance for students or barristers in pupillage as it thinks proper, due regard being had to the level at which similar provision is made by the other Inns to the financial needs of the Council of Legal Education and to the importance of providing adequate accommodation for the practising Bar; and

        (2) the facilities which it has hitherto afforded to its members generally.

(c) Unless otherwise agreed between the Inns, the annual contributions of each will be equal in amount except to the extent that in the case of any particular Inn this would involve exceeding the limit mentioned in the preceding paragraph.

(d) In settling the contributions of the Inns to any special project of a capital nature regard will be had to the general principle that no Inn will be required except with its consent to make a contribution in an amount which would involve it realising or raising money on the security of any of its capital assets.

(e) The consent by an Inn to contribute an amount in excess of the limits mentioned in paragraphs (b) or (d) will not be withheld unreasonably and will be given through its representative on the Finance Committee to whom the Inn will delegate authority wide enough to enable him to act promptly without reference back to that Inn.

(f) In deciding the annual rates of subscription of members regard will be had to the general principle that taking one year with another the annual running costs of the Senate together with the costs of any special project of an income nature, and any deficit in the annual budget of the Council of Legal Education should be borne as between subscriptions of members and contributions from the Inns:

    (i) up to an amount equal to the present annual running costs of the Bar Council together with those of the former Senate, in the same proportions as at present; and

371

(ii) as to any excess, in equal proportion or such other appropriate proportions as may be determined by the Senate, having regard to the services rendered to the Bar as a whole through the new Bar Council to the responsibility of the Inns for the education and training of new entrants to the profession and to the extent to which the resources of the Inns are derived from rents of professional chambers of barristers in London.

(g) In carrying out "agreed policy" as respects the provision within the Inns of Court of professional accommodation for barristers or their pupils or the rent to be charged therefor each Inn concerned will be entitled to keep such number of residential flats as is required to preserve the character of the Inn, due regard being had to the needs of the profession as a whole.

ANNEX 12.4

Inns of Court

Summary of balance sheets at 31 December 1974, 1975 and 1976

(paragraph 12.57)

	Lincoln's Inn			Inner Temple			Middle Temple			Gray's Inn		
	31 December 1974	31 December 1975	31 December 1976	25 March 1975	31 December 1975	31 December 1976	31 December 1974	31 December 1975	31 December 1976	31 December 1974	31 December 1975	31 December 1976
	£'000	£'000	£'000	£'000	£'000	£'000	£'000	£'000	£'000	£'000	£'000	£'000
Fixed assets	10	36	40				56	149	146	2,581	2,606	2,612
Investments	536	456	349	212	217	208	504[1]	376	350	44	70	88
Current assets:												
stocks	32	35	47	10	11	11	35	40	47	35	37	39
tax recoverable	—	—	—	—	—	—	—	19	36	—	—	—
debtors	124	179	270	159	234	286	145	153	171	99	91	235
bank	46	32	—	3	21	31	1	1	1	3	8	—
	202	246	317	172	266	328	181	213	255	137	136	274
Current liabilities:												
overdraft	—	—	—	69	—	88	73	44	46	73	81	78
tax	8	—	—	—	—	—	6	—	—	128	30	37
creditors	122	162	146	171	240	136	65	63	135	48	66	140
	130	162	146	240	240	224	144	107	181	249	177	255
Net current assets/(liabilities)	72	84	171	(68)	26	104	37	106	74	(112)	(41)	19
Repayable student deposits	(143)	(172)	(153)	(86)	(87)	(80)	(127)	(99)	(86)	(104)	(69)	(64)
Net assets	475	404	407	58	156	232	470	532	486	2,409	2,566	2,655
Accumulated funds:												
general funds	}155	(102)	(82)	(132)	(14)	96	196	62	71	}2,409	238	374
collegiate funds		190	173	183	164	109	26	182	177		2,328	2,281
special reserves	320	316	316	7	6	27	248	288	238	—	—	—
	475	404	407	58	156	232	470	532	486	2,409	2,566	2,655

[1] Includes the assets representing the Middle Temple's special reserves.

373

SECTION 13
Partnerships at the Bar

Paragraph 33.60 of Volume 1 mentions briefly the occasions since 1950 in which the rule forbidding partnerships between barristers has been considered by the profession. A full account of these and of the arguments for and against the rule are contained in the report of the special committee appointed by the Bar Council in April 1968, under the chairmanship of Sydney Templeman QC.

The report of the Templeman Committee is reproduced below by permission of the Senate of the Inns of Court and the Bar.

Report of
Special committee on partnerships

Contents

Part I.   History of the rule against partnerships
1   1902 Ruling
2   1952 Russell Vick Committee
3   1955 Bar Council Retirement Benefit Committee
4   1956 Finance Act; Retirement Pensions
5   1957 and 1959 Discussions
6   1961 Lawrence Committee Majority and Minority Reports

Part II.   Developments since the 1961 Lawrence Committee Reports
7   *Rondel* v. *Worsley*
8   1968 Finance Act. Post-Cessation Receipts
9   1969 Conditions
10   Bar Reviews of Practice

Part III.   Appointment of the present committee
11   April 1968. Terms of Reference
12   Composition of the Committee; First Schedule

Part IV.   Evidence
13   June 1968. Bulletin of Information
14   June 1968. Law Guardian Article
15   October 1968. Evidence Received

Part I

History of the Rule Against Partnerships

1   **1902 Ruling.** We have no evidence that partnerships were considered prior to 1902 when the Bar Council ruled that no practice in the least degree resembling partnerships is permissible between Counsel.

2   **1952 Russell Vick Committee.** In 1952 a Committee under the Chairmanship of Sir Godfrey Russell Vick was appointed by the Bar Council to examine and report upon the question of having something in the nature of partnerships in Chambers with special reference to the suggestion that this might assist in solving the difficulty of making a living until a practice can be built up and in solving the difficulty of saving for retirement. The Committee did not consider that the mere establishment of some form of partnership would by itself contribute much if anything to the problem of the young man starting at the Bar. The Committee thought that without some change in the basis of taxation, the problem of saving for retirement could be solved and solved only by some form of joint purse arrangement. The Committee recommended that further consideration of the whole problem of the rule against partnerships be deferred until after the Tucker Committee had reported on the provision of retirement pensions for the self-employed.

3   **1955 Retirement Benefit Committee.** In 1955 the Bar Council's Retirement Benefit Committee was asked to reconsider the Report of 1952, and the question of permitting joint purse arrangements and the Committee expressed the general view that joint purse arrangements would be far less valuable from the point of view of the Bar than those which could be obtained from the implementation of the second Tucker Report.

4   **1956 Finance Act: Retirement Pensions.** Relief against income tax and surtax was provided in respect of annual premiums, not exceeding £750 or one-tenth of earnings, paid by a self-employed person for a pension.

377

5 **1957 and 1959 Discussions.** The subject of the rule against partnerships was raised in a special meeting for Members of the Bar of under ten years' standing in June 1957 and was discussed by the Bar Council in February 1959 when proposals for the approval of a joint purse arrangement were disapproved.

6 **1961 Lawrence Committee Majority and Minority Reports.** In April 1959 the Bar Council appointed a Special Committee, Chairman Geoffrey Lawrence Q.C., to go further into and examine all aspects of the question of whether and how far partnerships and other organisations should be permitted at the Bar. The Majority Report of this Committee recommended in April 1961 that partnerships should not be permitted. The Majority Report was adopted by the Bar Council. A Minority Report saw no reason on ethical grounds for the rule that partnerships should not be permitted. The Minority considered however that a change-over to partnerships would open up opportunities for tax avoidance and would inevitably also make taxable the genuine post-cessation receipts of barristers and this would involve hardship in some cases, and in all cases would involve the withdrawal of a fiscal advantage which older practitioners had become entitled to expect. The Minority considered therefore that partnerships should not be permitted while the tax law remained unaltered.

Part II

Developments Since the 1961 Lawrence Committee Reports

7 **Rondel v. Worsley.** The judgment of the House of Lords in *Rondel* v. *Worsley* opened up the possibility of actions against Counsel in respect of advisory work.

8 **1968 Finance Act: Post-Cessation Receipts.** The Finance Act 1968 abolished, subject to some transitional relief, the exemption of post-cessation receipts from tax.

9 **1969 Conditions.** Increased prosperity at the Bar has resulted in young men being able to get started more rapidly. There is evidence of shortage of Counsel, particularly in the Provinces. Some local authorities now award grants to enable students to study for Bar examinations. In consequence of these developments, it is expected that there will be an increase in the number of persons qualified and prepared to practise at the Bar if there is accommodation for them, and if the prospects remain favourable.

10 **Bar Reviews of Practice.** The Bar reviewed several of its rules and practices in the light of modern developments.

Part III

Appointment of the Present Committee

11 April 1968. Terms of Reference. In April 1968 the Bar Council appointed this Special Committee "To consider the extent to which the operation of the rule against partnerships is open to justifiable criticism; the extent of the demand amongst Members of the Bar that partnerships should be permitted; and in the light of such examination to make proposals (if so advised) for the abolition or modification of the rule".

12 Composition of the Committee: First Schedule. This Committee, as constituted after co-options, consisted of the persons named in the First Schedule to this Report.

Part IV

Evidence

13 June 1968. Bulletin of Information. The Committee first met on the 27th May 1968 and on the 14th June 1968 the Bar Council issued a Bulletin of Information to Heads of Chambers for distribution to Members of Chambers drawing attention to this Committee, the Lawrence Committee Reports, and developments since the Lawrence Committee Reports, and inviting Members of the Bar to submit their views to this Committee, if possible by the end of July.

14 June 1968. Law Guardian Article. In June 1968 an article was published in the Law Guardian concerning the work of this Committee and the problem of partnerships at the Bar, and parts of this article were reproduced in the Daily Telegraph.

15 October 1968. Evidence Received. The Committee met for the second time on the 9 October 1968. By that date there had been received a Memorandum from the Young Barristers Committee of the Bar Council, letters from nine Members or former Members of the Bar (5 of whom asked that Partnerships be permitted) and a Memorandum from the Barristers' Clerks' Association.

The Committee noted that there was a singular lack of spontaneous demand amongst Members of the Bar that partnerships should be permitted, and determined to seek further evidence before attempting to reach any further conclusions.

16 November 1968. Second Bulletin of Information. In November 1968 the Bar Council in another Bulletin of Information drew attention to the appointment of this Committee and urged Members of the Bar to submit their views.

17 January 1969. Further Evidence Received. The Special Committee met for the third time on the 21 January 1969. Some 41 further expressions of opinion had been received.

18 (1) Evidence from Organisations. Members of this Committee had two interesting and fruitful discussions with Members of the Contentious Business Committee of the Law Society. This was followed by a letter from the Secretary of the Contentious Business Committee of the Law Society to the Secretary of the Bar Council. The Committee also received helpful information regarding American practices, the experience of the British Medical Association and the Barristers' Benevolent Association, and instructive memoranda from the Barristers' Clerks' Association, the Chancery Bar Association, the London Common Law Bar Association and the Young Barristers' Committee.

(2) **Evidence Analysed.** 18 of the Letters and Memoranda received by this Committee from Members and former Members of the Bar were in favour of the Abolition of the Rule against Partnerships and 32 were in favour of the Retention of the Rule against Partnerships. Some Letters were written not only on behalf of the writer but also on behalf of other Members of the same Chambers.

There were in October 1968, some 2,379 practising Members of the Bar in England and Wales organised in approximately 245 sets of Chambers. This Committee regard the demand amongst Members of the Bar that partnership be permitted as relatively small.

Part V

Definitions

19 "Partnerships". Partnerships are arrangements whereby two or more Members of the Bar agree to share fees and work. Partnerships involve the pooling of receipts and the pooling of services. Partners share profits, losses, responsibility and liability.

20 "Joint Purse Arrangements". Joint purse arrangements are arrangements whereby two or more Members of the Bar agree to share fees but not to share work. Joint purse arrangements involve the pooling of receipts but do not involve the pooling of services. Members of Joint Purse Arrangements share nothing but fees.

21 "Devilling Arrangements". Devilling arrangements are arrangements whereby one Member of the Bar agrees to remunerate another Member by a fixed sum or by a share of the fees received for work devilled. Devilling arrangements do not involve a pooling of receipts or services.

22 **"Chambers Arrangements".** Chambers arrangements are arrangements whereby Members of Chambers agree that the expenses of maintaining Chambers shall be shared in proportions which reflect the fees earned by each Member or by some other method whereby, in general, little or no expense is borne by a Member who has little or no work. Chambers arrangements do not involve a pooling of receipts or services.

23 **Present Rules.** Partnerships and joint purse arrangements are not permitted. Devilling arrangements and Chambers arrangements are permitted.

Part VI

The Criterion

24 **The Test.** (1) The Rule against partnerships is a restrictive practice in the sense that the Rule prevents barristers who wish to form partnerships from carrying on their practice in the manner they think best.

(2) The Rule should be abolished unless the public interest requires the Rule.

(3) The public interest requires the Rule if its abolition will lead to a fall in the numbers or quality of barristers available to a member of the public seeking representation or advice, or a fall in the numbers or quality of barristers available for judicial appointments.

(4) The Rule was not invented and its preservation is not sought for the purpose of limiting the number of practising barristers or for the purpose of improving or maintaining the financial position of barristers.

(5) If there is a conflict between the interests of the public and the interests of the profession the conflict should be resolved in favour of the public.

(6) A partnership itself imposes restriction on members of the partnership and on those who wish or are obliged to enter the profession via a partnership.

(7) Similar considerations apply to the Rule against Joint Purse Arrangements.

Part VII

Consequences of Abolition

25 **Inevitable Limitations.** The advantages and disadvantages of the Rule against partnerships cannot be considered without first deciding whether the rule can be abolished simpliciter or whether the Rule could in any event only be abolished subject to certain limitations on Members of the Bar entering into partnerships.

We have no doubt that if the Rule were abolished, the following limitations would be necessary.

(1) Members of the same partnership could not be allowed to represent conflicting or potentially conflicting interests.

(2) A member of a partnership could not be allowed to appear as an advocate before another member acting in a judicial capacity.

(3) A member of a partnership could not be allowed to appear as an advocate before a former member of the same partnership acting in a judicial capacity, so long as that former member was entitled to any pension or other rights for himself or his dependants from the continuing partners.

26 **Arguments against Limitations.** At present members of the same Chambers represent conflicting interests and it has been argued that the position will not be different if members of the same partnership represent conflicting or potentially conflicting interests. We cannot accept this argument. A client who instructed a partnership firm would expect and be entitled to the services of that partnership. He would not expect and could not understand how any member of the partnership could act for the enemy. If a partnership firm acted for two clients whose interests were potentially conflicting, and subsequently a conflict arose, not only would both clients feel aggrieved but both would then lose the services of the partnership.

27 **Partial Limitations Considered.** We have considered and rejected the possibility of compiling a list of litigious or non-litigious work in respect of which members of the same partnership could be allowed to act for different interests where the area of conflict was small or where a potential conflict was unlikely to cause difficulties. Such a list would introduce difficulties of definition and application and only cause embarrassment to members of the Bar and confusion in the minds of the public. The difficulties which have arisen in the past when one firm of Solicitors has attempted to act both for a willing vendor and a willing purchaser illustrate the problem.

28 **Segregation of Fees Considered.** We have also considered and rejected the possibility of allowing members of a partnership to appear for conflicting or potentially conflicting interests provided that the fees were segregated from the partnership fees. That there would be some difficulty in effecting segregation on a completely just basis seems obvious. More to the point however, we think that if barristers who were adversaries were known to be in partnership with each other there would be understandable concern on the part of the public. To permit this would be to cause cynicism and perhaps hostility.

29 **Consequences of Limitation that Members of a Partnership must not represent conflicting or potentially conflicting interests.** We consider therefore that members of the same partnership could not be allowed to represent conflicting or potentially conflicting interests. In practice this limitation alone makes unde-

sirable and in many cases impracticable the formation of partnerships in many branches of work at the Bar. In some provincial centres there are very few sets of Chambers. Similar conditions apply to those Chambers which specialise in Revenue work, Company law, Admiralty work, Commercial law, and to some extent the Chancery Bar. In criminal Chambers prosecution Briefs might prevent any members of the partnership being available for the defence of prisoners at an Assize.

It was suggested that members of the Bar wishing to form a partnership should require the consent of the Bar Council and that this consent could be withheld if the Bar Council considered that the suggested partnership would result in a monopoly or in a serious reduction of the number of barristers available to every member of the public in a particular field of law. We consider that such a system would be unfair to the Bar Council and unfair to those barristers who were refused permission to form a partnership in a field in which some partnerships had already been permitted.

It was also suggested that if partnerships reduced the number of Counsel effectively available, then new partnerships would spring up to provide competition and to meet the demand for separate representation. We think that under present circumstances this is an unrealistic expectation. There is at present grave difficulty in meeting the demand for places in Chambers and in forming new Chambers. The glamour and activity of London and the reluctance of existing Chambers to divide are inhibiting factors in recruitment to Provincial Bars. In London shortage of space and the reluctance of Solicitors to go outside familiar territory impose limitations on the number of barristers who can practise successfully. These difficulties will not we think be diminished by a partnership system. On the contrary established partnerships will be powerful, may well be monopolistic, and will effectively deter individuals or new partnerships from taking the risks which attach to newcomers in any field.

It has also been suggested that one set of Chambers might be divided so that there would be more than one partnership within a set of chambers or possibly partnerships and individuals within a set of Chambers. We see substantial difficulties in the administration and management of a set of Chambers which included more than one partnership or which contained some members operating in partnership and others acting as individuals. Reasons of space and economy prevent the introduction of extra clerks or office managers. In practice we think that if the majority of members of a set of Chambers resolved to enter into partnership, the position of the minority outside the partnership would not be very secure, particularly if the partners wished to expand their practice and their membership.

30 **Consequences of Limitation that Members of a Partnership must not appear before another Member acting as a Judge.** An equally serious limitation is the limitation which principle and authority require, namely, that a member of a

partnership should not be allowed to appear as an advocate before another member acting in a judicial capacity. See *R.* v. *Sussex Justices* (1924) 1. K.B. 256. No one has suggested that this limitation will not be necessary. This limitation would have serious repercussions on the administration of criminal law. Members of the Bar act as Recorders, as Chairmen of Quarter Sessions, and accept other part-time judicial appointments. A member of a partnership could of course refuse these appointments, but this would not be in the public interest. If a member of a partnership accepted an appointment, his acceptance would debar his partners from accepting briefs to appear before him and would deprive Solicitors and the public of the services of all members of the partnership to that extent. No one has suggested any solution to this difficulty.

31 Consequences of Limitation that Members of a Partnership must not appear before a former Member acting as a Judge and retaining Pension Rights. On principle a member of a partnership could not be allowed to appear as an advocate before a former member of the same partnership acting in a judicial capacity so long as that former member was entitled to any pension or other rights for himself or his dependants from the continuing partners. In practice this limitation might not be serious because pension arrangements can be made with an insurance company so that there need not be any financial connection between a judge on the one hand and any of the advocates who appear before him on the other hand.

32 Application of Limitations to Joint Purse Arrangements. The limitations which we believe will be necessary to impose on partnerships which are set forth in paragraph 25 of this Report must apply equally to joint purse arrangements.

Part VIII

Consequences of partnerships on administration and taxation

33 Selection and Work of Partners. Full partners share losses and liability for negligence. A barrister would therefore normally expect to become a salaried partner in the first instance. The selection of full partners would be very carefully considered and promotion might be slow. It has been suggested that a partnership might provide a comprehensive service and include specialists in different fields such as Company law, Revenue law, Trust law and so on. We do not consider that this is practicable. We doubt whether it is desirable in the public interest, because a member of the public who consulted a partnership would be under some moral pressure to seek advice on all problems from the narrow field of that partnership, whereas under the present system he seeks advice on each problem from the widest possible field, namely all practitioners who specialise in that type of problem.

34 Capital. A full partner might be required to purchase goodwill or to provide working capital. An incoming partner who does not possess free capital may undertake to acquire an outgoing partner's share of goodwill by assuming liability for some annual payment arising from the profits of the continuing partnership activities. Working capital can be provided, if there is no free capital committed to the partnership enterprise or available to that end, by the retention of profits otherwise available for distribution among the partners.

35 Control. The Partnership Deed must provide for the duration of the partnership, the right to retire or expel, and the consequences of retirement or expulsion. The Partnership Deed must also provide machinery for regulating the distribution of profits and for regulating drawings, working hours, holidays and the employment and control of staff. Control could be exercised by a majority in number of the partners, or by partners representing a majority of shares in goodwill or profits. Control we think would tend to move to the senior partners.

36 Taxation. (1) The computation of profits arising from the profession of barrister is at the present in the great majority of cases related to cash receipts; it is accepted by the Inland Revenue that the earnings basis may be claimed and if claimed must be conceded to the barrister. A computation on a cash basis ascertains the profit of the relevant period by including fees received in that period and deducting therefrom the expenses paid. The earnings basis involves a more scientific appraisal of the income and expenditure of the relevant period, and it becomes necessary to place a money value upon debtors and creditors, and, it may be, work in progress. Such a system of income and expenditure accounting necessitates the maintenance of much fuller records.

(2) The assessment on partnership profits is made in one sum in the partnership name; thus the most important single tax consequence of partnership in a profession is that each partner becomes jointly and severally liable to the tax referable to the partnership profits, for any period during which he was a member of that partnership. The assessment is divided among the partners according to the ratio in which they share the profits in the year of assessment itself, not for the basis period in which those profits were earned, and since income tax is a partnership liability, some provision is necessary for restrictions on the drawings of each partner so as to provide for the tax chargeable upon him.

(3) In the case of a continuing partnership the profits of the basis period ending on or before the 5th April in any year will form the measure of assessment for the year commencing with the following 6th April. The method of computing those profits is therefore of considerable significance, not the less so because by the Finance Act 1968, there is now imposed a charge of tax under Case VI of Schedule "D" on post-cessation receipts of all those assessed on the cash basis.

(4) Whether profits are computed on the basis of cash or earnings the consequences of a change in partnership can be radical so that any partnership agreement must provide for its operation during a defined period of years in which there can be no withdrawal of a partner. Should there be a change, for example by death of a partner, it is necessary to reserve a right to the continuing partners should they see fit to elect, and by election to secure, that the change should not be treated as involving a discontinuance for income tax purposes.

(5) The existence of the agreed but variable profit-sharing ratio will enable a more even spread of income and of liability to tax, but on the footing only that partner "A" is agreeable to forgo some part of his share of profit in favour of partners "B", "C", and "D". He may be but we assume will look for some return. This is particularly relevant to the stage of retirement, since here there can be provision made which has beneficial tax consequences. Thus if some form of goodwill exists this can be purchased by an annual payment which operates as a charge upon the partnership profits accruing to the continuing partners and thereby diminishes their liability to surtax and this payment can be made to a widow as well as to the retiring partner. The position can equally be met by an appointment of the retiring partner on a part-time basis as consultant at a salary.

(6) There are certain disadvantageous consequences in the sphere of capital gains tax and estate duty. Goodwill is an asset and if it is sold for a payment not otherwise chargeable with tax, that is to say for a capital sum, which exceeds the price paid by the seller, this excess will attract capital gains tax at the rate of 30 per cent. As to estate duty, at present the Inland Revenue accept that outstanding fees do not pass on the death, but it must be otherwise if there pass a share in the assets of a partnership.

Part IX

Criticisms of the rule against partnerships and advantages of the abolition of the rule

37 Encouragement of Beginners. (1) If the Rule were abolished partnerships could provide work and a secure income for the beginner. Under the present system a man of talent may be discouraged from joining the profession or driven to abandon it for financial reasons. The public are deprived of the services of those who cannot afford to begin or cannot afford to survive.

(2) *Comment.* Partnerships could help the beginner financially. However, beginners can be helped financially under the present system by devilling arrangements and Chambers arrangements. The main obstacle in the path of a beginner is not finance but shortage of space in Chambers. Partnerships would not supply a single additional space. So far as persons leaving the profession are

concerned we are not convinced that the numbers or quality of the Bar would improve as a result of partnerships. The departure of practising barristers for commerce or industry does not seriously denude the Bar of talent.

38 Distribution of Work. (1) In some Chambers, some members may be under-employed, others over-worked. In a partnership the work will be distributed between all members and the public would be served more speedily and more efficiently.

(2) *Comment.* If this distribution took place there would be a substantial advantage to the partners, particularly to those partners who were able to decide the distribution of work. At present work is distributed as a result of selection by Solicitors. Even if partnerships were permitted, we feel sure that Solicitors would continue largely to insist upon their work being done by selected member or members of the chosen partnership (see para 44). Moreover the public interest is unlikely to be promoted by changing to a system whereby work is distributed by a member of the partnership for this could preserve the mediocre and restrict the younger members to the less important and more monotonous work thereby depriving them of experience.

39 Provision for Illness. (1) A barrister who is ill ceases to earn and may be driven to abandon the profession.

(2) *Comment.* At present a barrister who falls ill is not infrequently able to depend and should be able to depend on Chambers Arrangements to reduce or eliminate his expenses and to preserve his place in Chambers. In some cases members of Chambers who take over the work of a sick barrister do so on a devilling basis so that the sick barrister has some source of income while he is ill. A barrister who fears sickness may effect insurance on terms which have greatly developed and improved in the past few years. Nevertheless we think that a partnership system offers substantial advantages to a barrister who falls ill, or to a barrister with family responsibilities who fears that he may fall ill. It must however be the position and is to be remembered in this context, that no relationship of a business nature can cope with the associate who is permanently or semi-permanently ill.

40 Provision of Substitutes. (1) If a Member of the Bar returns a Brief he is under no obligation to provide a substitute and if he does provide a substitute the Solicitor may object. If a member of a partnership could not conduct a case it would be the duty of the partners to provide a substitute and the Solicitor could not object to a substitute who was a member of the partnership unless he had delivered a Brief on the express understanding that a particular barrister would perform the work.

(2) *Comment.* A Solicitor selects his own advocate and the lay client tells his story to that advocate. In these circumstances grievances over substitutes and returned Briefs will not be cured by a partnership system.

41 Improvement in Office Efficiency. (1) Under a partnership system the Clerk would become an Office Manager, he could concentrate on office administration and office efficiency would be increased.

(2) *Comment.* Under any system someone must be the main influence in determining whether Instructions can be accepted, when the completion of written work can be promised, and when a Brief must be returned. We do not believe that a competent and busy Member of the Bar could or should carry out this task more efficiently than the Clerk and we do not believe that office efficiency will increase if the Head of Chambers becomes a senior partner and the Clerk becomes an Office Manager.

42 Improvements in Standards. (1) Members of a partnership can help one another; a partnership can provide specialists in different fields and their work can be combined and co-ordinated.

(2) *Comment.* There is no doubt that partnerships would confer on the members of the partnership a comfortable feeling of support and reduce the present anxiety of individual responsibility. In our opinion however it is an illusion to think that the work of a barrister can be carried on by a committee. The main work namely advocacy cannot be delegated and must depend entirely on the individual. We do not consider that a senior partner engrossed with problems entrusted to him could properly supervise the work of junior partners. So far as help and supervision are possible and desirable we are of the opinion that devilling arrangements plus the present convention whereby every Member of the Bar assists another by his advice confer in practice advantages which differ little from the corresponding advantages offered by partnerships. So far as specialists are concerned, the present system enables a Solicitor to choose his own specialists from any Chambers. A system under which a partnership introduced specialists in different fields would not in our view improve the overall quality of advice available to the lay client and would in practice inhibit the choice of the Solicitor.

43 Provision for Retirement. (1) A barrister cannot sell his goodwill and cannot arrange with other members of Chambers to pay him or his dependants a pension. Talented men may be driven to abandon the profession in order to provide for their old age.

(2) *Comment.* The possibility of providing for pensions and for the sale of goodwill undoubtedly presents an advantage of partnership which requires to be weighed carefully against any disadvantages. However now that retirement pensions can be purchased out of gross income we do not believe that talented men refuse to come to the Bar or elect to leave the Bar because of the lack of adequate pension arrangements. If the maximum pension obtainable by the self-employed is inadequate, the remedy lies in persuading the legislature that the maximum should be increased. So far as goodwill is concerned, we do not

believe that young men should be saddled with payments for goodwill and we understand that Solicitors and members of other professions are abandoning the sale of goodwill, except that goodwill may continue to be an element in fixing retirement and consultant pensions and benefits. In general we do not consider that the public will benefit if practising Members of the Bar are able to secure pensions and other payments from other members. To some extent there is a contradiction here between the advantages claimed for partnerships. A beginner may be attracted by the prospect of an assured income, but repelled by the prospect of working in his successful years partly for himself, partly for other beginners and partly for retired partners.

Part X

Advantages of the rule against partnerships

44 Freedom of Choice (1) Solicitors can choose any Member of the Bar. They can form judgments of the capacity of individual Members of the Bar and can select the individual best suited for each case. In our discussions with the Law Society it became clear that Solicitors attached the greatest importance to their right to choose for example a leader from one set of Chambers and a junior or specialist from another set. The limitations set forth in paragraph 25 of this Report would seriously limit the present freedom of choice of Solicitors.

(2) *Comment*. A Solicitor acting for a plaintiff could seriously embarrass the defendant by instructing a leader who was a member of one partnership and a junior who was a member of another partnership. The defendant would be seriously embarrassed by being deprived of the opportunity of instructing any barrister in either of the two partnerships. The importance attached to obtaining the services of the right man for the job is considerable and of itself illustrates the fact that the work of a specialist barrister is and must remain primarily the work of the individual and not of a group. We feel it vital in the public interest that the principle whereby the services of every individual barrister are available to any member of the public should not be eroded.

We have found no acceptable method of combining the benefits of freedom of choice with the benefits of partnership.

45 Availability of Barristers for Judicial Appointments. (1) At present many of the ablest barristers are ready and willing to accept part-time and permanent judicial appointments. Under a partnership system many would be deterred from accepting appointments. The ablest barrister would be the largest earner in the partnership, supporting the young and old members of the firm. He could not be expected to earn as a part-time judge anything like the fees he could earn during the time in question as an advocate; he could not accept a part-time appointment without reducing the profits available to his partners. He could not, because of the limitations noted in paragraph 30 of this Report, accept any appointment without debarring his partners from accepting Instructions to appear before him. He could not accept a full-time appointment without dealing a blow at the profits of his partners. The barrister offered a part-time or full-time appointment would be forced to consider whether he ought to decline in the interests of his partners and in the interests of retired partners and their dependants in receipt of partnership pensions. It would be surprising if his co-partners did not view with misgivings the possibilities of their largest earner being appointed to the Bench. The pressures on a barrister to decline an appointment would be indirect and probably unspoken but persuasive for all that. We believe that to some extent the pressures would have their effect and indirectly the public interest would suffer.

(2) *Comment.* It is in the public interest that barristers should be freely available for judicial appointments and we believe that the number and quality of barristers available would be reduced under a partnership system.

46 Individual Responsibility. (1) Each Member of the Bar is individually and openly responsible for the advice he tenders in litigious and non-litigious business. He cannot shelter behind the anonymity of a partnership or leave decision-making to his partners. Difficult questions or problems which perplex the beginner are canvassed with other Members of the Bar, particularly with other members of Chambers, so that the individual does not suffer isolation, although he bears the ultimate responsibility.

(2) *Comment.* This individual responsibility results in a high level of competence amongst practitioners and results in good training for those who eventually make decisions in some judicial capacity.

47 Equality. (1) There is equality between Members of the Bar, irrespective of their relative seniority.

(2) *Comment.* The public pay for competition and experience but not for seniority. We do not consider that it is in the interest of the public or the profession that there should emerge two classes of barrister, on the one hand the advocate or advisor who speaks and writes with the authority of a full partner, and on the other hand the advocate or advisor who is only a salaried employee.

48 Standards. (1) The individual barrister finds his own level of work according to his talents and his industry; those who do not succeed are obliged to make way for others. Partnerships may attract and preserve the mediocre to the exclusion of the able and to the detriment of the public. Under a partnership system a junior or salaried partner might in the interests of the partnership be obliged or requested to spend long hours on research in connection with a major problem of great importance financial and otherwise to the partnership, whereas in his own interests and thus in the long term interests of the public he ought to be increasing his knowledge and experience in some minor matter in, for example, a Magistrates' Court or a County Court.

(2) *Comment.* There remains some criticism of the lack of training of beginners. We trust that the new scheme of training for the Bar will in large measure meet this criticism. So far as advocacy is concerned, training can only come from experience.

Part XI

Consideration of the rule

49 Advantages of Partnership not Substantial. (1) There are some advantages to barristers of a partnership system. For example there are some financial advantages available for barristers who begin at the Bar. There are some financial advantages for barristers who fall sick or who wish to retire. There are administrative advantages for the barristers who are now over worked. Some, but not all, of these advantages can be obtained by individual insurance, or by generous Chambers Arrangements and devilling arrangements. We consider that the criticisms of the rule against partnerships which we have received from Members of the Bar who have urged the advantages of partnerships would have been fewer in number if there had been a full appreciation of the inevitable limitations applicable to partnerships of barristers referred to in Part VII of this Report.

(2) The advantages to the public of partnerships are in our view uncertain and speculative. We do not consider that a partnership system would produce barristers in greater number or of a high quality.

50 Fundamental Criticism. Is Prohibition Necessary? (1) There remains a more fundamental criticism expressed by those who ask whether it is necessary to *prohibit* partnerships. Prohibition can only be justified if freedom to enter into partnerships is likely to cause harm to the profession or public or both. At the outset of this inquiry there was in the Committee a fairly widely held view that it appeared difficult to justify the continuance of the Rule. As different aspects have been considered it has become increasingly clear that whilst the abolition of the Rule might have some advantages for the Bar, the Rule operates in a number of important respects to protect the public, and the abrogation of the Rule would, we consider, adversely affect the public.

(2) So far as the profession is concerned, we believe that partnerships would make it difficult for a beginner to enter the profession save as a salaried employee of inferior status, difficult for a beginner to prove his capabilities to Solicitors, and difficult for a beginner to gain the individual practical experience and reputation necessary to enable him to develop and exhibit his talents to the best advantage.

(3) So far as the public are concerned, we believe that partnerships would restrict the freedom of Solicitors and lay clients to choose amongst all barristers and would restrict the number of able barristers available for judicial appointments.

(4) The public would also suffer if partnerships created undesirable monopolies or preserved the less competent. We believe that there is a danger of this. A barrister is at present a member of a small profession of specialists, his work is the work of an individual, his strength and weakness are exposed to the public by open competition, and his survival is dependent on his success. The Bar prepares for the isolation of the Bench. A partnership system would or might well substantially change all this for the worse.

(5) Of course if barristers were free to enter into partnerships but did not take advantage of their freedom, no harm could arise. If substantial numbers of barristers did enter into partnerships it could be argued that they were the judges of their own best interests. But for the reasons we have endeavoured to express, we consider that it would not be in the interests of the public and therefore of the profession itself in the long run that partnerships should develop on any substantial scale.

51 **Prohibition Necessary.** Applying the test set forth in paragraph 24 of this Report, we consider that the abolition of the Rule will, or is likely to lead to a fall in the numbers and quality of barristers available to a member of the public seeking representation or advice, and to a fall in the numbers and quality of barristers available for judicial appointments, and we consider therefore that the Rule should be retained.

52 **Joint Purse Arrangements.** The views we have expressed concerning the Rule against partnerships apply *mutatis mutandis* to Joint Purse Arrangements.

53 **Conclusions.** (1) The Rule against partnerships is not open to justifiable criticism.

(2) There is no substantial demand amongst Members of the Bar for the abolition or modification of the Rule.

(3) There are positive advantages of the Rule. We accordingly do not recommend the abolition or modification of the Rule.

The First Schedule

Sydney Templeman, QC, Chairman.

Desmond Miller, QC.

R A MacCrindle, QC.

James Fox-Andrews, QC.

Richard Du Cann.

Donald Rattee.

David Pitman.

Ian Glidewell, QC.

Printed in England for Her Majesty's Stationery Office by Oyez Press Limited
Dd. 595222 K40 10/79